LAW AND ETHICS IN ACADEMIC AND STUDENT AFFAIRS

This valuable resource provides academic and student affairs practitioners with the tools to make informed legal and ethical decisions in their college and university contexts.

Law is constantly changing and is interpreted differently from campus to campus based on institutional culture and history. This text provides higher education practitioners with tools to anticipate practical and responsible action, engaging readers in anticipatory and reflective practice. In this text, Boettcher and Salinas introduce the Institutional Intelligence Model, a helpful framework that guides practitioners in examining a wide variety of campus issues. Throughout the book, readers can explore perspectives from current practitioners and utilize case studies to examine specific topics, including admissions, academics, student living, confidential resources, and graduate student experiences. By using the strategies in this book, practitioners will be equipped to successfully navigate legal and ethical issues on their campuses. This text is ideal for graduate students, student and academic affairs professionals, and those in leadership positions responsible for working with and supporting students and staff teams.

Michelle L. Boettcher is Associate Professor of Educational, Organizational, and Leadership Development at Clemson University.

Cristóbal Salinas Jr. is Associate Professor of Educational Leadership and Research Methodology at Florida Atlantic University.

LAW AND ETHICS IN ACADEMIC AND STUDENT AFFAIRS

Developing an Institutional Intelligence Approach

Michelle L. Boettcher and Cristóbal Salinas Jr.

Routledge
Taylor & Francis Group
NEW YORK AND LONDON

ACPA
College Student Educators International

Designed cover image: © Getty Images

First published 2024
by Routledge
605 Third Avenue, New York, NY 10158

and by Routledge
4 Park Square, Milton Park, Abingdon, Oxon, OX14 4RN

Routledge is an imprint of the Taylor & Francis Group, an informa business

ISBN: 978-1-642-67432-3 (hbk)
ISBN: 978-1-642-67433-0 (pbk)
ISBN: 978-1-003-44270-7 (ebk)

DOI: 10.4324/9781003442707

Typeset in Galliard
by SPi Technologies India Pvt Ltd (Straive)

ACPA
College Student Educators International

CONTENTS

PREFACE: *IT DEPENDS*

Hello and welcome to our book. In the preface, we describe how this project came to be, our thinking behind why this work is essential, and a snapshot of who we are and how our experiences inform what you will read in other chapters. This preface focuses on some core concepts and how we imagined this book into existence.

We met biweekly via Zoom for two years (2020–2022) to imagine, plan, write, edit, work through struggles, celebrate successes, and finish this book. We recorded our meetings and reviewed our conversations periodically as we wrote. Our biweekly meetings held us accountable, provided us with community, and allowed us to celebrate (or sometimes commiserate about) our progress. If you, the reader, would like to write a book with someone, we recommend that it be someone with whom you enjoy spending time and whom you trust to challenge and support you through difficult things.

We understand that law and ethics are not everyone's favorite topics. We get it. We want this book to be practical and *maybe* even enjoyable. We are storytellers and have incorporated stories about our experiences to explain concepts and share our perspectives. Our goal is for our stories to help you understand, and we hope our stories provoke you to reflect on your stories, experiences, and expertise.

We are proud of this work. It can stand alone to guide critical thinking, strategic planning, training, and professional development. This book also works in conjunction with more traditional law texts. At a time when students are often worried about doing things the "right way" (as if there were one "right way"), we offer strategies focused on utilizing critical thinking and our Institutional Intelligence Model to understand position and context.

In other words, we hope this book helps you figure out what you need to know *before* taking action.

Every campus is different. Every incident is different. Every student is different. Every staff member is different. And every reader is different. This text embraces these realities instead of oversimplifying the complex and essential work that student-facing staff members do daily.

Michelle

In the fall of 2015, I taught law and ethics for the first time as an assistant professor in the student affairs program at Clemson University. From 2007 to 2014, I worked as an Assistant Dean of Students and Director of Student Conduct at Iowa State University. It was a job I loved, working with a phenomenal team. I entered into my teaching that first year with a book selected and intended to lean hard into my experiences as a practitioner. The book I chose to use was a few years old and focused on the vocabulary of the law and drew heavily from legal cases.

In my graduate program at the University of Arkansas (U of A), we used *The Law of Higher Education* (3rd ed.) by Kaplin and Lee (1995). I loved reading "the big red book," dense with case law, and discussing the cases with our instructor, Dr. John Murry—an attorney who brought his expertise and a legal lens to his teaching. Upon finishing my M.Ed. at the U of A, I worked in housing at the University of Cincinnati and Ohio University, later in academic affairs at Dartmouth College, and then back in housing and finally in student conduct at Iowa State University, where I also earned my undergraduate and PhD degrees.

While I love case law, that was not the focus I wanted to bring to the classroom with my students. In my experience as a student affairs practitioner, I was never once asked about case law, and rarely did legal vocabulary come up in my work—even as a conduct officer. Instead, I made decisions with legal and ethical implications daily. So, after that first year of teaching law and ethics in higher education, I searched for a new text, as the book I had used in class did not answer many of the questions that students had. Do not misunderstand me; case law and a sense of history around legal and ethical issues are essential to student learning in a student affairs graduate preparation program. Therefore, in this book, you will find references to case law and legal vocabulary.

This book comes from my failure to find the book I wanted—a book, it turned out, that did not exist. When I asked others for recommendations, they suggested books I had already read and considered. The books were valuable but did not engage in law and ethics the way I thought was most relevant to student and academic affairs staff.

Yes, higher education (and the larger U.S. society) has become more litigious in recent years. For me, however, it is far more important for student affairs graduate students and higher education practitioners to understand how to navigate situations with legal and ethical implications than it is to memorize precedent or legislation. I served in an on-call role for 20 years. When I got called in the middle of the night, my first thoughts were about students and safety. Next, I thought about who needed to be informed about the situation. My third thought was about a variety of things. *It depends* on the situation. Regardless of what you face, it is unlikely that one of your first thoughts will be about legal precedent. However, all our thoughts, decisions, and actions when dealing with crises have legal and ethical implications—for example, student well-being, facilities issues, community impact, impact on the staff responding to the situation, and risk management.

So, what do we do? On what do our decisions depend? That is what this book is about. How we respond *depends* on who is involved. Is the person handling the situation a new employee in their first weeks on the job or an established associate dean of students? If handling a situation depends on the relationship between student accessibility services and the chemistry department, what is the history of collaboration and communication between those areas? What related incidents have happened on campus in the past? Is the incident on a public or private institution's campus? All these things and so many others matter.

On the first day of class in *Legal and Ethical Issues*, I tell students, "If you don't learn anything else in this class, know that the answer to any legal or ethical question in student affairs is: *It depends*."

Of course, the follow-up question is "What does *it depend* on?" Hence, this book.

As I imagined this book and it began to take shape, I knew I wanted a collaborator. I wanted a good writing partner who had areas of academic and student affairs expertise different from my own. I also wanted someone who philosophically had a similar vision of serving students in higher education.

The answer came to me immediately, and I reached out to my friend and colleague, Dr. Cristóbal Salinas Jr. In the past, he invited me to write with him about hazing (Salinas & Boettcher, 2018; Salinas et al., 2018). The subject of hazing overlaps with this book, and—more importantly—he was an outstanding writing partner and collaborator. We also had a relationship so embedded with trust that I knew he would be comfortable letting me know if I got too far off-track or used too much of a conduct-centric lens.

I owe gratitude to my friend and co-author for this book. He makes me a better writer, faculty member, friend, and human being.

Cristóbal

First, I am thankful that Michelle invited me to be part of this book. In our first conversation about this critical project, I vividly remember Michelle describing the idea of this book and her teaching experiences. Through this initial conversation, I understood that her concept of *it depends* is true in student affairs and higher education. *It depends* can be the answer to many questions. However, its purpose is not to answer or avoid answering a question but to help us stop and inspire us to think, analyze, and strategically consider how our decisions connect to law and ethics. Law and ethics impact our decision-making within student affairs, higher education, and beyond.

The concept of *it depends* is centered on my thinking and doing. For example, as a Multicultural Liaison Officer at Iowa State University, I learned that when I thought about what programming I would develop, my response was "*It depends.*" *It depended* on student and faculty needs and wants. What I was able to do also depended on budgets and discussions with my supervisor or colleagues. Even when I planned diversity presentations, the audience informed how I approached the work. It depended on the people, topic or case, location, and situation. This book will provide critical questions and scenarios for you to think about, analyze, and strategically consider. This text will move you from just responding with "*It depends*" to figuring out what things affect your decision in preparation for action.

It depends is a concept that creates opportunities for us to think, do, and feel about legal and ethical issues in student affairs and higher education. Nevertheless, law and ethics inform where we start with the concept of *it depends*. The law and ethics around us and our experiences inform how we think about factors in future situations. Like law and ethics, who we are and how we engage depend on history, geography, identity, and culture—and law and ethics are part of each. All of this affects how we understand the world.

For example, during my elementary and middle school years in Mexico, I learned that there are six continents in the world: Asia, Africa, America, Australia, Antarctica, and Europe. Then, in high school, in the United States, I re-learned that there are seven continents: Asia, Africa, North America, South America, Australia, Antarctica, and Europe. In Mexico, America is one continent, but in the U.S., it is two. In comparison, other textbooks for people in other countries might not consider Antarctica a continent. So how many continents are in the world? Again, *it depends* on where you went to school, where you learned, who taught you, who wrote the textbooks, and a variety of other points.

As an associate professor of higher education leadership at Florida Atlantic University, I find that law and ethics play a significant role in my course:

Introduction to Higher Education. In *Introduction to Higher Education*, I ask students to reflect and write about the following:

- What is the purpose of higher education?
- What methods do we use to study the history of higher education?
- Who controls/should control higher education?
- Who attends/should attend higher education institutions?
- What is/should be taught/studied in higher education?

In this class, I have learned that our understanding of higher education, student affairs, and academic affairs most often comes from our own college experiences and through positions that we hold or have held at colleges or universities. Although this is a great starting point, the field of higher education—past, present, and future—is vast and complex and goes beyond our individual experiences.

As presented in Chapters 2 and 3, the law has dictated much of the history of higher education. However, the historical perspectives of higher education are told and examined in various ways that impact how we think about and analyze college and university settings. Therefore, I hope this book provides a new perspective for you as a reader, a new way to view and question the history of student affairs and higher education.

Because when you think about what you know and the actions you might take in a situation, *it depends* on how you learned, with whom you engaged, and where you attended school. What you bring through identity, experience, and training also affects how you will make decisions in your job. Throughout this book, we provide critical scenarios that will engage you in different ways of strategically thinking, analyzing, and planning within higher education's ever-changing context now and in the future.

Guiding Information

In addition to relying on personal knowledge, perspective, resources, and expertise related to specific functional areas, we drew from legislation and case law for this book (Chapters 2 and 3). While this book is not about memorizing cases or policies, it is essential to be at least familiar with the law and court cases related to our work. We included history and terminology for additional context.

Beyond the initial chapters, student affairs organizational information guides this book. ACPA and NASPA provide several excellent resources for student affairs, legal and ethical issues, concerns, and practice. Other organizations also have ethical statements and resources specific to their members' work. Examples are the Association of College and University Housing

Officers International (ACUHO-I), the Association of College Unions International (ACUI), the Association of Fraternity/Sorority Advisors (AFA), the Association for Student Conduct Administration (ASCA), the National Academic Advising Association (NACADA), and the Association for Orientation, Transition, and Retention in Higher Education (NODA).

Other higher education organizations beyond those most directly connected with student affairs also have codes of ethics. These include the American Association of Community Colleges (AACC), the American Association of University Professors (AAUP), the Association for the Study of Higher Education (ASHE), the American Association of Colleges and Universities (AAC&U), the Association of American Universities (AAU), the National Center for Public Policy and Higher Education, and the National Center for Educational Statistics (NCES). We encourage you to seek out ethical guidelines for any of your organizations.

ACPA and NASPA Organizational Guidance

As the leading organizations for student affairs, ACPA and NASPA guide the way that organizations and specific functional units think about their work. Additionally, these national organizations provide insight into how different units across organizations work together to support college students. Here, we highlight a few aspects of law and ethics that support our approach to this book.

ACPA Statement of Ethical Principles and Standards

ACPA based its *Statement of Ethical Principles and Standards* on four standards: professional responsibility and competence, student learning and development, responsibility to the institution, and responsibility to society (ACPA, n.d., pp. 1–5). This document states:

> Contextual issues must also be taken into account. Such issues include, but are not limited to, culture, temporality (issues bound by time), and phenomenology (individual perspective) and community norms. Because of the complexity of ethical conversation and dialogue, the skill of simultaneously confronting differences in perspective and respecting the rights of persons to hold different perspectives becomes essential.
>
> *(ACPA, n.d., p. 1)*

This statement underscores the philosophy of this book. Legal and ethical issues are complicated, and doing legal and ethical work is hard. If you are looking for a checklist of what to do to avoid legal and ethical problems, it does not exist. Exercise healthy skepticism when anyone offers you a document and says, "If you do all of this, you will never get in legal or ethical trouble."

Instead, embrace the complexity. Learn what you can. Do the best you can—document what you did and why or who told you to do what. Learn from your mistakes. Center care for students. Does that read like a checklist of things to do so you never get into legal or ethical trouble? It is not. Instead, these are good practices. They do not guarantee that you will be immune from lawsuits or ethical challenges. Instead, this advice will help you explain (if asked) why you did what you did.

NASPA Standards of Professional Practice

This 1990 document outlines 19 areas of consideration for practitioners. It leans toward the legal rather than the ethical and speaks to institutional obligations, conflicts of interest, legal authority, research, confidentiality, references and hiring, and assessment, among other topics. The document states, "We hope that our members use these standards in developing their codes and guide them daily as they continue their work" (NASPA, n.d.-a, p. 1). This language acknowledges that each institution is different, as is each division or unit. It is essential to consider institutional culture and history, student needs and demographics, and individual expertise to customize how we address legal and ethical issues in our unique contexts.

ACPA/NASPA Competencies

As in the ACPA/NASPA Competencies (ACPA/NASPA, 2015), we agree that personal and ethical foundations "are stronger together" and work better as "a single competency area" (p. 5). Personal and Ethical Foundations (PEFs) consititute the first competency area listed. By focusing on the individual practitioner, the associations highlight that the work starts with each of us as people. The tools and materials we each bring to teams determine what we build in the community.

We encourage you as individual students, practitioners, and those working in and connected to higher education to explore your knowledge and opportunities for growth in the PEF competency. After that initial step, we hope you will come together to learn others' perspectives and further develop competence, resulting in a more profound commitment to understanding yourselves. This work can also help us create positive change informed by conversation and reflection. While individuals can easily use this book throughout their careers, the foundation of student affairs includes the idea that we learn best in community with others. We designed this text for both individuals and teams.

It is important to remember that the PEF competency includes "Distinguish the legal and moral influences on varying codes of ethics" (ACPA/NASPA, 2015, p. 17) as an intermediate outcome. This competency shows the connection between law, ethics, personal practice, and policy. These issues are intertwined in our work and similarly intertwined in this book.

In the Law, Policy, and Governance (LPG) competency, the theme is for students and practitioners to be able to identify, describe, and comply at the foundational level. It is not until the intermediate and advanced outcomes that organizations expect individuals to examine systems, policies, and processes critically. At the advanced levels, ACPA and NASPA expect individuals to develop, implement, and influence policies and practices to effect change.

We highlight PEFs and LPG here because they are part of the foundation for this book. However, we address relevant competencies in each of the functional area chapters. Ultimately, all competencies inform the work of all functional areas. Our goal was to highlight a few of the most relevant for each section.

We acknowledge the expertise of graduate students and emerging practitioners in student affairs and higher education. The phrase "we are the ones we have been waiting for" comes to mind. While the origin of this phrase is unclear, it describes the attitude of college students who are becoming new student and academic affairs practitioners. These new and emerging staff members are coming to higher education and student affairs work with a dedication to creating change. Many new staff members already have extensive experience creating change in and beyond higher education. As a result, as you engage with this book, we as authors do not assume that new practitioners start at foundational competency levels and move through intermediate outcomes to advanced outcomes as they move through their careers. New staff may function at advanced levels in some competencies, just as experienced practitioners and leaders are still learning in some areas.

The Institutional Intelligence Model

One of the gifts that emerged as we worked on this book was the Institutional Intelligence Model. This model took shape throughout our early conversations about how higher education staff navigate complex campus issues. How staff members handle a situation on one campus will differ from another. The way one leader handles a situation differs from another. What one student needs in a situation differs from another.

During one conversation, we realized that asking *who*, *what*, *where*, *when*, *why*, and *how* questions about situations was an effective way to get the information we need before making decisions—especially when first learning about an institution. In Chapter 5, you will find an introduction to the Institutional Intelligence Model. This model centers on the idea that you have to know your institution to make good decisions and take the most effective action in any situation. Who are the people involved, what is happening, where are you working, and other questions help provide us with institutional intelligence. We have embedded the Institutional Intelligence Model throughout the book and provided context about how to apply it, particularly in connection with the critical scenarios for each functional area.

Continuing the Conversation

As you engage in this book, we have created a companion online space for additional conversation. Legal issues are constantly in flux. New challenges emerge in higher education all the time. You have experience in functional areas and leadership roles and on campuses different from ours. Please share if you have critical scenarios, questions to ask, or provocations with which we should wrestle. We encourage you to write your own critical scenarios.

In thinking ahead, we want to encourage you to reflect, and we also want to provide a space to share. If you have scenarios that you encourage student-facing practitioners to consider, please submit them to **institutionalintelligencebook@gmail.com**. We will review all new critical scenarios submitted and share those that reflect situations that frequently occur, particularly compelling scenarios and those we want to offer to others for more consideration. We will publish these scenarios on our professional websites (https://www.mlboettcher.com and https://www.drcrissalinas.com).

This shared space is open to everyone. We hope students will share emerging and ongoing issues they are navigating. We hope instructors will encourage students to write and submit Institutional Intelligence scenarios for courses. In many ways, graduate students are the most current practitioners, given their level of student engagement. As frontline staff, they have insights that are invaluable.

We encourage student affairs, academic affairs, and other higher education practitioners to write and share critical scenarios. While we have both been practitioners, we have not worked outside our faculty roles for several years. Your firsthand accounts and perspectives are essential to continuing to do excellent work on campuses.

Conclusion

Again, welcome to this book. We worked to make sure that this is a valuable resource. We sought to bring a connection to real-world practice to the text by partnering with current practitioners on the critical scenarios in each chapter. Along with critical scenario co-authors, we designed these scenarios to foster discussion, reflection, and anticipation of issues that might emerge. Many thanks to the team of colleagues who supported that work.

We also brought ourselves into this text. Throughout the book, we reference our own experiences and thinking on topics. We did this intentionally to be transparent about our positionalities related to the topic. We want you—as much as possible—to understand who we are in the context of higher education law and ethics. We learned a lot through writing this book and look forward to learning more with you as we move to what comes next in academic and student affairs.

Finally, we tried to include some humor. Law and ethics can be a dense and intense area of study. Humor is our way of coping with challenging situations. Of course, humor must be used appropriately and never to mock, shame, or cause harm. We used humor throughout our work together, and it helped our collaboration. We hope that you find that our humor enhances the text.

Thank you for your attention to this work. Engaging in legal and ethical issues in productive ways is essential to the success of individuals, units, divisions, and institutions. These issues inform higher education every day. Nearly every decision we make has ethical implications. Most also have legal implications. That said, the work does not need to be overwhelming. Instead, practicing and strategically planning for issues make us more confident and competent practitioners and educators. We are excited to partner with you in the work.

FOREWORD

We need look no further than the docket of the Supreme Court of the United States to see the importance of legal issues in student affairs practice. From affirmative action to the recognition of the legal rights of gay, lesbian, bisexual, and transgender members of our society to reproductive rights, the Court's decisions have monumental implications for higher education. While the United States Congress seems more incapable of action than ever, there are still pieces of legislation with significant implications for student affairs under consideration at any time, in addition to the continued funding of the federal student financial aid system. In recent years, the actions of state legislatures have become increasingly important with bans on the teaching of Critical Race Theory considered in many states, legislative proposals to allow firearms on campus, passed in about a dozen states, proposals to protect students' free expression rights and paradoxically limiting the rights of protestors, to name but a few. The legal and legislative landscape facing student affairs practitioners is complex and at times contradictory. As Benjamin Cardoza (1921) observed, "Law never *is*, but is always about to be" (p. 126).

More than 25 years ago, as a doctoral student at Bowling Green State University, I had the opportunity to take higher education law with Dr. Donald D. Gehring, whose legal syllabus was famous for its length and the seemingly endless list of cases with which students were expected to be familiar. Was this the best approach? As Michelle and Cristóbal so often ask in this work, *it depends.* We were doctoral students preparing for careers as senior administrators and faculty. I had already established a clear research agenda with legal and legislative issues at its heart. I continue to engage with that agenda. I have also served as an expert witness and consultant on these issues working with numerous colleges and universities around the country. In my case, I think it was.

In the years since, I have taught legal issues in student affairs and higher education at multiple institutions to several different audiences—masters students, doctoral students, and working community college professionals. Each time, I had to consider multiple factors and finding the right approach to the course—striking a balance between practice and case law, student affairs–specific aspects and broader higher education issues, and the environments and roles for which my students were preparing. Like Michelle, I have searched for alternative current textbooks for the class but found myself returning time and time again to *The Law of Higher Education* by Bill Kaplin and Barbara Lee in its various editions (currently Kaplin et al., 2020) supplemented with other articles and materials—even court decisions (in moderation).

Law and Ethics in Academic and Student Affairs: Developing an Institutional Intelligence Approach offers a practitioner-oriented approach to understanding legal and legislative issues in student affairs and helps to address this gap in the literature. The most significant contribution in my view is the Institutional Intelligence Model introduced in Chapter 5 and expanded upon in the next four chapters. This model provides a thoughtful framework well suited for master's students examining cases with legal and ethical dimensions. I particularly appreciate the inclusion of ethical issues because while the law may tell us what we must or even what we could do, it does not tell us what we should do. One of the most exciting and frustrating aspects of legal and legislative issue in higher education is that it is constantly changing. The Institutional Intelligence Model offers students a framework that is not dependent on a static body of knowledge. Its utility is not limited to legal issues either—the framework can be helpful in examining a wide variety of campus issues. I also appreciate the intentional integration of American College Personnel Association (ACPA) and National Association of Student Personnel Administrators' (NASPA's) *Professional Competency Areas for Student Affairs Educators* (2015) throughout this work.

Not since Peggy Barr (1988) published *Student Services and the Law: A Handbook for Practitioners* has there been a work so clearly focused on the intersection of the law and student affairs practice. While there are scattered chapters across numerous works that address legal issues in specific functional areas, no work since *Student Services and the Law* has brought together a collection that examines legal issues across numerous functional areas. The chapter authors also clearly connect the legal issues in that functional area to the Institutional Intelligence Model and provide multiple Critical Scenarios so that readers can apply these concepts in practice.

Many lawyer jokes are based upon an assumed fondness among lawyers for the phrase "On the other hand," but with any good joke there is a kernel truth. Michelle and Cristóbal offer a far more productive response to the question "What should we do?": *it depends. Law and Ethics in Academic and Student Affairs: Developing an Institutional Intelligence Approach* offers a helpful framework for working through the obvious follow-up question "What does *it depend* on?" with the Institutional Intelligence Model. As I read the draft of this work to write the foreword, I was again preparing to teach Legal Issues in Student Affairs at Indiana University of Pennsylvania. I found myself, time and time again, making notes about how I might fine-tune my approach to my own class, which is for me the highest endorsement possible.

John Lowery
Professor of Student Affairs and Higher Education,
Indiana University of Pennsylvania

SECTION 1
Setting the Stage

1

USING THIS TEXT

"Hey, Michelle and Cristóbal, it's a book. I know how to use a book," you say. While we do not doubt you, we think our book is unique and want to make it enjoyable to use and read. We use books in various ways, including learning, application to practice, as door stops, in classes, for staff training, to raise our laptops for virtual meetings, and so on. We wrote this book to help you navigate the changing contexts of higher education.

As authors, we see change as an opportunity, not an obstacle. When change happens, we can reflect on what we have done, what we could do, who is affected and involved, and whom we need to invite into the work and learning. Institutions change based on students, leadership transitions, and public expectations. As individuals, we may take on new roles where we are or take positions at different institutions. We must navigate changing roles, campuses, and relationships.

Here is an example of institutional change. Think about a time when a new graduate student or practitioner joined your team. The new person might say or think, "That's not how we did it at my former institution. That way was better." You *know* people like that, or you *are* that person. Rarely can we cut and paste initiatives from one place to the next. We must learn to transfer experiences effectively as we change institutions. Change—even positive change—is difficult. This book can help, and here are a few ways you might want to use this book:

- In the classroom: This book encourages readers to develop questions to understand their institutional context by critically examining how decisions can have different results on different campuses.

DOI: 10.4324/9781003442707-2

- In the job search: Using the Institutional Intelligence Model (see Chapter 5) can help us learn about institutions as we apply and interview for jobs there.
- Onboarding: The Institutional Intelligence Model helps new students, staff, and faculty on campus and supervisors prepare for their arrival. Even practitioners established on campus need to revisit their specific culture, history, and other issues to transition new team members effectively.
- Training: This book provides tools to help us anticipate what we need to know to respond to crises effectively.
- Impact of external factors: Higher education is affected by alumni, community members, donors, employees, government, parents, students, and other stakeholders. Understanding relationships with each of these constituents is part of developing Institutional Intelligence.
- Reflective practice: The book can guide reflective practice after an incident or event.

These are a few examples of how this book can be helpful to academic and student affairs practitioners and others in higher education.

The Philosophy of This Book

Law and Ethics in Academic and Student Affairs: Developing an Institutional Intelligence Approach focuses on how academic and student affairs practitioners can make informed legal and ethical decisions. Knowledge of critical laws and court cases is essential, and you can find an overview of those topics in this book (see Chapters 2 and 3). However, it is much more important for student affairs and higher education staff to know how to navigate issues on campus.

Law is constantly changing and is interpreted differently from campus to campus based on the culture and history of an institution. This text provides higher education practitioners with tools to anticipate practical and responsible action. *Law and Ethics in Academic and Student Affairs: Developing an Institutional Intelligence Approach* provides tools and engages readers in preflection (reflecting before and during the incident, training, or onboarding) and reflection on emerging situations in higher education. By using these tools, practitioners are more equipped to navigate legal and ethical issues successfully.

Student affairs and higher education work has become increasingly complex. Issues of campus culture, institutional history, student identity, the debate around the purpose of higher education, and many other issues—contemporary and historical—frame the work of students, staff, and faculty on college and university campuses. Ethical decisions are made every day in almost every moment, and legal issues significantly impact all student-facing practitioners, not just student conduct hearing officers and university counsel. Increasingly, everyone from an undergraduate student resident assistant to the vice president of student affairs can be held responsible for institutional responses to situations. As a result, we need new strategies and approaches for our work.

Knowing First, Doing Second

When I (Michelle) teach law and ethics to the second-year cohort in our student affairs program each fall, students often want to know how to avoid every legal and ethical issue they might encounter in their career. When discussing hypothetical legal and ethical situations, they ask, "So what do I do?" It is both impossible and dangerous to attempt to answer that question. Early on, as a faculty member, I decided that "It depends" was a better response to their questions than "I have no idea." As a result, *it depends* has become the foundation for this text. The "it" being—"What should I do?"

Ultimately, the answer to any legal or ethical question is: *It depends.* The purpose of this book is to help practitioners understand what our actions depend on. A few examples of the factors to consider as we work through incidents on campus are the following:

- *Who* are you, and how long have you been at your institution?
- *What* is a student or organization's history with the university?
- *Where* do you work?
- *When* were you made aware of the situation?
- *Why* are you being consulted about the incident?
- *How* has the institution navigated similar incidents in the past?

As you can see, *it depends* on many things. This text aims to help students and practitioners explore what *it depends* on before moving to action. Think of this book as a guide to help you answer not just "What should I do?" but "What do I need to know before I do anything?" *It depends.* On what? This book will help you figure that out.

Institutional Intelligence Model

In this book, we introduce the Institutional Intelligence Model. One day when we were meeting about the book, we talked about how we make difficult decisions during times of change or crisis. We found that we both try to understand things first (time permitting) and then respond based on our best information and institutional knowledge. As a result, we realized we had come up with a model we and others often use intuitively. We built the Institutional Intelligence Model on *who*, *what*, *where*, *when*, *why*, and *how* questions. These questions help engage student affairs staff in preflective (before incidents emerge) and reflective (after the fact) processes.

The Institutional Intelligence Model is about knowing the elements that guide the behavior of individuals, groups, and organizations.[1] To develop Institutional Intelligence at an institution, we must understand the people, mission, vision, history, culture(s), practices, norms, beliefs, language/terminology, finances, policies and guidelines, bureaucracy, and unwritten rules that guide individual and group behavior. Each of these influences policy and ethical action and is influenced by local, state, and federal law and the ethics of students and employees on campus and other constituents.

This book asks critical questions to help us understand institutional *who*, *what*, *where*, *when*, *why*, and *how* questions and to analyze critical scenarios that can arise. We encourage you to develop critical scenarios to understand institutional factors on your campus. For example, who are great campus partners for your office? What are common issues that emerge for students your area serves? How does information about where you work (e.g., institutional type and institutional history) inform how you might respond to situations?

Additionally, you can use the Institutional Intelligence Model in self-reflection about who you are as a practitioner. Questions you might consider: Whom do you want to help? What experiences have shaped your ethics? Where do you want to work? When might you want to change jobs? Why did you choose this career? How do your ethics and values align with the institution where you work? Institutional Intelligence can help you clarify and articulate your ethical philosophy.

Ethical and legal issues do not exist separately; they influence each other and can help us understand human behavior and how we define right and wrong. This book is about thinking critically and strategically to make good decisions rather than providing a list of rules to follow. Through each chapter of this book, we further unpack Institutional Intelligence. The answer to "What should I do?" *depends* on people (*who*), events (*what*), place (*where*), timing (*when*), cause/rationale (*why*), and situational details (*how*). The Institutional Intelligence Model can help you explore each of those areas.

The Organization of the Book

We organized this book into four sections. Section 1 (*Setting the Stage*) focuses on how to use the text, a brief overview of the history, legislation, terminology, and legal issues in student affairs, and an overview of ethics. Chapter 2 provides the foundation for higher education, especially student affairs in history and law. Chapter 3 provides legal terminology and relevant case law. Chapter 4 focuses on a foundational understanding of ethics and their relation to values, morals, and beliefs.

Section 2 introduces and describes the Institutional Intelligence Model (Chapter 5) and offers tools to help you understand your specific work environments. This section takes you through the Institutional Intelligence Model questions in Chapters 6 through 9 (*who*, *what*, *where*, *when*, *why*, and *how*) to show you how these questions can help you develop a deeper and more comprehensive understanding of your institutional context.

Section 3 (*Functional Areas and Critical Scenarios*) focuses on student and academic affairs units. This section may be helpful for academic coursework, interview preparation, staff development, and training.

In addition, we developed and included critical scenarios to further explore the issues raised in the text. We labeled the situational descriptions as "critical scenarios" rather than case studies. The label "case study" can apply to a research methodology, a means of keeping clinical records, and requires significant detail related to context, complexity, ambiguity, and relevance (Fossey & Crow, 2011). Because our goal is for readers to clarify their institutional context and understand the elements that make their college or university unique, we present not fully developed case studies. Rather than providing a case—bounded by a specific setting and context (Merriam, 2009), we provide critical scenarios that have utility across institutional types, information about the positionality of the actors in the scenario, and other individual and institutional variables. We designed the critical scenarios to develop critical thinking skills. Additionally, the goal of the scenarios is not to figure out "What should Billy do?" but rather to answer the question "What does Billy need to *know* before they *do* anything?" Of course, you may be trying to figure out "Who is Billy?" but that is not the point we are trying to focus on here.

Additionally, we have included the word "critical" in describing our scenarios; this is for two reasons. First, many of the scenarios in this text unfold during a crisis. It is *critical* that staff know resources and be prepared to respond quickly and appropriately, not only for legal and ethical reasons but for issues of safety. Second, we encourage readers to consider critical frameworks in examining these situations. In this process, when examining a situation, readers must engage in critical thinking and decision-making to resolve the issue(s)/challenge(s) while considering the roles of power and oppression. Systemic and historical issues in higher education matter in the scenarios, but these concepts also matter in our work and lives outside these hypotheticals. The American College Personnel Association/National Association of Student Personnel Administrators (ACPA/NASPA) competencies state that in order for a practitioner to be successful at the intermediate level, staff must be able to "identify systemic barriers to social justice and inclusion and assess one's own department's role in addressing such barriers" (ACPA/NASPA, 2015, p. 31). This critical examination is central to our work with others and our own learning.

People are always involved in and affected by decisions. Therefore, we must also consider the intersection of people's identities in these scenarios. We have provided pronouns for each person in our scenarios but have refrained from providing additional information. We intentionally left other identities out of the descriptions to encourage readers to consider how identity might inform these scenarios. We encourage readers to think about how a situation could be very different depending on the identities of the people involved.

Finally, Section 4 concludes the book by focusing on reflective practice and how to use the Institutional Intelligence Model in the context of change. As examples of change, we focus on human resources—job search and hiring—and campus crises. In the afterword of this section, we ask you to consider the future of higher education with a particular focus on academic and student affairs practitioners.

We also discuss ways to continue conversations about law and ethics. Section 4 includes a brief afterword and additional information about the websites affiliated with this book. There are new and emerging issues every day. To keep the conversation going, we invite you to join us in additional discussions about the legal and ethical issues we face.

Section 1: Setting the Stage

Chapter 1 (Using this Text) provides readers an overview of how the book can be helpful in both practice and academic spaces. Chapter 1 contextualizes the book as a practitioner manual rather than a history of higher education law and policy. The chapter also provides a brief summary of the Institutional Intelligence Model. Finally, Chapter 1 gives an overview of the other chapters in the book. You are reading it right now. Is it helpful?

Chapter 2 (A Brief History of Higher Education and Related Legislation) provides an overview of U.S. higher education history and legislation (thus the title) focusing on student affairs.

Chapter 3 (Case Law and Higher Education) highlights terms and student-related court cases in higher education. The first section defines basic legal terms. The second section focuses on cases that have impacted higher education. Like Chapter 2, this chapter aligns with the ACPA/NASPA Law, Policy, and Governance (LPG) competency (ACPA/NASPA, 2015).

Chapter 4 (An Ethics Primer) provides an overview of ethical frameworks, primarily consequentialism, ethics of care, professional ethics, and applied ethics. Additionally, this chapter offers readers reflective prompts to engage in understanding their ethical philosophies, how those ethical philosophies developed, and the role that ethics play in student affairs practice. This chapter aligns ethics with the ACPA/NASPA Personal and Ethical Foundations (PEF) competency (ACPA/NASPA, 2015). This chapter also includes tools for student and academic affairs practitioners to use to engage in ethical practice.

Section 2: The Institutional Intelligence Model

Chapter 5 (Institutional Intelligence) introduces this new model to help you analyze situations and make sound decisions informed by your specific institutional culture to make effective legal, ethical, and contextually informed decisions.

Chapter 6 (*Who*) helps practitioners identify other individuals on and beyond campus who need information, may be impacted, or can assist as events unfold. Legal and ethical issues do not exist in isolation, and we must consider the implications for others as we make decisions. This chapter is a guide for managing institutional and individual risk/harm while centering on student support. Additionally, this chapter provides prompts to help us consider who we are.

Chapter 7 (*What*) situates issues at the forefront. Before identifying steps to take in a given situation, we must define the situation and understand situational complexities. This chapter helps us explore issues by asking: What is the issue? Is it legal, ethical, or a combination? Is the issue anticipated, currently unfolding, or in the past? What previous decisions, events, or incidents inform decision-making about the current situation? What information do staff members have or need? These questions help us identify the next steps as we make decisions.

Chapter 8 (*Where*) focuses on institutional type, location, culture, and history. Learning culture and history is challenging for new students, staff, and faculty. Student affairs and higher education practitioners often uncover historical and cultural issues through mistaken assumptions about campus. Furthermore, we can make mistakes when we apply our experiences at one institution to another. This chapter helps readers ask critical questions to understand where they work.

Chapter 9 (*When, Why, and How*) explores other questions we need to ask to understand our institutional contexts. For example, questions about why to respond to a situation have both legal and ethical considerations. When and how questions help us focus on the strategic responses for the most effective and efficient decision-making related to emerging issues.

Too often, student affairs graduate students, practitioners, faculty, researchers, higher education professionals, and those working in higher education–adjacent areas respond first (often out of care and concern for others or driven by a sense of urgency) without considering or recognizing the full impact of their decisions. By helping student affairs practitioners gather necessary information before or early in an incident, the practitioners themselves are more protected. Students or colleagues in crisis also get the support they need.

Section 3: Functional Areas and Critical Scenarios

Each discussion of a functional area in Section 3 opens with a direct quote from a student affairs practitioner, higher education leader, or scholar to help frame the chapter. We intentionally sought out key practitioner-leaders to provide practical context for the functional areas across student affairs. While we have practitioner experience in various student and academic affairs areas, we are not current practitioners. The world has changed dramatically since we were in those roles. We partnered with current practitioners whose insight is more timely, relevant, and accurate than ours.

We provide a brief overview of each functional area, starting with how it emerged as part of higher education. We include vital moments or changes as well. These are not comprehensive histories but concise summaries that provide background to each area.

Finally, we partnered with current student affairs and higher education practitioners to write a critical scenario specific to each functional area. We sought to provide the most robust possible scenarios and honor practitioners' expertise as holders of wisdom and expertise that we, as the authors of this book, do not have.

The goal of this section in each chapter is to provide a realistic situation for discussion in various individual and institutional contexts so we can use the book in classroom and practitioner settings. Each critical scenario prompts current student affairs and higher education practitioners to consider and identify what steps to take next at their institution. Each critical scenario concludes with a set of *who*, *what*, *where*, *when*, *why*, and *how* prompts to get you started developing your Institutional Intelligence skills and practicing analyzing situations.

Chapter 10 (Student Identity-Based Center Services) addresses the specific student experiences with identity-based centers and services that promote student success. We chose to open with this functional area because student affairs practitioners must learn about and honor students' identities to attend to them holistically. Our identities inform all we do in our work. The critical scenarios in this chapter consider intersections of identity informed by race, ethnicity, gender, first-generation college student status, and immigration status, among other social identities and aspects of multifaceted students' lives.

As mentioned earlier, we partnered with practitioners on the critical scenarios; we did not include identity-related information. In keeping with the idea that *it depends*, we encourage you to consider how these scenarios could play out differently depending on each actor's identity. How does identity potentially inform the experiences of individuals in each scenario?

Functional Areas covered in this chapter: *African American Cultural Centers; Asian American Cultural Centers; Latino Cultural Centers; Native American Cultural Centers; Lesbian, Gay, Bisexual, Transgender, and Queer Centers; Women's Centers; International Students Services*; and *Student Accessibility Services.*

Chapter 11 (Admissions, Financial Aid, and Orientation) focuses on critical first steps to the college experience. Admission, money to pay for school, and learning what it means to be a member of a particular institutional community set the stage for college students' experiences. Staff in these areas significantly impact students' experiences in higher education. This section discusses the role that each of these areas plays and provides scenarios for wrestling with the complex work done by staff in these units and offices.

Functional Areas covered in this chapter: *Admissions, Financial Aid*, and *Orientation.*

Chapter 12 (Academics) focuses on the relationships between academic advisors, coaches, and other academic success staff and the students they serve. Academic relationships vary from student to student, but academic support staff members are essential to student success. Academic advising and coaching involve much more than simply fulfilling administrative tasks and completing paperwork. Academic support staff often have information about students' lives and the opportunity to engage with student tutors, faculty, and peer mentors. Because of their relationships with students, this staff team receives information and supports students in times of stress and crisis.

Functional Areas covered in this chapter: *Academic Advising, Academic Coaching*, and *Academic Support.*

Chapter 13 (Student Living and Well-Being) combines student living environments with student behavior and wellness resources on college campuses. Issues related to physical and mental health often surface, and these areas have direct connections to specific policies such as the Family Education Rights and Privacy Act (FERPA), the Health Insurance Portability and Accountability Act (HIPAA), Title IX, and the Americans with Disabilities Act (ADA). However, while specific legal guidelines exist for each area, no policies are free of ethical implications.

Functional Areas covered in this chapter: *Campus Recreation, Wellness Programs, Fraternity and Sorority Life, Housing, Student Behavior Intervention*, and *Student Conduct.*

Chapter 14 (Student Involvement) focuses on student organizations, leadership, and service. These functional areas are essential to campus life with various activities and opportunities for engagement on college campuses. Student organizations, leadership, and service areas often involve risk management, conflict negotiation, and contracts. As a result, staff working in these areas must understand the institutional policy and history and know where and to whom to go as they support student initiatives. This chapter explores student organizations, leadership, and service issues through relevant critical scenarios with implications for other areas of student affairs.

Functional Areas covered in this chapter: *Civic Learning, Leadership, Community Service Learning*, and *Student Activities.*

Chapter 15 (Confidential Resources) emphasizes the specific staff who are able and obligated to provide confidentiality to students. In terms of university officials, all staff should respect students' privacy. However, the only staff able to offer complete confidentiality—a promise that they will not share information—are medical and counseling staff and religious advisors. Even in those instances, staff may have expectations or legal obligations to share some information. This chapter focuses on how to effectively partner with others on campus who may have student information that they cannot share with colleagues while working collaboratively to support students.

Functional Areas covered in this chapter: *Counseling Centers, Health Centers*, and *Spiritual Life/Campus Ministry.*

Chapter 16 (Graduate Students) highlights the unique position of graduate students as both employees and students. This transitional experience requires emerging practitioners to navigate a shift from having the rights, freedoms, and obligations of being undergraduate students to not only being students but also being connected to institutions as staff members. Navigating this experience requires special attention and guidance, different from other staff roles covered in Section 3.

Topical Areas covered in this chapter: *Academic Program Expectations, Graduate Assistantships, Graduate Assistant Supervision, Role Conflict*, and *Transitioning into Full-Time Roles.*

Section 4: Reflection and Recommendations

Chapter 17 (Engaging in Reflective Practice) guides readers on how to engage in reflective practice related to legal and ethical issues. While crises often take significant time, reflecting and learning are essential to improving policies, processes, responses, and resources. More importantly, this reflection provides tools and strategies to improve student support. Reflection is critical in our work and can make us aware of more efficient responses in the future. The investment is worth the return.

Topical Areas include *Change*, *Job-Seeking*, *Hiring*, and *Campus Crisis.*

Chapter 18 (Afterword: The Future and Continuing the Work) acknowledges the ever-changing nature of student affairs and higher education as well as the law and ethics; therefore, this book closes with both a summary and future implications. This chapter provides insight into how to adapt to different situations and use the critical scenarios presented throughout the book to anticipate potential and successful change in and beyond student affairs practitioners. We also share the opportunity to submit future critical scenarios based on your experiences.

Conclusion: Why This Book, and Why Now?

This book will be an essential resource for academic and student affairs practitioners, students, and other student-facing staff across higher education. While several texts outline the history, law, and policy of student affairs, no book takes the approach we have. We have focused on how higher education students, staff, and faculty navigate the growing and increasingly complex legal and ethical issues of higher education in our increasingly complex campus communities. The foundational assertion of this book is that there is not a one-size-fits-all approach to legal and ethical issues. In response, this book provides a multi-context thinking approach (Salinas & Guerrero, 2018) utilizing the Institutional Intelligence Model. By using this model, we can be better prepared to face crises—even the most unexpected events—with an understanding of our actions' ethical and legal implications. As we reiterate throughout the book, the answer to any question related to law and ethics is that *it depends.* This text helps higher education practitioners determine what *it depends* on.

Note

1 We use "institutions of higher education" and "organization(s)" interchangeably. In this book's context, we approach higher education institutions as organizations.

2

A BRIEF HISTORY OF HIGHER EDUCATION AND RELATED LEGISLATION

This book is neither a complete listing of higher education case law nor a history of higher education. However, it would be irresponsible for us to exclude foundational information to set the stage for the rest of the text. As a result, we made compromises. There is always more to know, understand, read, and study. While this chapter provides some historical context, we encourage you to read more about the history of higher education and relevant legislation and to read regularly about current events. Additional reading and study help us get a deeper understanding of the world and the specific higher education context in which we work.

It is disappointing to hear students say, "I hate history" or "history is so boring." We believe that people who hate history never had a great history teacher. History is storytelling. Of course, many stories are under-represented or completely absent, and we must do more work to uncover some stories than others.

A line in the play *The Niceties* by Eleanor Burgess speaks to this point. In the first act of *The Niceties*, there is an argument between a Black woman undergraduate student and her white woman faculty member about a lack of evidence in an essay the student has submitted for the professor's history course. The student, Zoe, responds to the critique by saying, "But if you say you need evidence... You're excluding the people who couldn't leave evidence behind. People who couldn't write. Anyone without money, or an education. Anyone with no possessions for historians to dig up" (Burgess, 2019, p. 23). As you consider the legislation in the rest of this chapter, do not forget that access to courts and lawmaking has never been equitable in the United States.

DOI: 10.4324/9781003442707-3

As a result, the story told by these pieces of history is a partial history at best. So, when you read this chapter or any record of any area in higher education, any movement or moment, not only consider whose perspectives are missing but do your homework. Seek out other sources of information to learn about what people not represented in the book, the course, or the training might have experienced or have to say about the topics you are exploring. What we offer in this chapter is a compromised history, as all accounts are.

For student affairs practitioners, it is essential to understand how the law sets the stage to avoid "getting in trouble" or "breaking the rules." We encourage practitioners to develop sophisticated and complex personal and professional ethics centering people rather than policy. Understanding how our complex history informs the legal history in our education systems is also essential. This history relates to power, privilege, classism, racism, sexism, and other marginalizing systems. Neither the U.S. educational nor government systems are perfect, but we can work to improve systems (and ourselves) over time with a thorough understanding of how higher education and other systems have come to be.

Competencies

Part of the history of an organization comes from organizational documents. These documents can capture our history, provide context for where we are today, and offer guidance for the future. Among the guiding documents for the umbrella student affairs organizations, the American College Personnel Association (ACPA) and the National Association of Student Personnel Administrators (NASPA) are the shared competencies (see Appendix) these groups developed together. The competencies include areas such as law and ethics, which directly relate to this text, but also leadership and human resources and other competencies for which there are additional legal and ethical considerations.

You can map any ACPA/NASPA competencies to any chapter of this book. Throughout the book, we highlight the competencies most closely connected to the topics in specific chapters. In the case of history and legislation, we encourage you to focus on Law, Policy, and Governance (LPG) and Values, Philosophy, and History (VPH). We also encourage you to work on the Social Justice and Inclusion (SJI) competency as law, policy, history, and other relevant factors have rarely emerged in our society in socially just and equitable ways.

Chapter Organization

The remainder of this chapter consists of two sections, followed by a brief conclusion. First, we include a discussion on the eras of higher education.

There is no consensus about the eras, so we provide examples from different scholars. This section provides a general understanding of the establishment of higher education and its evolution over time.

Next, the chapter includes legislation related to higher education and student affairs. This list and the following chapter on legal cases are in chronological order. As legislation and law build on what has come before, the chronology of laws and court cases reflects social and cultural priorities related to education over time. This format also provides an opportunity to see how issues once absent have slowly emerged and influenced higher education.

Eras of Higher Education

When you read about histories, you will find that scholars often put things into eras or periods or other categories. Authors on the history of higher education are no different. A few examples are the following:

Cohen and Kisker (2010): *The Shaping of American Higher Education: Emergence and Growth of the Contemporary System* (2nd ed.)

- Establishing the Collegiate Form in the Colonies: 1636–1789
- The Diffusion of Small Colleges in the Emergent Nation: 1790–1869
- University Transformation as the Nation Industrializes: 1870–1944
- Mass Higher Education in the Era of American Hegemony: 1945–1975
- Maintaining the Diverse System in an Era of Consolidation: 1976–1993
- Privatization, Corporatization, and Accountability in the Contemporary Era: 1994–2009

Hutcheson (2020): *A People's History of American Higher Education*

- Colonial and Early Republic College
- From the Beginning: Leadership, Exclusion, and Stratification in the Colonizing Colleges and the Early Republic
- Progressive Era and Its Enduring Impact on Higher Education: Efficient, Rational Solutions to Moral and Social Problems
- War: Meanings of Patriotism in Higher Education
- Sex and Love! Beer! Football! And Other Important Student Activities
- The Research University, Revised
- From the Colonial Colleges to the Colleges and Universities of Today: Processes of Exclusion and Stratification

Lake (2011): *Foundations of Higher Education Law & Policy*

- The Era of Legal Insularity: 1636–1960s
- The Civil Rights Era: early 1960s–1970s
- The Bystander Era: 1970s–1980s
- The Facilitator Era: 1980s to the publication of the book

Thelin (2019): *A History of American Higher Education* (3rd ed.)

- Colleges in the Colonial Era
- Creating the "American Way" in Higher Education: College-Building: 1785–1860
- Diversity and Adversity: Resilience in American Higher Education: 1860–1890
- Captains of Industry and Erudition: University-Builders: 1880–1910
- Alma Mater: America Goes to College: 1890–1920
- Success and Excess: Expansion and Reforms in Higher Education: 1920–1945
- Gilt by Association: Higher Education's "Golden Age": 1945–1970
- Coming of Age in America: Higher Education as a Troubled Giant: 1970–2000
- A New Life Begins? Reconfiguring American Higher Education in the Twenty-first Century: 2000–2010
- Prominence and Problems: American Higher Education since 2010

As you can read in the lists above, there is no agreement on how scholars and historians break down different eras of higher education. How historians do this work *depends* on their view of the world and their own lived experiences—in this case, their experiences with higher education. Additionally, these are historians, not always practitioners. Each of you brings expertise that might inform how you would group different periods in student affairs.

Despite our individual areas of expertise and insight or how we might organize the history of colleges and universities in the U.S., there are some themes across the history of higher education related to legal issues. The following is not a comprehensive list but a general guide to provide some preliminary context for the rest of this chapter and book.

The founding of higher education in the U.S. is linked to legal issues such as college access and the role of *in loco parentis* in the lives of students. After the first 150 years of higher education, there was a dramatic increase in school growth and the rise of small colleges. This era was accompanied by legal issues related to schools' contractual obligations to students, a clarification of what higher education in the United States would include, and legal issues about who was able to attend colleges and universities—particularly related to issues of race and gender.

The largest growth in enrollment in this nation's history of higher education came following World War II with the introduction of the Servicemen's Readjustment Act or the G.I. Bill. This was an era of civil rights legislation, a decline in campus *in loco parentis* responsibilities, and legislation about college access related to financial aid, disability accommodation, and equity on campus through integration and Title IX obligations. Beginning in the 1980s, colleges and universities saw tremendous increases in college costs and student loan debt without corresponding increases in the minimum wage, while issues of student safety were increasing in the face of the Clery Act, Title IX expansions related to sexual violence, and increased shootings on college campuses. Then, in 2020, everything stopped for a moment, then we all stumbled forward and have yet to determine what this new era entails, though, from a legal standpoint, efforts have centered student safety on issues of vaccinations and masks as well as questions about the quality of college education in increasingly online learning spaces where equitable internet access touches on issues of socioeconomic status, rurality, and race. All of this is in the midst of the racial pandemic, which college campuses must navigate as Black and Brown students, faculty, and staff are the targets of violence on and off campus. We see where we have been, but where we are headed next is unclear.

Another issue with capturing history is accuracy. There are many questions up for debate. Questions such as, who was the first Black woman to graduate from college in the U.S.? *It depends.* Was it Mary Jane Patterson, the first Black woman to graduate with a diploma from Oberlin College in 1862, or was it Lucy Ann Stanton, who graduated from Oberlin College in 1850 with a certificate instead of a diploma? Or maybe it was Grace A. Mapps, who graduated in 1852 from New York Central College at McGrawville, but we do not know what degree she earned. *It depends.*

We have provided some examples of how some scholars have outlined the history of U.S. higher education. Understanding how different scholars have made meaning of higher education is important because by breaking down and categorizing the past, we can look at key areas of influence on the laws and ethics today and anticipate what might come next. Still, this chapter will focus on critical cases and legal issues in higher education. These cases and laws provide another lens through which to examine the history of higher education in the United States.

Legislation and Higher Education/Student Affairs

Laws do lots of things for us. Laws provide funding, address safety issues, and specify what the government can and cannot do. If you do an internet search for "types of law," you will find seven different types of law, four types of law, eight types of law, and two types of law. In other words, when you are describing the types of law, *it depends* on what you are seeking.

As you read through the following section, you will find that most of the legislation listed here involved college access, creating and funding colleges, institutional obligations, and students' rights. Law changes, and how different institutions deal with legislation varies. This text provides some information, but you will want to work with supervisors and others on your specific campus to figure out how the laws outlined here impact your work at your college or university.

The Morrill Act of 1862

Rationale

The Morrill Act expanded college education across the United States by allocating land and other support to the states. It broadened access to higher education with an emphasis on agricultural and mechanical arts.

Elements

Vermont Senator Justin Morrill first proposed the Morrill Act in 1857, but President James Buchanan vetoed it in 1859 because it failed to include military tactics in the curriculum. It was resubmitted in 1861 and signed into law by President Abraham Lincoln on July 2, 1862.

The law gave 30,000 acres to each state for each senator and representative in that state. This process served to benefit the more populous eastern states. Primarily new institutions were built in the Midwest and West, while funding went to existing schools in some Eastern states. Some previously existing institutions became land grant schools. For example, Yale (founded in 1701) became Connecticut's land grant institution in 1863, and Rutgers was founded in 1766 and designated the land grant university for New Jersey in 1864.

There is some dispute about the first land grant institution in the country. Iowa State University (formerly known as Iowa State Agricultural College and Model Farm) was founded after the Iowa Legislature made Iowa the first state to accept the terms of the Morrill Act (two months after the act passed in 1862). Michigan State (founded in 1855 as the Agricultural College of the state of Michigan) is considered the pioneer land grant institution as it was the first institution to teach scientific agriculture. Finally, Kansas State University (originally Kansas State Agricultural College) was the first institution to be established (1862) and opened (1863) as a result of the Morrill Act. In addition to land grant institutions, there are now sea, space, and sun grant institutions across the country. We provide an overview of different institutional types in Chapter 8.

Takeaways

While the first Morrill Act increased access to higher education, it did little for African Americans, Indigenous people, and other People of Color. The initial institutions under the first Morrill Act were not obligated to admit all students, so segregated schools in the South were built or expanded but continued to admit only white students. Additional legislation extended college access to those students. In 1890, states were directed to admit all students or build another institution to serve particularly Black students but also other Students of Color not allowed at the existing land grant institutions. It was not until more than 100 years later that Morrill Act benefits and resources were extended to Indigenous people. The actual support provided to 1890 and 1994 institutions was not equitable to that offered to the colleges and universities founded because of the original Morrill Act.

Additionally, the impact of the Morrill Act on Indigenous people was significant. Lee and Ahtone (2020) wrote that, to create what are now sometimes referred to as "land grab" institutions, nearly 11 million acres were "taken from nearly 250 tribes, bands, and communities through over 160 violence-backed land cessions" (para. 5). The irony that land was taken from Indigenous peoples for higher education without providing higher education to Indigenous peoples is often overlooked, ignored, or invisible in discussions, policies, and practices on college and university campuses.

The Morrill Act of 1890 (Also Called the Agricultural College Act of 1890)

Rationale

Because there were states that prohibited African Americans from attending colleges and universities, the original Morrill Act did nothing to expand educational access for African-American students in those states. Before the 1890 legislation, some state public institutions and private universities such as Fisk University and Howard University did admit African-American students. However, owing to the lack of access at most land grant institutions in the South, a second Morrill Act was passed 28 years later. In 1890, this "Second Morrill Act" prohibited the distribution of federal funds to land grant colleges that discriminated based on race. Instead of obligating institutions to admit all students, states could now access federal funds if they accepted African-American students or established or designated a separate school to educate African Americans. Most of these institutions are found in the South, including the University of Kentucky, which admitted the first Black student at the institution, Lyman Johnson, in 1949, five years before the Brown v. Board of Education (1954, 1955) rulings, and Clemson University, which admitted Harvey Gantt, the institution's first Black student, in 1963, almost 10 years after the Brown ruling that found state laws establishing segregation were unconstitutional.

Elements

It is important to note that while the original land grant gave colleges and universities land (thus the name), that was not the case for the colleges established under the 1890 act. The 1862 Morrill Act directed institutions to sell the land given to institutions on which each state would establish a college and then sell the additional land to invest funds generated in stocks that were expected to yield at least 5% interest. These investments would "constitute a perpetual fund… and claim the benefit of the act to the endowment, support, and maintenance" (Morrill Act, 1862) of the land grant institutions.

Several historically Black colleges and universities (HBCUs) existed before the Second Morrill Act and later became land grant institutions. The oldest of the land grant HBCUs is Lincoln University, founded in 1866 by African-American Civil War veterans. Alcorn State University was the first to be deemed a land grant institution, which received funds under the first Morrill Act in 1862. Finally, the first HBCU established by/after the Morrill Act of 1890 (when there were already 12 existing institutions that would become land grant HBCUs) was Delaware State College (now Delaware State University), established in 1891.

Takeaways

The land grant institutions founded under the 1890 Act received neither land nor money despite promises under the act. Funding disparities have continued as many HBCUs have been underfunded and have had to wage legal battles with the states (e.g., Maryland and Tennessee, among many others) to get their designated state appropriations.

The Elementary and Secondary Education Reauthorization Act (1994), or the Third Morrill Act of 1994

Rationale

The Elementary and Secondary Education Reauthorization Act of 1994 included the "Third Morrill Act," designating tribal colleges as land grant institutions. The first tribal college was Diné College in Arizona, founded by the Navajo Nation in 1968. Today there are 32 tribal land grant institutions.

Elements

The act established a $23 million endowment for tribal colleges, which receive interest payments each year and funding for agricultural and natural resources and extension funding for collaboration between 1862 land grant institutions and tribal colleges.

Takeaways

It was more than 300 years between the founding of Harvard University and the establishment of Diné College. It would take 132 years from the first Morrill Act and over 100 years from the second Morrill Act for the United States to consider higher education for Indigenous people as part of the Morrill Act's mission to expand education. Instead, during this time, the U.S. focused on building Indian Residential Schools. The history of these schools is one of eradication more than education, as their primary goal was to assimilate Indigenous people into European-American religion, culture, and society (Carasik & Bachman, 2019).

The Servicemen's Readjustment Act of 1944

Rationale

This act was part of an effort to create opportunities after World War II when the United States was still recovering from the Great Depression and soldiers were returning to the United States after the war.

Elements

Also known as the G.I. Bill, the Servicemen's Readjustment Act provided veterans with funds for college, housing, and unemployment insurance. The impact of this bill was significant, with nearly half of the 16 million World War II veterans using their education benefits, causing considerable growth at institutions and diversifying the student body in terms of age, parental status, and socioeconomic status. By 1947, 49% of students enrolled in college were veterans (Wilson, 1995).

Takeaways

The G.I. Bill was created to stave off tremendous unemployment when nearly 16 million service members returned home after World War II.

Within seven years, about eight million veterans took advantage of the benefit, and within 50 years, the number of Americans with advanced degrees rose by nearly 20% (U.S. Department of Defense, 2019). This bill had an impact on society beyond education, as it included a home loan benefit which led to a positive impact on the economy and increased national prosperity for many (U.S. Department of Defense, 2019).

The G.I. Bill did not serve veterans of color or women veterans well. There was blatant racial discrimination, particularly against African-American veterans. Colleges and universities open to African-American students could not all support the influx of students. In other situations, state branches of federal agencies would force African-American soldiers into vocational schools or deny their benefits. African-American veterans experienced discrimination in terms of home ownership programs, as banks refused to loan them money, and suburban neighborhoods implemented restrictive covenants prohibiting African Americans from buying homes in those areas.

Executive Order 10925, 1961

Rationale

This executive order from President John F. Kennedy mandated government contractors to "take affirmative action" in hiring employees. This approach was not new, but this was the first time that affirmative action appeared as the concept is known today.

Elements

This executive order focused on protection related to "race, creed, color, or national origin" (Exec. Order No. 10925, 1961). The protected classes expanded over time.

Takeaways

In 1970, the first affirmative action case in higher education went to court. In the case, DeFunis v. Odegaard (1974), Marco DeFunis, a white student, was denied admission to the University of Washington School of Law and believed that less qualified students had been admitted over him solely based on their race. The case became moot, and the Supreme Court refused to hear appeals as DeFunis had been provisionally admitted and was about to graduate from law school when the case got to the Supreme Court. A later case, Regents of the University of California v. Bakke (1978), would eventually be heard by the Supreme Court, which would find quotas to be unconstitutional but affirmative action to be acceptable in some cases.

The protected classes grew over time. Currently, the Equal Employment Opportunity Commission (EEOC) Protected Classes include the following:

- **The Civil Rights Act of 1866**—prohibited discrimination on account of race, color, or previous condition of servitude.
- **Civil Rights Act of 1964, Title VII**—prohibited discrimination in employment on the basis of race, national origin, and religion for Public Accommodations and Public Funding (any program receiving federal funds must treat the protected classes fairly). As the result of amendments, the act would eventually prohibit discrimination on the basis of race, color, religion, sex, or national origin in employment (requiring employers and labor unions to treat protected classes fairly).
- Also created EEOC.

Congress added the following:

- **1967—age**
- **1972—women/gender**. The government expanded protected classes and clarified gender through various cases.
  - Meritor Savings Bank v. Vinson (1986)—gender harassment
  - Price Waterhouse v. Hopkins (1989)—sexual stereotyping
  - Baldwin v. Department of Transportation (2015)—sexual orientation
  - Bostock v. Clayton County (2020)—sexual orientation and gender identity
- **1973—disability** in government employment; 1990—disability in all employment with the passage of the Americans with Disabilities Act.

The Civil Rights Act of 1964

Rationale

Proposed in June of 1963 amid widespread protest, the act sought to address civil rights issues related to access, employment, housing, and voting. Additionally, the act provided resources for handling civil rights complaints, grievances, and lawsuits.

Elements

Title I: Provisions to ban discrimination in voting.
Title II: Provisions to ban discrimination in public accommodations.
Title III: Provisions to ban discrimination in public facilities.

Title IV: Provisions to desegregate schools.
Title V: Expanded the power of the Commission on Civil Rights.
Title VI: Provisions to ban discrimination in government programs.
Title VII: Provisions to ban discrimination by private employers (including private institutions).
Title VIII: Voters and Fair Housing Act (applicable to campus residence halls).
Title IX: Included a provision to make it easier to move civil rights court cases from state to federal court.
Title X: Established the Community Relations Service to address community discrimination.
Title XI: Established criminal contempt punishment for Civil Rights Act obstruction.

Takeaways

While this act was monumental in that it prohibited discrimination in public accommodations and federal programs, it did not address all concerns. It failed to include other initiatives promoted by activists at the time, including protection against police brutality, discrimination in private employment, and granting the Justice Department authority to address desegregation and job discrimination through lawsuits.

Higher Education Act of 1965 and Related Legislation

Rationale

Initially designed to increase access to higher education for low- and middle-income students, the Higher Education Act (HEA) has been reauthorized many times since its inception. This law administers financial aid and enforces privacy, civil rights laws, and other issues for institutions that accept federal funding.

Elements

Much of the original HEA focused on financial support to institutions and students. Additionally, the act included support for teaching and learning. It consists of the following:

Title I: Funding for extension and continuing education.
Title II: Funding to enhance libraries.
Title III: Strengthening developing institutions.

Title VI: Need-based financial support of students through loans, scholarships, and the creation of work-study programs.
Title V: Improvement of teaching.
Title VII: Improvement of undergraduate education.

Takeaways

The HEA has been reauthorized eight times, most recently in the Higher Education Opportunity Act of 2008. The impact of different reauthorizations of the act and related policies includes the following:

- **1968**: The establishment of TRIO programs (the first three were Upward Bound, Educational Talent Search, and Student Support Services). Expansion of the Guaranteed Student Loan program.
- **1972**: Basic Educational Opportunity Grant (BEOG). Expansion of other need-based assistance.
- **1976**: Expanded need-based awards.
- **The Middle Income Student Assistance Act of 1978**: Not part of reauthorization but closely connected to the HEA, this act focused on middle-income students' needs, stimulating rapid borrowing expansion.
- **The Tribally Controlled College or University Assistance Act of 1978** authorized the Secretary of the Interior to provide educational grants to tribally controlled Indian community colleges to be controlled by Indian tribes. Specifically, this act addressed the needs of Native Americans (Title I), extended construction grants for Indian community colleges (Title II), and allocated specific appropriations through the Navajo Community College Assistant Act. The act provided $60 million over three years (Title III) (Tribally Controlled Community College Assistance Act, 1978).
- **1980**: BEOG, renamed the Pell Grant in honor of Senator Claiborne Pell.
- **The Omnibus Budget Reconciliation Act of 1981** was not part of reauthorization but was closely connected to HEA. This act focused on slowing the growth of the Guaranteed Student Loan (GSL) programs and provided unsubsidized loans, including Parent Loan for Undergraduate Students (PLUS) loans.
- **1986**: Established eligibility guidelines for all guaranteed loan borrowers. Increasing the amount students could borrow continued loan growth and the shift toward borrowing rather than grants. It was renamed National Direct Student Loans Perkins Loans in honor of Carl D. Perkins, who helped initiate Head Start and the school lunch program.

- **1992**: The federal government increased Pell Grant awards and created unsubsidized Stafford Loans (the new name of the Guaranteed Student Loan Program in honor of Robert Stafford, who had chaired the Senate Subcommittee on Education, Arts, and Humanities). The creation of these unsubsidized loans primarily benefited middle- and upper-income students. At the same time, Pell Grants failed to provide sufficient appropriations to students, especially low-income students who became increasingly dependent on borrowing to pay for college. The government also piloted direct lending at 300 institutions.
- **The Taxpayer Relief Act of 1997**: Another initiative that benefitted middle- and upper-income students while doing very little for low-income students, this act provided tax credits based on tuition and fees, the Lifetime Learning Tax Credit, and tax deductibility for student loans. It was not about access as the HEA of 1965 had been, but one of the most extensive federal aid bills for an increased commitment to higher education.
- **1998**: Increased maximum Pell Grant and reduced interest rates on Stafford Loans.
- **Higher Education Opportunity Act of 2008**: Made changes to allow broader qualifications for student loan discharges for people with disabilities. Provisions included efforts to combat illegal file-sharing. Pell Grant award maximums increased, there were reduced interest rates on subsidized loans, and the program enacted loan forgiveness for public servants, among other loan changes. Additionally, college cost transparency increased through implementing net price listings, state higher education spending charts, net price calculators, consumer information, multi-year tuition calculators, and state commitments to an affordable college education.
- **Coronavirus Aid, Relief, and Economic Security (CARES) Act of 2020**: Allocated $13.95 billion because of COVID-19. Half of the funds allotted to institutions provided direct emergency aid to students (food, housing, health care, childcare, course materials, and technology). The remaining funds were to offset expenses incurred because of the pandemic. Institutions could not use funds for endowments, athletics, religious activities, or enrollment recruitment. The act also suspended student loan payments.

The Freedom of Information Act (1966)

Rationale

The Freedom of Information Act (FOIA) gives citizens the right to access information from any federal agency.

Elements

Requests must be in writing (electronic or by mail) and reasonably describe the information requested (not too broad), and submissions must comply with agency and other federal requirements. There may be fees for these requests (staff time, copies, redacting information, and computer usage).

Takeaways

Public institutions and the Department of Education are among the units obliged to FOIA requests. The Family Educational Rights and Privacy Act (FERPA) applies to and protects some records. It is important to remember that FERPA applies to records, not conversations. Notes taken about student meetings may or may not constitute educational records.

The Education Amendments of 1972

Rationale

These amendments updated the HEA of 1965.

Elements

Title I: Higher Education—Community Service and Continuing Education Programs. This extended funding outlined by the HEA of 1965 provided grant funding, review of extension programs, appropriations for libraries, and emergency funding available for higher education. Finally, it offered various financial aid options for students, including grants, loans, and work-study.

Title II: Vocational Education—primarily edited to clarify language and extend dates from 1972 through 1975 items under the Vocational Education Act of 1963.

Title III: Amendments Relating to the Administration of Education Programs—created an Assistant Secretary for Education over the Office of Education as part of the Department of Health, Education, and Welfare. The administration of Jimmy Carter created the Department of Education in 1979.

Title IV: Indian Education—addressed funding for elementary and secondary school programs for Indigenous children.

Title V: Miscellaneous—included several edits and clarifications across elementary, secondary, and higher education.

Title VI: Investigation of Youth Camp Safety—this was an investigation of accidents and illness at youth camps across the country (hence the name).

Title VII: Emergency School Aid—provided for funding to eliminate segregation and discrimination in elementary and secondary schools.

Title VIII: General Provisions Relating to the Assignment or Transportation of Students—prohibited transporting students (or teachers) to different schools to overcome racial imbalance.

Title IX (renamed the Patsy Takemoto Mink Equal Opportunity in Education Act in 2002)—prohibited gender discrimination.

Title IX's primary author was Patsy Mink, a U.S. Congresswoman from Hawai'i and the first Woman of Color in Congress.

Title X: Assistance to Institutions of Higher Education—addressed funding to schools, including that based on undergraduate enrollment, student veterans, and graduate education.

Takeaways

These amendments addressed various issues across elementary, secondary, and higher education. The most referenced of these and arguably the most influential was the Patsy Takemoto Mink Equal Opportunity in Education Act (Title IX). Focused initially on admissions and participation in higher education, it has since been the foundation for addressing sexual misconduct (see Alexander v. Yale, 1980) and other gender inequity issues.

Rehabilitation Act of 1973 (Section 504)

Rationale

To afford broader access to higher education, Section 504 prohibited colleges, universities, and postsecondary education institutions from discriminating on the basis of ability against students who are otherwise qualified for admission.

Elements

This act covers all public and private schools receiving federal funding. In addition to access, this act requires institutions to include students—regardless of ability—in participation and benefits of higher education. Students are obliged to provide notice to the college to get accommodations and auxiliary aids.

Takeaways

While this act provided more access to students with disabilities, there are still facilities on campuses that are not accessible at institutions across the country. Additionally, many schools focus solely on "compliance," the lowest level of accommodation for students, rather than a more holistic and inclusive approach to supporting this student population.

Family Educational Rights and Privacy Act of 1974 (FERPA)

Rationale

FERPA protects the confidentiality of student educational records (grades and conduct records). The act covers public and most private schools (those that receive federal funding).

Elements

FERPA has three parts: The first gives students (or students' parents/guardians in P-12 educational settings) permission to review records. The second part allows students (or parents/guardians depending on the context) the right to request inaccuracies in records. The final element of FERPA has to do with the release of records. While institutions generally must have the student's permission to release records, there are exceptions to this section of FERPA. Those exceptions include school officials with a legitimate educational interest in the records, transfer institutions, audit and evaluation releases, financial aid staff, organizations conducting research or responsible for accreditation, releases for judicial (including juvenile justice) processes, and the release of records for health and safety emergencies. The second part prohibits sharing of documents without student consent. Exceptions for the second part include sharing information with

- school officials with a legitimate need to know
- other schools where students wish to enroll
- auditing and accreditation agencies
- financial aid
- organizations for study purposes
- agencies with a subpoena for records
- health and safety managers
- juvenile justice system

When a student becomes an eligible student (regardless of age), the rights accorded to and the consent required of parents under FERPA transfer to a student. An "eligible student" is a student who is 18 or who is enrolled at a postsecondary institution (regardless of age). At that point, FERPA rights transfer to the student. Additionally, it is essential to remember that FERPA applies to records, not conversations, as most conversations do not generate records. Notes from student meetings may or may not be FERPA-protected. Information entered into a database will likely create an educational record.

Takeaways

Student affairs practitioners and other higher education professionals should be familiar with the FERPA processes at their institution. Violating a student's FERPA rights can result in penalties for individuals and institutions, including monetary damages. See more information in Chapter 15.

Drug-Free Schools and Communities Act (1989) (DFSCA)

Rationale

To curb the use and abuse of harmful and illegal drugs.

Elements

Institutional harmful and illegal drug policies must be comprehensive and distributed to students and employees annually. Additionally, colleges and universities must implement prevention programs.

Takeaways

Since 2012, there has been a significant increase in DFSCA enforcement, resulting in fines from $10,000 to $35,000 at higher education institutions across the country.

Americans with Disabilities Act (ADA) of 1990

Rationale

Prohibits discrimination based on disability.

Elements

The act includes four sections (employment, public entities, public transportation, public accommodations, commercial facilities, and telecommunications). Existing legislation such as Section 504 of the Rehabilitation Act of 1973, the Fair Housing Amendments Act of 1988, and the Individuals with Disabilities Education Act (passed in 1975) provide the foundation for the ADA.

Takeaways

Public and private institutions receiving federal funding must provide equal access for students with disabilities. Higher education institutions must provide access to extracurricular activities, campus buildings, residence and dining halls, and academic opportunities. Strategies for giving access can include various accommodations, including sign language interpreters, assistive listening devices, testing accommodations, and permitting service animals. Accommodations are not required when they would fundamentally alter the service, program, or activity or cause an undue financial burden.

The Jeanne Clery Disclosure of Campus Security Policy and Campus Crime Statistics Act (1990)

Rationale

Jeanne Clery was a 19-year-old Lehigh University student who was raped and murdered in her college residence hall in 1986. The university had not informed students that there had been 38 violent crimes on campus in the preceding three years. The Clery Act provides increased transparency through the annual reporting of crime statistics on college campuses.

Elements

The Clery Act requires institutions to provide an annual security report (most schools do this in October once the fall term has begun). The act requires a public crime log, timely warnings (often text messages or email alerts), and crime statistics for at least the past eight years.

Takeaways

Several high-profile violations of the Clery Act resulted in significant penalties for institutions. These incidents have resulted in fines, legal settlements, and termination of some leaders, administrators, and staff. Some examples are the following:

- **Michigan State University**'s failure to respond appropriately to allegations of sexual misconduct by Larry Nasser from the 1990s through 2015. This incident resulted in a $4.5 million fine for Michigan State and a 175-year prison sentence for Nasser.
- **Virginia Tech** failed to issue a timely warning to students in response to on-campus shootings in 2007. This tragedy resulted in a $32,500 fine and inspired many campuses to implement student behavioral intervention teams.

- **Eastern Michigan University**'s 2008 mishandling of information and process following the murder of Laura Dickinson. It paid $350,000—the largest Clery Act violation fine until that time—and a $2.5 million settlement with Dickinson's family. The violations went back as far as 2003 and included failure to adequately disclose crime statistics and failure to provide a timely warning.
- **University of California at Berkeley (UC Berkeley)** had several administrative violations related to Clery reporting between 2009 and 2016, including misclassification of incidents, technical errors, failure to issue annual security and fire safety reports, and failure to issue emergency notifications. The U.S. Department of Education fined UC Berkeley $2.3 million.
- **Baylor University**'s misreporting of crime statistics between 2011 and 2016 resulted in a $461,656 fine. Among the violations at Baylor were a lack of administrative capability to provide Clery reports, failure to report accurate crime statistics, failure to issue timely warnings, and a failure to maintain an accurate daily crime log.
- **Penn State University**'s 2012 failure to address issues related to Jerry Sandusky's sexual abuse of boys on campus. The Department of Education issued a $2.4 million fine for the Clery Act violations. Additionally, the university has paid more than $100 million to those who filed claims against the university concerning this case.

The Violence Against Women Act of 1994 (VAWA) (see also the Campus SaVE Act)

Rationale

VAWA expanded Clery Act regulations and requirements.

Elements

Congress has reauthorized and updated it four times since 1994 (2000, 2005, 2013, and 2022). Key elements of the act include the following:

- **1994**: acknowledged domestic violence and sexual assault as crimes.
- **2000**: created a victims' legal assistance program and added dating violence and stalking to VAWA.
- **2005**: added prevention initiatives, housing protections, funding for rape crisis centers, and cultural and linguistic services.
- **2013**: enhanced access to safety and justice for Indigenous and LGBTQ survivors.
- **2018**: VAWA was allowed to lapse.

- **2022**: extended authorization to 2027. Among other things, the reauthorization expanded the criminal jurisdiction of Tribal courts to cover non-Native perpetrators and increased services and support for survivors from underserved/marginalized communities. It established a federal cause of civil action for distributing intimate images without consent.

Takeaways

Colleges and universities must report domestic violence, dating violence, and stalking and adopt specified disciplinary procedures (such as notifying reporting students of their rights), adopt policies, and engage in prevention efforts.

Equity in Athletics Disclosure Act (EADA) (1994)

Rationale

The act provides accountability for higher education and transparency in equity of intercollegiate athletic programs to institutions that receive Title IV federal student financial aid.

Elements

Through the Equity in Athletics Data Analysis site (https://ope.ed.gov/athletics/#/), the public can access general information about institutions (undergraduate enrollment and gender breakdown) as well as information about the athletic department (director, reporting official, and contact information). Finally, the site provides information about the sports at each institution, the number of athletes by gender and sport, and the total number of teams by gender.

Takeaways

Because of the EADA, the public can get data for a single school, compare data among many schools, and download and generate trend data about college and university athletics.

The Health Insurance Portability and Accountability Act (HIPAA), 1996

Rationale

HIPAA provides for the privacy of physical and mental health records.

Elements

- Title I—availability of group health plans.
- Title II—fraud and abuse prevention, administrative simplification, and medical liability reform.
    - Privacy Rule—regulation of Protected Health Information (PHI) records.
    - Security Rule—focuses on the security of electronic PHI records.
    - Enforcement Rule—sets penalties and establishes investigation and hearing procedures for HIPAA violations.
- Title III—tax provisions for medical savings accounts.
- Title IV—application and enforcement of group health insurance requirements.
- Title V—offset of health plan tax deductions.

Takeaways

HIPAA does not protect health records considered educational records. However, FERPA protects educational records. HIPAA does not prevent universities or colleges from asking for medical information from employees and students if there is a legitimate business reason for doing so. See more details in Chapter 15.

Digital Millennium Copyright Act (DMCA) (1998)

Rationale

The act protects copyrighted material and makes the production and dissemination of copyrighted material illegal. It focuses liability on individuals, not internet providers.

Elements

A DMCA claim or "takedown notice" directs users to remove copyrighted material from online spaces.

Takeaways

It is illegal for college students and others to copy or share intellectual property (e.g., games, movies, and music) without permission. Usually, embedded videos are not a violation of this act.

Victims of Trafficking and Violence Prevention Act of 2000

Rationale

Provided strategies for the prevention of trafficking, protection of victims, and prosecution of perpetrators of human trafficking.

Elements

The Campus Sex Crimes Prevention Act (CSCPA) is part of the Victims of Trafficking and Violence Prevention Act of 2000. This part of the act required sex offenders to provide notice of enrollment or employment at colleges and universities.

Takeaways

Not only must individuals disclose if they are sex offenders, but the university is required to provide the campus community guidance on where it can find this information.

Homeland Security Act of 2002

Rationale

This act consolidated 22 agencies and bureaus into the Department of Homeland Security (DHS) to coordinate responses to natural and man-made disasters and terrorism.

Elements

The act fostered partnerships with colleges and universities for training on risks and threats. Additionally, the act fostered collaboration between federal and campus law enforcement agencies in planning and response to security issues.

Takeaways

In 2011, the DHS Office of Academic Engagement (OAE) was established to work with the academic community on engagement, resilience, and outreach. There are many concerns about DHS, often in partnership with Immigration and Customs Enforcement (ICE), and the handling of international student visas.

Predominantly Black Institution Act of 2007

Rationale

The Predominantly Black Institution (PBI) Act of 2007 is an amendment to the HEA of 1965 designed to help address the persistent gap between the graduation rates of Black students and those of white students.

Elements

Institutions are eligible for grants and other financial support if they have a particularly low per-student expenditure compared with other institutions. These schools must also have an enrollment of at least 40% Black American students, with particular attention to first-generation college students, students from underserved P-12 schools, and low-income students (Predominantly Black Institution Act, 2007).

Takeaways

PBIs are not the same as HBCUs, but there can be some overlap. The federal government has continued to try to increase educational equity between Black and white students. However, there is a gap between these students' graduation rates that is informed at least in part by historical issues of inequitable funding, access, and support into and through higher education.

The Campus Sexual Violence Elimination (SaVE) Act (2014)

Rationale

The Campus SaVE Act increased transparency about sexual violence on campus, provided equitable treatment to reporting and accused students in situations involving sexual violence, and provided federal resources supporting mandated education and awareness programming in higher education.

Elements

The Campus SaVE Act expanded the categories of violence that must be reported annually to those previously established by VAWA and the Clery Act: domestic violence, dating violence, and stalking. Additionally, the act added "national origin" and "gender identity" to hate crime categories under the Clery Act.

The Campus SaVE Act also specified victims' rights and college responsibilities to students reporting incidents, including the following:

- Information on obtaining protective and no-contact orders.
- Details about the protection of victim confidentiality.
- Written notification of mental health, advocacy, legal, and other resources.
- Written notice of victims' right to change academic, living, transportation, or work situations.
- Notifying victims of their rights is part of student discipline procedures.
- Publishing procedures for reporting sexual violence, including the right to decline to file a formal report.
- The accuser and accused have rights to an advisor and to receive the final results of the proceeding in writing and have the right to appeal disciplinary decisions.

Finally, the Campus SaVE Act requires education and training on sexual violence. Education and training include the following:

- A statement by the school that it prohibits sexual violence.
- A definition of sexual violence acts.
- Education on bystander intervention.
- Sexual violence risk reduction programs.
- Information on institutional reporting and disciplinary systems.
- Annual training on sexual violence for officials conducting disciplinary hearings.
- Prevention and awareness education for new students and employees.
- Ongoing prevention and awareness campaigns, including information from this list.

Takeaways

Colleges and universities have done much related to violence on campus. Campus violence is a topic that continues to put students at risk and challenge educational leaders. The interpretation of this and other policies and the impact on campus procedures vary significantly from one campus, community, and state to the next. Additionally, the influence at the federal level on legislation, policies, implementation, and practice around sexual violence can cause dramatic shifts depending on the leaders at any given time.

Conclusion

It is important to note that what we have highlighted here does not include all aspects of law relevant to higher education. For example, this text does not address issues of academic freedom related to faculty, college governance, and other campus challenges. Instead, we have focused on laws most relevant to student affairs practitioners. As the U.S. and states pass new legislation, staying current with what is happening at the local, state, and national levels is essential.

According to Justice Ruth Bader Ginsburg, "A great man once said that the true symbol of the United States is not the bald eagle; it is the pendulum, and when the pendulum swings too far in one direction, it will go back" (BBC, 2017). We can study the evolution of Title IX as it relates to sexual misconduct to see Justice Ginsburg's idea in action. Whereas in the early 2000s, many processes were (re)designed to focus on supporting students who reported violations, today is different. Increasingly, accused students file lawsuits against colleges and universities because they feel judicial processes compromise their rights. Additionally, the federal guidelines can change dramatically based on who is in the White House and who controls Congress.

Mental health issues on campus are another reason to pay attention as laws in higher education change. Whether students' mental health issues involve self-harm or violence against another person or people, the university's obligation to provide a safe environment involves considerations and actions that are different from the past. Not long ago, no one knew what a Behavioral Intervention Team was. Today institutions put themselves at huge risk for harm, violence, and lawsuits if they do not have a team monitoring concerning behaviors not only of students but of faculty, staff, guests, and others.

As historian Letitia Woods Brown said, "Somehow I am both historian and futurist. One basic question haunts me: what do students need to know about themselves and about the past that will help them face their world understanding and commitment?" (1974, p. 19). That question drives this text and, specifically, this chapter. Legislation, like society, is constantly changing. This chapter's foundational information in preparation and work in student affairs is helpful. That said, the law is far from the final word when guiding the work of higher education and student affairs practitioners.

3

CASE LAW AND HIGHER EDUCATION

Chapter 2 focused on the laws passed in the United States related to higher education. In this chapter, we look at how the courts have helped shape higher education law. It is essential to acknowledge that the United States' legal history is not rooted in equity and the justice system is historically unjust. Regardless, it is important to understand legal issues, history, court precedents, legislation, and other concepts related to the law in higher education. We encourage readers to carefully look at who participates in these court cases, who is absent, and what voices are privileged and oppressed. There is much work to be done—to advocate for those oppressed by the system—just as there is with all education, government, and society.

Memorizing dates and names of court cases provide only the *when* and *who* of history, which is a superficial understanding of past events. For issues of law, much of that history takes the form of legal cases, which—on the surface—can be dry. For example, "Morse v. Frederick, 2007 is a free speech case" is not exciting or intriguing for most people. However, framing that same case as the "Bong hits for Jesus case" provokes more curiosity for most of us as readers, right? When engaged, we are more likely to remember the story in the history and the concepts related to the case. History helps us understand change, culture, and the world and provides crucial contextual information to navigate past issues and create change in the future.

Competencies

We connected this chapter to the same competencies (see Appendix) in Chapter 2. Case law and the related terminology directly connect to Law,

DOI: 10.4324/9781003442707-4

Policy, and Governance (LPG). Again, we stress that LPG issues are informed directly by the Social Justice and Inclusion (SJI) competency issues. Similarly, we must use SJI to examine the Values, Philosophy, and History (VPH) competencies of student affairs. For example, one of our founding documents, the Student Personnel Point of View (1937), mentions women but nothing about race or other identities, citizenship, or an understanding of the larger society or development of a global perspective. The following version of the document mentioned women once but used only "his" (68 times) and never "hers" when referring to students throughout the document (ACE, 1949). The 1949 version presents the role of students as world citizens, filling a gap in the earlier version. However, the document does include the following:

> Personnel specialists and administrators, both men and women, should be available in all personnel departments. That is, competent men counselors should be available for those students who prefer to consult a man. In like manner, competent women counselors should be available for those men and women who prefer to consult a woman about scholastic or personal adjustments. Both men and women administrators should be members of top policy-making councils.
>
> *(ACE, 1949, p. 10)*

In addition to utilizing the gender binary, this section of the Student Personnel Point of View overlooks other identities that staff bring into their work. We must look to the past to understand how we came to the present. Additionally, we must consistently reflect on what and whom we include in policies and processes. We must also ask ourselves what and who is omitted through historical practice, carelessness, or intentional exclusion.

Chapter Organization

We divided this chapter into two sections. The first provides definitions of terms. As most student affairs practitioners do not have legal degrees and few will ever work exclusively in conduct roles, a glossary of terms can prove helpful. While we have provided the commonly used terms, it is essential for you to understand what terms and language your institution uses in codes of conduct, contracts, and other documents, as the vocabulary can differ from one campus to the next.

The second section highlights critical court cases related to higher education and student affairs. While this is not a comprehensive list and does not include every detail about each court case, the section provides a helpful overview of the judicial impact on higher education. As in Chapter 2, most of these cases relate to access, funding, institutional obligations, and/or students' rights. This chapter includes the name of the court case, who was involved, issues, and takeaways related to student affairs. Some court cases also have a list of related cases for those who want to explore the issues more thoroughly.

Legal Terms

The law has terminology and jargon like other professional languages. This use of language is not random, of course. Benson (1984) did an excellent job of highlighting how these choices, related to the language of the law, alienate and set the public up for exploitation and manipulation founded on social status, power, and elitism. He asserted that this language serves as a form of social and political control by causing problems for non-attorneys to comprehend what they are reading or being told (Benson, 1984).

While higher education has been encouraged not to mirror codes of conduct in the civil and criminal judicial systems (Martin & Janosik, 2004), there are still issues with legalese in terms of student conduct codes and higher education law and policy. This section provides definitions of language commonly found in student codes of conduct, policies, and other legal documents.

Academic dishonesty/misconduct—An effort to create an unfair academic advantage (or disadvantage) for self or others.

Accused—A person alleged to have done something criminal or violated policy. Some processes use other words such as "respondent" or "defendant" in public legal proceedings; someone accused of a crime is a criminal defendant, while a civil case defendant is the person/people/organization against whom a civil suit has been brought.

Advisor—Someone students or student organizations select to support them through a student disciplinary process. In most situations, this person cannot represent the students but simply advises them. Attorneys may or may not be allowed to serve as advisors in these cases.

Appellant—Person(s) appealing a previous court or institutional decision.

Appellate—Related to an appeal, an appellate court hears appeals of other courts' decisions.

Brief—Written statement submitted by attorneys explaining why a judge should decide a case (all or part) in favor of the attorney's client.

Burden of proof—The responsibility of proving a point.

Case law—The same as "precedent" and means law established by an earlier court decision.

Civil case—A case that does not include a crime, usually between private parties or businesses.

Class action—When a large group (class) of individuals or entities sue on behalf of the entire class.

Confidentiality—The obligation to protect individuals by not sharing information about them and their situations. Confidentiality in higher education applies to legally protected or privileged relationships such as licensed medical and clinical staff, mental health professionals, and ordained religious advisors. Personal attorneys also must keep the information confidential. At some institutions, victim advocacy staff may also be considered confidential resources.

Contract—An agreement that creates an obligation. Examples: contract with a stand-up comedian for a campus event, housing contract between residents and the university.

Complainant—Individual(s) named as reporting parties in a policy violation; someone who brings forth allegations against another party or group. Some institutions use other terms, such as "accuser" or "reporting student," to convey the same concept.

Compliance—Organizational adherence to laws, guidelines, regulations, and specifications. Compliance is the lowest standard of following law or policy.

Complicity—Acting to abet, aid, encourage, facilitate, or promote a prohibited act by another person.

Criminal case—A situation where a person, group, or organization is accused of criminal violation of the law.

Damages—Money asked for or awarded in a civil case. Damages may be compensatory (for loss or injury) or punitive (punishment to deter future violations).

Decision—The outcome of a hearing or other judicial process.

Due process—The rights of the accused to have a hearing or trial. In higher education, the core elements of due process are the right to have your case heard, notification of charges against you, and the right to a description of evidence against you (Kaplin & Lee, 2014; Stoner & Lowery, 2004). Most institutions afford more due process than this (such as the right to a hearing, an opportunity to *review* evidence, and—in some cases—the right to appeal), and institutions are bound to follow the process they have outlined.

Evidence—Information presented to the judge, jury, hearing board, or other deciding body related to each side of a case.

Failure to comply—Ignoring or disregarding the legitimate directives of authorized university officials (e.g., not providing identification or information when asked).

Felony—A serious crime generally punishable by imprisonment for more than one year.

Foreseeability—The ability to have anticipated a situation, action, or outcome.

In loco parentis—Acting in place of the parents. Historically, colleges and universities acted *in loco parentis* to protect students. This concept has changed over time depending on the larger society.

Harassment—An act intended to alarm, annoy, or intimidate another person.

Hazing—Forcing/subjecting individuals to physically or psychologically stressful/dangerous activities, rituals, and rites of passage to gain organizational membership. Other facets of hazing may include humiliation, impairment of physical liberty, violation of law/policy, and interference with academics.

Hearing—The process through which an accused student engages in the conduct process, which results in a determination of being responsible or not responsible for the alleged violation(s).

Hearings in absentia—A campus hearing is held when the accused student(s) or organization(s) choose not to attend.

Impact statement—Usually in cases involving physical or sexual assault or other egregious behavior, an impact statement is the opportunity for a reporting student or person to tell how the behavior of a student or group of students affected them personally, academically, or in other ways.

Injunction—Court order preventing a party from taking a specific action.

Interim actions—When an individual or organization allegedly engages in an activity that poses a risk for the individual(s) or the larger community, the university may take action. In contrast, the university investigates and adjudicates a case. Interim actions may include registration or records holds, interim suspension, removal from university housing, no contact notices, or suspension of organizational recognition or privileges.

Jurisdiction—Area of responsibility. An area of responsibility may be a geographic, policy, or conduct area.

Malfeasance—Intentional conduct that is wrongful and unlawful. A more significant level of wrongdoing than nonfeasance or misfeasance.

Misdemeanor—Criminal offense less than a felony. Generally punishable by a fine and imprisonment for less than one year.

Misfeasance—Inappropriate but not unlawful conduct.

Negligence—Failure to use the level of care a reasonable person would take in a similar situation.

Nonfeasance—Failure to act despite having a duty to act.

Not responsible—When a charged student or group of students is found not to have violated a policy or rule outlined in the code of conduct. This is the campus equivalent of "not guilty."

Plaintiff—Person, group, or organization that files a formal complaint with the court.

Precedent—This is the same as "case law" and means law established by an earlier court decision.

Preponderance of evidence—A standard of responsibility used by many colleges and universities where, having considered all evidence, it is more likely than not that a violation occurred. Preponderance is sometimes known as the 51% rule and is a lower standard of evidence than "beyond all reasonable doubt."

Prima facia—Face value, first impression, accepted as fact until proven otherwise.

Prior restraint—The act of the government or other official or agency to prevent certain forms of free speech because of what *might* happen as a result of the speech. Prior restraint is generally considered a violation of the First Amendment but may be permissible in limited circumstances, such as when the nation is at war or when speech will incite violence.

Privacy—A responsibility of many university officials (including conduct staff) to keep information private. Privacy is not the same as confidentiality. In instances based on privacy (which applies to nearly all university employees), the obligation is to tell only those with a legitimate need to know about personal information. Confidentiality is more restrictive than privacy.

Probation—A period of review when an individual or organization must demonstrate their ability to comply with policy, regulations, rules, and law.

Sanction—Penalty or punishment as the result of having been found responsible for a violation.

Reinstatement—A student or organization that has been suspended from a university but is allowed to return.

Release of information—When a student wants their student conduct or other protected information shared with a specified person or persons, they must sign a release of information. These releases are generally limited to a specific incident for a specific period.

Reprimand—An official warning.

Responsible—Finding that a person or group has engaged in behavior violating policy. This is the campus equivalent of "guilty."

Retaliation—Anything that would discourage a reasonable person from reporting a violation or participating in a hearing, including threats, intimidation, harassment, or coercion.

Sanction—A requirement imposed when students or organizations are found responsible for violating a policy or law. An educational sanction focuses on student or organization learning and development. A punitive sanction focuses on punishment for a violation (e.g., a monetary fine).

Standard of proof—Level of certainty and degree of evidence necessary to establish proof in a criminal or civil proceeding.

Upheld—When a decision-maker agrees with a previous decision or finding in an appeals process.

What Is That Called on My Campus?

While there are some standard terms and definitions for different legal issues, this does not mean that all things are consistent in all contexts. Just as definitions or classifications of crime can vary from one state to the next (thus, attorneys have to be licensed to practice law by state), so do codes of conduct vary from one college or university to the next. As you move from one place to another, figuring out what constitutes a violation, what the potential consequences are for the violation, and what institutions call the violation will vary.

Since the answer to "What do I do if a student gets in trouble on campus?" is "*It depends*," it is imperative to learn your institution's policies, processes, and vernacular. For example, students involved in the conduct process can be called different things. A student who has allegedly stolen every fire extinguisher from a residence hall might be called an accused student, a defendant, a student in an alleged violation, a respondent, or something different. Similarly, a student who comes forward to report another student who copied from them during an exam might be the accuser, complainant, or the reporting student. The language colleges and universities use to describe students in their processes varies. While this is one example, there is a different language for many aspects of student codes of conduct (or employee codes of conduct, for that matter) from one institution to the next.

Key Court Cases

This section is little more than a cheat sheet of cases. Of course, do not cheat since that would likely violate the academic integrity policy of your institution (see Chapter 4: "An Ethics Primer" or the "Student Conduct" section in Chapter 13). This section can give you a sense of cases, who was involved, and the critical components for each case. As in the chapter on legislation (Chapter 2), most court cases discussed here deal with college access, funding, institutional obligations, students' rights, or a combination of these issues. Because case law, like legislation, also builds on what has come before—in case law on precedent—this section is also organized chronologically.

Trustees of Dartmouth College v. William H. Woodward (1816)

Who Was Involved

Dartmouth College and the state of New Hampshire.

Issue(s)

This case focused on contract law. Dartmouth was founded in 1769 by Eleazar Wheelock as a private institution with a charter from England. In 1816, after the American Revolutionary War, with a new party in power, the state legislators decided they would rather have Dartmouth as a public, secular institution. They appointed new trustees and reinstated John Wheelock (Eleazar's son), whom the existing trustees had removed. The existing trustees then got Daniel Webster (Dartmouth alumnus) to sue William Woodward, Dartmouth's secretary and treasurer. Webster had sided with those who wanted to establish a "new" Dartmouth as a public institution overseen by the state government and took the college's charter, records, and seal.

The Supreme Court, under Chief Justice John Marshall, heard the case. The original trustees argued that changing Dartmouth violated Dartmouth's rights, the state constitution, and the U.S. Constitution's contract clause. The Supreme Court reversed the state court's decision and found that New Hampshire had violated Dartmouth's charter. In short, "new" Dartmouth lost and "old" Dartmouth won.

Takeaways

In addition to the contract clause aspects of the case, student affairs practitioners must remember that this case set a precedent and told states that higher education institutions could expect private institutions like Dartmouth to have the same protections as public institutions.

People v. Wheaton College (1866)

Who Was Involved

E. Hartley Pratt and Wheaton College.

Issues

The university suspended Pratt for joining a secret society. The Illinois Supreme Court found in favor of the college, saying that the institution had the power to oversee college discipline but only as long as its policies did not violate the laws of God or man. The court added that it did not have any more right to tell a school how to discipline its students than it did to tell a man how to discipline his family.

Takeaways

The courts continue to support colleges and universities regarding *in loco parentis* controls and authority.

RELATED CASES

Gott v. Berea, 1913; Stetson University v. Hunt, 1924; Anthony v. Syracuse University, 1928; Dixon v. Alabama State Board of Education, 1961.

Tape v. Hurley (1885)

Who Was Involved

Joseph and Mary Tape (parents of Mamie Tape) and Jennie M.A. Hurley (and others). The parents and students sued Principal Hurley, Superintendent Andrew Moulder, and the board of education.

Issue(s)

Eight-year-old Chinese-American Mamie Tape was denied admission to the San Francisco public school because of her ancestry. Her parents sued and won based on the Equal Protection Clause of the Fourteenth Amendment.

Takeaways

Following the court decision, Superintendent Moulder wrote to the state legislature, which passed a "separate but equal" education bill allowing for separate schools for Chinese students.

North v. Board of Trustees of the University of Illinois (1891)

Who Was Involved

Foster North, a student at the University of Illinois, and the Board of Trustees of the University of Illinois.

Issues

North violated the University of Illinois policy requiring mandatory religious service attendance. The Supreme Court of Illinois found in favor of the university. The court said that once students enroll at a university, they give up many individual and Constitutional rights. The court referred to the institution as a student's master whom students must obey.

Takeaways

The courts continue to support colleges and universities regarding *in loco parentis* controls and authority.

RELATED CASES

People v. Wheaton College, 1866; Gott v. Berea, 1913; Stetson University v. Hunt, 1924; Anthony v. Syracuse University, 1928; Dixon v. Alabama State Board of Education, 1961.

Plessy v. Ferguson (1896)

Who Was Involved

Homer Plessy, a railroad passenger, and John H. Ferguson, a judge for the criminal District Court of the parish of Orleans.

Issue(s)

Plessy, a multiracial passenger, rode on a white railroad car instead of the car designated for Black passengers. Police arrested him for violating an 1890 statute requiring railway companies carrying passengers to provide equal but separate accommodations for Black and white passengers.

The Supreme Court found in favor of Ferguson, stating that separate-but-equal coaches did not violate the Thirteenth or Fourteenth Amendments under the equal protection clause.

Takeaways

This case set a precedent for "separate but equal," not only on railroad cars but in terms of education.

Berea College v. Kentucky (1908)

Who Was Involved

Berea College and the state of Kentucky.

Issue(s)

When Berea College was founded in 1855, it was coeducational and desegregated. In 1904, Carl Day introduced what came to be known as the "Day Law," prohibiting the teaching of Black and white students in separate branches of the same school or within 25 miles of each other. The Supreme Court found in favor (5–2 decision) of the state of Kentucky.

Takeaways

In 1855, segregation was permissible—the location of private institutions dictated to which state laws institutions were subject. According to the Supreme Court, when the Fourteenth Amendment says that no state can deny a person equal protection, it means that you can provide separate accommodations, services, and education, but those options must be equal.

Gott v. Berea College (1913)

Who Was Involved

Restaurant owner J. S. Gott and Berea College.

Issue(s)

Gott purchased a restaurant across from Berea College in September 1911. The summer before, Berea College—a private institution—updated the student code of conduct and forbade students from eating at establishments not owned by the college.

Takeaways

The court found in favor of Berea College, saying the school was acting *in loco parentis* on behalf of its students and that the school had contractual obligations to students but, as a private institution, did not have the same obligations to the community.

RELATED CASES

People v. Wheaton College, 1866; North v. Board of Trustees of the University of Illinois, 1891; Stetson University v. Hunt, 1924; Anthony v. Syracuse University, 1928; Dixon v. Alabama State Board of Education, 1961.

Stetson University v. Hunt (1924)

Who Was Involved

Stetson University and Helen Hunt, a Stetson student.

Issues

Hunt allegedly rang cowbells, paraded through the residence hall after hours, and turned off lights. The university suspended her without a hearing. The Florida Supreme Court upheld the university's decision and action. The court asserted (using nearly identical language to *People v. Wheaton*) that the institution could make policies so long as they did not violate the laws of God or man. Additionally, the court asserted that it could not interfere in this situation, just as it could not interfere with how a father disciplined his family.

Takeaways

The courts continue to support colleges and universities regarding *in loco parentis* controls and authority.

RELATED CASES

People v. Wheaton College, 1866; North v. Board of Trustees of the University of Illinois, 1891; Gott v. Berea, 1913; Syracuse University, 1928; Dixon v. Alabama State Board of Education, 1961.

Anthony v. Syracuse University (1928)

Who Was Involved

Beatrice Anthony, a student, and Syracuse University, the institution she attended.

Issues

Anthony signed registration cards each year as part of her enrollment. The cards stated that the university could dismiss students for any reason, and the university may or may not choose to tell students the reasons for the dismissal. Syracuse dismissed Anthony for behavior based on rumors that school authorities had heard about her, indicating that Anthony did not represent a "typical Syracuse girl." The court found in favor of Syracuse.

Takeaways

The courts continue to support colleges and universities regarding *in loco parentis* controls and authority.

> **RELATED CASES**
>
> *People v. Wheaton College, 1866; North v. Board of Trustees of the University of Illinois, 1891; Gott v. Berea, 1913; Stetson University v. Hunt, 1924; Dixon v. Alabama State Board of Education, 1961.*

Mendez v. Westminster (1947)

Who Was Involved

Thomas Estrada, William Guzman, Gonzalo Mendez, Frank Palomino, and Lorenzo Ramirez are five Mexican-American fathers of students in Westminster, Garden Grove, Santa Ana, and El Modena school districts in Orange County, California.

Issue(s)

Attorneys for Mendez and the others argued that "Schools for Mexicans" in four school districts in Orange County, California, were unconstitutional because the plaintiffs were white. Separate schools were not in place in other parts of California, and often in segregated parts of the country, Mexican students were placed in white, not Black, schools. The court found in favor of Mendez, not because the court considered the Mexican students to be white but because the Equal Protection Clause of the Fourteenth Amendment does not allow for separate-but-equal schools.

Takeaways

Separate but equal does not stand in educational practice.

> **RELATED CASES**
>
> *Maestas vs. George H. Shone*, 1912; *Del Rio Independent School District v. Salvatierra*, 1930; *Roberto Alvarez vs. the Board of Trustees of the Lemon Grove School District*, 1931; *Delgado v. Bastrop Independent School District*, 1948; *Cisneros v. Corpus Christi Independent School District*, 1950; *Hernandez v. Texas*, 1954.

Sipuel v. University of Oklahoma (1948)

Who Was Involved

Ada Sipuel and the law school at the University of Oklahoma.

Issue(s)

Ada Lois Sipuel, a Black woman, applied to law school at the University of Oklahoma (OU). Sipuel argued that she should be admitted because there was no "separate but equal" law school for her to attend in Oklahoma. OU President George Lynn Cross acknowledged that Sipuel was academically qualified for admission, but Oklahoma statutes prohibited Black and white students from attending classes together. Should the university choose to violate these laws, the University would be fined $500 a day (about $6,200 in 2022 dollars), instructors teaching Black and white students together would be fined $50 a day (about $620 today), and students attending the classes would be fined $20 a day ($247 today).

The Supreme Court ruled that Sipuel—a Black woman—must be provided the same legal education opportunities as other citizens. Instead of admitting Sipuel-Fisher (she was married by this time), the Attorney General ordered the state Board of Regents to create the "Langston University School of Law." It created the school in five days in space in the state capitol. In the meantime, OU admitted George McLaurin, a Black man, and, rather than take another case to the Supreme Court, also admitted Sipuel-Fisher. She would graduate and become a member of the OU Board of Regents.

Takeaways

Black students have the same rights as white students regarding access and quality of legal education. Additionally, it is worth stressing that access is not the same as an equitable experience. Although Ada Lois Sipuel-Fisher was admitted to the OU law school, she was forced to sit at the back of her classes in a roped-off chair marked "colored."

RELATED CASES

Sweatt v. Painter, 1950; *McLaurin v. Oklahoma State Regents for Higher Education*, 1950; *Florida ex rel. Hawkings v. Board of Control*, 1956.

Brown v. Board of Education Topeka I (1954)

Who Was Involved

This case represents similar complaints from four states and the District of Columbia. Oliver Brown—the only man among the plaintiffs—was assigned as lead plaintiff in the case, where he advocated for admission for his eight-year-old daughter Linda to the white school closest to their home: Sumner School in Topeka, Kansas. Future Supreme Court Justice Thurgood Marshall was one of the attorneys representing Brown.

Issue(s)

The lower courts had found that the segregated schools were substantially equal to white schools in terms of facilities, books, and teacher qualifications, and thereby in compliance with the Fourteenth Amendment as interpreted by Plessy v. Ferguson. "The Supreme Court held that 'separate but equal' facilities are inherently unequal and violate the protections of the Equal Protection Clause of the Fourteenth Amendment" (Brown v. Board, 1954). The Court's decision was unanimous.

While Brown v. Board is the name of the case with which we are most familiar, there were four other cases filed along with Brown in Kansas. The other cases are Briggs v. Elliott (South Carolina), Davis v. County School Board of Prince Edward County (Virginia), Belton v. Gebhart / Bulah v. Gebhart (Delaware), and Bolling v. Sharpe (District of Columbia).

Takeaways

The courts mandated that separate but equal was no longer the law of the land. The goal was to provide more equitable educational opportunities for all students. Still, much of the conversation around this issue focused on the differences between educational opportunities for Black and white students—particularly in the South.

RELATED CASES

Clark v. Board of School Directors, 1867; *Belton v. Gebhart / Bulah v. Gebhart*, 1952; *Briggs v. Elliott*, 1952; *Davis v. County School Board of Prince Edward County*, 1954; *Bolling v. Sharpe*, 1954.

Brown v. Board of Education Topeka II (1955)

Who Was Involved

Same as Brown v. Board of Education Topeka I (see the previous case).

Issue(s)

While the Supreme Court had decided that schools must integrate, many all-white schools did not follow the ruling. The Court found that different schools and communities would require other solutions. Instead of mandating a deadline, the Court ordered all schools to integrate with "all deliberate speed" (Brown v. Board, 1955).

Takeaways

Cases related to desegregation continued for nearly 20 years. Additionally, Brown v. Board set a precedent for equal access pertaining to gender (Title IX, Chapter 2) and physical and mental ability (Section 504 of the Rehabilitation Act, Chapter 2).

In the context of higher education, examining the experiences of students who integrated colleges and universities is an essential additional context. Those first to integrate their institutions included John Chavis (Washington & Lee University, 1799), Alexander Lucius Twilight (Middlebury College, 1823), Mary Jane Patterson (Oberlin College, 1862), Rebecca Lee (New England Female Medical College, 1864), Henry Ossian Flipper (U.S. Military Academy at West Point, 1877), Autherine Lucy (University of Alabama, 1956, but Lucy was suspended three days after she began at the university over fears for her safety and later expelled), Hamilton Holmes and Charlayne Hunter (University of Georgia, 1961), James Meredith (University of Mississippi, 1962), Vivian Malone and James A. Hood (University of Alabama, 1963), and Henry Gantt (Clemson University, 1963).

RELATED CASES AND LEGISLATION

Cooper v. Aaron, 1958, the Civil Rights Act of 1964; *Green v. County School Board of New Kent County*, 1968; *Alexander v. Holmes County Board of Education*, 1969; *Swann v. Charlotte-Mecklenberg Board of Education*, 1971; *Wright v. Council of the City of Emporia*, 1972; *United States v. Scotland Neck City Board of Education*, 1972; *Lau v. Nichols*, 1974; *Milliken v. Bradley*, 1974.

Dixon v. Alabama State Board of Education (1961)

Who Was Involved

St. John Dixon and the other Black plaintiffs—Bernard Lee, Marzette Watts, Edward English Jones, Joseph Peterson, and Elroy Embry—students at Alabama State College (today Alabama State University), university president Harper Trenholm, Alabama Governor John Patterson, and the Alabama State Board of Education.

Issue(s)

Six Black men students at Alabama State College were engaged in a Civil Rights protest by taking "whites only" seats at a lunch counter in the Montgomery County Courthouse for 90 minutes, after which they returned to campus. The students said they were engaging in free speech and had protection under the First Amendment, and as a result, the police did not arrest them. Gov. Patterson called President Trenholm, demanding the students' expulsion. When Trenholm asked for leniency, Patterson contacted the Alabama State Board of Education, which expelled nine students and put 20 others on probation for protest participation. The Board of Education said that, owing to *in loco parentis* authority, they could expel students without notice or hearing.

Takeaways

This case initiated the end of universities acting *in loco parentis*. Public institutions cannot expel students without basic due process, including notice of charges, a right to be heard on the charges, and notification of the outcome of the hearing process. It is important to remember the tremendous risk these students took in assuring due process for all college students.

RELATED CASES

People v. Wheaton College, 1866; *North v. Board of Trustees of the University of Illinois*, 1891; *Gott v. Berea*, 1913; *Stetson University v. Hunt*, 1924; *Anthony v. Syracuse University*, 1928; *Dixon v. Alabama State Board of Education*, 1961.

Tinker v. Des Moines Independent Community School District (1969)

Who Was Involved

Five Tinker siblings aged eight to 15 at three schools and the Des Moines Independent Community School District.

Issue(s)

The students wore black armbands protesting U.S. involvement in the Vietnam War. While there was no policy prohibiting this in the elementary school, the middle and high schools suspended the three older children for wearing the armbands in violation of the schools' policies.

Takeaways

Siding with the students, the court found that free speech under the First Amendment applied to public schools and that there would have to be a constitutionally valid reason to restrict it in the classroom.

RELATED CASES

Schenck v. the United States, 1919; *Sweezy v. New Hampshire*, 1957; *Bethel School District v. Fraser*, 1986; *Hazelwood v. Kuhlmeier*, 1988; *Castorina v. Madison County School Board*, 2000; *Defoe v. Spiva*, 2010.

Healy v. James (1972)

Who Was Involved

Catherine J. Healy, seven other Central Connecticut State College (CCSC—today Central Connecticut State University) students, and college president F. Don James.

Issue(s)

Students attempted to organize a chapter of Students for a Democratic Society (SDS). CCSC President James, rejecting the recommendation of the Student Affairs Committee, denied official recognition to the campus chapter of SDS because the organization had been involved in violence on other campuses. The students argued that denying the organization recognition was an infringement on their rights to free speech and an unconstitutional exercise of prior restraint.

Takeaways

Building on *Tinker v. Des Moines* (1969), the court asserted that college campuses must provide First Amendment protections to their students. The court found that CCSC engaged in prior restraint by not recognizing the organization. The majority decision stated that neither students nor teachers at public secondary institutions "shed their constitutional rights of freedom of speech or expression at the schoolhouse gate" (Healy v. James, 1972). As a result of the decision, universities could not prohibit student organizations from being recognized based on organizational focus or content.

Regents of the University of California v. Bakke (1978)

Who Was Involved

Allan Bakke, a 35-year-old white man, and the University of California Medical School at Davis.

Issue(s)

UC-Davis medical school rejected Bakke both times he applied. The school reserved 16 of 100 spaces in each class for qualified minorities. Bakke's GPA and test scores exceeded those of the admitted minority students. He argued the university excluded him solely based on his race.

Takeaways

The court found in favor of the university, writing that race as a criterion for admission is acceptable but that racial admissions quotas violate the Equal Protection Clause of the Fourteenth Amendment.

RELATED CASES

Hopwood v. Texas, 1996; *Grutter v. Bollinger*, 2003; *Gratz v. Bollinger*, 2003; *Fisher v. Texas I*, 2013; *Fisher v. Texas II*, 2016; *Students for Fair Admissions, Inc. v. University of North Carolina*, 2023; *Students for Fair Admissions, Inc. v. President and Fellows of Harvard College*, 2023.

Bradshaw v. Rawlings (1979)

Who Was Involved

Donald Bradshaw and Bruce Rawlings—both college sophomores at Delaware Valley College—named the college, a beverage distributor, and a student organization (Maennerchor Society) as defendants in the lawsuit.

Issue(s)

Rawlings drove Bradshaw to a Maennerchor Society off-campus event where the group served alcohol. On the way home, Rawlings lost control of his vehicle and crashed into a parked car. Rawlings was severely injured and sued the defendants named above as a result.

Takeaways

The circuit court ruled that given the change in the role of the university away from *in loco parentis*, universities were no longer obligated to guarantee student safety and did not have a duty to protect students from all potential harm.

RELATED CASES

Baldwin v. Zoradi, 1981; *Beach v. University of Utah*, 1986; *Rabel v. Illinois Wesleyan University*, 1987; *Whitlock v. Denver*, 1987.

Southeastern Community College v. Davis (1979)

Who Was Involved

Frances Davis and the Southeastern Community College (SCC) nursing program.

Issue(s)

Davis, who could not understand speech without lip-reading, was denied admission to the nursing program at SCC. The Supreme Court found that SCC did not violate Section 504 of the Rehabilitation Act of 1973 in denying admission. The unanimous court found that she was not "otherwise qualified" even with an improved hearing aid.

Takeaways

A person must meet program requirements "in spite of" their handicap rather than "in every respect except as to limitations imposed by their handicap" (Southeastern Community College v. Davis, 1979).

RELATED CASES

Pushkin v. Regents of the University of Colorado, 1981; *Wynne v. Tufts University School of Medicine*, 1991, 1992; *Ohio Civil Rights Commission v. Case Western Reserve University*, 1996; *Guckenberger v. Boston University*, 1997; *Dudley v. Miami*, 2016.

Alexander v. Yale (1980)

Who Was Involved

Yale students Ronni Alexander, Margery Reifler, Pamela Price, Lisa E. Stone, and Ann Olivarius; Yale University; and Keith Brion, Michael Cooke, and other Yale faculty members.

Issue(s)

The plaintiffs alleged that Yale failed to provide a process for addressing sexual misconduct. They did not look to sue the university but instead wanted to ensure that Yale instituted a process for students to report sexual misconduct. Ultimately, they did not win the case in court. However, they lost because Yale had done what the plaintiffs had requested and created processes for taking reports, investigating, and adjudicating sexual harassment complaints.

Takeaways

This case was the first time a lawsuit used Title IX this way, the rationale being that sexual misconduct disproportionately impacted women in higher education. As a result of this case, campuses across the country began implementing processes for reporting sexual misconduct on campus.

RELATED CASES

Meritor Savings Bank v. Vinson, 1986.

Bob Jones University v. the U.S. (1983)

Who Was Involved

Bob Jones University and the United States government.

Issue(s)

Before 1971, Bob Jones University did not admit Black students because of its interpretation of the Bible's stance on interracial dating. After admitting married Black students from 1971 to 1975, it finally admitted all Black students in 1975 as long as they were not engaged in and did not advocate for interracial dating. Because of racially discriminatory policies on campus, the U.S. government revoked the university's tax-exempt status.

Takeaways

When the government has an overriding obligation to the public interest (such as eradicating racial discrimination in education), that outweighs the burden of a denial of tax benefits to a college or university.

RELATED CASES

Goldsboro Christian Schools v. U.S., 1982; *Grove City College v. Bell*, 1984.

Mullins v. Pine Manor College (1983)

Who Was Involved

Lisa Mullins, a first-year college student at Pine Manor College.

Issue(s)

Mullins, required to live on campus as a first-year student, was attacked in her on-campus apartment by an unknown assailant. The court found that the university has a duty to students regarding safe housing (as any other landlord would be obligated to) and that the campus must make reasonable attempts to prevent foreseeable harm.

Takeaways

Universities are required to make sure on-campus housing is safe. Ensuring safety is the same obligation any other landlord would have to occupants. Additionally, the university must make reasonable attempts to prevent foreseeable harm to students.

Doe v. University of Michigan (1989)

Who Was Involved

Doe, a student and the University of Michigan.

Issue(s)

In the 1980s, there were multiple racist incidents at the University of Michigan. In response, the university developed a campus speech code. A guide that included examples that appeared to violate the First Amendment supplemented the code. When the university implemented the code, Doe, a University of Michigan graduate student in psychology, taught courses that explored controversial theories purporting differences in the mental abilities of men and women on the basis of biology. Because he was afraid that teaching these theories might violate university speech codes (which covered classrooms, libraries, labs, and other spaces), he filed suit against the university. The federal district court held that the campus speech code adopted by the University of Michigan violated the First Amendment as it was overbroad and vague.

Takeaways

The First Amendment on college campuses protects free speech. University speech codes must not violate the freedoms outlined therein.

Related Case

UWM Post v. Board of Regents, 1991.

Furek v. The University of Delaware (1991)

Who Was Involved

Jeffrey Furyk, Sigma Phi Epsilon fraternity, and the University of Delaware.

Issue(s)

During a hazing incident, the student was in the process of joining the Sigma Phi Epsilon fraternity when a member poured oven cleaner on Furyk, resulting in significant burns on his body.

Takeaways

Repeated hazing warnings to the university from the Dean of Students and other university officials constituted an assumed duty on the part of the university to protect students. The court found that, when they know that potential risk exists, colleges and universities should take reasonable steps to prevent harm to students.

Hopwood v. Texas (1996)

Who Was Involved

Cheryl J. Hopwood, three other white law school applicants, and the University of Texas School of Law.

Issue(s)

Hopwood, Douglas Carvell, Kenneth Elliott, and David Rogers applied to the University of Texas law school in 1992. After being denied admission, the plaintiffs filed suit because they felt the university racially discriminated against them. They had higher LSAT scores and GPAs than 36/43 Latin*[1] students and 16/18 Black students admitted.

Takeaways

Race cannot be used as a factor in admissions to diversify the student body or eliminate the effects of past discrimination.

RELATED CASES

Regents of the University of California v. Bakke, 1978; *Grutter v. Bollinger*, 2003; *Gratz v. Bollinger*, 2003; *Fisher v. Texas I* (2013); *Fisher v. Texas II*, 2016; *Students for Fair Admissions, Inc. v. University of North Carolina*, 2023; *Students for Fair Admissions, Inc. v. President and Fellows of Harvard College*, 2023.

Ayers v Fordice and United States v. Fordice (2002)

Who Was Involved

Jake Ayers, Sr., Mississippi state Governor Kirk Fordice, and the state of Mississippi.

Issue(s)

Initially filed in January of 1975, this case focused on Mississippi's separate-but-equal higher education systems. Ayers, the father of a student at Jackson State University, claimed that the Mississippi legislature had historically underfunded historically Black colleges and universities (HBCUs) in the state (Jackson State University, Alcorn State University, and Mississippi Valley University). The court did not find that the current system was unconstitutional; rather, the court found that the system was insufficient and had not done enough to eliminate segregation in higher education.

Ayers v. Fordice was originally Ayers v. Waller and later Ayers v. Musgrove. The U.S. government eventually took on this case as a class action suit.

Takeaways

Race-neutral admissions policies cannot eradicate prior policies and practices related to segregated education systems. The three HBCUs and the state reached a $503 million settlement. However, many people criticized this amount as insufficient to help the schools compete with historically white universities in the state, which had been resourced inequitably over time.

RELATED CASES

Geier & United States v. Sundquist, 2001.

Grutter v. Bollinger (2003)

Who Was Involved

Barbara Grutter, the University of Michigan law school, and University of Michigan President Lee C. Bollinger.

Issue(s)

The University of Michigan denied Grutter, a white applicant, admission to its law school. The law school admitted that it used race as one consideration for admission because of a compelling interest in diversifying the student body.

Takeaways

Race can be used as a factor for admissions as long as it is not the only factor considered. The Supreme Court also found that the practice at the University of Michigan did not function as a quota.

RELATED CASES

Regents of the University of California v. Bakke, 1978; *Hopwood v. Texas*, 1996; *Gratz v. Bollinger*, 2003; *Fisher v. Texas I*, 2013; *Fisher v. Texas II*, 2016; *Students for Fair Admissions, Inc. v. University of North Carolina*, 2023; *Students for Fair Admissions, Inc. v. President and Fellows of Harvard College*, 2023.

Gratz v. Bollinger (2003)

Who Was Involved

Jennifer Gratz and Patrick Hamacher, the University of Michigan, and University of Michigan President Lee C. Bollinger.

Issue(s)

The University of Michigan denied Gratz and Hamacher admission to the institution. The university used a point system for admissions. The Supreme Court favored the students as the University of Michigan had not narrowly tailored its admissions policy to achieve the diversity goal.

Takeaways

Universities can consider race in admissions policies so long as institutions narrowly tailor those policies to align with university goals. The definition of "narrowly tailor" varies, but the focus tends to be on the smallest racial preference needed to achieve the compelling interest of the institution (Ayres & Foster, 2007).

RELATED CASES

Regents of the University of California v. Bakke, 1978; *Hopwood v. Texas*, 1996; *Grutter v. Bollinger*, 2003; *Fisher v. Texas I*, 2013; *Fisher v. Texas II*, 2016; *Students for Fair Admissions, Inc. v. University of North Carolina*, 2023; *Students for Fair Admissions, Inc. v. President and Fellows of Harvard College*, 2023.

Fisher v. Texas, I (2013)

Who Was Involved

Abigail Fisher and the University of Texas at Austin (UT Austin).

Issue(s)

Fisher, a white woman, was denied undergraduate admission to UT Austin in 2008. She claimed that discrimination based on race violated the Equal Protection Clause of the Fourteenth Amendment. The court remanded the case back to the Fifth Circuit Court and directed them to apply strict scrutiny review to the case.

Takeaways

The Supreme Court required no admissions changes as a result of this case.

RELATED CASES

Regents of the University of California v. Bakke, 1978; *Hopwood v. Texas*, 1996; *Grutter v. Bollinger*, 2003; *Gratz v. Bollinger*, 2003; *Fisher v. Texas II*, 2016; *Students for Fair Admissions, Inc. v. University of North Carolina*, 2023; *Students for Fair Admissions, Inc. v. President and Fellows of Harvard College*, 2023.

Fisher v. Texas, II (2016)

Who Was Involved

Abigail Fisher and UT Austin.

Issue(s)

This case also involved Abigail Fisher claiming that UT Austin violated the Equal Protection Clause when she was discriminated against because of her race. Upon review, the Fifth Circuit Court again found in favor of the admissions policy utilized at UT Austin. The Supreme Court agreed and found that the university's use of race as an admission factor promoted "cross-racial understanding" and increased diversity, which aligned with university goals.

While the Supreme Court heard this case in 2016, it is worth noting that in 2012 Abigail Fisher graduated from Louisiana State University.

Takeaways

The Supreme Court affirmed that race could be a consideration in admissions policies so long as institutions could pass strict scrutiny from the courts.

RELATED CASES

Regents of the University of California v. Bakke, 1978; *Hopwood v. Texas*, 1996; *Grutter v. Bollinger*, 2003; *Gratz v. Bollinger*, 2003; *Fisher v. Texas I*, 2013; *Students for Fair Admissions, Inc. v. University of North Carolina*, 2023; *Students for Fair Admissions, Inc. v. President and Fellows of Harvard College*, 2023.

Students for Fair Admissions, Inc. v. University of North Carolina, 2023

Who Was Involved

Students for Fair Admissions, Inc. and the University of North Carolina.

Issue(s)

This case involved the Students for Fair Admissions, Inc. (SFFA), a nonprofit organization focused on eliminating racial preferences in college admissions. The group alleged that the University of North Carolina (UNC) made admissions decisions based on a number of issues, including grades, recommendation letters, extracurriculars, and race. The SFFA alleged that UNC's admissions decisions made on the basis of race were unlawful under the Equal Protection Clause of the Fourteenth Amendment because they discriminated against white and Asian applicants by preferencing Black, Hispanic, and Native American applicants. The Supreme Court agreed, overturning a federal trial court decision and ruling in favor of the SFFA.

Takeaways

The decision effectively overruled *Grutter v. Bollinger* (2003) and eliminated race as an admissions criterion. It is important to note that UNC is obliged to not only the equal protection clause but also Title IV of the Civil Rights Act of 1964. Title IV prohibits discrimination on the basis of race by institutions that receive federal money. As a result, Title IV applies to UNC as a public institution but not to Harvard, which is a private institution. Service academies were exempted from the court's decision.

RELATED CASES

Regents of the University of California v. Bakke, 1978; *Hopwood v. Texas*, 1996; *Grutter v. Bollinger*, 2003; *Gratz v. Bollinger*, 2003; *Fisher v. Texas I*, 2013; *Fisher v. Texas II, 2016; Students for Fair Admissions, Inc. v. President and Fellows of Harvard College*, 2023.

Students for Fair Admissions, Inc. v. President and Fellows of Harvard College, 2023

Who Was Involved

Students for Fair Admissions, Inc. and Harvard University.

Issue(s)

This case involved the Students for Fair Admissions, Inc. (SFFA), a nonprofit organization focused on eliminating racial preferences in college admissions. The group alleged that Harvard University made admissions decisions based on a number of issues, including grades, recommendation letters, extracurriculars, and race. The SFFA alleged that Harvard's admissions decisions made on the basis of race were unlawful under the Equal Protection Clause of the Fourteenth Amendment. An additional element in the Harvard case was the university's discrimination against Asian students through the use of subjective standards to measure likability, courage, and kindness in admissions, resulting in a ceiling for the admission of Asian American applicants. The Supreme Court ruled in favor of the SFFA and overturned federal trial and federal appeal court decisions.

Takeaways

The decision effectively overruled *Grutter v. Bollinger* (2003) and eliminated race as an admissions criterion. Service academies were exempted from the court's decision.

RELATED CASES

Regents of the University of California v. Bakke, 1978; *Hopwood v. Texas*, 1996; *Grutter v. Bollinger*, 2003; *Gratz v. Bollinger*, 2003; *Fisher v. Texas I*, 2013; *Fisher v. Texas II, 2016; Students for Fair Admissions, Inc. v. University of North Carolina*, 2023.

Conclusion

As we have said, this chapter does not encompass every case related to higher education and student affairs. Additionally, new cases are constantly emerging, so we encourage you to stay current with incidents on campuses across the country. This chapter provides a brief overview of the court cases that have impacted higher education. Since precedent matters in legal issues, these cases can help us understand where we are and how we got here.

Note

1 Latin* is an all-inclusive term that critically considers the fluidity of social identities of people of Latin American descent or origin. Latin* invites to the conversation those who do and do not identify with Latinx, Latino, and Latina. For example, Latin* considers Latinx, Latiné, Latinu, Latini, Latino, Latina, Latina/o, Latin@, Latin, or Latin American (Salinas, 2020; Salinas & Lozano, 2022).

4

AN ETHICS PRIMER

If we think about law as what we can do, then ethics are what we should do. These do not always align. I (Michelle) was once a hall director in a new residence hall. There were several Americans with Disabilities Act (ADA)-compliant rooms throughout the building—at least one on each floor. The Honors Program had a learning community on the first floor, and students had to be in honors to live there. The result was that anyone who was not in honors and who needed an ADA-compliant space could not live on the first floor. The ADA spaces in the building met legal standards. The building was ADA-compliant. However, the situation meant that students who may have had issues evacuating the building during a fire alarm or other emergency when the elevators were not functioning could not get themselves out of the building. The decisions made were legal, but were they ethical?

Much of our work in higher education will involve ethics more than laws. This emphasis on ethics is stated repeatedly throughout the text. Sundberg and Fried (1997) wrote that "making ethical choices and thinking through ethical issues are at the very core of our work as student affairs professionals" (p. 67), and Sandeen and Barr (2014) called ethics a cornerstone of student affairs. As such, this chapter is foundational in the context of this book and in how we engage with students, colleagues, and other constituents daily.

Student affairs graduate students and academic and student affairs staff often worry more about legal than ethical issues. This heightened attention to the law over ethics is problematic because we make ethical decisions multiple times daily—in and out of work. We make decisions related to law far less frequently.

DOI: 10.4324/9781003442707-5

So, why do we not think more about our ethics? Often, we are good at seeing the ethical issues in others' work. Maybe we even discuss others' lack of ethics in-depth with our friends. However, we sometimes fail to use a critical lens on our own behavior, and we also fail to acknowledge that by gossiping about others' mistakes rather than going directly to them, we are engaging in a potential breach of ethics.

Sexual misconduct, social media, freedom of speech, issues of equity and justice, access to higher education, and relationships between student affairs practitioners and students, staff, faculty, parents and families, alumni, donors, and community leaders—these and other issues inform our work each day. The challenges faced by academic and student affairs staff can range from a quote on the closing of a resident assistant's email signature to workplace harassment. The work involves addressing a variety of behaviors in others, but ultimately the work starts with how we engage in ethical practice or fail to do so.

Competencies

This chapter relates directly to the Personal and Ethical Foundations (PEF) competency. PEF focuses on maintaining integrity in work and life. According to the competency description, "integrity has an internal locus informed by our internal voices of care, experiences, and a combination of external ethical guidelines... [which grow through] curiosity, reflection, and self-authorship" (p. 12). We wrote this text to provide opportunities to engage curiosity and practice reflection as we engage in self-authorship.

Chapter Organization

This chapter provides an overview of ethics with particular attention to how ethics inform student affairs practice. It sets the stage for future chapters on functional areas that focus on specific situations that have emerged in the past, are surfacing now, or could become concerns in the future. Essentially, this text is designed to help put ethics into practice so that we as practitioners can think about ethical situations rather than learning ethics through trial-and-error in work with a direct impact on students and others around us.

Ethics Distinguished from Law

Ethics and law are intertwined but not synonymous. Ruggerio (2015) wrote, "law is not possible without ethics" (p. 4). Lawmakers, like all of us, bring their perspectives to work; as a result, who the lawmakers *are* impacts the creation of laws. We know that people make laws, yet their lived experiences and social identities will shape how they support, challenge, or vote for new laws. However, lawmakers are not always ethical or at least may not always consider ethics since laws often do not address the needs of all stakeholders and often have a disproportionately negative impact on historically marginalized individuals and communities. While this chapter focuses on law and ethics, it is important to understand what these terms mean and how they differ from related concepts. See Table 4.1 for definitions and examples of these terms.

It is important to note that ethics are both personal and communal. The guidelines exist in the community but are put into action individually. As Reybold et al. (2008) wrote, "professional ethics are ultimately defined and put into practice by the individual based on personal values" (p. 112). Professional organizations have professional ethics—such as those of lawyers and doctors—but people violate those ethics. Student affairs also has ethical guidelines (e.g., American College Personnel Association [ACPA's] Statement of Ethical Principles and Standards; ACPA, n.d.), but how people enact those ethics varies greatly. Table 4.1 provides definitions, sources, and student affairs examples of law, ethics, morals, values, beliefs, and virtues.

TABLE 4.1 Definitions, Sources, and Examples of Terms

Term	*Defined*	*Source*	*Example*
Laws	What we are required or not allowed to do	Collective, Society	The Clery Act
Beliefs	What we think is true	Individual	Only the best and the worst of people go into student affairs.
Morals	What is good or bad	Individual or collective codes of conduct. Taught by family, church, school, and others.	Personal perspective that student affairs staff should not drink with students, regardless of age
Values	What is important, how things should be	Individual	Assistantship and field experiences should not exploit graduate students.
Virtues	Traits that individuals possess	Individual	My supervisor is incredibly patient in helping me learn about my new position.

Consider this example; you are working in a leadership office at a university in the Midwest. A horrible blizzard is beginning, and while the university has not decided to close early, the roads are getting dangerous. There are three associate directors (ADs) in the office. One AD tells her team to leave if they need to. The public schools are releasing early, and if people need to leave to make it home safely or meet their kids, they should go. The second AD says that until the university closes, he expects everyone to stay at work or take vacation time. The third AD tells everyone except the administrative staff they can go home. The admin team needs to stay in case calls come in or someone comes to the front desk with questions.

Is each of these decisions legal? Probably. Is each of them ethical? If yes, how can they all be ethical and all be different? If not, which of the three is ethical? Of course, this puts aside the idea that the inconsistency across a single office will create challenges to morale. Our ethical decisions are individual and communal, impacting those around us. This chapter explores these ethical ideas and challenges.

The Philosophy of Ethics

There is an old saying, "Just because you can, doesn't mean you should." Ethics sometime push against the law. Legal guidelines are fundamental parameters, not aspirational goals. On the other hand, ethics are the standards we hold ourselves to.

Ethics Overview

Ethics stem from philosophy but are not solely things we think about and reflect upon. Instead, ethics inform our thinking, behavior, and engagement with others. Ruggerio (2015) described normative ethics as "involving the collection and interpretation of data on what people from various cultures believe, without any consideration for the appropriateness or reasonableness of those beliefs" (p. 5). Normative ethics involve how people subjectively choose between wrong and right. Reybold et al. (2008) focused on professional ethics, which they defined as strategies "for professional reasoning and conduct in the workplace" (p. 111).

In the context of student affairs, scholars have examined ethics and ethical decision-making in conjunction with moral development. Piaget (1932) conceptualized moral development by examining children's moral reasoning. He saw morality as an exchange between thinking and action, ultimately describing it as a constructivist process. Kohlberg (1973, 1984) built on this, identifying three levels and six stages of moral reasoning:

- Preconventional level—Stage 1: Obedience & punishment; Stage 2: Individualism & exchange
- Conventional level—Stage 3: Good interpersonal relationships; Stage 4: Maintaining the social order
- Postconventional level—Stage 5: Social contract & individual rights; Stage 6: Universal principles

While Kohlberg's work is important, Gilligan (1977) noted that the sample he used for his study comprised only boys/men. There are additional concerns with the research design for Kohlberg's work; however, Colby et al. (1983) replicated Kohlberg's study and addressed those concerns with results similar to those of Kohlberg's original work.

There are several scholars whose work has contributed directly to ethics in student affairs. The following is a summary of critical studies related to the topic.

Gilligan (1977) studied women's moral development and devised an Ethic of Care model. This model includes the same levels as Kohlberg's (1973, 1984) model, but Gilligan identified two transitions between each level, paying particular attention to the positionality of self in relation to others, instead of additional stages. The preconventional (individual survival) stage is followed by a transition from selfishness to responsibility to others. Subsequently, the conventional (self-sacrifice is goodness) stage is followed by a transition from goodness to truth and then to the postconventional (principle of nonviolence: do not harm self or others) stage.

Rest (1994) developed schemas (patterns in memory) in a staircase model rather than specific and rigid stages:

1. Moral awareness (sensitivity and recognition)
2. Moral judgment
3. Moral intention
4. Moral action.

Mathieson (2003) identified seven elements of moral maturity:

1. Moral agency and sense of self – Individuals have the right and ability to make and act on decisions and understand themselves as moral agents.
2. Harnessing cognitive ability – the ability to recognize issues, those involved, and conflict and create new systems of meaning as a person addresses or resolves (or ignores) issues

3. Harnessing emotional resources – managing emotions and using them to inspire action at the right time in pursuit of the proper outcomes
4. Using social skills – understanding relationships, norms, and social pressure and navigating those issues in pursuit of goals
5. Using principles – beyond simply following principles, seeing how they interact with one another and influence communities
6. Respecting others – See inherent worth in others, understand concepts of interdependence with others, realize the cultural impact on social norms, and have the ability to interact with those holding different worldviews without feeling threatened.
7. Developing a sense of purpose – can be a goal or a process of living life; reinforced by the work of other scholars (Chickering, 1969; Frankl, 1984; Maslow, 1968).

Ruggerio (2015) wrote that four things influence ethics:

1. The role of the majority—While the majority has a voice, we must remember that "there is no magic in majorities" (Ruggerio, 2015, p. 21). However, occasionally institutions start to believe that "the majority view is the wisest, most informed view" (Ruggerio, 2015, p. 21). Higher education ethics are enmeshed in the history of higher education where the majority has been white people of privilege making educational decisions with significant impact on those historically disenfranchised from access to higher education.
2. The role of feelings—This approach is grounded in Carl Rogers's humanistic psychology. Graduate programs and supervisors train student affairs practitioners to help students recognize their feelings, needs, desires, and preferences rather than feeling "shameful," "odd," or "bad."
3. The role of conscience—Ruggerio (2015) summarized this as knowing "what we have done or are tempted to do is wrong" (p. 38). Conscience is our internal monitor speaking to us about our actions (or inaction).
4. Comparing cultures—Each culture—in this book, each college and university culture—has values, rituals, and customs that reflect geography, history, and economic circumstances. Therefore, it is vital to make sense of individual aspects of each institution (mission, vision, history, culture(s), practices, norms, beliefs, language/terminology, financial resources, policies, bureaucracy, and unwritten rules) without comparing one place with another.

Scholars have taken a variety of approaches to understanding ethics and moral development. While Ruggerio (2015) provides a general overview of ethics, other scholars have focused on moral development in children

(Piaget, 1932; Kohlberg, 1973, 1984) or women (Gilligan, 1977) or college students (Mathieson, 2003). Rather than examining development, Rest (1994) examined what needs to happen for moral behavior to take place, whereas Reybold et al. (2008) examined professional ethics. These overlap and connect in various ways—Gilligan's (1977) work built on Kohlberg's (1973, 1984), which has been critiqued for equating reasoning with behavior and for cultural, age, and gender biases (Snarey, 1985). We must continue to explore these issues in terms of the development of individuals as that information informs the ethical practice of organizations.

Student Affairs and Ethical/Moral Development

Navigating ethical issues in student affairs is complicated not only by institutional context, culture, and history but also by the concept of ethics. Work teams structure expectations around ethics, including group and personal accountability. Group accountability mirrors responsibility to the supervisor and other leaders, the public, and the law but also accountability to one another as individuals (Cooper, 1998). We each bring our values, morals, and beliefs to our work, and each of those informs how we put personal and organizational ethics into practice.

Additionally, student affairs staff are uniquely situated to influence the ethical development of students (Wilcox & Ebbs, 1992). Through our practice and ways of engaging with students, we role-model ethical practice for students. As a field of practice, we focus on the holistic development of students. Reybold et al. (2008) wrote that we often choose careers that align with our values and the ethics of those career fields and professions.

It is important that ethics be incorporated into the training and learning of student affairs practitioners. While Kitchener (1986) worked primarily with counseling graduate students, her work has been adapted more broadly to a variety of helping professions and is relevant to the learning and practice of student affairs professionals. Kitchener (1986) identified the five goals of ethics training for counseling and student services:

1. Stimulating ethical sensitivity—"help students become aware of the variety and complexity of moral issues that pervade professional practice and the value conflicts inherent in them" (p. 308).
2. Improving ethical reasoning—focuses on providing students a way to evaluate cases coherently and consistently.
3. Developing moral responsibility—providing students an opportunity to make and justify ethical decisions.

4. Tolerating ambiguity—connects to the previous goals reinforcing the idea of the complexity of these decisions and how various factors impact situations in practice.
5. Fidelity—in the context of loyalty and faithfulness, someone working in the helping professions must meet their obligations to the people they serve (students, clients, etc.).

King and Kitchener (1994) developed the Reflective Judgment Model composed of seven stages.

Pre-reflective thinking: Knowledge is gained by

Stage 1: Direct, personal observation.
Stage 2: Direct, personal observation or from authority figures.
Stage 3: Authority figures.

Quasi-reflective thinking

Stage 4: Knowledge is uncertain and always involves ambiguity.
Stage 5: Knowledge is contextual and subjective.

Reflective thinking

Stage 6: Knowledge is constructed into individual conclusions based on information from various sources.
Stage 7: Knowledge is the outcome of constructing solutions evaluated in terms of evidence and re-evaluated when new evidence is available.

Dalton et al. (2009) also identified five ethical domains: student welfare, the institution, the profession, the community, and personal conscience. They described the ethical practice as "more an art than science" (p. 160). The Reflective Judgment Model and these ethical domains highlight the need for the Institutional Intelligence Model (IIM) and other tools to make meaning of specific and changing contexts in our work.

Reybold et al. (2008) studied staff perceptions of ethics in student affairs. They found that participants focused on "doing the right thing," but some followed the rules explicitly, and others imposed personal values on their decisions related to rules and guidelines (p. 120). Most participants in the study conflated professional ethics and personal morality. Regulation and sanction, as well as situating decisions in a social and cultural context related to mission and relationships, also emerged from this study. These aspects align with the IIM discussed in Chapter 5, as IIM centers on the institutional context in navigating issues as they emerge.

Liddell et al. (2010) wrote about personal and institutional barriers that can inhibit moral development and the potential role of moral elders in helping student and professional development.

Personal barriers to personal, ethical, and moral development

1. Conformity
2. Lack of ethical awareness
3. Failure to "push away from the dock"
4. Lack of self-efficacy

Personal barriers exacerbated by organizational culture

1. Cultural norms
2. Territory wars
3. Peer group pressure
4. Fear of being ostracized
5. Inadequate learning opportunities

Strategies for successful ethical mentoring

1. Know yourself
2. Know others' perspectives
3. Coach for growth
4. Balancing individual and community needs
5. Know your institution

This scholarship builds on what came before it. Kitchener (1986) identified goals for training, then King and Kitchener (1994) developed stages for that learning to take place. Reybold et al. (2008) later moved from learning to action in that people sought to "do the right thing" by either following rules or following personal values. Dalton (2009) identified places where ethical decision-making shows up, and Liddell (2010) identified barriers to ethical development. Whether focusing on work and training, thinking, or action, these scholars provide a framework for building or reflecting on ethical practice in action.

Additional Resources

Ethics are standards shared across a profession or applied field. Many of us have at least a passing familiarity with medical ethics, legal ethics, and business ethics. Many organizational documents and statements guide our ethics in student affairs. Here is a summary of some of those guiding documents.

ACPA Statement of Ethical Principles and Standards

ACPA has provided a document related to ethics designed to support student affairs students and full-time staff. The document states, "The principal purpose of this statement is to assist student affairs professionals… in regulating their behavior by sensitizing them to potential ethical problems and by providing standards useful in daily practice" (ACPA, n.d., p. 1). The document has four sections: professional responsibility and competence, student learning and development, responsibility to the institution, and responsibility to society.

The statement is an essential resource as it centers on students but also includes obligations to institutions, the practice of student affairs, and each of us as individuals. According to the ACPA/National Association of Student Personnel Administrators (NASPA) competencies, "Personal and ethical foundations are aligned because integrity has an internal locus informed by a combination of external ethical guidelines, an internal voice of care, and our own lived experiences" (ACPA/NASPA, 2015, p. 12). So while this chapter focuses specifically on ethics, much of this text's goal is to explore that "internal voice" to develop and maintain integrity in student affairs practice.

ACPA/NASPA Competencies

There are ethical considerations in each of the ACPA/NASPA competency areas (see Appendix). This section summarizes the ethical implications embedded in each competency area and should not replace full consideration of the competency document.

Personal and Ethical Foundations (PEF)—focuses on developing personal integrity and aligning personal and organizational values.

Values, Philosophy, and History (VPH)—ensures that work toward the future builds on the past and connects our values to our work. In other words, how do we engage in the work honoring (and challenging) the past while building toward a more equitable future?

Assessment, Evaluation, and Research (AER)—focuses on the ability to design, conduct, critique, and use various methodologies to create an assessment, evaluation, and research to inform policy, practice, and research. What are we studying, and who is invited as a holder of knowledge and insight? Are our approaches equitable, and do they go beyond the low bar of compliance in our treatment of participants and partners in the research?

Law, Policy, and Governance (LPG)—focuses on the ability to understand implications for each of these areas on an individual campus with work toward understanding the work in these areas more broadly across higher education. What are the rules, who made the rules, and to whom do the rules apply? What are the consequences for not following the rules and are those consequences equitable?

Organizational and Human Resources (OHR)—the ethics of hiring, supervision, management, staff development, resource allocation, and the interaction between human and organizational resources. Whom are we hiring and inviting to do the work with us? Who decides who gets opportunities? How do our processes today disrupt past discriminatory practices?

Leadership (LEAD)—focuses on individuals' ability to lead with integrity and on fostering ethical leadership in others. Who gets to be a leader? How do our ethics inform how we treat others?

Social Justice and Inclusion (SJI)—an ethical student affairs practitioner develops an understanding of oppression, privilege, and power and knows how to enact social justice processes to pursue socially just goals. Additionally, ethical practitioners focus on the connections between leadership and advocacy in an SJI context.

Student Learning and Development (SLD)—ethical application of theory to practice centering students in the process is essential in the work of student affairs practitioners.

Technology (TECH)—an understanding of both opportunities and limitations of technology in student affairs is essential for ethical practitioners. Additionally, they should be actively engaging in technology as new platforms emerge.

Advising and Supporting (A/S)—communication, group dynamics, conflict, collaboration, and crises are the areas of focus and development for ethical practitioners related to A/S competencies.

CAS Standards—Statement of Shared Ethical Principles

The Council for the Advancement of Standards (CAS) reflects good practices agreed upon by the higher education profession at large. The CAS statement on ethics includes the following seven principles:

1. Autonomy
2. Non-malfeasance
3. Beneficence
4. Justice
5. Fidelity
6. Veracity
7. Affiliation

NASPA Standards of Professional Practice

These standards, endorsed in 1990, provide a list of considerations. The areas addressed in this document include the following: professional services, accountability to institutions (agreement with mission and goals, resource management, employment relationship, conflict of interest, campus community), recognition of legal authority, treatment of others (equal consideration, students, confidentiality), research, human resources (selection and promotion, references, performance evaluations), professional competence and development, and assessment (NASPA, n.d.-a). Professional organizations provide some guidance, but individually we must do additional work to develop integrity and personal ethics. We discuss this in the next section.

Ethics in Student Affairs: Practice

While each of us struggles with issues related to law, policy, process, and other structures in higher education, we face ethical decisions much more frequently. It is worth noting that while a fundamental component of this book is the concept of *it depends*, we are not suggesting that there is no room for consistency in work. It is essential to follow the policies that your institution has in place. In terms of student conduct, for example, it is most important first to have a policy and then to follow that policy. That said, staff must develop and use their Institutional Intelligence to do their work most effectively, legally, ethically, and appropriately for a given situation.

Common Issues

- Hiring and promotion
- Evaluations
- Financial decisions (funding, raises, and budgets)
- Having "favorites" (employees, students, and colleagues)
- The gray areas—drinking with students, work romantic relationships, and other things not forbidden but discouraged
- Abiding by policy

Several resources are available to provide ethical guidance and considerations. However, there is no single source of academic and student affairs ethics. Instead, we draw from a variety of areas and pools of information. These resources can be useful in educating, training, onboarding, planning and guiding reflection and assessment.

Student Affairs Ethics in Action: The Low Bar of Compliance

We opened this chapter with the story of the ADA rooms in a new residence hall and the honors community on the first floor of the building. The building followed the laws regarding accessibility. Having a learning community on the first floor was not illegal, nor was it against university policy. From an ethical standpoint, was it okay to prohibit non-honors students with mobility issues from living on the first floor where they could evacuate themselves from the hall in case of emergency? Was it ethical to force those students to depend on staff or students to communicate with emergency response personnel that there was someone on the third-floor landing who needed help evacuating the building?

We must face these issues to move beyond the very low bar of compliance and toward ethical practice in higher education. Also, after a year, the honors community moved to an upper floor of the building with more space for more students. Also relevant, one of two students who had expressed concerns moved to the first floor. The other student enjoyed his community on the third floor and stayed there. So, even when we make sound ethical decisions, we should never expect that we know what all students will want or need.

The example above illustrates that being ethical or putting ethics into practice is different from studying ethics. In order to be ethical, we must fully understand ourselves and practice and reflect on our professional ethics (Wilcox & Ebbs, 1992). We encourage you to engage with this chapter with student affairs history and legislation (Chapter 2), case law (Chapter 3), and the IIM (Chapter 5) as each of these areas relates to student affairs.

Other chapters related to functional areas throughout this book will give you opportunities to consider your ethics. You might ask, "Why don't the authors tell us what to do?" As mentioned previously, we cannot do that since we do not know your specific background or the nuances of doing work on your campus. This book provides opportunities to think critically about being ethical and practicing ethics in student affairs and how ethics influence our decision-making. Each of these is linked inextricably to Institutional Intelligence. Reading, discussing, and writing are the best ways to develop our ethical philosophy. Throughout the book, we present multiple questions to help us understand the law and ethics of our institutions.

We each must play a role in legal and ethical practice. Humphrey et al. (2004) wrote that student affairs practitioners function on campus as "both role model and moral conscience for the campus" (p. 676). With that responsibility, we must engage in reflective practice and ongoing education related to ethics to succeed as individuals, community members, and educators.

Ethics in the Context of Institutional Intelligence

While professional organizations have ethics, the institution where we work also develops community ethics. How we function ethically will vary depending on where we work—again, our Institutional Intelligence is relevant to how we make decisions and act. Reybold et al. (2008) wrote, "If professional ethics are a combination of institutional standards, personal values, and societal standards all situated in a particular context, we must consider these elements when defining ethical behavior in the workplace" (p. 112). With this concept in mind, what is necessary, expected, ethical, and legal on one campus may be less or not ethical on another. "Like what?" you ask. Let us give you three examples.

Religion

This topic is complex when put into practice. If you work on the campus of a religiously affiliated institution, faith discussions with students may be permissible by policy and encouraged or expected as part of your work. Sharing your religious practices and beliefs in conduct meetings, one-on-one supervision conversations with resident assistant staff, or staff meetings may be standard practices. A prayer before a training or workshop activity might be entirely appropriate. That same behavior may not be appropriate at a public institution that might prohibit these same activities in practice, policy, or both. The issue of religion can surface not only through face-to-face exchanges but through the items we have in our offices or the quotes we choose for our email signatures.

When and with whom is it okay to talk about religion in the office? Of course, *it depends* on more than just your institution. Geographic location, functional area, relationship with colleagues, and other factors may impact where and with whom you can talk about your faith or the topic of faith in general or religious practices. You might use the "Strategies for Successful Ethical Mentoring" (Liddell et al., 2010) to reflect on your work. That work suggests knowing yourself and others' perspectives as you coach for growth while balancing individual and community needs. In the end, Liddell et al. (2010) suggest getting to know your institution. If you are incorporating your religious beliefs into your work, how does that align with your institution?

Using strategies identified by Liddell et al. (2010) is one of many approaches to ethical and moral development you might use. You might also combine resources. For example, when you get to the prompt about knowing your institution, you might turn to the IIM in this text to help you learn more about your specific campus.

Intimate Relationships with Colleagues

Dating people at work is a thing. It could happen. Sometimes people are open about it, and other times they are not. Different institutions will have different policies about this. Often, these policies are informed by institutional history and events that occurred on campus in the past. Understanding the policies related to this issue is essential; however, considering yourself, your expectations, and your limitations is just as important. As we mentioned earlier, just because you can do something does not mean that you should do that thing.

This could be a moral decision for some people. Starting with awareness and moving through judgment and intention is a focused way that might help some staff determine the "moral action" they want to discuss (Rest, 1994). It is essential to consider how closely you work with someone you are interested in dating, your positional power in the workplace as it relates to the other person, and the potential implications for the relationship (or the end of the relationship) on your work and your workplace.

Special Treatment

Different people have different levels of influence on colleges and universities. If people hold financial or political influence on an institution as donors, legislators, or alumni, or in other roles, expectations can go along with power and institutional relationship. If a student gets into trouble for violating a policy and calls their parent, a state legislator, to intervene on their behalf, how might that influence the process? Does it make a difference if the parent calls you directly, the vice president of student affairs (VPSA), or the university president?

While this is a book of questions more than answers, we can assure you that the answer to those questions is—yes. Using King and Kitchener's (1994) model, you can engage in pre-reflective thinking as you observe those around you—particularly authority figures—the VPSA or the president or chancellor of your institutions. Moving into the quasi-reflective stage, you can see how you create your knowledge, which is always changing, contextual, and subjective. Finally, you will engage in reflective thinking based on what you have seen happen from others around you or based on the decisions you made and what you learned from those. You may not understand how much influence someone has on your work until a specific situation arises. That said, it is vital to understand who key campus influencers are and the history of their engagement with a university. It is just as important to reflect as situations unfold so that you can build your Institutional Intelligence and continue to develop your own ethical philosophy and make sure it aligns with your sense of integrity and, ultimately, your institution as well.

Conclusion

It can be frustrating not to have specific guidelines and checklists around ethics in student affairs practice. Reybold (2007) wrote that student affairs practitioners must interpret ethics in specific contexts. A purpose of this text is to provide the IIM as a guide for that interpretation. When personal beliefs and professional or organizational ethics conflict, this can present a challenge to practitioners. These struggles may signify that it is time to identify areas to work toward change or a time to consider changing jobs. By using the *who*, *what*, *where*, *when*, *why*, and *how* questions in this text, student affairs practitioners can begin to put student affairs and institutional ethics into practice.

SECTION 2

The Institutional Intelligence Model

5

INSTITUTIONAL INTELLIGENCE

Consider the following: A student comes to you because she wants to lead a protest on campus. There are several factors to consider—her free speech rights and university policy. What should you do? There is not enough information here to answer that question, right? Getting the relevant information is why we have developed the Institutional Intelligence Model—providing a tool to get the information you need before acting.

The Institutional Intelligence Model is a way of examining the personal and institutional context and understanding organizational bureaucracy. Sternberg (1985) defined intelligence as "mental activity directed toward purposive adaptation to, and selection and shaping of, real-world environments relevant to one's life" (p. 45). Our model takes this idea of intelligence and focuses it specifically on institutions—in the case of this text, higher education institutions. Taking the time to understand our context helps us interpret legislation and case law successfully. This model also helps us understand campus context and how our ethics align with our institutions and the people around us.

Law and ethics influence how student affairs personnel and administrators develop, interpret, and implement policies related to laws that directly or indirectly impact organizations. Institutions of higher education are complex organizations where change is constant. As change occurs, it can create (dis)comfort, increase (or decrease) responsibilities, and build or break down relationships among the organization's students, staff, faculty, administrators, and stakeholders.

DOI: 10.4324/9781003442707-7

Student affairs and work across higher education have become increasingly complex as our culture has become more litigious. Issues of institutional history, campus culture, student identity, and the debate around higher education's purpose frame practitioners' work on college and university campuses. We make ethical decisions every day, and legal issues dictate the future of student affairs work, from decisions about college access for undocumented students to the law relating to Title IX and federal legislation and guidance on sexual misconduct on college campuses. As a result, legal issues are no longer the focus of only hearing officers and university counsel. Increasingly, everyone from an undergraduate student organization to the vice president of student affairs is potentially held responsible for institutional behavior. Times have changed and will continue to change. The Institutional Intelligence Model is one tool to use to navigate that change.

The Role of History

Along with change, history is also part of Institutional Intelligence. History emerges through the interpretation of the law and the role of ethics in organizational change. These interpretations and changes combine to make a significant contribution to organizational history.

Institutional Intelligence is rooted in history. History informs an organization's recollection, memories, interpretation, and discovery. Chapters 2 and 3 provide an overview of higher education history, legislation, and case law in the U.S. This educational and legal history is part of the social history that has informed and guided change and helped create and develop Institutional Intelligence at the macro level to examine large-scale patterns across higher education.

Institutions will make decisions based on previous experiences. How individuals and institutions made decisions in 1965 differs from how we make decisions today. For example, *in loco parentis* began to disappear from many campuses in the 1960s and 1970s until the 1980s and 1990s. Today, as society has become increasingly litigious, how students and student-facing practitioners deal with situations has changed. As White (2007) wrote, colleges and students had a relationship that resembled that of landlord and tenant where "colleges and universities could not be liable to a student for damages" (p. 327). The "special relationship" between students and their colleges and universities continues to surface as institutions are held responsible for protecting students from their behavior (White, 2007). Higher education will continue to make decisions based on these precedents until a new era with new laws and expectations takes root.

Institutional Intelligence will continue to help us navigate change in the future based on place, law, people involved, and other contextual factors. More specifically, the *who*, *what*, *where*, *when*, *why*, and *how* will inform decision-making and can help us develop our Institutional Intelligence in an ongoing way. Table 5.1 provides a list of questions to help achieve Institutional Intelligence and move beyond *it depends* when answering "What do I do?" in situations we face.

TABLE 5.1 The Ultimate Cheat Sheet for Critical Thinking

Institutional Intelligence prompt	*Possible question*
Who(m)	... benefits from this action or decision?
	... does this action or decision harm?
	... decides/decided about this situation?
	... is directly affected by the decision or action?
	... else has faced this situation?
	... is the best person to consult about this situation?
	... deserves recognition for this work or accomplishment(s)?
What	... happened?
	... are the strengths/weaknesses of those involved and/or affected?
	... is another perspective or alternative in this situation?
	... is the best-/worst-case scenario?
	... is most/least important in this situation?
	... can we do to make a positive change in this moment or in the future?
	... is getting in the way of our actions?
Where	... did the incident or situation occur?
	... are there similar situations that we can learn from or that need to be addressed?
	... is there the most need for specific resources or support in this situation?
	... might this incident/response exacerbate a situation or create new problems?
	... can we get more information?
	... do we go for help with this situation?
	... are the areas for improvement in our process or on campus in the future?

(*Continued*)

TABLE 5.1 (Continued)

Institutional Intelligence prompt	*Possible question*
When	… did the situation, event, or crisis occur? … is this behavior, action, or reaction acceptable/unacceptable? … would this action, behavior, or response cause problems? … is the best time to act? … will we know if we have succeeded or resolved the situation? … has this situation happened before? … can we expect this situation to change? … should we ask for help?
Why	… is this situation a problem/challenge? … is the situation, event, or response relevant to me/others? … are people influenced by this decision, action, or incident? … should people know about this incident (or not)? … did this situation or incident happen? … is there a need for this action or decision?
How	… is this situation or action similar to ___? … is this situation or action disruptive? … do we ascertain facts in this situation? … will we approach this situation safely? … does this response or decision benefit us/others? … does this response or decision harm us/others? … can we create positive change based on this situation and what we learned?

Adapted from Future Focused Learning (2021).

Institutional Intelligence

The Institutional Intelligence Model can help people and organizations analyze any micro-level situation as individual actors. First, we define Institutional Intelligence and its terms. Next, we provide context to understand Institutional Intelligence at the macro level. We use Institutional Intelligence as individuals (micro level) to understand patterns and trends across higher education (macro level). In other words, we develop Institutional Intelligence as staff members to understand the institutional context. In this book, we define the term "institutional" as pertaining to a large organization or institution. In higher education, our institutions are systems that govern people and (re)create rules and policies that create culture(s), beliefs, and practices.

Additionally, we define the term intelligence as the collection of information and the ability to acquire, learn, and apply knowledge informed by culture, society, and people. Intelligence promotes logic, reasoning, planning, creativity, problem-solving, critical thinking, and ethics. These definitions provide an overview of Institutional Intelligence as a model to understand institutions at the macro level. However, institutions are composed of various units and departments, which can have unique cultures and practices and individual practitioners with their own beliefs. Smaller units within institutions and the staff members who make up those units govern themselves at the micro level in the context of the macro context. Knowing that we develop Institutional Intelligence most effectively at the micro level is essential as we use the model to understand individual cases, situations, events, and crises.

Red Onions

To further unpack "institutional" and "intelligence," we use the metaphor of the red onion[1] to represent an organization. Layers of red skin protect the outside of the red onion. As we peel the onion layers, "the skin changes texture from papery and fragile to something stronger" (Shankman & Allen, 2009, p. 20), and colors change from red to purple and white. In this metaphor, the red onion represents an institution at the macro level. At the same time, each layer represents the institution at the micro level. Whether macro- or micro-level, the red onion has the same general characteristics—smell, flavor, and name. At each level, an organization has the same mission, vision, history, and culture. Yet the layers of a red onion change in texture and color.

Just as each layer is different from the entire onion, each unit and department of a large organization has different people, practices, norms, beliefs, language/terminology, financial resources, policies, guidelines, bureaucracy, and unwritten rules. While an organization has a shared mission, vision, history, and culture, individual units also have a unique history, culture, and other characteristics. The unit characteristics are ideally (though not always) aligned with the institution's mission, vision, history, and culture.

The center of the onion is the most pungent part and can be a reminder that an institution's core is powerful, and the other layers grow around and are affected by what is at the center. Things at the center include how an organization allocates resources to express institutional values, the history around which the institution has grown, and even the emotional attachment that people have for institutions. This attachment can exist for students, alumni, donors, employees, and others connected to the institution.

The growth of an onion builds around the center. Similarly, organizations are constantly changing. Onions are also affected by internal and external factors such as the health of the onion, nutrients, pests, sunlight, temperature, and water. There are a variety of factors that affect institutions. For this text, we focus on the impact of law and ethics. How law and ethics are enacted on campus is influenced by the *who*, *what*, *where*, *when*, *why*, and *how* questions that guide individual and group behavior.

Just like red onions, developing Institutional Intelligence can make you cry. You will make mistakes (that is part of learning), and some of those might be painful. Our goal is to maximize learning while managing the struggle. Just as you can slice that onion and cry, you can develop Institutional Intelligence by making a massive mistake during a crisis. However, you might also chill the onion, cut it under running water, or wear goggles so you will not cry as much. Similarly, you can try to develop Institutional Intelligence before an incident to minimize the mistakes (and crying) when a situation emerges and you need to respond. Just as a red onion can help you make a great dish, Institutional Intelligence can help you make informed and effective decisions to succeed in your work.

Terenzini (1993) wrote about the knowledge and skills that institutional researchers need. He described "contextual intelligence" as knowledge that "involves understanding the culture both of higher education in general and of the particular campus" (Terenzini, 1993, p. 5). He added that this knowledge reflected "organizational savvy and wisdom" (Terenzini, 1993, p. 6). However, Terenzini (1993) stressed that this knowledge could be acquired only through working at a university, and he centered institutional research. Furthermore, he did not provide a specific model for developing contextual intelligence.

Institutional Intelligence, in our model, is rooted in law and ethics that provide context and process to interpret, develop, and implement an organization's existing or new policies and guidelines. As Winston and Saunders (1998) wrote, "no ethical standard or law can be adequately understood outside the framework of the culture that devised it" (p. 80). Therefore, the *who*, *what*, *where*, *when*, *why*, and *how* of a campus inform Institutional Intelligence and guide the behavior of individuals and groups.

At the institutional/macro level, achieving Institutional Intelligence will take time and be challenging. Large organizations have various units and departments. You cannot learn everything about the *who*, *what*, *where*, *when*, *why*, and *how* of a campus in a day, month, or probably ever. You can develop insight over time, and if you do the work on an ongoing basis, you can keep building your Institutional Intelligence about the specific place where you work.

Throughout this book, we present and provide examples of Institutional Intelligence at the micro level as we delve into functional areas. Keep in mind that even at the micro level, Institutional Intelligence can be challenging. Office and team cultures and histories are not always apparent at first. Additionally, change (see Chapter 17) affects units in the form of staff turnover, reorganization, increases or reductions in resource allocation, and other ways. When states or the federal government pass legislation, campus policies are changed, or an institution's five-year plan is updated, individual units are impacted.

The Institutional Intelligence Model

The Institutional Intelligence Model consists of three parts (Figure 5.1). First are law and ethics. We must understand the laws that affect our work and how ethics (our own, others', and organizational ethics) inform what we do and how we engage with others. Second, at the core is Institutional Intelligence, which is what and how we develop information learned about our campuses and the role of law and ethics in our institutions. The third element is the foundational questions – *who*, *what*, *where*, *when*, *why*, and *how*. These questions help us understand our institutional contexts. Using these foundational questions and combining them to understand law and ethics on our campuses develop our Institutional Intelligence.

The people (*who*), mission (*what*), vision (*what*), history (*who, what, where, when, why, how*), culture(s) (*who, what, where, why*), location (*where*), practices (*what*), norms (*what, why*), beliefs (*what, why*), language/terminology (*what*), financial resources (*how*), policies and guidelines (*what, why*), bureaucracy

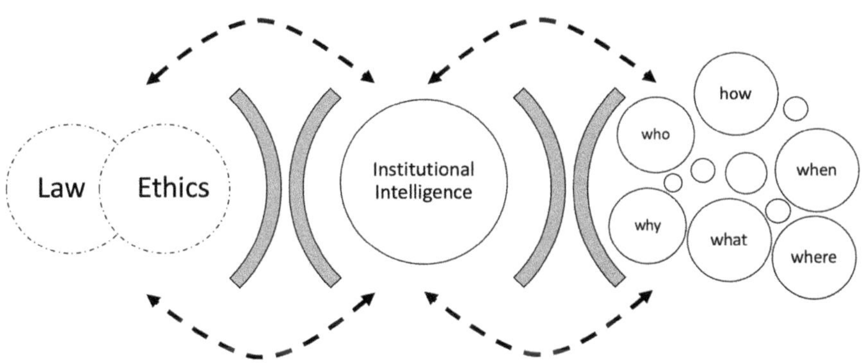

FIGURE 5.1 The Institutional Intelligence Model.

(*who, why, how*), and unwritten rules (*why, how*) guide and influence the behavior of individuals and groups in an organization. The law and ethics that inform Institutional Intelligence affect all of these elements (and more).

At the beginning of this chapter, we presented the example of free speech on campus. A student wants to lead a protest on campus. Among the factors to consider, we listed her rights and university policy. But there are other questions as well: Who is the student? With whom is she connected on campus? What has her past activity been on campus? What positions does she hold? Where does she want to hold the protest? Why is it important to her to protest at this specific time? When does she need an answer or need to fill out relevant forms? How does she plan to protest—silently? With speakers? Megaphones? A march? Anticipating and attempting to understand the unique complexities of legal and ethical situations were the catalysts for our creation of the Institutional Intelligence Model.

We can use this same process to develop questions, analyze situations, and understand how an academic department or the Dean of Students Office might handle a report of student plagiarism or how an academic advisor might navigate a situation with a student who is trying to navigate a difficult domestic situation and meet academic requirements for the term.

Law informs a student's due process rights and how institutions protect those rights (or not) at a specific college or university. Conduct officers must consider a variety of processes (e.g., student codes of conduct and honor codes), policies (e.g., policies related to housing), constituent documents (such as student organization by-laws and constitutions), and laws at the local, state, and federal levels as well as institutional history, norms, and informal practices and processes. Additionally, just as law informs the policies and processes on campus, ethics have an impact. Institutional ethics inform the process, as do the ethics of the specific conduct officer hearing the case.

Applying *who*, *what*, *where*, *when*, *why*, and *how* to a case provides hearing officers with information that may help them make decisions that are more just. Additionally, these questions help others—the accused student, the faculty member making the report, the student's parents, and those who might hear an appeal of the case—understand the decision. Anyone concerned about a hearing decision can use these questions to assess a conduct hearing.

That said, different people will have access to different information. For example, other hearing officers may know the outcomes of previous cases, whereas parents may not. A brand-new staff member may not understand the history of academic integrity on campus as a longer-term employee does. A faculty member reporting their first academic integrity violation will be less familiar with the process than someone who has previously reported cases.

In Table 5.1, we provide some exemplar *who*, *what*, *where*, *when*, *why*, and *how* questions to help develop Institutional Intelligence.

These and other questions can help us proactively (during onboarding and training), reactively (as an incident unfolds or people make decisions), and reflectively (as we look back on incidents, events, and decisions). Additionally, these prompts can help us document important information to share with supervisors or others who need to know about situations.

Institutional Intelligence is about knowing the *who*, *what*, *where*, *when*, *why*, and *how* elements that guide the behavior of individuals and groups in an organization. These questions help us understand our organizations. For example, you cannot understand the *where* of a university (location, politics of the region, history, and so on) without understanding the *who* or the *why*; alternatively, if you do not understand the *what* of an incident (what happened) or *who* (who is involved or affected) of a specific college campus and you do not know the *where* (history and bureaucracy) aspects of your campus, you have not fully developed Institutional Intelligence. Because units, institutions, and society are constantly changing, no one fully achieves Institutional Intelligence, so the work to develop in this area is ongoing.

Applying Institutional Intelligence

The intended goal of the Institutional Intelligence Model is to understand how law and ethics, and institutional characteristics, affect an organization. Consider the following (very short) play.

Scene: Something has happened.

You: What should I do?

Michelle and Cristóbal: (together) *It depends.*

You: On what?

Michelle and Cristóbal: (together) On law and ethics as well as the *who*, *what*, *where*, *when*, *why*, and *how* of your organization.

You: Oh. On *Institutional Intelligence*?

Michelle and Cristóbal: (together) Exactly. Also, document everything as you go.

End scene.

When facing a challenge, we ask, "What should I do?" Since we know the answer is "*It depends*," Institutional Intelligence is what we use to determine what "it" (the thing you should do) is. Throughout this book, we use the statement *it depends*; in each case, our location and individual experiences are unique. What we have the capacity and knowledge to do in response to an event is based on the places, spaces, relationships, and cultures we know.

For example, we both (Michelle and Cristóbal) worked full-time as staff at Iowa State University, and we now work as faculty at Clemson University (Michelle) and Florida Atlantic University (Cristóbal). The way our previous and current institutions handle disciplinary cases is different. It is different because *it depends* on the laws and policies of the state, institution, and the background and ethics of the people working in the case.

Also, we use the *who* (Chapter 6), *what* (Chapter 7), *where* (Chapter 8), and *when*, *why*, and *how* (Chapter 9) to help us analyze different scenarios. The following four chapters go into more detail about each of these questions. Each of these questions matters, and each question relies on the others to provide full context or fully developed Institutional Intelligence. Without understanding the *who* or *why* of a specific campus, we cannot understand where we work. Alternatively, suppose you understand *what* an office does and *who* the good partners on campus are without knowing campus history. In that case, you might not provide the best response since you will not have fully developed your Institutional Intelligence.

For example, you know the staff in the conduct office well. A student in an organization you advise comes to you and says that residence life fined them for throwing a water balloon out of their window, and they do not have the money to cover the fine. At your previous institution, there were ways that students could do community service instead of paying fines. You call a colleague in conduct and explain the situation. They say they did not hear the case; because it was a residence hall violation, a hall director (HD) heard the case.

You call the HD, whom you do not know well, leave a message explaining the student's situation, and ask for an alternative to the fine. Instead of hearing back from the HD, you get a terse call from the area coordinator who supervises the HD. She says that it was inappropriate of you to call the HD and that the student is responsible for the consequences of their actions. A few hours later, your supervisor asks you what you did to frustrate the area coordinator, who called you since they were in a meeting together, and the area coordinator went off about your supervisor not training their staff very well.

There could be several reasons for this. Not being connected with the housing staff is a challenge (*who*), and not understanding the process at play for this conduct violation is a challenge (*what*). Not understanding the hierarchy of residence life, their policies, the history of the fine system, the history of this student's behavior in the residence halls, not keeping your supervisor informed, and other factors (*where*, *why*, *when*, and *how*) all contribute to the miscommunication. Because of your lack of a more developed sense of Institutional Intelligence, your efforts to help a student not only have failed but have potentially created additional challenges and tension between you, your office, and the housing program. Therefore, the *who*, *what*, *where*, *when*, *why*, and *how* questions are essential to practice Institutional Intelligence.

Imagine instead that you have a more fully developed level of Institutional Intelligence. After reviewing the housing terms and conditions online, you touch base with your supervisor about your plan to reach out the area coordinator who oversees student conduct in the residence halls. Your supervisor says that sounds like a great idea. You call and say, "I wanted to follow up after this student reached out. Can you help me understand the policy and how you work with students who cannot financially afford to pay the fine?" In this version of events, you still contact the right office, consult consult the information you have about the policy and process, and then contact the right person. You can partner with the area coordinator to assist the student while continuing to develop Institutional Intelligence about how things work in housing at your institution. You conclude by sending your supervisor a short email letting them know what happened. You used your existing Institutional Intelligence, continued to develop your contextual knowledge about your institution, and documented what happened. As a result, the student is supported, you continue to build good relationships on campus, and your boss wants to give you a raise and a promotion—or at least a good review at the end of the year.

Institutional Intelligence in Action: Free Speech

Let's continue to put the Institutional Intelligence Model into action. In this book, we use critical scenarios to explore different functional areas. Here, we will use critical scenarios as a warm-up for what is ahead in the text.

Looking at the First Amendment and free speech on campus, we will find that every campus handles this topic and issue differently. Of course, institutional culture and history impact policies and practices related to free speech, as do other events in society and on other campuses. Let us break this issue down into some Institutional Intelligence questions that a practitioner might want to ask before deciding what to do (thinking before acting).

Who is the speaker, and who has concerns about the speaker or the speech?
What issues on campus or in the community might impact the institutional response?
Where on campus is the speech being exercised?
When is the speech event taking place? Or has it already taken place?
Why are you involved in this situation?
How has the campus historically acted with similar speech issues in the past?

Each of these questions is essential to developing Institutional Intelligence about speech on a given campus. Of course, these are not the only questions to be asked, but they provide an example and help us understand our institutional context. In addition, we must consider legal and ethical issues. What state and federal laws are relevant to this situation? How do our ethics, as well as the ethical perspectives of others, help guide or potentially hinder an appropriate response to a given situation?

While Institutional Intelligence might sound complex, it requires asking the right questions to understand the current context. As a result, higher education and student affairs practitioners consider the law, ethics, and institutional context before acting to get the best outcome to help people. Nevertheless, people will have a different understanding of the law and ethics in any situation.

Institutional Intelligence in Action: Search Committees

Search committees are essential for institutions and play a significant role in daily work on college and university campuses. A hiring decision-maker will get members from across all functional areas. Using the red onion metaphor, search committees are often within a single layer of an organization but impact the entire onion or university. A bad hire in one area can hurt the institution, just like a bad spot in an onion can spread.

Similarly, the search committee's decision-making will impact an organization at the micro and macro levels. New hires require us to continue to learn, as change is a catalyst for our Institutional Intelligence. As a new person enters an organization, they will have to learn the institution, but others will also have to get to know that new employee.

All that said, not all search committees are created equal. Some are effective and have support from human resources, talent acquisition, or other campus partners, and their members have tremendous integrity. Other search committees might have less support or guidance and lose their way in the process.

Every search committee member holds some Institutional Intelligence. Their work experiences inform their level of Institutional Intelligence, as do the departments where they work, their past service on search committees, their understanding of unit and institutional mission, vision, and goals, and a variety of other factors. The decision-making of the search committee as a team will also change Institutional Intelligence at the micro and macro levels. A search committee's goal should be to have a strong pool of diverse candidates. From that pool and the subsequent interviews, the committee should work to make recommendations to the hiring individual. The goal is to bring in someone who will benefit from and grow in the role and can simultaneously support the unit and organization with their talents, experience, and skills.

With any search committee, law and ethics play a role. There are policies and processes to follow at the university level that must comply with state and federal employment laws. Similarly, there are ethical considerations—should you share that no one knows who will be supervising this new employee? Is it ethical to hire someone based solely on Zoom interviews without giving them a chance to be on campus and meet people face-to-face? These and so many other questions are important for committees to navigate. Being part of a successful search committee requires confidence and trust. The recommendations or rankings of applicants by the search committee will impact the decision-makers. Therefore, as a search committee member, you are responsible for bringing as much Institutional Intelligence to search committees on your campuses as possible.

Critical Scenario 5.1 Institutional Intelligence

Co-Authors: Abigail Beadle, Access Consultant, University of Iowa, and Andrew Kutcher, Client Services Manager, Leepfrog Technologies, Inc.

For this critical scenario, you are on a search committee, and one of the applicants works at another institution where you have a colleague-friend who works in a different area. The candidate has not listed your colleague-friend as a reference. Do you contact your colleague-friend about the applicant? What are the legal and ethical implications of reaching out (or not reaching out)? If you reach out to your colleague-friend, will you notify the search committee regardless of the outcome?

The Law

- What are the relevant legal issues in this scenario?
- What institutional policies, procedures, or processes are applicable in this scenario?

Ethics

- What are the relevant ethical issues in this scenario?
- What information would you need to make sound ethical decisions?

Identity

- How might the social identities that you and others hold affect how this scenario would unfold?
- How do the situation and the information you would need change depending on the identities of those involved?

Scenario-Specific Questions

- Who is on the search committee? Who makes the hiring decision? With whom should you consult before calling your colleague-friend?
- To whom does making the call give an advantage or disadvantage?
- What are the past practices of search committees? What guidelines have the search chair provided the search committee? What are institutional policies and guidelines?
- What are the expectations of the search committee members? What are relevant state and federal laws?
- What training or resources on search committee ethics does the institution provide?
- Where do you work? Where are your colleague and applicant working?
- When should you contact your colleague?
- When do you tell the committee that your colleague and the applicant work at the same place?
- Why have you been appointed to the search committee?
- How does your role on the search committee matter? (For example, are you in the hiring department, a campus collaborator from another area?)
- How well do you know your colleague, and how well do they know the applicant?
- How will you be working with this new colleague (peer, supervisor, supervisee)?
- How does making the call enhance or compromise the search process?

What other questions might you add to this list? What other questions related to searches would you have if you were asked to serve on a committee? What have you seen or experienced in the past that might provide you with good questions in the future? What role might documentation play in this process? What search information or questions should you include (or not) in emails?

Developing questions to ask before acting is a foundational element of the Institutional Intelligence Model. You could call your colleague and ask, but what do you do with the information? You could call, ask, then share with the committee, but what if there is a problem with your making that call that compromises the search process? Understanding before acting is vital in these scenarios and making good decisions in other situations. You may not always have time to ask many questions first, but this scenario is one situation where you have time to check.

Institutional Intelligence in the Classroom

We have designed this text and this section to address the "*it depends*" issues and help guide the development of Institutional Intelligence. Do you want to know the answer to every legal and ethical issue? The answer is: *it depends.* Does that answer lack depth and detail? You ask, "Okay, authors, so what does *it depend* on?" *It depends* on the *who*, *what*, *where*, *when*, *why*, and *how*.

In her writing on critical thinking, hooks (2010) wrote that in order to understand how life works, children ask questions to understand the "who, what, when, where, and why of life" (p. 8). As you face challenging situations, you have to consider the incident, context, your role, and others who are involved or affected. It would be helpful to think about why you were involved when the incident happened and how your decisions impacted this situation, those involved, and future situations. Our focus on Institutional Intelligence incorporates all of these aspects as you work through campus events legally, ethically, and with a focus on the impact on others.

Disclaimers

While it is hard to measure Institutional Intelligence, we recognize that few (if any) people in an organization will achieve Institutional Intelligence at the macro level. However, we can achieve Institutional Intelligence at the micro level. Engaging with *who*, *what*, *where*, *when*, *why*, and *how* questions enhances your Institutional Intelligence. All of this will help make you a better professional, a better resource for students and colleagues, and a more effective leader and collaborator.

Furthermore, we must learn how to navigate systems to develop and create Institutional Intelligence. Part of this learning relates to law and ethics, part of it relates to institutional culture and history, and part of it to knowledge about who the people are at a given institution. Developing Institutional Intelligence is complicated and ongoing work. Additionally, since the law, policy, goals, human resources, financial resources, and culture are constantly changing, there are several different ways of navigating and understanding Institutional Intelligence. In effect, we are never fully "institutionally intelligent" since we always learn amidst change.

Another thing to remember is that you can do all the Institutional Intelligence work in the world and still make a problematic decision or action. People and organizations are both complicated. There are internal and external stakeholders with different priorities and expectations. Making as informed a decision as possible will often leave some people or teams unhappy. Your decision may not stand. Others may question the action you took. That is the reality of doing difficult work in challenging circumstances as part of a complex organization.

It is essential to document what you do, why you have done it, and whom you consulted as you made your decisions. Documentation is crucial in situations with significant implications or decisions you suspect will be unpopular or challenged. Given how busy everyone is, without documenting things, you may forget timelines, precisely with whom you communicated, and other vital details.

Conclusion

Working with students in higher education – particularly around difficult situations – can be overwhelming. However, this work can also be tremendously rewarding. A member of the university counsel team I (Michelle) worked with, Keith Bystrom, once said, "Do you want to go to court because you tried to do something, or do you want to defend yourself for doing nothing at all?" Some people might respond, "Keith—I do not want to go to court at all!"

While that might be the aspiration, it may not be the reality. I found Keith's words comforting. Do your best and be able to explain why you made the choices you did. I did that when I was in housing, then in conduct, and now as a faculty member. The implications are different in each role I have held, but the advice has stuck with me.

So perhaps the takeaway from this chapter is to think before you act. Document the actions you take. Take action to help. The Institutional Intelligence Model can help with thinking, guide the documentation process, and explain the action.

Note

1 Some people argue that it is a purple onion.

6
WHO

Institutions are not people. We can give institutions human characteristics (i.e., creative, uncaring, or [your institution's name here] is just one big happy family), but while people run and invest in institutions, institutions are not people. Therefore, looking at the *who* element of Institutional Intelligence, we are talking about the people in higher education. Someone once said, "Remember, people love institutions. Institutions do not love people." Institutions are not people. As a result, we must consider the human element of higher education as we seek to understand the institutional context. This chapter focuses on the people part of colleges and universities.

Chapter Organization

We encourage you to keep law and ethics in mind as you go through the rest of this chapter. We start with *who*—**you**—since you are part of the people of higher education. Besides, who is more interesting than you? We know ourselves as thoroughly as we can know anyone. Who we are matters.

We then move to those we are in a relationship with—colleagues, supervisors, supervisees, students, and others. Others on our campus and how we engage with them affect our work. Next, we examine the vast ripple effect of relationships that make up the complex human by unpacking the idea of *who*. Finally, we put this all into practice by examining what the *who* elements of the Institutional Intelligence Model look like in action. Who needs help? Who needs to act? Who needs to be informed? Whom are we overlooking? Using the Institutional Intelligence Model, we explore these and other questions through the final critical scenario.

DOI: 10.4324/9781003442707-8

Legal and Ethical Considerations

When we examine internal and external constituents in higher education, there are no more essential elements than the human beings who participate and engage with our institutions. We offer you a chance to reflect on who you are and critically examine others and how you are in a relationship with them at your college or university.

Our legal obligations to human beings in higher education usually surface formally through employment contracts, student enrollment, housing contracts, vendor and entertainer contracts, and other two- (or more) party agreements. These contracts outline what everyone involved does, their compensation, and so on. People can still challenge these agreements, but they provide an initial understanding of expectations between people or groups.

Beyond contracts, other documents also guide our legal obligations in higher education. The Family Educational Rights and Privacy Act (FERPA), the Health Insurance Portability and Accountability Act (HIPAA) (see Chapter 2), and other legislation and regulations provide legal parameters and guidelines. "Dear Colleague" letters from the federal government can give insight into laws and policies like Title IV (financial aid) or Title IX (gender equity, especially in sports and sexual misconduct). Additionally, laws in the surrounding community can carry obligations for institutions (the drinking age mandated by the U.S. government, state marijuana laws, or community noise ordinances, for example).

However, each university has its policies that it expects students and employees to follow. These may not be mandated by law, but they are guidelines for members of the university or college (housing contracts, for example). Some of the *who* elements related to campus policy include whom the policy addresses, whom the policy affects, whom the policy controls (or liberates), and who was involved in creating the policy.

Not only is who you are as a member of the university community an important aspect of your personal ethics, but your ethics inform institutional ethics and integrity. You are the starting point to making meaning of your role within the institutional context. Knowing yourself informs whom you center in your work, whom you consult, and whom you potentially overlook—intentionally or not. How you see your ethical obligation to other human beings on campus will drive your decisions.

Consider this reframe on "the trolley problem." The trolley problem is a philosophical exercise where people must decide between letting a runaway train kill several people or taking action. If you take action, the train switches tracks and kills only one person. When it comes to *who* ethical decisions in our work, we may be called upon to decide whether we use our energy and resources (our trolleys) to help a single person or a community of people.

Do we use it to benefit a small group of students or to give the most benefit to all students on campus, perhaps at a cost to smaller groups?

Who Are You?

Consider your current role at your current institution. If you are a graduate student, you may have access to less information or resources than full-time staff. If you are a brand-new employee in the first weeks of a new job on a new campus, you likely have many questions, the first of which is, "Where can I park?" Then you have questions about policies, processes, and resources that oblige you to consult with others. If you are an assistant director and have been at the same institution for 11 years, you may not have as many questions as some of your newer colleagues. However, you will likely need to consult and partner around significant issues to get answers—time and experience influence the *who* at our institutions.

Who you are is more than positional identity in an organization. Therefore, it is vital to know who you are:

- Who are you regarding your identities and the experiences you bring into a given situation?
- Who are you in relation and connection to other offices on campus?
- Who are you in connection to constituents beyond the campus?
- As situations emerge, who are you to those involved—colleague, mentor, teacher, supervisor, friend?

Fully understanding who you are involves the ability to be reflective and humble. Are you the best person to be the liaison for a given student? Are you the best person to manage a crisis on the scene? Are you the person with the most access to needed resources? The answer cannot always be "Yes." The answer is "*It depends*" or "sometimes." We must acknowledge that we cannot always be the go-to person for every situation. We do not want that to be the case. We want diverse experiences and knowledge to use in our work.

That said, we cannot be the holders of all information at an institution. It is not possible. Instead of being the person with all the abilities, knowledge, and resources, we are supposed to know who can help, and we should build collaborative relationships with those partners. Rousseau (1990) wrote that relationships in the workplace cut across behaviors, norms, and expectations. Additionally, relationships between academic and student affairs staff are essential as soon as new practitioners begin their job searches after graduate school (Boettcher, 2019). By centering the people in our work (*who*)—including ourselves—we can respond ethically and legally, guided by our institution's policies and practices.

Who Else?

After reflecting on who we are as individuals, we must examine our relationships with others. This section examines relationships with students, colleagues, supervisors, and other constituents. Our work in higher education does not happen in isolation—at least not the most productive work we do. Thinking about how we will build relationships and maintain them over time is an important aspect of our work that is best achieved through intentional planning and ongoing reflection.

Relationships with Students

While knowing who you are and how your social identities play a role in each space, situation, and decision-making is essential, you must also understand other actors. You cannot reasonably know everyone at an institution. However, you can learn about existing networks and build your own networks across campus.

Students are at the center of higher education. Of course, this is debatable when we look at their power and influence on campus and where institutions allocate resources. Also, the role of students varies from campus to campus. How much power do students have? You guessed it! *It depends.* However, regardless of their power on campus, students are often the holders of knowledge (Salinas, 2020) about what campus culture is like since interactions with students can often provide "the clearest picture … of institutional culture" (Boettcher, 2019, p. 106).

Some questions to consider as you engage with and learn from students on your campus:

- What is your job role, and how do you engage with students (programmatically, in a class, in student conduct hearings, as an organizational advisor, or in other ways)?
- How often do you engage with students?
- What has the history of student involvement been in creating (or resisting) change on your campus?
- What relationships do others in your unit or office have with students?
- How do you set and maintain appropriate boundaries with the students you serve?

These and other questions can help you prepare for, build, and sustain relationships with students. If you want to learn more about students, asking the students themselves is an excellent place to start. Other sources for information about students on your campus include student government and the campus newspaper. Other student organizations may have helpful information as well since each organization—like each student—has a unique relationship with a college or university.

Students hold essential knowledge, and we often overlook their institutional insight. In their four or five (or more) years at an institution, they may be on campus longer than many staff. As a result, their knowledge is essential to understanding campus and discrete units within the campus context.

What do students know and think, and what are their perceptions? I (Michelle) had a mentor who used to say, "Perception is reality." Knowing how students perceive you, your office, your unit, and your division is an essential first step to understanding history and culture. It also helps us identify the work ahead to build better relationships with students.

Relationships with Colleagues

Understanding your colleagues in and out of your specific functional area is essential. Learning about your colleagues will take time, just as the skills in other elements of the Institutional Intelligence Model take time to develop. It will be time well spent as you build relationships and get to know your colleagues. Their experiences and identities contribute to your unit's strength, history, culture, and the larger university.

Each of us carries our own history and relationships. Understanding our team members' connections across the university and community is essential.

Think about your relationships in your current context. Here are some prompts to help you understand your connections now (and in the future).

- To whom are you connected and why?
- With whom have you collaborated around past issues?
- What ongoing programs, events, or training have you facilitated with partners?
- What committees have you served on, and whom did you meet as part of that work?
- Where else on campus have you worked previously, and whom do you know there?
- Who else has worked in your area and moved to another office or unit?

Just as important as understanding functional relationships, we must look at strained or compromised connections on campus.

- With what other functional areas on campus is there tension? Why?
- Who has instigated or sustained the disconnection with those areas? Are those individuals still part of your team? The university?

- How might you bridge gaps and help heal compromised relationships at your institution?

Building a professional network on campus takes time. In a new job, you can start by asking your supervisor and other colleagues who the key partners for your area are. Set up a meeting with each area or person in particular areas to introduce yourself. As you become more established, reach out to new employees to offer to meet with them. You may not interact regularly, but at least you have established an initial connection before the stakes are high in the midst of a crisis or emergency.

Establishing connections: One strategy. An example from my (Michelle's) past work involved connecting with faculty. As a conduct officer, one of the areas I oversaw was academic integrity. Each fall, I would send an invitation/request to all new faculty on campus—usually between 80 and 100 people. I would ask whether I could come by their office for a 15-minute meeting.

While I said my purpose was to discuss the academic integrity process, another reason for my meeting with them was to let them know how the dean of students' office could help them if they had concerns about student behavior. I got a pretty good response rate by offering to come to them and asking for only 15 minutes. Each fall, I met with between 50 and 60 faculty. I never interacted with many of them again, but at least they knew who I was if they ever had questions or concerns.

Furthermore, all credit to Dr. James Rhatigan, who established this outreach as Dean of Students at Wichita State University, and Dr. John Schuh, who replicated it when he was associate vice president of student affairs (VPSA) on the same campus. Further, Dr. Schuh discussed this in a class he taught in my doctoral program at Iowa State University. Rhatigan and Schuh (2003) wrote about this practice in their article "Small Wins," which provides several other examples of how to build relationships in support of our work.

Supervisors and Reporting Lines

Who is your supervisor, and who is their supervisor? These questions are fundamental considerations as you navigate a situation. First, this speaks to your supervisor's position, title, level of authority, and responsibility. Who is likely to ask them about situations you are handling? What role does your supervisor play in the lives of students, staff, or faculty on campus? Will they be called upon to speak to the media about a situation with which you are involved?

We (Michelle and Cristóbal) both worked for a VPSA whose motto was "It's my job to make my boss look good." Agree or not, that gave us information about what the leader of our division expected of the rest of us. He could not do his job if we were not communicating about things that could come up in conversations he had with the university president. As a result, we needed to keep our supervisors apprised of situations so they would not be surprised in meetings with the VPSA.

Regardless of your title and role, you should never be the only one holding information about crises, trauma, and emergent situations. Your supervisor is likely someone you will need to keep informed. None of us likes to appear out of the loop or without critical information when our boss or others ask us questions.

Again, asking critical questions is part of developing Institutional Intelligence. Ask for time for you and your supervisor to get to know one another better. Show an interest in the person who is providing leadership for your team, unit, department, or division. Work on building connections with your supervisor. Consider the following questions:

- Who is your supervisor? Who is their supervisor? Furthermore, who else are they supervising?
- Is your supervisor a mentor or a friend?
- Is your supervisor a recently promoted former peer?
- Is there tension between you and your supervisor?
- Are you concerned about your supervisor's ability to lead or manage a situation? If so, why?
- What are your supervisor's strengths and talents?
- What motivates your supervisor?
- What are your supervisor's personal, professional, and team goals?

In order to work effectively with others, we must understand their motivations, talents, limitations, and spheres of influence. For example, if your supervisor has been on your campus for more than a decade and has an outstanding reputation as a student-centered leader and collaborator and as someone who is always seeking creative initiatives to enhance the community and experiences of students, staff, and faculty on campus, great. You will likely receive support and be inspired by that person. Or, if your supervisor is new and relatively unknown on campus or if your supervisor was recently involved in an issue of their own making and, as a result, they as an individual and your office or unit are in poor standing with students, your work will likely be more challenging. Alternatively, you and your supervisor may have a personality conflict that has affected the working relationship.

Regardless of your history with your supervisor, you likely will need to keep them informed of situations that arise.

Documentation

Documentation raises another important aspect of navigating legal and ethical issues in your work. It is essential to document incidents and responses to those incidents. Take notes or follow up conversations with emails. Documentation helps you track what you and your team need to do and provides a record for future reference as you work to improve or if there are problems. From the most self-centered ways of thinking about the work, it is a form of protection to document who gave directives, what those directives were, and why you did what you did in a situation.

It is essential to think about how you will document. Consider the implications of putting things in email messages (see the Freedom of Information Act in Chapter 2, for example). There may be times when email is appropriate. There may be other ways of documenting information, but those might also be records that the media and others could request. Discuss this with your supervisor, mentors, and others as you establish your communication and documentation practices in new roles and at new institutions.

However, moving beyond the low bar of covering yourself, documentation plays a crucial role in reflective practice. Documenting what you did and why you made certain choices allows you to go back and see whether what you, your collaborators, and other colleagues did was effective and supportive as well as legal and ethical once you have gone through a situation. Reflection provides us a chance to see what might have worked better. It can be much more challenging if you do not document along the way. You think you will remember the steps you took and why, but situations are complex and can take time. Additionally, it is doubtful that dealing with a single incident is the only work task you will have at a given time.

We discuss reflective practice in more detail in Chapter 17.

Other Constituents and Stakeholders

We all know that colleges and universities are influenced by more than students, staff, and faculty on campus. Others invested in our institutions include alumni, parents, donors, boards, local communities, legislatures (state and federal), and other individuals and groups.

Institutional Boards

Senior leadership and boards of trustees or boards of regents provide leadership and oversight of higher education organizations. Therefore, we have to ask ourselves: "Who are the leaders of the institutions? Moreover, who are the members of the board of trustees or board of regents?" More likely, the board of trustees often influences any policy or institutional changes, as they have power politically and economically at the state and local levels.

Legislators

Elected state and national officials also regularly weigh in on higher education issues. Legislatures and governors often play a role in appointing people to state boards of regents. Political leaders (current and former) also serve as members of university boards of trustees and other oversight groups for specific institutions. There can be positive things that come from these relationships related to funding and other forms of support. These relationships can also allow inappropriate influence on college presidents and other college and university leaders.

The role of boards and government officials in work at the university level varies from campus to campus and state to state. It is essential not to make assumptions about how one campus functions versus another—learning who is in these roles and the history behind different oversight groups is an integral part of Institutional Intelligence. These individuals and groups can affect funding, student affairs programs at an institution, and even the college or university's curriculum.

Alumni and Donors

"Money talks!" is a common saying because it is true. Donors can have a tremendous impact on a specific university. That does not mean that donors will always get what they want when they try to dictate policy. However, it is important to understand that donors will likely have different levels of influence as a result of their contributions to and support of the university.

There is a myth that a farmer and his wife went to see the president of Harvard. Their son died after his first year at the university, and they wanted to make a gift to dedicate a memorial to him. Put off by their appearance, the president dismissed them. They went on to found Stanford University.

Almost all of this is a lie. The Stanfords did have a son who died, but he was 15 and never attended Harvard. Leland Stanford was governor of California, and when their son died, he and his wife dedicated time, energy, and resources to building the Leland Stanford Junior University. They did meet with the president of Harvard but only to get information about how to set up an endowment for the university they were founding (Stanford History, n.d.).

This urban myth still circulates as a message about either treating people with respect or being careful how you treat potential donors because you could lose out on significant funds. Either way, donors have historically played a vital role in building and developing higher education. The bequest for a 400-volume library and the money John Harvard gave to New College in 1638 transformed the college into what we know today as Harvard University.

If you want to see whether or not alumni and donors influence your campus, suggest changing the university mascot or the alma mater. There are probably better ways to gauge alumni and donor influence. We suggest having conversations with your supervisor and others before changing the mascot. However, if you look at current events, you will often see that alumni and donors have opinions and threaten to stop supporting universities when things on campus change.

These situations can have both ethical and legal implications and financial implications. In the case of using Indigenous peoples as mascots in higher education, there are ethical questions of appropriation. There can also be legal and financial questions, as outlined by McEwan and Belfielf (2010):

> Campus debates [about Indigenous nicknames, symbols, or mascots] often hinge on two issues. The first is whether Native American nicknames damage the education experience of Native American students, an opinion expressed by a range of organizations, including the U.S. Commission on Civil Rights. The second is the revenue impact of changing a school's nickname or symbol.
>
> *(p. 127)*

The authors assert that the actual long-term impact of giving is minimal and usually seen only with recent graduates (McEwan & Belfielf, 2010). However, the importance of "the brand" in higher education continues to impact institutional decision-making in mascots, donor behavior, and other contexts.

Parents and Guardians

Parents and guardians can be donors, elected officials, trustees, and alumni and hold other relationships with colleges and universities. In some instances, parents with a student on campus might be their only tie to an institution. As a result, parents and guardians are invested in various ways and will reach out to you and your campus about many issues. A few examples include the following:

- "My student moved into the residence hall yesterday, and I haven't heard from him in the past six hours."
- "When my student gets arrested for underage drinking, does she get kicked out of school?"
- "My son has a hearing next week, but I can't make the time of the meeting, so you need to reschedule it."
- "My daughter's roommate is a different [race, sexual orientation, religion, or another social identity] than my child, so we need to find her a new room."
- "I need my son's RA [resident assistant] to make sure he takes his medication every day and doesn't drink any alcohol while he's taking it."

These are all calls that I (Michelle) received as a hall director or a conduct officer. I received many calls where parents or guardians would be very agitated. At one point in my career, I sometimes realized my job was to get yelled at.

Around that time, I realized when parents or guardians called, the underlying emotion was not anger and rarely was the yelling at me specifically as a human being. The underlying emotion is fear. It does not matter whether you are on a campus of 2,000 or 40,000 students or 15 minutes or 1,500 miles from where the parent lives. Parents are afraid that no one at a college or university knows or cares about their students. Additionally, families hope for the best and want success for their students. Sometimes families' definition of what is best aligns with the student and the institution. Sometimes not.

While our instinct might tell us to help, we must consider significant legal and ethical implications. Not every student has a good relationship with their parent(s) or guardian(s). Not every student wants their parent(s) or guardian(s) at their conduct hearing. Believe it or not, sometimes students misrepresent the circumstances that got them in trouble. I will not go so far as to say that sometimes students lie to their parent(s) or guardian(s), but if you say it, I will not argue with you.

The point is that there are legal and ethical considerations when dealing with parents. See FERPA in Chapter 2 for one example. You must also develop Institutional Intelligence on your specific campus. What rights do students have? What rights do parents and guardians have? What is your ethical role in navigating students, parents, guardians, and policies? The *who*, in this instance, is not just students and parents/guardians but also you.

Unpacking Who

Other considerations about the people (internal and external to the college or university) with whom you work have to do with their relationships with the campus and others invested in a given situation. Here are some examples:

- Is your colleague or supervisor new to campus? Do you, having been on campus longer, have more Institutional Intelligence than they do?
- What relationships do you and others rely on within the team and outside of your functional area?
- What experience do your colleagues and supervisor (and their supervisor) have specifically managing situations similar to what you are facing?
- Is the person involved an alum of the institution where you work?
- Is your colleague or supervisor someone who comes to campus with a background in something other than student affairs, such as law or business?
- Is your colleague or the constituent involved currently, or have they ever been, a member of a student organization or club (i.e., fraternity or sorority) involved with an incident on campus?
- Does the parent or alum have unique political power or connections related to the institution?
- What relationship does the external constituent have with the university president? Did the person call the president first, and then the message trickled down to you?
- Is the student involved a legacy student? How might that matter?

We must consider these and other questions. You may make the same decisions regardless, but how you communicate what happens might differ depending on who is involved.

Chapter 2 provided an overview of the history of higher education and legislation related to colleges and universities. Chapter 3 explored relevant case law. People created those laws and policies for other people. In Chapter 4, we provided an overview of ethics and their relationship to the law. As people establish laws and policies, we must pay attention to how laws and policies often disproportionately impact marginalized communities negatively. Law is influenced by those making the laws and those for whom the laws are made. Not all lawmakers are ethical. Remember the following: "Just because we can doesn't mean we should." Unpacking who has power and influence and who has advantage and privilege versus who is absent, disregarded, or overlooked is vital to developing Institutional Intelligence.

When we ask people why they got into student affairs, most of us have one of two reasons. Reason 1: "I needed something when I was in college, and someone helped me. I want to do that". Reason 2: "I needed something when I was in college, and no one helped me. I want to make sure that does not happen to anyone else".

For example, I (Cristobal) received an anonymous threat when I ran for student body president at the University of Nebraska at Kearney (UNK). It said, "Chris, take your name off the ballot before you get hurt. We do not want a Mexican or fag as student body president" (Salinas, 2018, p. 748). This anonymous hate crime affected me negatively. Nevertheless, it inspired me to continue my academic career in higher education and student affairs to help other students who might have similar experiences. Behind this hate crime was the person who wrote the anonymous note (*who*) that affected me (*who*). I vividly remember asking myself, "Who did this?" and other people would ask, "Who would do such a hateful thing?" Again, the *who* played a significant role in understanding this hate crime. While the university administrators and police asked:

- What happened?
- Where did it happen?
- When did it happen? When did you find the note?
- How did you find out?

They completely overlooked the *who* aspects of the situation. The focus was not on me, as a person, or who might do such a thing. Instead, what mattered most were the investigation, the process, and other details. As a result, I felt like I mattered very little. No one involved in the investigation asked me whether I was okay. Again, it is essential to center the *who* in our work.

It was never clear who wrote the note. Unfortunately, while I do not wish anyone to experience anything like what I faced, hate crimes continue perpetuating across college and university campuses targeting historically marginalized individuals and communities. From my experience with the anonymous threat, I hope the university learned how to handle hate crimes properly. It is these experiences that shape our values and beliefs.

Having been the victim of a hate crime in college prompted me to continue with my education career in higher education and student affairs to address issues that continue to challenge, oppress, and disfranchise historically marginalized communities of people. In this sense, I have learned that people (*who*) are the center of my scholarship and praxis.

Like Cristóbal, many of us continued our education in student affairs because of our experiences with people. People can help and inspire us. People can be both positive and negative role models for us. Therefore, the *who* comes and sets the stage for other Institutional Intelligence questions. As we navigate legal and ethical issues, we must consider multiple aspects of the who element.

Who in Action

Suppose you pay attention to current events, which we highly recommend. In that case, you will see that as issues emerge on campus, many people and organizations expect to have input, make demands, or offer unsolicited (and sometimes unwanted) critique. Critique and feedback appear in emails from strangers, newspaper editorials, social media, and various other ways.

The first response of academic, student affairs, and other higher education staff can be easy: "They do not know what they are talking about. They don't have the full story." As a former conduct officer, I (Michelle) would see this frequently. A campus incident would get local news coverage, and people would share their perspectives on what should happen to a particular student. First, they did not usually have all of the information, and second, they often were not familiar with how the university conduct process worked.

So what do we do when people or organizations ask for their wants or expectations? Let us give you a moment. You know the answer. That is right! *It depends.* What *it depends* on is determined partly by institutional culture and history and the role of individuals on campus. Here are some questions to get us thinking about what we may want to consider:

- Who are the people? Parents, alumni, donors, lawmakers? How about a graduate of the institution who is a major donor, has two children currently attending the university, and also happens to be the governor of the state where the university is located? It could happen.
- Who decides the outcome?
- Who decides what is shared with others about the outcome?
- Who benefits from a decision, and whom might this decision harm?
- Who is invited to give feedback about this decision?
- Who is accountable (likely multiple people) once the decision is made?

Who questions will generate additional questions about *what*, *where*, *when*, *why*, and *how*. As we answer those questions, we develop our Institutional Intelligence and avoid "*it depends*" as a final answer. Chapter 5 provides a resource for critical thinking, including various prompts. Other chapters present more questions to help us gain a deeper understanding of our specific contexts and an understanding of the Institutional Intelligence Model.

Who *Needs to Know?*

In student affairs, we face many situations. Even the same situation has different points we need to consider, so no two challenges, crises, or incidents are the same. As we engage in our work and students or colleagues come to us with concerns, we have to ask ourselves, "Who else needs to know this information?" It is also essential to consider "Who has a legitimate need to know this information?" Many people might like or want to know, but your focus should be on who needs to know.

FERPA is addressed in more detail in Chapter 2, and ethics in Chapter 4. To summarize, those with a legitimate need to know are university officials who need to review educational records as part of their job, acting in the student's best educational interest or related to individual or campus safety issues. Additionally, students have the right to review, seek amendment, and consent to disclose their records.

As mentioned earlier in this chapter, your supervisor is likely someone who will need to know about major issues or incidents. Who else might need the information you have? Here are some possible considerations:

- Do medical officials need to be informed?
- Is law enforcement needed?
- Are there other staff on campus who have significant relationships with the student who might need to know if that student is facing a crisis?
- Do faculty need to be notified that a student may be absent from class?
- Is the student under 18 or in significant enough danger to notify the family?
- Do university officials responsible for communicating with the media need to be informed?
- What information should you share with other staff who have been working with the student in this situation?

As stated previously, each situation is different, and multiple factors will play a role in who needs to know. However, we advise communicating with your supervisor and necessary stakeholders as soon as possible.

When you reflect on Cristóbal's experience of a hate crime when he ran for student body president at UNK, whom do you think needs to be informed? Should the student body and/or student government be notified? Should the Dean of Students, university police, the director of the Office of Multicultural Affairs, the faculty, and/or the university president and provost be notified? Should Cristóbal's parents be notified? Also, who should be involved? Moreover, what role does each individual play in the decision-making on how the case will be handled? Most important, who is the central point of contact for the student? While there could be many people and units involved, it is crucial to remember that the student should be centered as the primary person who matters and might have other needs (e.g., speaking with a psychologist, getting an extension on assignments deadlines, or taking a break from student organizations).

Who is the Central Point of Contact?

Next, we use history to think about who needs to know all the information and who should connect all the information at an institution. Following the tragedy at Virginia Tech University, where 33 people died and 23 were injured, the Virginia Tech Review Panel reviewed the situation and made recommendations. A significant finding from the panel was that "[a]lthough various individuals and departments within the university knew about [previous incidents related to the perpetrator's behavior on campus], the university did not intervene effectively. *No one knew all the information, and no one connected all the dots*" [emphasis added] (Virginia Tech Review Panel, 2007, p. 10). Think about who the central points of contact are at the institution.

The Dean of Students Office (DSO) will often be the central point of contact. Finding out who holds information about students on your campus is essential. Remember, when in doubt, fill it out—if you are unsure whether you should report something, report it. Higher education institutions would rather have you report information that may not be a crisis than not report something that could be. By reporting concerns, the institution can take the necessary steps to get control of the situation. Also, we cannot know everything about a student, a situation, or an emerging issue. The information can provide additional insight into the situation and may be essential to providing the best resources at the optimal time to act.

Who Needs to Act?

Once we share information through the appropriate channels with the appropriate offices and individuals, the next question is, "Who needs to take action?" Those responding may be a single person or—more likely—a team of people who will need to act in different ways. As stated earlier, you will not always be the only or the best person to implement a plan or take initial action. Within each organization, there should be trained people to handle various situations. While we work in student affairs, we are not experts on everything about students. Instead, we should direct them to the person with the right expertise.

For example, a student navigating a parent's terminal illness may need someone to be their single point of contact in the DSO. Still, that liaison may be reaching out to an academic advisor, the counseling center, residence life, and a mentor who advises an organization the student is involved in to take on different aspects of support for the student. Each situation is different, and each student's needs are different. Clear and ongoing communication is essential, as is an understanding of FERPA. We should regularly ask ourselves, "Who has a legitimate need to know about this situation?" Once we have the answers, we can notify the appropriate people.

Whom Are We Overlooking?

Those who need support around situations go beyond the student or employee most directly involved. While we must respect FERPA regarding what information we share, we must also abide by ethical practices in providing support and care to others that an event impacts. In a non-crisis situation—perhaps where we are developing policy or changing processes—we also need to discover who may be inadvertently impacted by our decisions.

Think about going on a trip. After you have packed, consider, "What will ruin my trip if I forget to take it?" If you have everything on that list, you can figure out the rest later. If you overlook packing your passport and you are headed to Canada, that will negatively impact your trip. If you forget your toothbrush, you might be able to navigate more easily on your travels.

This approach can be helpful in a crisis. "Who has to be involved right now?" is the first question—the "What don't I want to forget on my trip?" question. As the situation evolves, new questions emerge, and you can deal with them. Questions might include the following: "Who can help and needs to know about this situation?" "Who else will be asked about this situation and needs information to respond?" or "Who else needs support related to this situation?"

Answering these emergent questions is another place where relationships matter. For example, relationships and communication are the foundation for successful Behavioral Intervention Teams (BITs). These teams bring together people with different areas of expertise to process situations and develop strategies and plans for addressing issues and supporting those affected. Additionally, these teams are essential for identifying gaps in our processes. Often, we are focused on a single aspect of a situation and fail to consider other implications. Teams and colleagues can bring their own experiences and unique perspectives.

Critical Scenario 6.1 Who

Co-Author: Alonso Reyna Rivarola, Senior Director for Institutional Equity, Inclusion, and Transformation, Salt Lake Community College

Reflect on the spring of 2020 when the United States was learning about the COVID-19 pandemic. Higher education institutions responded to the pandemic based on their geographical and political contexts, including state mandates, campus leadership, and other factors, such as infrastructure and resources. Many institutions quickly transitioned to remote learning; some continued this learning modality the following summer and fall semesters. Remote learning raised new challenges as students, staff, and faculty sought to engage meaningfully while witnessing the effects of COVID-19 on loved ones and the world. As the pandemic was unfolding, the United States was reckoning with the murders of Black people—including Breonna Taylor, George Floyd, and Tony McDade, among many others (Rest in Power)—at the hands of police officers. Further, during this time, the country faced other crises, including acts of racism and violence perpetrated on communities of color, including Black and Asian communities.

The Law

- What legal issues emerged during this time?
- What policies, procedures, or processes did institutions change or maintain?

Ethics

- How were our ethics challenged or affirmed during this time?
- What leadership decisions from this time did you see as ethical? Which were unethical?

Identity

- How might social identities affect the experiences of students, staff members, and faculty during this time?
- How did institutional leaders consider or overlook people's social identities in making decisions?

Scenario-Specific Questions

- Who was centered and privileged in university decisions related to the pandemic?
- Who was in power, and who made the decisions?

- Who benefitted from the decisions and actions, and whom did universities harm with their decisions and actions?
- Who was disproportionately affected by the pandemic? By university decisions?
- Who were the helpers? Who were the advocates for students, staff, and others?

We can also ask about the people (*who*) affected with more specific *what* and *how* questions:

- How did leaders prioritize the health and well-being of live-in residence hall staff during the pandemic?
- How did institutions attend to students without a permanent home when halls closed?
- How did the university leaders support parent employees through the era of work-from-home and virtual schooling?
- What did the university provide to students without computer or internet access?
- How did the university provide ongoing mental health support for students when the pandemic disrupted their campus mental health partnerships?

Conclusion

We began this chapter with the idea that "People love institutions. Institutions do not love people." We do not remember where we heard it (or we would give them credit). However, people should keep this idea in mind when they expect human behavior or care from an institution. Do not let this make you angry. It is not the job of institutions to love us. They do not have that capacity, no matter how often the people at those institutions use words like "community" or "family."

Also, do not misunderstand. There are times when we want institutions to rely on us as individuals. Part of me (Michelle), when I left my conduct role at Iowa State University, wanted the university to shut down. I wanted my absence to create such a hole in the organization that it simply could not go on without me, and it had to close its doors. It did not. The area where I worked continued to thrive under the leadership of my friend and colleague Sara Kellogg.

Institutions persist. The people, the *who* of organizations, are what help craft our colleges and universities. We, as people, create cultures. We can sustain or disrupt unhealthy practices. We can center human beings or exploit labor and center dollars or “the brand” of where we work. Ultimately, it is the people who support stagnancy, or it is the people who make a difference. People drive the history, culture, and work of colleges and universities.

7

WHAT

When you work in crisis response and get an emergency call, your first thought may be, "What happened, and what can I do?" This response is the same in many other situations, too. When a student sits down in your office and asks to talk with you, the responses are similar: "What happened, and what can I do?"

While at the moment *what* questions inspire us to act, it is essential to consider that the *what* questions give us past and future perspectives. For example, some *what* questions include the following: In a given situation, what is the campus history (precedent) for action or decisions? What have others tried that worked or did not work? What are the implications for situations like this in the future if I take a particular action? What precedent am I setting?

In this chapter, we encourage you to use *what* questions to provide additional institutional context. As part of the Institutional Intelligence Model, *what* questions lead us to action, inspire us to reflect, and anticipate the future. In a crisis, for example, asking "What has happened in the past?", "What is happening right now?", and "What does this mean for the future?" can help us frame our responses thoughtfully and strategically.

Chapter Organization

This chapter focuses on the *what* questions. What is happening, and what are the implications for what is happening? What do the people who are affected need? What can I offer? Specifically, we use *what* questions to understand the issue (or multiple issues), needs, and our role in responding

DOI: 10.4324/9781003442707-9

during an incident. It is difficult to know what action to take until you understand the situation and what you bring to it.

Legal and Ethical Considerations

Because *what* questions are often related to action, they can also have implications for individuals and organizations in terms of liability. Risk management forms, waivers, and releases of information (ROIs) are examples of documents that might connect with our *what* questions. Example questions are "What are the university vehicle guidelines?" (risk management), "What do we need students to acknowledge before they participate in an outdoor recreation trip?" (waiver), and "What else is going on with this student that I need to know about to help him?" (ROI).

We also use policies related to *what* questions regarding permission and obligation. "What am I allowed to do given my role?" or "What am I required to do given my role?" are examples. What our policies say about situations is incredibly important.

"Have a policy and follow that policy" is something you have seen already in this text. When we have policies and do not follow them or have policies and do not know about them, we open ourselves up to problems down the road. Indeed, the problems might include lawsuits, but more importantly, we put people at risk of harm. Generally speaking, institutions create policies to prevent or respond to past incidents.

Ignorance of a policy, process, or procedure is not an adequate excuse for mishandling a situation. As a result, understanding the *what* issues at your institution is essential. Knowing and following policy help you, the institution, and most importantly, the human beings (students, staff, and faculty) on your campus.

Navigating What

There are two strains of *what* questions in the work of student affairs practitioners—internal and external. Internal questions focus on the self. What do we have to offer, and what are our limitations? External questions look at what has happened, what is happening, and what needs to happen in the future.

Here are some internal questions related to *what*:

- What is my role in this situation?
- What skills or training do I have that apply to this situation?
- What knowledge, resources, and connections do I have that can be useful?

- What are my limitations in this situation?
- What are my ethics related to this situation?
- What am I expected to do according to my job description?
- What expectations do students, colleagues, parents, and others have of me in this situation?

Here are some external *what* questions:

- What has created this situation?
- What has already happened to address the situation?
- What is currently happening?
- What resources are available on campus and in the community?
- What is the protocol for this and similar issues?
- What are the legal and ethical implications for my immediate action, inaction, or delayed action?
- What is the policy? What is the law?
- What is the process?
- What could potentially happen?
- What could be positive next steps or outcomes?
- What could the negative next steps or outcomes be?
- What has happened in situations like this in the past?

Maybe the most succinct way to boil this down is to these three questions: What do I bring? What is happening? What do I do?

Okay, you have done your homework and read the policies and procedures. You do not have them memorized (and should not try to—you can pull up things instantaneously, so save the brain space for something else). Once an incident is brought to your attention, understanding the policy and procedures will inform your next steps.

The *what* stage can be complex or straightforward. Many times there may be multiple *whats* in a single situation. For example, a drunk student who has chosen to go off medication for a mood disorder breaks a window in a residence hall, pulls a fire alarm, and passes out in a parking lot. That is not a single event, and it raises multiple concerns—the more complicated the situation, the more your knowledge of *what* becomes important. Again, even with complex situations, we can start with some foundational questions: What do I have to offer? What is happening, and what needs to happen next?

Internal What

As described above, the internal focus is on what we bring (or not) to our work and includes knowledge, competence, experience, confidence, resources, and influence, among other skills and tools. Many student affairs graduate programs stress the amount of reflection in their learning and curriculum. This reflection is also essential in practice. Reflection fosters individual growth, learning, and better work—ethical, legal, and practical.

The internal aspects of *what* are best understood and explored through reflective practice. Thinking about and documenting—through journals, emails, reports, and resumes—the *whats* of our work help foster reflection alongside the action. Areas to consider include training and expertise, personal limitations, issues of control, and personal needs. We discuss the role of reflection more in Chapter 17. As we explore each of these areas, consider the process outlined but also put the process into action and think about your strengths, gifts, background, and limitations.

Training and Expertise

So, what do you know? What training have you had through professional organizations or certifications? What training and staff development have you had on your campus or the other campuses where you have worked? What experience do you bring to your work? All these things inform what you will do as you prepare for, engage with, and reflect on situations that emerge in your career.

To get started in this reflection process, consider the following prompts related to your graduate preparation program:

- What did the program emphasize? Was it focused on developing excellent practitioners, or was it focused primarily on social justice issues, or was it a policy program? All programs will have elements of each, but no program can be all things for all people. What was at the center of your program?
- How does what you learned in your graduate program inform how you now engage in student affairs work?
- What are things faculty said that stayed with you (whether you agreed or disagreed)?
- What are things you saw practiced in your graduate assistantship or field experiences you have sought to replicate (or eliminate) in your work as a team member, supervisor, or mentor?
- What have you seen your peers do that has shaped how you do your job now?
- What legal, ethical, policy, and scholarly work and thinking were you prompted to participate in during your graduate experience or throughout your career?
- What things were missing from your experience, and how did you realize they were missing? What have you done to fill those gaps?

You can go through these and many other questions for different aspects of your work: certifications, onboarding experiences, committee work, and training. The set of tools you bring to your job is diverse and likely unique to you. We are not suggesting that you spend the rest of your career thinking about everything that has come before. However, knowing your skills is essential to being able to help or when you need to ask for assistance.

Another way to look at this idea of what you have to offer is to read over your resume. Please do not read it through the lens of simply working on updating the document. Instead, consider the following:

- What are my primary job responsibilities?
- What training and education do I have around those responsibilities?
- What are the legal and ethical implications of the work I do?
- What gaps exist between what I know and what is dictated by law, policy, and ethics?
- What do I need to do to fill those gaps?

Doing this in partnership with a supervisor or mentor can give you an additional perspective beyond what you know about yourself. Alternatively, conducting peer reviews and analyses of how job responsibilities and personal skills align can provide richer insight and a more thorough consideration of the *what* issues related to training and expertise in our student affairs and higher education work.

Personal Limitations

Our circumstances are constantly changing. Awareness of what we can or cannot do in a given situation is essential to legal and ethical practice. This knowledge also makes us better collaborators, leaders, and community members. When I (Michelle) was an assistant dean, I served in an on-call duty rotation with other Dean of Students Office members. One weekend morning, I got a call from a colleague working with the family of a student who had died. She was going to the airport to meet two family members coming to campus.

She called me to see whether I would be willing to go with her to the airport. She admitted she had not worked with families in this way. She said she would appreciate having a colleague with her. I immediately said I would go and acknowledged I had never met with the family of a student who had died before either.

While neither of us had been in this situation before, we also both knew the other brought knowledge about campus resources, a sense of care in our work, and the ability to get answers to whatever questions the family might have. In addition, because we had both been at the university for a while, we each had our own set of Institutional Intelligence skills we could use to support the family in that challenging time.

However, our limitations perhaps made for the greatest strength in working together. Well, maybe not the limitations themselves, but our willingness to be transparent about those limitations with ourselves and one another. We drove to the airport together, not expecting the other to have all the answers but knowing we would be reaching out for help from campus police, housing, counseling, the registrar, and many other areas.

With the idea of limitations as assets, we ask you to consider your limitations. The set of tools we bring to our work is incomplete—hence our need to partner with others whose experiences and tools are different from ours. We do not work in isolation and should not take on complex tasks alone. Needing a partner or team to manage a situation is a sign of wisdom. Insisting on handling things alone shows ego, ignorance, or both.

We have all had experiences where we failed to do something or at least would have done a better job if we had asked others for help. Instead, we said "I got it" and were less effective and less efficient and provided less intentional care and attention to detail than if we had worked with others.

We are ethically obligated to say no to tasks we are not equipped to perform. In worst-case situations, we can put others at risk and do significant harm. Knowing our limitations and being transparent with those is an ethical obligation we have to one another.

Instead of simply focusing on "What can I do?", we need to ask ourselves:

- What am I not able to do right now?
- What is going on in my life that might compromise my ability to help in this situation?
- What do I not have the appropriate training to address?
- What harm might I do by saying yes when I am not the best person to take on this task?
- What relationships do I have with people better equipped to help here?
- What else can I do that would be helpful right now?

Let's go back to the scenario from earlier. If my colleague called about going to the airport and I was struggling with issues at home, I could have said:

> I cannot help you with that right now, but let me help you find someone who can go with you. While I cannot meet with the family directly, let me call about arranging a hotel and meals and schedule meetings with

campus partners for them."I cannot do that, but I can do this" is better than saying yes to something and not helping and potentially causing harm.

We are formally and informally trained to put others before ourselves. However, we can do the work well only if we have what we need. It may be training or certification. It may be space to process a difficult situation. It may be more hands to help. It might be a moment to pause and think before moving on to more action and response. While all situations can feel like emergencies, that is not the case. There are relatively few true emergencies (including physical injury, threat of harm, facilities emergencies such as a fire, or other situations where student, staff, or faculty well-being is at risk). That said, for many of us, a stressful situation can feel like a crisis. This is true for students as well. For example, a roommate conflict can bring a sense of urgency to a student, resulting in crying, yelling, or other forms of frustration. There is usually time to negotiate this situation unless there is imminent danger.

Legally, training is essential. You do not want someone without appropriate training administering CPR. Similarly, you do not want someone not trained on Title IX to investigate, adjudicate, or support students impacted by sexual misconduct. Ask for help or training when you are out of your depth in terms of knowledge and skill.

Even with training, we must navigate each situation that emerges differently. There are a few essential questions regarding information amid a crisis, project, or other situation.

- What information do you need to act?
- What do you need to share, and with whom?
- What students have the greatest immediate needs? What are those needs?

These are triage questions to help you manage the situation at the moment. These help you prioritize, but as you figure out the answers to these questions, other needs and concerns may surface that can inform what additional steps you need to take.

If someone tells you to do things beyond your training, skill, and ability, even when you share your limitations, that is something you need to document. An example: I (Michelle) was the hall director in a brand-new residence hall. In addition to living in a hall still being built, I was assigned to the building for overflow housing. I had to hire staff for that hall but did not know how long they would have positions as we gradually moved residents out of the building.

I then got an email informing me that I would also be responsible for temporary international student housing. It was too much for me. I wrote back to my supervisory team and said:

> I need help with international student housing. I am feeling overwhelmed. My apartment is not finished—though I've already moved in per your instructions. I am trying to hire staff and manage the daily changes for overflow housing. I need someone to take on the international student temporary housing.

With the support and guidance of a mentor, I offloaded that task so I could complete the other duties I had been assigned.

External What

External *what* issues include issues that provide structure or otherwise influence what our responses should be as staff and faculty in higher education. Policies may guide our behavior as employees or students' behavior on campus. Procedures and protocols can provide direction and expectations related to steps or order of response to situations on campus. Understanding these *what* issues is important as we navigate campus situations.

Policies, Procedures, and Protocols

Being familiar with campus policies, procedures, and protocols is essential. If you are working in student affairs or student-facing roles in academic affairs or engaging with students in any way in higher education, reading the student handbook is a necessary first step.

The student handbook(s) on your campus should give you a sense of the policies, procedures, and expectations for students enrolled at your institution. In addition, the graduate student handbook, the university catalog, and other publications may include policies related to student behavior, academic expectations, student safety, and other issues. Reading those and related documents as part of your onboarding at a new institution is essential. Ideally, you may even review these documents before your interview. Not only can you get more information before accepting a position as a potential hire, but it will also prepare you for an interview if you have reviewed policies related to your potential future role on campus.

General policy areas include academic issues (integrity, plagiarism, and research), safety (alcohol and other drugs, assault, hazing, threats, bullying, sexual misconduct, and weapons), campus speech (chalking, fliers, and hate speech), facilities issues (authorized use of facilities, building access, fire safety, and property damage), and student behavior (classroom behavior, conduct, harassment, and intimidation). These areas overlap. For example, harassment could fall under safety, free speech, and expectations for student engagement.

A review of campus-specific policies for students is also a chance to look into the history of a given campus community. If a policy seems unusual or unexpected, asking about how that policy came to be can provide meaningful context.

Additional Considerations

In many student conduct codes, you will find a category of "violations of local, state, or federal law." Consider this the "other duties as assigned" section of codes of conduct. In short, if it is not legal, it is also not legal on campus. That said, the enforcement of laws on different campuses may vary. Knowing the process for dealing with legal violations on your campus can help you understand your unit/department/division and further develop institutional intelligence. The following are examples of common college campus issues. This is not an exhaustive list but a set of considerations and how *what* issues are related to each.

Contracts

A good contract protects all the parties involved in the event, service, or other contracted relationship. It is essential to read contracts carefully and ensure that an appropriate designee signs all contract sections. There can be financial and safety repercussions if a contract is not read and followed.

There is a relevant story about the band Van Halen. One of the "demands" in their contract was a bowl of M&Ms for them backstage—with the brown M&Ms removed. Some people thought this was a bit of an urban myth. Others thought this demand was an example of the egotism and self-centeredness of rock stars. This clause was in the contract as a safety precaution.

The band included this because it allowed them to see whether the promoter read the entire contract. Because of the lighting needed for Van Halen concerts and some venues being too outdated to support their equipment, they needed to be sure they would be safe going on stage. If they saw brown M&Ms, they knew they would have to do an additional check because the promoter had not read the entire contract (Zeveloff, 2016).

Contracts are important but useless if you do not read them.

Employment Contracts

The contract between the employee and the institution outlines each member's obligations. The law, institutional context, history, and other factors inform these documents. These documents outline what employees do for the university and what the university will do for employees. The contract should include job expectations, ongoing performance reviews, promotion and raise processes, and the types of work done by an individual in their role.

Event, Speaker, and Entertainment Contracts

Contracts between student affairs programs and outside entertainment or speaking agencies are documents that newer staff members need to be prepared to review. Anyone with contract-signing responsibility must read and discern specific requirements or requests from the speaker or experience provider to ensure that the office and institution can honor those obligations. Additionally, risk management is a significant consideration in planning events and contracting with others for campus entertainment. Remember the brown M&Ms.

Housing Contracts

The contract between a student and a housing program can often entail obligations beyond campus policy, codes of conduct, or state or federal law. An example is the prohibition of candles or other open flames in residence hall rooms. While this can seem straightforward (no open flame, fewer potential fires in the building), it can become complicated. If, for example, a student's religious practice requires lit candles, housing programs must navigate how to balance students' religious and faith traditions with contractual obligations and safety guidelines in the building.

Policies

Free Speech

Free speech is another critical topic that has received national attention from students, staff, and faculty. Free speech and academic freedom are part of the core of higher education learning. However, what is an employee allowed to say? What implications does the speech have on an employee's work and employment? In a world where the separation between public, private, work, and personal spaces is increasingly blurred, what employees and students can say and what universities can do in response to things said are constantly tested.

Institutional type affects the exchange of ideas on and off campus for students, staff, and faculty. A private institution can enact and enforce speech-related policies that are far more restrictive for students and employees than public institutions. That said, you still need to read campus policies because often institutions—public and private—afford students more rights than what the law requires.

Social Media Guidelines

Free speech on social media is constantly changing in terms of higher education. The public constantly scrutinizes what students, staff, and faculty post on social media. In any given week, you can find stories about someone affiliated with a university posting an unpopular opinion, potential threat, or hate speech online. Additionally, there are legal and ethical implications for our use of social media.

Poor decision-making can threaten a person's relationship with their college or university or an institution's reputation. Another way this topic surfaces on campus is from student organizations whose posts promoting upcoming events or photos of events that have taken place include inappropriate images, hashtags, or labels. Social media can also be a tool to threaten or harass others. The guiding *what* issues for these situations come down to the following:

- What did someone post?
- What concerns are there about the post?
- What are the guiding policies at the university that relate to the post?
- To what extent is the post protected by freedom of speech?

These are complex questions with complicated answers. "*It depends*" and "It's complicated" come to mind regarding these situations, but neither of these responses is sufficient.

Some excellent advice is "Have a policy and follow your policy." This concept does not mean we should try to develop a policy for every possible violation that might occur. Instead, campus partners advised me (Michelle) in my role as a conduct officer to make sure we had policies that addressed issues broadly and followed the policies we had in place. The commitment to following the policies we have is why I am not a fan of making policies that we cannot enforce or that we know we will not follow.

An example is when you are in a class, workshop, or conference session and someone says, "What is said here stays in here." That promise is not guaranteed, and, at worst, it offers a false sense of security. Furthermore, you cannot do anything if someone does share what is said. Most people know it is not true as soon as it is said.

As far as policies regarding social media go, focusing on a policy about a specific social media platform is both unnecessary and short-sighted. Things evolve too quickly, and social media outlets that are popular today will not be popular within a couple of years (if they last that long). Additionally, focusing on the content of the speech is often problematic. See Chapter 3 for more information about speech cases such as Tinker v. Des Moines (1969), Healy v. James (1972), Papish v. Board of Curators of University of Missouri (1973), and other relevant case law.

It is likely and perhaps even preferable if your institution does not have any policy related to specific speech on social media. Instead, policies that address threats, harassment, misuse of computers or technology, retaliation, rules of personal conduct, and teaching disruption policies can address the more significant issues of concern. Different functional areas may face different issues related to social media use among students, staff, and faculty. Therefore, it is crucial to be familiar with student and employee policies and guidelines when addressing social media or other campus behavior concerns.

Space Reservation Guidelines

The policies for speakers and campus events can have a tremendous social, educational, legal, and ethical impact at a specific institution and across higher education. Having and following space reservation guidelines in working with students, student organizations, and other groups—both on and off campus is essential. While this can be relevant to free speech zones on campus, there are more significant implications about who can reserve space for other lectures and events.

An interesting case related to this topic is white supremacist Richard Spencer's 2018 attempt to speak on the Michigan State University (MSU) campus. Spencer wanted to speak at MSU, as he previously had at the University of Florida and Auburn University. The MSU policy allowed speakers without university affiliation to request to speak on campus.

What MSU did regarding the space reservation was an example of the university having and following a policy for speakers to reserve space. Their policy allowed speakers to register on campus but also allowed the campus to move sites and adjust dates for speakers. MSU took advantage of this policy in the situation with Spencer. The university relocated Spencer's speech after a statement by MSU President Lou Anna K. Simon about the university's dedication to free speech despite the speaker's racist messages. The Foundation for the Marketplace of Ideas—Spencer's organization—was responsible for fees related to the venue, but the university—following its policies—got to choose the time and location for the event. MSU chose Monday, March 5, 2018 (the first day of spring break on the campus) and provided Spencer space in the MSU Pavilion for Agriculture and Livestock Education. This building sits on farmland on the edge of the campus (Wolcott, 2018).

While the university did not endorse the content, it allowed space for exchanging ideas. The president spoke against what Spencer stood for but did not prohibit space reservation on the basis of the speaker's words and ideas. The university did not violate the First Amendment and followed its policies, allowing administrators to choose where and when the event would occur. It is worth noting that despite these efforts, the event cost MSU more than $18,000 (primarily to pay overtime for law enforcement and safety staff and equipment), and there were violent protests and 25 arrests when the event took place (Associated Press, 2018).

Safety Considerations

In addition to the risk management issues mentioned in connection with housing and campus events earlier in this chapter, there are other safety considerations that student affairs and universities must anticipate, plan for, and respond to. These include active shooter situations, campus safety reporting, campus threat situations, emergency alert protocols, mental health concerns, natural disasters, self-harm situations, behavior concerns (for students, staff, and faculty), suicidal ideation, weapons on campus, and a variety of other issues. Students, staff, and faculty must be aware of policies and procedures related to these potential emergencies on campus.

Other considerations inform these issues of Institutional Intelligence. For example, inclement or severe weather planning will look one way in Iowa, where issues related to tornadoes or snow and ice may be seasonal, and another way in Florida, where people will be more concerned about hurricane protocols and planning. Schools in California would likely include earthquake and wildfire responses in their planning. We discuss inclement weather issues in more detail in Chapter 8.

During the COVID-19 pandemic, institutions learned they could face issues that require every facet of institutional work and learning to change. In these situations, campuses often watch one another to see what works and what does not. They then adapt based on how they interpret other institutions as successful or unsuccessful.

In large-scale situations like a pandemic, another *what* can emerge—what does the institution value? Institutions put their values on display in a crisis through how they engage with students, staff, and faculty.

- What workers are deemed essential, and how are essential workers supported and protected or exposed and made more vulnerable?
- What are the university's fiscal priorities—undergraduate education? Research? Salaries and hiring?
- What institutional learning occurs because of crises, tragedies, and other significant incidents?

- In what ways is a campus innovative and reflective, taking lessons learned to transform work practices to meet the changing needs of the people the campus serves?

In summary, what do we do when things happen on our campuses? Well, *it depends*. How successful will you be navigating incidents on your campus? *It depends* on how well-prepared you are and how familiar you are with campus policies and procedures.

Title IX

Knowing how a specific campus handles Title IX related to sexual misconduct is essential for everyone on campus. As a defining issue of our time, this topic is handled differently from one university to the next. Additionally, policies related to sexual misconduct have undergone tremendous shifts over time. While policies tended to favor students reporting violations, at other times, the pendulum has swung to privilege and focus protection on those accused of violations. Knowing where your campus stands on the issue can help prepare you for situations and inform you how to support students navigating institutional processes related to sexual misconduct.

It is imperative to understand your obligations under Title IX. Are you a mandatory reporter? What are you able to keep private? Remember, very few people on campus can promise confidentiality—counseling and health center staff, religious advisors, and sometimes campus advocates (find out whether that is true on your campus). Most of us working with students will do our best to protect their privacy—that is, we will let only those with a legitimate need to know have information about a given situation. However, hardly any of us can legally promise confidentiality. The difference between privacy and confidentiality is a crucial distinction we must understand in order to protect students and—secondarily—to avoid putting ourselves and our institutions at risk.

Student-Specific *What* Issues

Student Athletes

Too often, people without a clear understanding of student athletics see them simply as hyper-privileged, entitled celebrities on campus. Most student athletes have higher GPAs than non-athletes (NCAA, 2021a). Furthermore, nearly all pursue careers, graduate education, and other endeavors unrelated to their sport or athletics. Staff working with student athletes need to understand and help the athletes understand the accountability levels they are responsible for during their college careers.

As with all other college students, student athletes must follow the institution's student code of conduct. In addition, however, student athletes are obliged to abide by coach and team rules, athletic department rules, and NCAA guidelines. Each of these sets of rules, guidelines, and policies is complex in its own way. Because these policies overlap, student athletes who violate them may be held accountable on several levels.

As an example, I (Michelle) once worked on a college campus as a hall director for a building that housed many of the men's basketball players. When I received a conduct report involving any player who lived in my building, I had to email a copy of the report to the head coach (whether the report alleged that the player violated policy or not). The players told me they had to do additional running early in the morning until they met with me.

Just as students can waive some of their Family Educational Rights and Privacy Act (FERPA) rights to allow parents and family members to access their grades or other educational records, student athletes, on some college campuses, sign a similar waiver. As a result, offices can share records with a coach, athletic director, or another athletic department designee. This process can help athletics address any issues that might impact an athlete's eligibility and potentially provide the athlete support through the process.

In the case of my conduct work with the men's basketball team, the athletes were sanctioned by their coach (mandated to run) before they were found responsible for any violation. In nearly all cases where a player on the men's basketball player was named, they were in the report simply because they were present when an incident occurred. They still had to run until they met with me, and I let the coaching staff know we had met.

Athletes sometimes violate policies. Athletes also enjoy some privileges related to their status as sports team members. However, this section provides insight into the multiple levels of policy and accountability that these athletes must navigate. In addition, the NCAA's name, image, and likeness (NIL) policy adopted in June 2021 provides another level of complexity to the student athlete experience in higher education (NCAA, n.d.). As amateur college athletes can monetarily benefit from the use of their NIL (through video games, social media, advertising, etc.), new legal and ethical issues are likely to emerge. We will see how this policy plays out on different campuses and whether or not centralized oversight for NIL emerges.

Student Organization Guidelines

Student organizations are a strength of higher education. They allow students to engage in a community around academics, personal interests, or future careers. The policies guiding these organizations can be as diverse as the organizations themselves. Some considerations for these groups include the following:

- What is the purpose of the group?
- What are the guidelines for membership?
- What are the institutional expectations for student organizations?
- What activities, goals, and initiatives are related to the organization?
- What is the history of the organization on campus or across higher education?
- What is the leadership structure for the organization?

These questions are relevant for organizations in general and subsets of organizations. For example, sports clubs, fraternities and sororities, and clubs affiliated with academic majors may have additional guidelines specific to those organizations.

Other Student Considerations

In addition to athletes and organizations, many other students or groups warrant special consideration regarding *what* questions. Student government and other leaders are often highly visible on campus. When involved in incidents, they risk dismissal from their positions, and their actions can significantly impact others.

Student employees have complicated relationships with colleges and universities. They are employees and students. Their primary relationship with the university is as students, but issues in the workplace can impact not only their employment status but their student status. Some student staff has high levels of responsibility that can create complicated power dynamics between student staff and other students. Examples include resident assistants, peer mentors, and students with access to other students' information, such as students working in the Dean of Students Office, campus safety student employees, and residence hall front desk staff.

There are a variety of other student roles on campus where students would have to abide by contracts, other documentation, or additional/different expectations. Part of your job is to figure out those roles on campus, the expectations of those student employees, and what your job requires of you (legally, ethically, and in terms of campus policy).

What Do Others Expect of You?

There can be a variety of constituents for any unit, organization, or institution. These include students, colleagues, supervisees, supervisors, unit leaders, parents, alumni, donors, regents/trustees, elected officials, media, and other stakeholders. Not only might each constituent have different expectations for you or your team, but those expectations may also conflict. The following scenario provides an example of where there may be several people in different positions on or beyond campus with opinions about how this situation should be handled.

Critical Scenario 7.1 What

Co-Author: Larissa Jenkins, Senior Catalyzer, Arizona State University

Darnell (he/him) is a student security aide for campus police. His primary job is to make rounds of academic buildings, lock doors, and report any issues during his shift. One evening, Darnell sees a broken window in the Admissions Building, Evans Hall. He calls to report the situation. The shift supervisor tells Darnell to enter the building to see whether there is further damage. Darnell goes in and keys into the room with the broken window. He sees some blood, a passed-out person, and written on a dry-erase board in the room are the Greek letters for a fraternity chapter on campus. The writing on the board is blue, and there is a blue dry-erase marker in the person's hand.

The Law

- What are the relevant legal issues in this scenario?
- What institutional policies, procedures, or processes are applicable in this scenario?

Ethics

- What are the relevant ethical issues in this scenario?
- What information would the characters need to make sound ethical decisions?

Identity

- How might characters' social identities affect how this scenario would unfold?
- How do the situation and the information you need change depending on the identities of those involved?

Scenario-Specific Questions

- What are the potential issues in this situation?
- What resources might Darnell and campus safety need in addressing the situation?
- What areas of training would be helpful to Darnell in addressing the situation?
- What needs to be communicated or documented related to this situation?

Conclusion

"It's not what you know. It's who you know," according to an old saying. We disagree. What you know *and* whom you know as well as what we do in partnership with one another makes all the difference—legally and ethically, personally and professionally. You can know 99% of the people on campus, and if you act without considering your campus policies, procedures, history, and culture, you may be responsible for uninformed decision-making and could be held accountable by others. You can have 99 problems, and a lawsuit might be one—at least not if you know and follow good policy. (Pause.) Okay, you still could get sued, but you can show why you did things the way you did. Consider keeping records of the decisions you and others make and other artifacts. Know the *what* issues on your campus—policy, procedure, and history—and know your own *what* issues—what you know, what you are responsible for, and what you can do to help.

8

WHERE

The answer to "Where do you work?" is more than the name of an institution.

More thoroughly and deeply consider where you work. Yes, your institution has a name and is in a specific state and city/town. However, what differentiates your institution from others? What defines where you work and differentiates it from other places?

Instead of "Where do you work?" as a starting point, consider the question "Where are you from?" What makes your hometown distinct? What are the points of pride? What are the struggles and shortcomings in your community? What assumptions do people make about where you are from? Who lives in your hometown? What does your town produce? What is the history of your home community? If you moved a lot growing up, what aspects do you remember about different places where you lived?

Now think about those same things in the context of your workplace. What is the relationship between your institution and that community? What is the history of your institution? Think again, where do you work? How would you answer that question if you could not give the name of your institution?

Understanding *where* factors in your work is critical to performing your job as a student affairs practitioner. So, *where* you work matters, and your work depends on the type of institution, location, history, politics, people, and so much more related to that place. Hirt (2006) stated that providing a history of student affairs through the lens of institutional type matters to student affairs practitioners, and where one works varies in other ways; not every higher education institution is alike. Where you work is influenced by

DOI: 10.4324/9781003442707-10

law and ethics. The idea that place matters is true philosophically and in practice.

Sometimes, we learn some of the issues related to a specific college or university before starting at an institution as a student or employee. When I (Cristóbal) think about Iowa State University, I knew several things before going there. I knew the university had a nationally regarded student affairs master's program and faculty, graduate school scholarships, and an active and united chapter of Sigma Lambda Beta International Fraternity, Inc. Additionally, the campus was a four-hour drive from home (Schuyler, Nebraska).

Once I got to campus, I learned more. I realized I needed support and created a sense of community. To do so, I had to build relationships because I knew that some people would care about me if I got to know them. As I built a community with people who cared about me, I understood that most of these people were white—my faculty, administrators, and mentors. In addition, as I engaged and learned more about Iowa State's culture, I had to cope with the lack of diversity and support for Latin* students. However, I knew my fraternity was active on campus, and I found social connections and support from them.

Regardless of what we think we know, we learn more about a campus once there. We choose particular institutions on the basis of access, geographical location, finances, degree(s) offered, student (or staff or faculty) demographics, family, and other factors. There are many considerations when choosing where to work or study. For example:

1. What type of institution is this (public, private, regional, religiously affiliated)?
2. What social identities are valued, represented, and privileged at the institution regarding students, faculty, and staff?
3. What is the campus culture like?
4. For employees, how competitive is the salary, what is the standard of living, and does the salary make a living in the area affordable?
5. What are the job responsibilities, and how have those responsibilities historically been achieved on this campus?

Once you are on campus, understand that your location directly affects decision-making at your institution. Consider the following:

1. Where is student affairs situated on campus (organizational charts, where are office spaces)?
2. Where is student affairs connected off campus and in the surrounding community?

3. Where are students on campus? Is it a residential campus?
4. Are there specific organizations that involve many students (student government, fraternity and sorority life, intramural sports)?
5. Where are the faculty? Where are their offices, and where are they in relation to academic and student affairs? Are there active partnerships in place? Additionally, given the current context, are they located on campus, teaching remotely, and potentially living in a different geographic area?
6. Where is your space? Where do you find community? Where do you feel like you belong? Where do you feel unwelcome?

We can thoroughly learn many of these things only once we live and work in a place. Getting others' perspectives can be helpful, but often we have to learn a place ourselves as we transition into new communities and workplaces.

We hope these questions help you think about and examine your institution's policies, procedures, and ethics and how they put local, state, and federal laws into practice. As we know, law and ethics influence each other. However, institutions may implement and enforce them very differently depending on location.

Chapter Organization

In this chapter, we provide scenarios of how information related to where we are can influence law and ethics in the work of academic and student affairs practitioners. First, we discuss institutional type, campus traditions, history, and culture. Finally, we examine how students, staff, administrators, and faculty help develop our institutions. All of these elements of institutional culture and history can inform ethics, policy, and practice on campus. As a result, understanding *where* issues on campus is essential to doing the most effective work on legal and ethical considerations.

Legal and Ethical Considerations

There are various legal and ethical questions about where we work and learn. For example, how do state laws relate to campus activities and processes? These can include everything from purchasing to curriculum, from community noise regulations to liquor laws, housing and zoning regulations to regulation of activities related to speech and activism.

Legal issues can vary significantly from one campus to the next. Some of these issues include ability/accessibility accommodations, gun laws, Title IX, trans*[1] student policies, and many others. Where you work and the influence of politics and regional issues have to do with more than whether you work in a "red state" or a "blue state." Doing your homework to understand how location informs college or university policy is essential during the job search. However, that work should continue as you begin on a campus and learn more about the *where* of your new campus.

Similarly, location, history, and culture inform campus ethics. You can turn to mission statements, job descriptions, and organizational charts to get a sense of the ethics of a division or institution. College newspapers also provide insight—at least from a student perspective—into the ethics of individuals and units on campus. What concerns and frustrations do students raise? What are the things that students celebrate? What organizations exist (or are absent)? Each of these can provide some ethical insight.

Institutional Type

Higher education institutions, broadly defined, focus on teaching, research, and service. Additionally, each campus is informed by demographic and mission characteristics, such as the size of the student body, regional location, the degrees granted (bachelor's, master's, or doctoral or a combination thereof), level of research productivity, and institutional affiliations. The following is a sample list of ways to classify institutions:

- Asian American and Native American Pacific Islander–serving institutions (AANAPI)
- Community and junior colleges
- For-profit institutions
- Hispanic-serving intuitions (HSIs)
- Historically Black colleges and universities (HBCUs)
- Land, sea, air, sun, and space grant institutions
- Liberal art colleges
- Military service institutions
- Minority-serving institutions (MSIs)
- Private colleges and universities
- Religiously affiliated institutions
- Research 1 universities
- Teaching colleges and universities
- Technical and professional colleges
- Tribal colleges and universities (TCUs)
- Women's colleges

To add another layer of complexity, institutions also have Carnegie Classifications. The Carnegie Classification helps contextualize and classify colleges and universities in the U.S. to identify comparable universities. Some institutional traits include degree-granting (doctorate-granting universities, master's-awarding or comprehensive universities, baccalaureate colleges, associated colleges, special focus institutions, and tribal colleges), enrollment profile, size, and setting (the Carnegie Classification of Institutions of Higher Education [CCIHE], n.d.).

Carnegie Classifications are also often used to differentiate teaching and research institutions. Teaching institutions have primarily undergraduate students and primarily confer baccalaureate degrees. Research universities also confer undergraduate and master's and doctoral degrees. Within research universities, classifications are "Very High Research Activity (R1)", "High Research Activity (R2)," or "Doctoral/Professional Universities." Master's colleges and universities must award at least 50 master's degrees and fewer than 20 doctoral degrees during an academic year to maintain the Carnegie Classification. The Carnegie Classification also includes Baccalaureate/Associate's Colleges, Associate's Colleges, Special Focus Institutions, and Tribal Colleges (CCIHE, n.d.). Visit the CCIHE website (https://carnegieclassifications.iu.edu/) for an overview of how colleges and universities are classified (CCIHE, n.d.).

Higher education institutions are also categorized by their history and original (or current) mission. These categories include private or public, religiously affiliated, and historically or predominantly white institutions. Furthermore, higher education institutions can be categorized by geographic location, namely suburban-large, rural-fringe, and city-midsize (National Center for Education Statistics, 2022).

Private Colleges and Universities (Non-Profit)

Private institutions spend their tuition on educational programs that help students learn. They spend most of their budgets on instruction, curriculum development, and recruitment to help improve the student experience and student success (National Center for Education Statistics, n.d.-a). Private institutions generally have higher tuition rates than public colleges and universities. These schools often offer more financial aid, scholarships, and grants to make their institutions more affordable. For example, in the 2019–2020 academic year, the average grant/scholarship aid at public four-year institutions was $8,600. The average award at private institutions was $25,200 (National Center for Educational Statistics, 2021). Examples of private non-profit institutions are the Massachusetts Institute of Technology (MIT), Princeton University, the University of Chicago, and Vanderbilt University.

Research 1 Universities (R1)

The R1 designation is the highest classification given to research universities. The CCIHE categorizes research institutions based on research activities and expenditures. Some research activity indicators that determine R1 status include annual expenditures in science and engineering (S&E) and doctorates awarded. R1 universities are institutions with the "highest research activity" and require faculty to focus on their research output, such as the number of peer-reviewed journal publications and research grants. R1 universities can be public or private; examples of R1 are Harvard University, The Ohio State University, Johns Hopkins University, Temple University, Texas Tech University, the University of California-Davis, and the University of Florida.

Teaching Colleges and Universities

Teaching colleges and universities are institutions with a commitment to teaching. They place importance on student instruction, assistance, and success rather than conducting research. Consequently, teaching colleges and universities value research but prioritize teaching. Faculty members will likely have heavier teaching loads at teaching colleges and universities than at research universities (R1 or R2). **Most colleges and universities that do not offer Ph.D. programs and junior and community colleges** are teaching institutions as they are committed to teaching. Examples of teaching colleges and universities are California State Polytechnic University-Pomona, Grand Canyon University, Grand Valley State University, and the University of Nebraska at Kearney.

Religious Colleges and Universities

These institutions are associated with a specific religion, denomination, church, or faith. **Religious or faith-related colleges and universities are primarily** liberal arts colleges with enrollments as small as 362 (Faith Baptist College and Theological Seminary) to nearly 15,000 (Baylor University) and almost 48,000 (Liberty University) undergraduate students (U.S. News Rankings, 2021). Some **religious colleges and universities** are considered large research universities (R1). However, nearly all religiously affiliated colleges **and universities are private or independent**. There are almost 1,000 colleges and universities with religious affiliations; some examples are the University of Notre Dame (Catholic, R1), Barry University (Catholic), Bennet College (United Methodist Church, all women's HBCU, liberal arts), Boston College (Catholic, R1), St. Olaf College (Lutheran), and the University of San Francisco (Catholic).

Junior and Community Colleges

These institutions are two-year postsecondary schools that offer affordable education to students. In most cases, community college degree programs align with the local community's needs, and these institutions have an open-door approach to students seeking postsecondary education. Community colleges can also serve as technical schools or schools for students who are not seeking or may need access to a four-year college. Programs at these types of institutions help students gain the skills needed to be prepared to enter the workforce. In addition, community colleges serve as a pathway to transfer to a four-year college for many students. Some community colleges also offer four-year bachelor's degrees. Community colleges are teaching colleges that serve the educational needs of their communities. Examples of community colleges are Modesto Junior College, Miami Dade College (which offers associate's and bachelor's degrees), Northeast Community College, Naugatuck Valley Community College, and Oregon Institute of Technology.

Technical and Vocational Colleges

Teaching and vocational colleges educate students for a specific trade or career. Technical colleges usually do not require general education courses as other colleges and universities do and instead focus entirely on career-specific skills. Technical and vocational colleges are two-year colleges, and examples are Eastern Idaho Technical College, Vatterott College, and Empire Beauty Schools.

Liberal Arts Colleges

These institutions originated in the classical era between the 8th century BCE and the 6th century CE when the Greeks focused on grammar, logic, and rhetoric as essential for the development of citizens to engage in public life (Brighouse, 2019). According to the American Association of Colleges and Universities (2022), liberal arts colleges today focus on the following essential learning outcomes: human culture and physical/natural world, intellectual and practical skills, personal and social responsibility, and integrative and applied learning (n.p.). Most liberal arts colleges are private. Examples are Bowdoin College (private), Pomona College (private), Spellman College (private; all-women's HBCU), Washington and Lee University (private), Truman State University (public), and the University of North Carolina at Asheville (public).

Women's Colleges

Women's Colleges are single-sex institutions of higher education that admit only women students. Women's colleges focus on transforming the world through the education and success of women. Some examples of women's colleges are Saint Mary's College (Catholic, private, liberal arts), Smith College (private, liberal arts), Sweet Briar College (private, liberal arts), and Wellesley College (private, liberal arts). There are also men's colleges, including Wabash College (private), Morehouse College (private, HBCU), and Hampden-Sydney College (private, liberal arts). Many schools that started as women's or men's colleges have since become coeducational. Examples are Texas Women's University (public), Sarah Lawrence College (private), and Pitzer College (private).

Land, Sea, Air, Sun, and Space Grant Institutions

These colleges and universities receive their designations and the ability to receive federal funding for research-intensive projects with a unique focus that benefits the larger community. For example, land-grant institutions use knowledge to respond to current social and economic concerns with specific services to the state. Sun-grant institutions are based on research and innovation to create renewable and sustainable local energy resources. Sea-grant institutions provide research and support for managing marine and coastal resources and development. Space-grant institutions have a focus on aerospace science and technology. Some schools hold one of these designations. Others may be involved in work across several or all of these research areas. Examples of land, sea, air, sun, *and* space grant institutions are Oregon State University, Penn State University, and Texas A&M University.

Minority-Serving Institutions (MSIs)

The U.S. Department of Education can also categorize higher education institutions as "minority institutions" (U.S. Department of Education, n.d.) based on the percentage of minoritized students enrolled. For example, there are historically Black colleges and universities (HBCUs), Hispanic-serving institutions (HSIs), Tribal colleges and universities (TCUs), Alaska Native and Native Hawaiian-serving institutions (ANNHSIs), predominantly Black institutions (PBIs), Asian American and Native American Pacific Islander-serving institutions (AANAPISIs), and Native American-serving non-Tribal institutions (NASNTIs). The following sections provide a brief overview of each type of MSI.

Alaska Native and Native Hawaiian-Serving Institutions (ANNHIs)

The Higher Education Amendments of 1998, under Title III of the Higher Education Act of 1965, designated the first Alaska Native and Native Hawaiian-Serving Institutions (ANNHIs). Title III provides institutional aid to improve and expand institutional capacity to serve Alaskan Natives and Native Hawaiians (Higher Education Amendments of 1998, n.d.). ANNHIs include Alaska Christian College, Chaminade University of Honolulu, Kapiolani Community College, Honolulu Community College, University of Alaska Southeast – Sitka Campus, University of Alaska Fairbanks – Interior Alaska Campus, University of Alaska Fairbanks, the University of Hawaii at Hilo, University of Hawaii Maui College, and Windward Community College.

Asian American and Native American Pacific Islander-Serving Institutions (AANAPISIs)

Established in 2007, AANAPISIs serve the fastest-growing population in the nation: Asian Pacific Islander Desi Americans (APIDAs). At least 10% of the undergraduate student population of these institutions must be APIDA students (Nguyen et al., 2020). AANAPISIs are eligible to apply for federal grants to improve their academic quality, increase their self-sufficiency, and strengthen their capacity to make a substantial contribution to the higher education resources of the Nation. AANAPISIs include American River College, CUNY Queen College, Guam Community College, Mt. San Antonio College, University of California-Irvine, the University of Hawaii at Hilo, the University of Hawaii at Manoa, and the University of Illinois at Chicago.

Hispanic-Serving Institutions (HSIs)

HSIs must have 25% or more total undergraduate Hispanic or Latin* full-time equivalent student enrollment to receive federal funding under Title V and Title III grants (Higher Education Amendments of 1998, n.d.). With the fast growth of HSIs, *Excelencia* in Education implemented the phrase "Emerging Hispanic-Serving Institutions" to focus on institutions with an undergraduate full-time Hispanic enrollment between 15% and 24% (Pennamon, 2019). Examples of HSIs are the American University of Puerto Rico, Arizona State University, California Lutheran University, Florida Atlantic University, Mesa Community College, and Union Institute & University.

Historically Black Colleges and Universities (HBCUs)

HBCUs are Black colleges or universities established before 1964 whose principal mission is the education of African-American communities. As of 2020, there were 101 HBCUs, of which 52 are public and 49 are private, and approximately 24% of the students attending HBCUs are not Black (National Center for Education Statistics, n.d.-b). HBCUs were founded and developed to provide access to higher education to Black Americans during a time of legal segregation; these institutions have played a significant role in African-American and Black students and students of other races receiving a quality education. HBCUs are federally recognized by the Higher Education Act of 1965. Some examples of HBCUs are Cheyney University of Pennsylvania, Florida A&M University, Hampton University, Howard University, Morehouse College, Texas Southern University, and Tuskegee University.

Native American-Serving Non-Tribal Institutions (NASNTIs)

These institutions have less than 10% Native American students and are not Tribal colleges or universities. Tribes do not govern NASNTIs, but these colleges and universities serve American Indian and Alaska Native students. These institutions are provided with federal grants to enable institutions to improve and expand their capacity to serve Native Americans. NASNTIs are federally recognized by the Higher Education Opportunity Act of 2008. In 2020, the following institutions received the NASNTI awards: Central Wyoming College, Fort Lewis College, Carl Albert State College, Connors State College, Eastern Oklahoma State College, Montana State University-Northern, Northeastern Oklahoma A&M College, Redlands Community College, Robeson Community College, University of Minnesota Morris, the University of North Carolina at Pembroke, and Utah State University Blanding.

Predominantly Black Institutions (PBIs)

Predominantly Black institutions (PBIs) "strengthen eligible institutions to plan, develop, undertake, and implement programs to enhance the institution's capacity to serve more low- and middle-income Black American students" (U.S. Department of Education, n.d.). PBIs increase college preparation and access and provide financial assistance to enhance academic success on these campuses. PBIs serve at least 1,000 undergraduate students, have at least 50% low-income or first-generation degree-seeking undergraduate enrollments, have low expenditures per full-time undergraduate student compared to other institutions offering similar instruction, and enroll at least 40% African-American students (Predominantly Black Institution Act of 2007, n.p.). PBIs are different from HBCUs. PBIs are federally recognized by the Higher Education Opportunity Act of 2008. PBIs include Albany Technical College, Baton Rouge Community College, Clayton State University, Edgecombe Community College, and Metropolitan College of New York.

Tribal Colleges and Universities (TCUs)

TCUs are federally supported public institutions that assist in bridging the divide in education for some American Indian, Native American, and Indigenous communities. Tribal identity is at the heart of all TCUs, and they all share the mission of tribal self-determination and service to their communities. TCUs are federally recognized by the Tribally Controlled College or University Assistance Act of 1978. Each institution was founded and authorized by its tribal government with a specific goal: to provide higher education options to American Indians through holistic, supportive, and regionally and culturally focused programs. Most TCUs are in the Midwest and the Southwest United States. Examples of TCUs are Aaniiih Nakoda College (Aaniinen and Nakoda tribes), Cankdeska Cikana Community College (Spirit Lake Dakota Nation), College of Menominee Nation (Menominee), Diné College (Navajo Nation), Fond du Lac Tribal and Community College (Chippewa, Ojibwe), Ilisagvik College (Iñupiat Nation), Nebraska Indian Community College (Omaha and Santee people), Saginaw Chippewa Tribal College (Anishinaabeg peoples, including Ojibwe, Odawa, Potawatomi, Mississaugas, Nipissing, and Algonquin), Sisseton Wahpeton College (Sisseton and Wahpeton Bands of the Dakotah), and Tohono O'odham Community College (Tohono O'odham Nation).

The Complexity of Identity at Minority Serving Institutions

While there is a variety of MSIs, how each campus navigates emerging opportunities and challenges is complicated. Minority institutions are eligible to receive federal funding to support increased enrollment and graduation. The National Science Foundation (NSF) and National Endowment for the Humanities (NEH) partnerships and opportunities with other federal departments, including the Department of Health and Human Services (HHS), the Department of Energy (DOE), the Department of Transportation (DOT), the Department of Commerce (DOC), and the National Aeronautics and Space Administration (NASA), also provide federal funding.

Regarding federal grants, some institutions have to choose which MSI designation to prioritize. For example, according to Dr. Robert Teranishi,

Helen Chu Endowed Chair in Asian American studies at UCLA, nearly half of AANAPISIs are also eligible as HSIs but ultimately have to choose which grants they can accept because they cannot accept both. As a result, the government does not allocate all grant funds (Herder, 2022). Without appropriate funding, institutions cannot support current students or increase the enrollment of minoritized student populations. For example, HSIs must have at least 25% Hispanic/Latin* undergraduate full-time students of the student population to receive access to federal funding.

Another example of how minoritized student populations are underserved and oppressed by law and policy is Tennessee State University (TSU), a public historically Black land-grant university. Since the 1950s, the federal government has failed to adequately fund TSU compared with historically and predominantly white land-grant universities (Chang et al., 2021).

"Minority institutions" can also intersect with other types of institutions presented earlier. For example, Bennet College is a private liberal arts institution affiliated with the United Methodist Church. Bennet is also an all-women's HBCU. Coastline Community College, Evergreen Valley College, and University of California – Irvine are all AANAPISIs and HSIs. Huston-Tillotson University (private) and St. Philip's College (public community college) are both HBCUs and HSIs.

Finally, racial identity categories are complicated and inconsistent across higher education, the government, and other institutions and agencies. For example, while there are ANNHIs, some reports group American Indian and Alaska Native students in one category and Native Hawaiian or other Pacific Islander students in another (Espinosa et al., 2019). This inconsistency complicates understanding what services, resources, and experiences students need.

The unique legal context for MSIs helps create the culture on those campuses. Boland (2018) wrote about how Title II and Title V grants have been used on MSI campuses. It is worth remembering that HBCUs and TCUs were "the original MSIs [and] educated students of color who were forbidden an education in the traditional colleges and universities of the day" (p. 1). This history is essential to understanding those and other MSI campuses today. Additionally, given the grant-funded nature of many MSIs, political partnerships (which have legal and ethical implications) are essential for funding and both public and institutional policy decisions to maintain MSIs (McLendon et al., 2009; Tandberg & Griffith, 2013).

To describe the unique ethical issues that MSIs face, Farrell-Cole and Cabrales (2020) focused on HSIs. The authors wrote, "HSIs are facing several tensions or realities, which could challenge or have unintended consequences on ethical standards" (Farrell-Cole & Cabrales, 2020, p. 139).

They also list changing demographics, college readiness, accountability, and scarce resources, as well as connections between institutions and communities, which are particularly relevant for Latin* students (García, 2017). MSIs play a significant role as they educate and provide educational opportunities for historically marginalized communities that have often been ignored and forgotten by law. Yet the *where* plays a critical role in understanding the population demographics of MSIs and communities.

Other *Where* Considerations

The *where* of higher education affects student affairs work in important, complex, and diverse ways. Here are a few areas for consideration:

- How does geographical location affect policies, planning, and resources needed for natural disasters?
- How might student organization guidelines be different at a large, public institution compared with a small, religiously affiliated one?
- What might a conduct officer need to communicate about alcohol to fraternity and sorority life (FSL) chapters on a campus where an alcohol-related hazing death recently occurred? How might that communication differ on campuses without a recent hazing death?
- How might the student experience differ at an urban institution compared with a rural institution?

These examples provide context to how policies and laws are affected by institutional *where* issues. An institution's location informs its culture, traditions, and people. Understanding geographical and regional context is part of developing Institutional Intelligence. The following examples examine *where* issues related to a statewide system, and we examine how university traditions and culture affect one institution within a larger system.

The University of Texas System

People matter. Students matter, staff matter, faculty matter, alumni matter, donors matter, and leaders matter (see Chapter 6). However, while the idea that people matter can seem simple, not only do people shape places, but places shape people as well. Individuals make up units, teams, organizations, and systems. To clarify how *who* shapes *where* in higher education, we offer an example of the University of Texas System (UT System, 2022). Statewide systems exemplify this complexity; the multiple stakeholders invested in institutional decision-making speak to issues of power and influence in crafting our college and university campuses.

Thirteen academic and health institutions across Texas comprise the UT System, which has an enrollment of 243,000 students. The UT System is one of the United States' largest public university systems. The UT System academic institutions include UT Arlington, UT Austin, UT Dallas, UT El Paso, UT Permian Basin, UT Rio Grande Valley, UT San Antonio, and UT Tyler. UT System health institutions include UT Southwestern Medical Center, UT Medical Branch at Galveston, UT Health Science Center at Houston, UT Health Science Center at San Antonio, and UT MD Anderson Cancer Center. Each of these places has its sense of *where* and a shared sense of *where* as part of the larger statewide system.

These 13 institutions' locations matter as location influences who is involved and what resources each campus has. For example, the UT System's main office is in Austin, near UT Austin. Because of proximity, UT Austin has more access to system leadership and potential resources than other UT institutions. Furthermore, the capitol and Texas legislature are in Austin, which may sometimes help UT Austin secure resources, support, and advocacy.

That said, because of its location, UT Austin may be more visible than other schools in the system. This visibility can mean more attention and criticism. While proximity to resources and visibility can be assets, they may also create additional work, challenges, or labor for staff working on the UT Austin campus.

UT Austin's location informs not only *where* issues but *who* issues. Connections between administrators, alumni, current students, faculty and staff, and the Texas legislature are more likely since they live and work in proximity to one another. Additionally, community stakeholders close to the state capital and the UT Austin campus will have common interests and easier access to leaders and legislators than community members around San Antonio or Tyler campuses. In this example, the *where* of an institution can translate into increased visibility, power, and influence. UT Austin shows how proximity to power can be a significant Institutional Intelligence consideration. Fans and alums often call UT Austin "UT" In contrast, the other 12 institutions in the University of Texas system are "UT-[name of city]" (e.g., UT Austin or UT Rio Grande Valley). Furthermore, "The Eye of Texas" is UT Austin's alma mater song; it is believed the song has racist origins. "The Eye of Texas" was first performed in a minstrel show in 1903 (Eubank, 2021). On September 3, 2021, the NAACP (National Association for the Advancement of Colored People) and UT Austin students filed a complaint with the U.S. Department of Education's Office of Civil Rights because the song is racially offensive, and every time it is played, it creates a "hostile environment" for Black students, faculty, and staff (Eubank, 2021). Because of the racist origins of "The Eye of Texas," student athletes wrote a letter requesting that the song be removed until the university addressed racial concerns, or they would not participate in university events (Levin, 2020), and for a week students who give campus tours to perspectives students refused to work (Mcgee, 2021). However, UT Austin administrators responded that "The Eye of Texas" has "no racist intent" (Eubank, 2021). "The Eye of Texas" is another example of how ethics and legal issues intertwine with the university's traditions, cultures, mission, and people.

Traditions and Culture

Just as higher education institutions are rooted in location, they are also rooted in traditions that contribute to campus culture. We define traditions as "inherited and established customs, beliefs, and values that have been passed from generation to generation" (Salinas & Boettcher, 2018, p. 4). People spread traditions through behaviors, memories, symbols, stories, and legends. These are communicated from person to person, from community to individual. Some behaviors, memories, symbols, stories, and legends become enduring customs, beliefs, and practices essential to the culture.

Time and space help define culture. Culture is more extensive than traditions, but our traditions are part of our culture. Culture is the way of knowing, believing, and doing, which becomes behavior guidelines of a community. Culture builds society and shapes values. These values include law, ethics, religion, history, language, economics, and the arts. Within cultures, there are subcultures, including, in the context of this book, campus cultures. Kuh and Whitt (1988) defined campus culture as

> collective, mutually shaping patterns of norms, values, practices, beliefs, and assumptions that guide the behavior of individuals and groups in an institute of higher education and provide a frame of reference within which to interpret the meaning of events and actions on and off-campus. *(p. 29)*

This definition is essential to help us understand our *where* in higher education. This definition also invites us to think about how the "norms, values, practices, beliefs, and assumptions" (Kuh & Whitt, 1988, p. 29) can guide us in making ethical decisions and interpret and apply the law.

Tarnished Traditions

On November 18, 1999, at 2:42 a.m., on the Texas A&M campus, the annual Aggie Bonfire was burning when it collapsed, killing 12 Texas A&M students and injuring 27 other people (Aggie Traditions, 2021).

Following the incident, the university struggled with whether to keep this tradition or eliminate it. The university put the bonfire on hiatus and created a memorial. According to the memorial website, "The Bonfire Memorial embodies many layers of meaning associated with the Aggie Spirit — a deep sense of belonging, a strong spirit of teamwork, and leadership and an enduring sense of tradition that unites thousands" (Aggie Traditions, 2021, para. 4). However, since that time, the bonfire has continued unofficially off campus. Student Bonfire is a 501(c)(3) nonprofit organization with bylaws and a board of directors consisting of A&M graduates (Eden, 2014).

This tradition and tragedy are woven into the fabric of Texas A&M. Every campus has its events—traditions and tragedies—that inform the campus culture and institutional *where*. Other examples:

- Building names, campus statues, and other commemorations of problematic historical figures (University of North Carolina at Chapel Hill, 2018)
- Campus disruption and violence related to protest or speech issues (University of Virginia, 2017)
- Celebrations associated with homecoming, athletics, graduation, or campus festivals (Iowa State University, 2014)
- Issues with alma mater lyrics (Harvard, 1998, 2018)
- NCAA championship celebrations or disruptions (e.g., University of Kentucky 2012, 2015)
- Problematic chants, cheers, or mascots (Indiana University of Pennsylvania, 2007)
- Instances of campus violence or tragedy (e.g., Kent State University, 1970; University of Iowa, 1991; Virginia Tech, 2007; Northern Illinois University, 2008; Umpqua Community College, 2015).

Since traditions create different cultures at colleges and universities, these traditions are part of the Institutional Intelligence on each campus. This Institutional Intelligence informs campus community practices and how the campus interprets law and ethics in its specific context.

In the Texas A&M bonfire tragedy, Fearn-Banks (2017) highlighted how the culture informed the response to this crisis. As the new executive director of university relations at the time of the incident (she had been in the role for four months), Cynthia Lawson had a unique perspective and insight into this situation. President Ray M. Bowen fostered a culture of trust and an investigation of the collapse "that was beyond reproach" (Fearn-Banks, 2017, p. 138). Texas A&M's honor code states, "An Aggie does not lie, cheat, or steal or tolerate those who do" (Texas A&M, n.d., para 2). That aspect of the campus culture potentially informs or at least mirrors how

Lawson described President Bowen's actions following the tragedy. The ethics of the campus were reflected in the ethics of the leadership, and the leadership investigated relevant legal issues with dedication and integrity.

Athletics

Another significant part of campus culture for many students involves athletics. High-profile teams, an affinity for a specific sport, or even an attachment to a mascot can provide social and community engagement for students. Students (and often alumni, staff, and faculty) label themselves through their attire as members of a community related to an institution and particularly sporting teams at a given institution. College athletics culture and challenges in an athletics context are handled differently based on the *where* of the institution.

Athletics in higher education institutions have received significant attention in mainstream media, contributing to a culture of traditions, attitudes, values, pride, competition, and goals about sports. We understand that not all institutions have athletic departments. Nevertheless, college sports can significantly influence traditions, legal cases, and ethical issues based on institutional type. Pride, connections, and community are things in which students and alumni invest tremendous time, energy, and emotion. When legal and ethical issues emerge in the context of a team, sport, or program, many people may weigh in on what institutions should do in a given situation. How these incidents unfold is informed in significant ways by campus location. Consider the following questions related to legal and ethical *where* considerations in athletics.

- Does the team generate revenue?
- Does the team involved have a history of winning championships?
- Does the situation involve a team, a single team member, a coach/coaches, or some combination?
- If the situation involves a single athlete, does that athlete excel in their sport?
- Has the coach been at the institution for a long time, or are they new to campus?
- To what level do alumni attend and support the team(s) involved in a situation?

These are a few questions about how place (and people connected to that place—both *where* and *who*) can affect legal and ethical issues. For example, there may be a difference between how an incident involving a star player from a Division I football player is handled and how the same incident is handled on the campus of a Division III program. At the very least, there are likely different levels of media coverage in those situations. The Family Educational Rights and Privacy Act (FERPA) may be an issue for the Division I player when the media want information about the player's conduct case. That may not be the case for the Division III player if no such requests exist for records. There are lots of other questions to consider.

As an example, the NCAA recently introduced the Name, Image, and Likeness (NIL) policy (NCAA, 2021b). NIL has provoked more questions about law and ethics related to student athletes' opportunities and behaviors related to their brand initiatives. How institutions navigate NIL is an ongoing situation that will evolve significantly in the coming years.

Defining Where *Individually*

As you work to develop your Institutional Intelligence, we encourage you to consult with others about how they handle law and ethics within a specific institutional context. Here are some questions to consider:

- Where do students, staff, and faculty feel safe/unsafe?
- Where can I go on campus to better understand campus history, culture, and traditions?
- Where are hubs for student engagement?
- Where are there good partnerships with faculty on campus?

Perhaps most importantly, ask yourself: What is this place to me?

As you learn about campus, be open to finding various spaces where people—including employees—build community, culture, and tradition. For example, people may create a community in virtual spaces, meetings, parties, and social network happy hours, among other events. Other people might feel safe at LGBTQ+ bars, coffee shops, businesses owned by People of Color, community centers, or outdoor spaces.

Critical Scenario 8.1 Where

Co-Author: Dr. Dax Boatwright, Assistant Director of Transfer Student Services, New Student Transitions and Family Engagement, Florida Atlantic University

Francisco (he/him) was recently hired as the Deputy Chief Diversity Officer at an HSI under the Office of Equity, Diversity Inclusion. Francisco reports directly to Elena (she/her), the institution's Associate Vice President and

Chief Diversity Officer. Francisco supervises the Director of Equity and Social Justice, the Director of Social Justice Education, and two graduate student researchers. Other personnel under the Office of Equity, Diversity Inclusion include the Director of Hispanic-Serving Initiatives, the Director of Black and Indigenous People of Color (BIPOC) Initiatives, the Director of Faculty and Staff Excellence Initiatives, and the Equity and Social Justice Analyst. During his first year at the institution, his boss Elena asks Francisco to propose a new organizational chart to restructure the office.

Elena says,

> "I want you to present an idea and the rationale. You and I will work on this as it moves forward, and ultimately, I will be responsible for final decisions. I want to get your ideas. Be careful as you put together your proposal. I don't want our team worried about changes that may not happen. It is possible nothing will change."

The Law

- What are the relevant legal issues in this scenario?
- What institutional policies, procedures, or processes are applicable in this scenario?

Ethics

- What are the relevant ethical issues in this scenario?
- What information would the characters need to make sound ethical decisions?

Identity

- How might characters' social identities affect how this scenario would unfold?
- How do the situation and the information you need change depending on the identities of those involved?

Scenario-Specific Questions

- Where should Francisco begin in order to understand the history and politics of the office and university?

- Where might Francisco situate himself and others in the organizational chart? What are the implications for Francisco's colleagues, supervisees, and Elena?
- Where does Francisco expect faculty, staff, students, and alumni to get engaged and supported?

In addition to *where* specific questions, the following can help Francisco develop Institutional Intelligence.

- What resources are in place to promote ethical decisions?
- What resources are available to help Francisco determine fair equity across all departments in the organizational chart?
- How is compliance determined in this scenario?
- How influential are cultural identity norms in this scenario?
- How does Francisco's understanding of power influence his organizational chart creation?

Conclusion

In this chapter, we explored how knowing issues related to *where* at your institution is essential for you as an employee. Understanding a place helps you choose the right campus in your job search. Understanding and seeking opportunities to learn more about where you work help you do your work more efficiently, ethically, and with an understanding of the campus approach to legal issues. Understanding where you work is essential. This learning can take time and energy, but cultivating Institutional Intelligence related to where you work will benefit you, your colleagues, and students, making the work of learning and understanding your campus worth the effort.

Note

1 Trans*: used to include explicitly both transsexual and transgender. The * in trans also indicates the inclusion of gender identities such as gender-fluid and gender-nonconforming, alongside transsexual and transgender.

9

WHEN, WHY, HOW

My (Michelle's) first major as an undergraduate student was journalism. The faculty told us repeatedly to remember *who*, *what*, *where*, *when*, *why*, and *how* as we wrote articles. In discussing this text, Cristóbal and I agreed that we needed to frame the book building on these questions. As a result, we have (re)introduced these questions via the Institutional Intelligence Model for understanding higher education contexts (see Chapter 5). To this point, we have talked about *who*, *what*, and *where*. We separated these three because of the significance of these considerations in navigating legal and ethical issues and developing Institutional Intelligence. Who is or should be involved? What is happening? Where do you work, and where are things taking place?

This chapter focuses on the remaining questions—*why*, *when*, and *how*. Some of these questions are important during an incident and even more so in reflecting on incidents, preparing training, and engaging in continual improvement in supporting students, constituents, stakeholders, and each other as academic and student affairs colleagues. As with the previous sections, we do not pretend to provide you with an exhaustive list of all the questions you may want to ask yourselves. Instead, we provide prompts in this chapter and throughout the text as starting points to guide your thinking. Given the unique institutional type, campus culture, history of the place where you work, and your individual experiences, talents, and insights, there may be other essential questions you need to include in your work.

In the previous chapters (Chapter 6: Who; Chapter 7: What; and Chapter 8: Where), we provided context on how our relationships and those involved (*who*) matter, how the nature of the incident (*what*) matters, and how the

DOI: 10.4324/9781003442707-11

culture, history, and law and ethics of an institution (*where*) matters. In this chapter, we combined the *when*, *why*, and *how* questions to help understand how the facets of each case interact and inform one another as situations arise and how Institutional Intelligence plays a role in each of us navigating situations as successfully as possible.

Academic and student affairs crisis work mirrors case management—similar to what counseling and social work staff do. Academic and student affairs staff work with students on self-harm, family illness/death, mental health issues, learning disabilities, and any other issues that students might face. Some staff might serve in on-duty rotations and may be the first staff member to respond to a crisis. As a result, it is essential to consider *when*, *why*, and *how* as intersecting and overlapping concepts. The intricacies of *who*, *what*, and *where* required independent chapters (see Chapters 6–8). However, *when*, *why*, and *how* fit better as a set, and we have combined them in a single chapter.

Chapter Organization

This chapter overviews the three remaining Institutional Intelligence questions—*when*, *why*, and *how*. The following section discusses how each fits into the Institutional Intelligence Model. We conclude the chapter with a series of critical scenarios to practice using the questions in this chapter and other Institutional Intelligence Model questions to practice putting the model into action.

When

When questions establish timelines and deadlines—when did things happen, and when do the following steps need to take place? A few *when* questions to build into your procedures might include the following:

- When did an incident take place?
- When were you or your team made aware of the situation?
- When were other campus partners made aware of the situation?
- When did a response take place?
- When did you or others provide resources?
- When can you anticipate updates?
- When will other people—including students involved, supervisors, communities impacted, parents, and stakeholders—be notified?
- When will the media, if involved, have information about this situation? When do you anticipate that the media will release information about this situation?

When questions require coordination; no single person will likely have the answers to all these questions or others that may emerge.

When questions help us plan, *why* questions help us understand, and *how* questions help us examine options for the process and next steps. More than any of our Institutional Intelligence Model questions, *when* questions—especially paired with *what* questions related to action—help us develop responses and then analyze those responses. *When* questions can help us adjust timelines to be more effective and ensure more support to students and safety for our campuses.

Why

When questions are specific and time-focused, and *why* questions help us examine the big picture around events and incidents. There are lots of questions beyond "Why me?" that we need to ask ourselves. A first question may be, "Why is this an issue or concern?" It may be a safety concern, a student mental health issue, or a pattern of concerning behavior escalating between groups of students. The issue may be a concern because what is happening may be a policy or legal violation on campus. Knowing why a situation is a concern helps us identify the next steps, such as connecting a student with campus resources, reporting a violation of the student code of conduct, or facilitating a conversation to address an issue between students or groups.

A question we often forget to ask ourselves is, "Why am I involved?" Understanding our role is crucial because it helps define our work moving forward. If you are involved because a student came directly to you with a concern, you may serve as a liaison between the student and other offices since you were reached out to specifically. They have shown trust in you and may be most receptive to your offers of resources and support.

Maybe you are involved because the student is a member of a program you coordinate. There may be nothing specific you need to do. However, you might have information to share with others about the student's past or recent behavior changes, life circumstances, or whether they are showing up to classes or meetings.

You may become involved because someone on campus needs your help with some aspect of a situation. Maybe you are teaching a course, and a student needs extra time to complete an assignment or will be absent from class or multiple class meetings. The student or their advocate may ask you to adjust due dates or assignments depending on the situation.

Regardless of why you are involved, it is vital to share information when asked, and it is just as important to ask the questions you might have. For example, if you get a call from someone on your campus letting you know that a student is no longer allowed to attend organizational functions for a group you advise, and you want to know why, then, by all means, ask, "Why?" The person may or may not be able to share that with you, but at least you will have asked.

Remember that the Family Educational Rights and Privacy Act (FERPA) (see Chapter 2) protects students' academic records. While not the same as confidentiality, the caveat on FERPA is that information should be shared only with those with a "legitimate need to know." If you are advising an organization and want to know why a student is no longer allowed to attend, the fact that a student is banned from the organization may be all the information you get. It can be frustrating, but it is incumbent on others in that situation to protect the student or others involved. Not everyone can know everything about each situation.

Why questions help us understand situations and motivations. *Why* questions also often serve to prompt other questions. We can always ask *why* questions—even about confidential resources (see Chapter 15). To abide by their confidential relationships with students, others may be unable to answer every question you have; that said, they will often provide some guidance even if they cannot provide specific details. Rapport, trust, and communication are why building relationships is integral to our work.

Finally, *why* questions can also help us understand more about the enactment of processes, procedures, and policies on our campuses. Asking these questions early in your career or role is essential to understanding your institution. Find good partners with whom you can anticipate and process situations to understand the culture, history, and other elements of your unit, department, division, and institution more thoroughly and quickly.

It is worth noting that asking the *why* questions requires sensitivity and care; without a thoughtful approach, *why* questions can come across as accusatory or victim-blaming or in other ways that can create barriers between responding staff and those who are directly impacted by a crisis or event. One strategy is simply affirming what a person did and asking for more information. "Thank you for sharing that with me. How did you make the decision to take that action?" or "I appreciate what you have shared. Can you tell me more about if you made that decision on your own or after consulting with others?" Or even "I need to ask follow-up questions to understand the sequence of events and how people made decisions." Focusing on collecting information rather than indicating that you are trying to assign blame will encourage people to share details with you more openly.

How

If *when* questions are about timelines and deadlines related to our responses and *why* questions are about the big picture, then *how* questions are about action. How did this happen, and how did we respond? *How* questions can focus on students or communities/organizations—how did the situation come to be? How did individuals or groups react? While those questions tend to help us collect information, we could also ask, "How did we respond? How did we make those decisions? How do we move forward?" to reflect on what we did and how effective our decisions were.

We can answer *how* questions by compiling lists of actions taken. *How* responses work best paired with *when* and *why*: "We took this action (*how*) at this time (*when*) because (*why*)." This sequence helps us process incidents to identify improvement strategies, barriers, and opportunities to build partnerships that are more effective.

Let's return to the student organization you advise—and the specific student who is no longer allowed to participate. In that situation, you might have several *how* questions, such as "How do I explain to other students if they ask why this person is not coming to meetings anymore?" Again, ask for information. The people you are asking likely have experience with these kinds of situations if you do not.

There are other *how* questions that center on you as an individual. These are best asked in advance of situations so we can prepare to address concerns and gaps before an incident arises. However, there are many situations that we cannot anticipate and must experience before we have enough information to ask ourselves some of the following:

- How can I help?
- How have I been trained to respond to issues?
- How am I limited in what you can do and offer in a given situation?
- How can I be better prepared for the future?
- How can I establish, strengthen, and maintain partnerships on campus for better responses in the future?
- How can I support others who may be the frontline responders in a given situation?

Additionally, you might ask, "Is there other information I can provide that might be helpful?" This question can be essential to helping formulate a complete picture of what the student involved is facing, how they have been engaging with others, or what resources they are already using. Past incidents on various campuses have taught us that centralizing information about struggling students is essential to providing the best response for the individual and the larger community.

Some questions supporting the Institutional Intelligence Model are less focused and concrete than others. *How* questions, for example, can be vague. *How* is often speculative—how can I do better? How can I help?

There may be room for creativity in responses to *how* questions. *How* questions can be both liberating and daunting because of the ambiguous nature of the responses to these questions. Answers to *how* questions are often "I'm not sure, but let's try this." However, that also means the response to *how* questions allows us to be flexible and adaptable—the Swiss Army knife in a given situation. "How can I help?" might be followed by "Well, in several ways. For starters, let's have you do this..."

Legal and Ethical Considerations

There are many legal and ethical considerations for *when*, *why*, and *how* in academic and student affairs work. *When* it is about time; staff must consider deadlines and dates included in handbooks, correspondence, and other communication with students, staff, faculty, and others. *When* also matters as people seek to understand timelines after an incident has occurred. For example: When did you know this incident had happened? When did you call the police? When did you let your supervisor know? When did you make other students aware of the incident? Of course, each situation is different, but considering when you should take action is essential to a good response. Being prepared to act promptly and to document your actions, conversations, and other details also helps you follow campus policy and abide by legal and other guidelines.

Why questions are about rationale and philosophy. As a new staff member in student veterans' services, you may want to know why your office reports to a particular area. As a new director of civic learning and leadership, you may want to know why your office does not partner with community grassroots organizations. These are essential questions to ask and explore. *Why* questions help us understand relationships, history, and some of the more complex issues in higher education.

Finally, *how* questions help us clarify policy and process. Knowing how academic integrity hearing officers and faculty share information is important. It is essential to ensure that FERPA is respected and that everyone involved has the necessary information. *How* can sometimes be where we get in the most trouble. We should not assume how one institution does things is the same as another. For example: How are things done here? How do you want me to document this? How do we handle situations like this here? Each of these *how* questions and so many others can help us avoid legal issues or provide an explanation based on policy about the decisions we make around an event.

When, *why*, and *how* also connect to organizational and individual ethics. For example, I (Michelle) worked at an institution where if a student was behind on their room-and-board payment, the first step was to change the lock on their room and ban them from the building. When were we required to act? Immediately. Why? Because the policy puts payment before other considerations. How? By changing the locks. This process exemplified the institution's and the functional unit's ethics in action. It was then up to me to decide whether those ethics aligned with my own.

Using the Institutional Intelligence Model

Now that we have covered all the Institutional Intelligence Model questions, let's take some time to look at how the pieces work together. These questions are not sequential. You do not ask all the *who* questions and then move on to *what*, followed by *where*, and so on. As you get answers to some questions, you must ask new questions. It is a constantly shifting process depending on your information and the information you need. With that in mind, we conclude this chapter with four examples of using the Institutional Intelligence Model in practice. As we reiterate through this text, the questions we include here are not a comprehensive list. Different individuals will have additional questions, and other institutions will have different answers. We provided these examples to give you a sense of how to use the information from Chapters 10 through 16 practically. In each situation, consider Institutional Intelligence Model questions but also think specifically about the legal and ethical implications in each critical scenario.

Critical Scenario 9.1 When, Why, How

Co-Author: Catrina Wagner, Associate Director, Office of Student Development, UC Davis

Dane (he/him) has just started as an academic advisor at the College of Business. He is excited but also nervous about having his first meetings with students. This is his first job out of graduate school, where he was a graduate assistant in the academic success center and partnered with many academic colleges, departments, and programs. While he has worked with academic programs and has met individually with students and has a general understanding of how academic advising works based on his experience as a student, there is a lot he has yet to learn.

Dane's supervisor, Pearl (she/her), has set up an extended one-on-one supervision meeting at the end of his first week of work. She asks him to bring questions to the meeting so that she can learn more about what he knows and what he feels he needs to know, and then Pearl can build training and meetings with campus partners around the list she has as well as Dane's list. Using the Institutional Intelligence Model, develop a list of questions that Dane might bring to his meeting with Pearl.

The Law

- What are the relevant legal issues in this scenario?
- What institutional policies, procedures, or processes are applicable in this scenario?

Ethics

- What are the relevant ethical issues in this scenario?
- What information would the characters need to make sound ethical decisions?

Identity

- How might characters' social identities affect how this scenario would unfold?
- How do the situation and the information you need change depending on the identities of those involved?

Scenario-Specific Questions

- Who are essential partners for Dane to meet?
- With what offices should Dane begin to build connections?
- Where might Dane go to find out about his campus to begin a list for Pearl?
- When would Dane want to meet with offices? (Which are most pressing, and which can wait?)
- Why might Pearl want Dane to bring ideas rather than her preparing a list without his input?
- How could this activity help Dane? How could it create issues for him in his new role?

Critical Scenario 9.2 When, Why, How

Co-Author: Brad Menard, Director of Housing and Residence Life, University of Toledo

Frank (he/him) is the area coordinator in charge of duty training for the resident assistants (RAs) and hall directors (HDs) on campus. Frank uses Behind Closed Doors (BCD) as an activity to help students process situations. RAs approach a room, knock on the door, and then address the situation inside. It could be a loud party, a roommate conflict, a student struggling with depression, or various other issues.

Rather than putting the first-year RAs on the spot, Frank decided that this year experienced staff (RAs and HDs) would be the responders, and first-year staff would be the actors performing a scene or situation. Frank develops the process using the Institutional Intelligence Model. Before the first scene, he asks staff to consider *who*, *what*, *where*, *when*, *why*, and *how* questions. He then allows the staff member confronting the scene to pause and ask for guidance or to bring in another staff member to assist. After the scene, the entire group uses the Institutional Intelligence Model to debrief.

The Law

- What are the relevant legal issues in this scenario?
- What institutional policies, procedures, or processes are applicable in this scenario?

Ethics

- What are the relevant ethical issues in this scenario?
- What information would the characters need to make sound ethical decisions?

Identity

- How might characters' social identities affect how this scenario would unfold?
- How do the situation and the information you need change depending on the identities of those involved?

Scenario-Specific Questions

- Whose interests does Frank center in his version of BCD (new staff, returning staff, residents, hall directors, others)?
- What are some Institutional Intelligence Model questions that Frank might use for the first part of BCD to help staff anticipate the experience as the incident unfolds and after the scene, during the debrief?
- Where might Frank encounter resistance?
- When might Frank want to share his ideas for changing BCD for this year's training?
- Why might Frank have decided to make the change to BCD?
- How might this BCD format challenge new staff? How might this BCD format challenge returning staff? How might Frank and his team connect these experiences to policies, procedures, laws, and ethics without overwhelming new staff? How might BCD be an experience that Frank and his team build on over the year to revisit or acknowledge changes on their campus?

Critical Scenario 9.3 When, Why, How

Co-Author: Wen Xi, Residence Director, Pace University

Elise (she/her) is a program coordinator in student activities and an advisor to the women's club softball team. One evening, she gets a call from Jennie (she/her), a team member, who says that another player was transported to the hospital because of an alcohol overdose. Jennie asks whether Elise can come to the hospital to be with her as they wait on more information about the other student.

The Law

- What are the relevant legal issues in this scenario?
- What institutional policies, procedures, or processes are applicable in this scenario?

Ethics

- What are the relevant ethical issues in this scenario?
- What information would the characters need to make sound ethical decisions?

Identity

- How might characters' social identities affect how this scenario would unfold?
- How do the situation and the information you need change depending on the identities of those involved?

Scenario-Specific Questions

- Who needs to know about this situation right away?
- What information does Elise need right away? What does Elise need to do to abide by university policies, procedures, and expectations?
- What campus partner relationships can Elise utilize to best support Jennie and the other student after the hospital transport?
- What are the possible consequences that Elise needs to consider before deciding to go to the hospital?
- Where can Jennie turn for help if she needs assistance managing the situation?
- When should Jennie notify the team, and what information can she share?
- Why might Elise wait to notify others at the university?
- How can the Institutional Intelligence Model help her navigate supporting Jennie, the hospitalized student, and the team?

Critical Scenario 9.4 When, Why, How

Co-Author: Meredith McDevitt, Ph.D. Student, Clemson University

Sally (she/her) is the campus Student Harm Intervention Team coordinator. The team has been following up after a tornado struck campus and damaged several academic and administrative buildings. While no one was hurt or injured, several people were displaced, and storms significantly disrupted students' experiences. The main areas affecting students' experiences beyond classroom buildings are damage done to the library, two dining halls on campus, and the student union.

As the campus moves into clean-up, repair, and rebuilding mode, how can Sally and her team use the Institutional Intelligence Model to identify the next steps that she and the team need to take to support students on campus?

The Law

- What are the relevant legal issues in this scenario?
- What institutional policies, procedures, or processes are applicable in this scenario?

Ethics

- What are the relevant ethical issues in this scenario?
- What information would the characters need to make sound ethical decisions?

Identity

- How might characters' social identities affect how this scenario would unfold?
- How do the situation and the information you need change depending on the identities of those involved?

Scenario-Specific Questions

- Who needs to be involved in recovery efforts? Who has the most pressing need?
- What information do Sally and the team need to collect to take action?
- Where have students and families been directed to get information about emergencies in the past? Where should resources be centralized?
- When might Sally and the team anticipate operations returning to normal?
- Why might Sally reach out to other institutions for help or guidance?
- How can Sally support her team through this work given that staff may be working extra hours?

Conclusion

You pick up the phone, and a student on the line says, "Something terrible happened, and people are hurt." Instinctively, you want to know who is hurt, what happened, where the students are, when it happened, why the student called you, and how you can help. This reaction is an example of the Institutional Intelligence Model in action. There are many other questions, but these help us know what action we might need to take immediately.

As you learn new roles, move to new campuses and communities, and face change, the Institutional Intelligence Model will serve you well. Even if you stay on the same campus for your entire career (rare but not impossible), your campus is constantly changing. Think about the questions and resources we have today that we did not have or utilize before the spring of 2020. While the pandemic was overwhelmingly negative and impacted so many people in so many ways, we developed new skills and strategies because of COVID-19. Furthermore, COVID-19 forever changed every single campus.

We must continually engage in our work with curiosity and a desire to learn. As soon as we stop, as soon as we are confident we "get it" and fully understand how things work, that is when we become stagnant. That is when we do harm. So ask questions. Seek to understand. It is the very best any of us can do in our work.

SECTION 3

Functional Areas and Critical Scenarios

10

STUDENT IDENTITY-BASED CENTERS AND SERVICES

> Based on my social identities, as a Latino gay male with an accent at a predominantly white institution, I felt the expectation from some of my peers, faculty, and staff members to engage in one identity-based center rather than others. For example, as a student, I was expected to be part of the LGBTQ+ Student Services Office; however, I was only engaged in the Multicultural Student Services Office because of the racism I experienced as a student of color.
>
> —Dr. Cristóbal Salinas Jr., Associate Professor, Florida Atlantic University

This chapter focuses on the diversity of student populations in higher education and how academic and student affairs practitioners can use the Institutional Intelligence Model to pursue inclusion and work toward equitable processes, opportunities, and outcomes for student populations. Hurtado (2007) wrote about the

> production of citizens for a multicultural society. This citizenship can produce leaders with greater social awareness and complex thinking skills to alleviate social problems related to inequality... [with a goal of] improving education for students from different racial, economic, and religious communities to achieve a pluralistic democracy.
>
> *(p. 193)*

Societal culture, economics, politics, and other realities impact students' experiences and learning. There are disparate effects of these realities on

DOI: 10.4324/9781003442707-13

students holding marginalized identities. This chapter outlines the vital work in this functional area and how to use the Institutional Intelligence Model to navigate emerging issues.

Chapter Organization

This chapter begins by examining current student demographics in higher education and the impact of more diverse students and student experiences in higher education. We move on to the role of practitioners and multicultural student services on campus for individual students and student groups/communities. Next, we examine how these staff members engage in significant work for the campus. Finally, this chapter includes a discussion on the range of social identities that students may hold to provide a foundation for future chapters. Students' identities inform their experiences across student and academic affairs. We must consider who the students are and learn about them as individuals to have the Institutional Intelligence necessary to connect them to opportunities and resources.

Legal and Ethical Considerations

So, what should you keep in mind and consider related to legal and ethical issues in the context of student identity-based centers? *It depends.* What is the political climate on your campus and in your state? What are students' concerns on your campus regarding accommodation, discrimination, harassment, racism, and safety informed by their social identities? The issues that students have in the classroom depend on the training that faculty get related to microaggressions, implicit bias, personal pronouns, and faculty members' willingness to enact an equitable classroom. The comfort and safety of students depend on facilities (e.g., gender-neutral bathrooms and classroom accessibility). Additional safety concerns include harassment, threats, and violence directed at students based on their identities (e.g., Asian and Asian-American students targeted during COVID, ongoing racist incidents directed at Black and Brown students, and women's safety on campus). Furthermore, there are legal and ethical considerations for the work that student identity-based centers and services do related to campus policy (e.g., housing assignments and campus policies affecting undocumented students).

Student identity-based center staff must navigate the law and campus policy even when it does not align with their ethics. It can be particularly challenging for staff to support students in the wake of local or national violence that disproportionately affects people who hold marginalized identities (e.g., shootings at the Pulse nightclub in Orlando, Tops Friendly Markets in Buffalo, the Tree of Life Synagogue in Pittsburgh, and Robb

Elementary School in Uvalde, Texas). When institutional leaders issue weak statements (or no statement at all) in response to these devastating events, students are left to wonder whether anyone cares about them. It is the center's staff who help students process those events. Therefore, staff must understand their institutional *who*, *what*, *where*, *when*, *why*, and *how* to effectively advocate for and support students.

Competencies

We begin our discussion of functional areas with student identity-based centers and services because the work done in these centers intersects with all of the American College Personnel Association/National Association of Student Personnel Administrators (ACPA/NASPA) professional competencies (see Appendix). For this chapter, however, we focus on Social Justice and Inclusion (SJI), Advising and Supporting (A/S), and Personal and Ethical Foundations (PEF). Because the centers in this chapter focus on student identities, how each of us individually and how our institutions collectively recognize, support, and celebrate these identities (or fail to do so) are central to students' campus experiences. Next, A/S is an essential competency in this area, given the significant connections that staff in these centers have with students. Finally, it is often by navigating unique, individual circumstances to support unique individual students that we develop in the PEF competency area. While other competencies are also relevant, these are the ones we encourage you to focus on in reading this chapter.

Student Demographics and Impact

College students from across the country and world are enrolled in colleges and universities and are changing the landscape of higher education in the United States. College students are diverse and have different goals, expectations, and learning preferences (Sharaievska & Harmon, 2021). As higher education practitioners, we must acknowledge that college students are changing demographically and in terms of their characteristics. Information from the National Center for Educational Statistics (2021), as seen in Table 10.1, highlights some of these demographic changes.

The percentage of racially and ethnically minoritized college students is increasing, "although this does not represent the ratio of the general population" (Sharaievska & Harmon, 2021, p. 1).

Students are changing the landscape of higher education's outcomes, culture, and policy. College students are diverse and bring their social identities, characteristics, and aspirations from home. While in college, they develop more expectations for their education and communities and set

TABLE 10.1 College Enrollment Rates of 18- to 24-Year-Olds by Race/Ethnicity: 2010 and 2019

Race	*2010 (%)*	*2019 (%)*	*Difference (%)*
White	43	41	−2
Black	38	36	−2
Hispanic	32	36	+4
Asian	64	62	−2
Pacific Islander	36	43	+7
American Indian	41	24	−17
Two or more races	38	47	+9
Total % of 18- to -24-year-olds enrolled	41	41	No change

Adapted from National Center for Educational Statistics (2021).

career, family, and personal goals (Vrontis & Thrassou, 2007). As we examine students' lives in higher education and the role of student affairs in support of students, we must acknowledge and continue to wrestle with our institutional histories and shortcomings.

Student populations change from campus to campus and dictate how an institution might be classified. For example, as we discussed in Chapter 8, an institution with 25% or more total undergraduate Hispanic or Latin* full-time equivalent student enrollment can be considered a Hispanic-serving institution. Women's colleges are single-sex institutions of higher education that admit only women students. Refer to Chapter 8 for more context on institutional types. Furthermore, students' characteristics can dictate institutions' unofficial classification and culture. For example, there are residential vs. non-residential campuses and traditional vs. fully online institutions, and some institutions might have a majority of part-time vs. full-time students. All these and many other characteristics influence how we engage with students.

In addition, social identities play a role in how we engage with students and how they engage with us, the campus, and programming. The National Survey of Student Engagement (n.d.) defines student engagement:

> Student engagement represents two critical features of collegiate quality—the amount of time and effort students put into their studies and other educationally purposeful activities, and how the institution deploys its resources and organizes the curriculum and other learning opportunities to get students to participate in activities that decades of research studies show are linked to student learning.
>
> *(para. 1)*

Student engagement has helped student affairs practitioners provide college experiences that support students' learning.

However, engagement opportunities are not one-size-fits-all. Like other activities, processes, policies, and structures on college campuses, not every approach to engagement serves all racial and ethnic groups equally well. Some initiatives can marginalize specific student populations (Museus et al., 2019). Therefore, we must consider how students self-identify when working with student populations. There is a great deal of variety among student identities, including intersections between race, ethnicity, gender, sexual orientation, age, socioeconomic status, (dis)ability, religion, faith, body type, immigration status, first-generation status, transfer, residential, non-residential, part-time, full-time, distance learners, traditional, and non-traditional. It is part of the work of higher education to foster communities where students are welcome, safe, and able to thrive regardless of the identities they hold and the backgrounds they bring to college.

The Role of Practitioners

Academic and student affairs practitioners are educators. As educators, we teach, research, and practice who we are (Hinojosa & De León-Zepeda, 2019). In other words, "we do human work" (García & Hinojosa, 2020, p. 297). For student-facing practitioners, we teach in formal settings (classes) and facilitate out-of-class learning opportunities through leadership development, career counseling, conduct meetings, and student organization communities.

Nevertheless, as Stewart (2011) wrote, "College life and administration continue to reflect the nation's bigotry and oppression" (p. 2). There continue to be systemic issues in society, and higher education is a microcosm of society that privileges some and disadvantages others. Whether intentionally designed or perpetuated through tradition and practice, these issues perpetuate inequity and injustice in and beyond college and university campuses. As we work to address these long-standing issues, we must utilize a variety of approaches, instruments, tools, and ways of innovative thinking to create sustainable change. The Institutional Intelligence Model provides an approach to include in the work to create equitable processes, opportunities, and outcomes for all students.

Just as history and the past inform our work, so do current events. We must constantly assess and adapt how we engage with students about issues and trends. For example, higher education and students' concerns looked dramatically different before the spring of 2020 than in the fall of 2022 because of the COVID-19 pandemic. The pandemic has change students engage inside and outside the classroom. We likely will not know the full impact of the pandemic for decades to come, but we need to continue to assess, adapt as new situations emerge, and apply what we are learning.

Chapters 2 and 3 of this book list historical events and legal cases that changed how we engage with students and how they engage with higher education. So students change, the environment and community change, and laws also change the higher education landscape. Because students are often changing, what happens when higher education fails to provide them with what they need? Additionally, what is the role of student wants and demands that go beyond their fundamental needs? We need only look at recent new residence halls and the amenities included to get a sense of the impact of student demands and expectations on some campuses.

Who is responsible for student engagement and success? What can we do to balance student wants with fiscal realities in higher education? Where do we utilize resources to make the most important differences in higher education? How can we make positive and transformative changes in the political contexts on our campuses? When do we address all of the demands on our time? Why is our specific institution where it is today? How do we not simply avoid failing students in our roles—how do we set them up for success and the ability to thrive? These are a sampling of the Institutional Intelligence questions we must ask as we seek to support and engage with the diverse students in higher education. Each of these has ethical and potentially legal implications for resource allocation as well as care and support of students, staff, and faculty.

Not all students are the same; they have different experiences and work toward individual goals. Furthermore, when students encounter obstacles, we must consider what institutional factors may be part of the problem. Using Institutional Intelligence to examine systemic issues critically helps us find gaps in personal, cultural, and institutional knowledge. For example, Patton (2019) wrote that student engagement work has historically focused on white students at historically white institutions. She encouraged us to consider the following: "1) Who are the students? 2) In what are they engaging? 3) Where is the engagement occurring? and 4) With whom are they engaging?" (Patton, 2019, p. xiii). Therefore, it is critical for student affairs practitioners to be aware of, respect, and validate students' social identities to serve them better and create learning opportunities. Furthermore, the Institutional Intelligence Model is valuable for fostering student engagement and identifying resources. By asking *who*, *what*, *where*, *when*, *why*, and *how* questions, we can better understand what an institution does and whom it serves.

Our job is to give students the tools to engage locally, nationally, and globally (Sasso & DeVitis, 2015). Therefore, we must create an inclusive and diverse community, a wide range of engagement opportunities, diverse educational pathways, and customized individual support to retain students. Higher education has built cultural and identity-based centers to develop safe spaces for diverse student populations. However, this work is complex. As Jenkins and Walton (2008) wrote, "Cultural practitioners have dual roles as educators and programmers. They do more than educate audiences on culture—they critically understand the architecture of various cultures and replicate, enact, and engage these experiences on campus" (p. 89). With these crucial roles in mind, this chapter provides an overview of different offices and departments that are the hub for many students with marginalized identities. In addition, this chapter presents different centers/offices that focus on supporting under-represented and systematically excluded students. Finally, this chapter highlights how this model can be used to address legal and ethical issues in higher education.

Multicultural Student Services

Multicultural Student Service offices have been part of colleges and universities dating back to the 1960s during the civil rights movement when Black students demanded that predominantly white institutions (PWIs) provide academic and cultural support and create inclusive change (Patton, 2010; Patton et al., 2011). Historically, Multicultural Student Services focused mainly on providing services for Black and Chicano students (Stewart, 2011). However, over the years, Multicultural Student Services have emerged as race and ethnicity cultural centers for Black/African-American, Latin*, Asian, and Native American Indian groups on college campuses (Patton, 2010; Stewart, 2011).

Multicultural Student Services has continued to support Students of Color and other marginalized student groups at the academic and cultural levels. These offices and staff have been at the entry and support point for many marginalized groups in higher education. Historically, Multicultural Student Services engaged with and created support for students who hold identities beyond race and ethnicity. For example, some Multicultural Student Services focused on LBGTQ+ student populations, others on inter/faith/religious identities and first-generation students. Other student group identities, such as women, international students, and students with disabilities, have historically been under-represented and systematically excluded in higher education. Many institutions have created centers to support students who hold these identities.

Multicultural Student Services is part of campus culture and history. Museus and Jayakumar (2012) noted that campus culture shapes students' experiences. Additionally, Multicultural Student Services can shape students' experiences (Stewart, 2011). In this chapter, we do not intend to homogenize all student populations by noting that they all are part of Multicultural Student Services. Instead, we introduce a range of identity-based student services designed to promote the success of diverse students on campus and better serve identity-based student groups. We also acknowledge that these identities intersect, creating both power and oppression. We must recognize the services provided at each institution to better support students, faculty, and staff.

Shared purposes across cultural centers include providing space where racially minoritized students can find community and support to navigate the larger campus community, particularly at PWIs (Liu et al., 2010; Patton, 2010; Yosso & Lopez, 2010). These spaces also serve as spaces that affirm and empower the value of historically under-represented and marginalized Students of Color on campuses (Yosso & Lopez, 2010) and serve as resource spaces for cultural knowledge (Liu et al., 2010). Additionally, cultural centers support the recruitment and retention of Students of Color (Foote, 2005; Shuford, 2011), help improve campus climate (Harper & Hurtado, 2007), and help educate the campus as a whole (Liu et al., 2010; Shuford, 2011).

Racial and Ethnic Cultural Centers

While multicultural centers serve a variety of student cultures on campus, specific centers focusing on students' identities are also important. Benitez (2010) wrote that as student composition changes, leaders must "continually revisit the fluidity of student enrollment and the newly created campus climate dynamics cultivated through these phenomena" (p. 122). Cultural centers have historically served as a "home away from home" for Students of Color (Patton, 2006). With this in mind, we set out to provide a cursory overview of centers on campus and their role in law, ethics, and student "learning and growth."

African-American Cultural Centers

The first African-American cultural center, The Center, was founded in 1969 at Rutgers University-New Brunswick (Patton, 2010; Rutgers University, 2022a). The center supported African-American students entering Rutgers University (2022b). In 1972, The Center was named the Paul Robeson Cultural Center after the singer, actor, athlete, and civil rights activist who was the third African American to graduate from Rutgers University (2022b). The Paul Robeson Cultural Center encourages students "to consider the complexities of their identity while celebrating Blackness in all of its expressions and embodying the founding legacies of academic excellence and intersectional social justice" (Rutgers University, 2022a, para. 1).

Black and African-American cultural centers "provide important university support and services, such as advising, career development, mentoring, and leadership skill building" (Sanders, 2016, p. 30) and space for students to "cope with a hostile, unfriendly or indifferent campus environment" (Foote, 2005, p. 191). The centers emerged as the number of Black and African-American students increased on college campuses through the 1960s (Patton, 2005). These centers serve many needs of students and campuses, including fostering community and belonging for Black students (Bennett, 1971), providing social support (Patton, 2005, 2006; Pittman, 1994; Young & Hannon, 2002), enhancing campus climate (Pittman, 1994) and student recruitment, transition, and retention (Patton, 2005, 2006; Pittman, 1994), and educating the broader campus (Shuford, 2011). These spaces provide Black and African-American students a community and support among peers and staff with shared identities within the larger campus community.

Asian American Cultural Centers

In 1968, following the Asian Political Alliance formation at the University of California at Berkeley—the first organization to use the term "Asian American" (Lee, 2015)—other Asian-American organizations and the first centers emerged on college campuses. The first Asian American Studies Center was founded in 1969 at the University of California at Los Angeles (UCLA) by students, alumni, and faculty during the Asian American Movement (Patton, 2010). The Asian American Studies Center published books on Asian American studies and is the home to the *Amerasia Journal*, founded in 1971 as the first journal to focus on Asian Americans (UCLA, 2019a). The Asian American Studies Center's mission is to "Expand our scholarly capabilities and deepen the public understanding of Asian-American and Pacific Islander lives towards a healthy, just, democratic, and compassionate society for all" (UCLA, 2019b, para. 1).

In addition to fulfilling the purposes for all cultural centers outlined earlier in this chapter, Asian American Cultural Centers facilitate intragroup interactions as a step toward fostering coalition-building (Liu et al., 2010). More recently, these centers have become sites to help address increasing violence against Asian and Asian-American students (Gonzalez, 2022).

Latino Cultural Centers

The first Latin* cultural center was *Aquí Estoy* (Here I am) at Northeastern Illinois University (NIU) in 1969 (Patton, 2010). *Aquí Estoy* initially opened "to serve as a field center with a focus on teaching English as a

Second Language (ESL) to Puerto Rican students" (Northeastern Illinois University, 2022, para. 4). In 1973, *Aquí Estoy* was renamed *Comunidad Latino Adelantando Sus Estudios Secundarios* (CLASES) to promote academic and community development for Hispanic/Latin* communities in Chicago. In 1975, NIU recognized *El Centro de Recursos Educativos* (Center for Educational Services), known as *"El Centro." El Centro* supports community-based academic programs for college credit. Its mission is "to provide educational opportunity for Chicago's diverse mix of cultures, coming together in an academic setting that serves as an affirming educational bridge to the promise of the future" (Northeastern Illinois University, 2022, para. 11).

Latino cultural centers provide students with a social network of staff and peers that support the link between ethnic identity and acculturation to higher education (Evans et al., 1998; Torres et al., 2003). These centers provide "cultural nourishment" (Gonzalez, 2000, p. 82). For Latin* students, these centers provide "an environment that is centrally focused on their culture" (Cheesman et al., 2008, p. 18) and space to see others who share their identities as leaders. As with other centers, these spaces provide community, a reprieve from the larger campus, resources, and opportunities for individual growth and development.

Native American Cultural Centers

American Indian peoples attended the University of North Dakota (UND) as early as 1968 (Kozel, 2008). In the same year, students from surrounding reservations and rural American Indian communities created the University of North Dakota Indian Association (UNDIA), a campus student organization. UND developed programs for Native American students to support them academically and culturally. The first Native American cultural center, American Indian Center, was formed in 1971 (Kozel, 2008; Patton, 2010). The American Indian Center is called "Anashinobay Aki," which means "Land of the Original People" in Chippewa (Kozel, 2008).

It is important to remember the historic atrocities perpetuated by the European education system established in the United States and Native communities. Early colonizer efforts focused on social assimilation at best, eradication, and genocide in many instances. Assimilation through education was a means of erasure of Indigenous identity, which in part has fostered tribes not valuing what Western institutions had or have to offer (Shotton et al., 2010).

For Native students who choose to attend PWIs, Native American centers provide support around alienation and racism through spaces that reinforce Indigenous culture and values (Guillory, 2009; Shotton et al., 2010).

This support is vital for Indigenous students who often do not have access to student services or mentorship programs since those students are such a small group on most campuses. Other essential but absent support for Indigenous students includes culturally safe spaces, Native American student organizations, and cultural activities (Wintermute, 2021).

Other Identity-Based Student Services

Student services in higher education provide students with academic and cultural support and often an inclusive space or culture (Patton et al., 2011). Student services can also motivate students to engage with student services offices or organizations (Guiffrida et al., 2012). In addition, student services support students from different backgrounds, create cultures and traditions, and promote student success. Additionally, student services offered on campus reflect an institution's priorities and goals. As student demographics shift and institutions evolve, student services should adapt to meet the needs of contemporary student populations.

Each university has different student demographics, goals, and priorities. Therefore, student services and centers are limited in what they can offer a university. The Institutional Intelligence Model can guide us to uncover other services and centers that institutions lack. We also acknowledge that the names of these services, centers, spaces, and units can change. Again, Institutional Intelligence is not stagnant. We must continue learning, relearning, and unlearning as students, campuses, communities, and social change.

International Students Services

International students have been studying in the United States since the 1850s. Yung Wing was the first student from China to graduate from a university in the United States (Yale University) (Jou, 2022). Yung helped create the first education exchange program with China in the US.

In 1952, the US government began the F-1 student visa (University of Wisconsin-Madison, 2022). Along with this change came an increased need for support of international students in higher education. International student services "support international students in their academic, social, and cultural transition" (Pérez-Encinas & Ammigan, 2016). International Student Support Services (ISSS) must have adequate resources to foster an inclusive campus student experience (Briggs & Ammigan, 2017). These functions include support in orientation programming, academics, health and wellness, and housing. Additionally, ISSS can be an essential partner with other student affairs units to support intercultural training

(Briggs & Ammigan, 2017). That said, the specific context, organization, and staffing models are unique to each office on each campus, again calling for Institutional Intelligence when building partnerships around programming and policy with ISSS.

Lesbian, Gay, Bisexual, Transgender, and Queer Centers

In 1966, the Student Homophile League, which became Queer Alliance, the first gay student organization in the country, was founded at Columbia University (Columbia University, 2021). In 1970, the University of Michigan recognized the Gay Liberation Front (GLF) and the Radical Lesbians as student organizations. GLF asked the administration for physial space to host a statewide conference. However, the University of Michigan president "denied the request, stating that homosexual activity was illegal, that a conference would necessitate the presence of the police, and that the conference was not educationally-oriented enough to use university space" (Burris, 2022, para. 2).

After pressure from student organizations and other students, the first LGBTQ center, Human Sexuality Office, was established in September 1971 at the University of Michigan (Burris, 2022; Sanlo et al., 2002). Two quarter-time Human Sexuality Advocates staffed the office (Spectrum Center, n.d.). The staff advocated for changes to make the curriculum more LGBT-inclusive, address community concerns, and get counselors and other university staff training on LGBT issues. The team also developed peer advisors and a speakers' bureau to attend classes and train residence life staff (Spectrum Center, n.d.).

LGBT offices have expanded in the past 50 years, and paid staff or graduate students support LGBT students on about 200 campuses (Postsecondary National Policy Institute, 2021). Beginning in the 1990s, educating others to foster a broader and complete understanding of sexuality and gender was part of the work done in centers on college campuses. This understanding included adding bisexuality and other queer- and trans-spectrum identities and experiences (Rankin et al., 2019). The work of these centers has increased visibility and understanding, impacting programming and campus policies.

Student Accessibility Services

People with disabilities and parents of children with disabilities had advocated for people with disabilities long before the Americans with Disabilities Act (Mayers, 1992). The disabilities rights movement secured equal opportunities and rights for people with disabilities. According to Elmer and colleagues (2018), "Many disabled students don't learn about disability as a community they are connected to and an identity to celebrate until and unless they encounter disability history and culture in college" (n.p.). In the wake of the civil rights movement in the 1960s and 1970s, colleges and universities engaged more actively in providing services for students with disabilities. In 1990, congress signed the Americans with Disabilities Act into law. The University of Minnesota established the Disabled Students Cultural Center (DSCC) the following year. Later, Syracuse University and the University of Washington established similar cultural centers (Elmore et al., 2018). It is important to note that centers are not the same as accessibility accommodations offices, although the areas may intersect. According to Elmore et al. (2018), today's students

> [w]ant a connection to the disability community and disability culture in college. When safer spaces devoted to supporting disability identity and culture on campus become part of the institutional landscape, students with disabilities will be less isolated and more integrated with campus life. *(para. 11)*

The authors add, "While similarities between centers exist, each center is as unique as the campus context from which it emerges" (Elmore et al., 2018, para. 12). This statement affirms an Institutional Intelligence approach to working with this group of students.

Women's Centers

In 1960, the Minnesota Plan for the Continuing Education of Women became the first women's center in the US. Its mission was "to address the needs of women whose education had been interrupted by marriage and motherhood" (University of Minnesota, 2023, para. 5). The center was renamed the Women's Center to specify and advance gender equity across identities. The Women's Center's mission is to "educate and inspire feminist leaders, advance an empowering intellectual environment, and advocate for an equitable University culture and community" (The Women's Center, 2022, para. 1).

A women's center is a place for women to share spaces, information, and support to ensure that women- and gender-related topics are centered and visible in higher education institutions. Byrne (2000) identified several roles that women's centers play on college campuses. These include enhancing learning, promoting community service and political activism, programming, intellectual empowerment, and peer support. Davie (2002) added that women's centers navigate the ongoing tension between "binding wounds" and "changing the world." In many ways, this speaks to helping the individual navigate what they are facing (binding wounds) and addressing systemic issues of power and equity on campus and in the larger community and society. Women's centers are also spaces of support and partnership with curricular and academic initiatives such as feminist pedagogy, partnership with academic programs, women's lecture series, and internship experiences (Byrne, 2000).

Today, many women's centers are wrestling with their legacies as spaces grounded in "white, middle-class feminist praxis" (de la Peña et al., 2018, p. 118). Those same scholars ask, "how can women-centered spaces incorporate an intentional race and class analysis within an intersectional feminist practice?" (de la Peña et al., 2018, pp. 120–121). Goettsch et al. (2018) also highlighted inclusivity, intersectionality, and social justice, merging identity centers and renaming them so that women's and gender centers can continue their work. The authors wrote, "they must understand their institution's current and projected context and politics and the current and future needs and concerns of their constituents" (Goettsch et al., 2018, p. 16). This need to understand campus context is an example of how the Institutional Intelligence Model can support the work of these and other centers. For example, the politics on a campus with an established women's center that has a history of events, programming, and campus and community partnerships is going to be different from the politics on a campus that has no established center but that is looking to create such a resource for students.

Additional Areas

There are social identities beyond those in this chapter. Some innovative centers emerging in higher education include those serving commuter students, first-generation college students, students who are parents, students with housing or food insecurity, transfer students, and student veterans. Each of these centers has their own areas of focus and legal and ethical issues that they must navigate. Legal issues might include federal guidelines or campus policies. Ethical issues can range from equitable distribution of resources to the ways in which we attend holistically to students—or how we fail to do so. Nonetheless, institutions still have work to do to make higher education welcoming for all.

Institutional Intelligence Questions

Who: Who is missing from this chapter? Who is absent from your campus conversations? Whom is your institution failing to serve? Who decides who is invited to conversations? Who is legally obligated to certain tasks or accountable in terms of institutional policy, practice, procedures, or processes?

What: What visible and invisible social identities do students hold? What identities do you hold? What is the history of centers on your campus? What are the political challenges for centers on your campus? What legal obligations do students, staff, faculty, administrators, and institutions have to one another and the larger community/society?

Where: Where do new students go to find community? Where do you provide information about centers on campus? Where are the student identity-based services and centers physically located?

When: When do students learn about institutional support and services? When are different centers open, and do those hours meet student needs? When do you collect student feedback on the services that centers provide? When do students make the most use of the centers (times of the semester, academic year, time of day)? When are reviews conducted to ensure that policies and practices follow campus guidelines? What other legal implications do centers have—for example, abiding by grant requirements for some areas or projects?

Why: Why do you partner with centers? Why do you not partner with centers? Why do different units and offices partner with centers? Why do centers partner with one another (or not)? Why do students say that they engage with centers (or not)?

How: How do students engage with centers in person, virtually, or in other ways? How can institutional leaders, faculty, and staff practice inclusive excellence to support minoritized student populations through partnerships with centers? How are centers making primary contributions on campus (social programming, educational programming, training, policy)? How does the staffing in each center on your campus meet the needs of students (or not)? How are resources allocated to different centers on your campus? How is ongoing assessment incorporated into centers' work to make sure goals and objectives are met and internal and external guidelines are being followed?

Critical Scenarios

Because of the importance of identity, community, and support, we are providing three critical scenarios in this chapter to give you opportunities to engage with different aspects of who students are. We encourage you to consider how these scenarios might change on the basis of students holding different or additional identities.

Critical Scenario 10.1 Student Identity-Based Centers and Services

Co-Author: J'Lissabeth Faughn, Director of LGBTQ* Resources, University of Kentucky

Fawn (they/them) is a new student on campus in the first few weeks of the fall term. They were very active in high school and their hometown community around justice and equity issues. Fawn wants to get involved with organizations celebrating their biracial and gender-fluid identities. After the first week of classes, Fawn also set up appointments on and off campus to identify and secure resources related to a recently identified learning disability. Rather than being frustrated by the newly identified cognitive/learning disability, Fawn hopes to find a community and learn more about this new aspect of who they are.

At an academic advising meeting, after discussing how Matt (he/him) can help Fawn with the accommodation process and get them connected to offices and resources on campus, Fawn says, "Can I ask you about a question that isn't about classes?"

"Of course," Matt replies, excited that he has built some rapport and trust with this new student.

"There are a couple of student organizations I really want to participate in. Two of them meet on the same day at the same time, and the learning disability meetings conflict with one of my classes. I'm not sure what to do since they are all important to me and are all organizations discussing issues about who I am and the communities I want to be involved with. What should I do?" Fawn pauses and adds, "There is one other thing."

Fawn goes on to share that yesterday when they were in the LGBTQI+ office on campus, there was an incident. They were in the lounge space with some friends when a student came in and started taking photos on his cell phone. When the desk worker confronted the student and said he was not allowed to take photos in the space, he yelled. "I don't even want to be here, but I have to come here to learn about resources for this stupid intro class!" The coordinator talked with the student, but Fawn is not sure what happened with the pictures the student took.

The Law

- What are the relevant legal issues in this scenario?

- What institutional policies, procedures, or processes are applicable in this scenario?

Ethics

- What are the relevant ethical issues in this scenario?
- What information would the characters need to make sound ethical decisions?

Identity

- How might characters' social identities affect how this scenario would unfold?
- How do the situation and the information you need change depending on the identities of those involved?

Scenario-Specific Questions

- To whom might Matt reach out to get more information for Fawn? Who would have the authority to change organizational meeting times? Who is advising the organizations that Fawn wants to join?
- What additional information does Matt need from Fawn about the organizations to provide the best help? Are there things he should not ask?
- Where does the university keep information about student organizations? Where can Matt refer Fawn to get more information?
- When does Matt need to respond to Fawn? When do student organizational meetings begin during the fall term?
- Why might the meetings for some organizations be scheduled at the same time?
- How are organizational meeting times decided? How are those times communicated to members? How does this scenario change based on what identities Fawn holds? How does the scenario potentially change based on the identities that Matt holds?

In what other ways can characters utilize the Institutional Intelligence Model in this scenario, and what additional questions should they be asking?

Critical Scenario 10.2 Student Identity-Based Centers and Services

Co-Author: Jared Logan, Assistant Director, New Student and Family Programs, Florida State University

Donney (he/him), a second-semester first-year student and a Black queer man at a predominantly white institution, decided to join a Latino-based fraternity he had recently learned about. He joined the Latino-based fraternity, the only multicultural fraternity on campus, to build community among the other fraternity members. In addition to joining the fraternity, Donney was engaged with the Multicultural Student Affairs (MSA) Office. He created a sense of connectedness and belonging with the MSA staff, students, and programming.

During Donney's sophomore year, he heard from a friend that a Black fraternity would be established on campus the following semester. He wanted to learn more about the Black fraternity and approached John (he/his), a staff member who told him of the Fraternity and Sorority Life Office. John told him, "Once you affiliate with an organization, that's it. You can't switch to another fraternity."

Donney went to get advice from Joyce, a staff member in MSA. Joyce suggested that maybe Donney should connect more with the LGBTQ+ student organization on campus as a new avenue to engage and not think about the Black fraternity.

The Law

- What are the relevant legal issues in this scenario?
- What institutional policies, procedures, or processes are applicable in this scenario?

Ethics

- What are the relevant ethical issues in this scenario?
- What information would the characters need to make sound ethical decisions?

Identity

- How might characters' social identities affect how this scenario would unfold?
- How do the situation and the information you need change depending on the identities of those involved?

Scenario-Specific Questions

- Who else might be a helpful resource for Donney? Who has the final say about whether or not Donney can join the Black fraternity?
- What other information would you need about the situation to help and support Donney? What units should be involved in this critical scenario? What policies might be relevant to this situation?
- Where might Donney go for meaningful support to validate all of his social identities?
- When do students learn about the support and services that an institution has to offer them? When are students expected to make decisions about which organizations to join? When can students decide to no longer engage with organizations?
- Why might a student want to leave one organization for another? Why would there be restrictions on organizational affiliation? Why might these restrictions be different for fraternities and sororities than for other campus groups or clubs?

How else can Donney use the Institutional Intelligence Model in this scenario?

Critical Scenario 10.3 Student Identity-Based Centers and Services

Co-Author: Anna Pietrzak (she/her), Residence Hall Coordinator, University of Delaware

Sydney (she/her) and Victoria (she/her) are roommates, and both are involved in the Women's Center on campus. At a recent Women's Center Advisory Board meeting (for which both Sydney and Victoria are representatives), the Director, Fiona (she/her), announced that the center might be changing its name. The Howard Women's Center is named for one of the first female graduates of the institution. She became a Dean of Women in the early years of the university when it became coeducational.

The center will now be called the Perez Gender Equity Center. Sydney and Victoria are excited about the center being named for a recently retired faculty member actively engaged in campus social justice and equity work. Dr. Perez served as the Director of the Women's Center for more than 10 years before moving into a faculty role.

However, Sydney and Victoria disagree about changing from "Women's Center" to "Gender Equity Center." Sydney feels that by giving up "Women's Center," the center will not serve women on campus in the same holistic ways it currently does. She told Victoria, "Changing it to a gender center waters down the work and again pushes women lower on the priority list."

Victoria disagrees. She then adds, "I think that a Gender Equity Center expands the community, potentially increases resources, and is a much more socially just approach to issues on our campus."

The disagreement, debate, and tension have gotten so intense that their resident assistant (RA), Doris has asked the hall director, Jeremy (he/his), to do a roommate mediation.

The Law

- What are the relevant legal issues in this scenario?
- What institutional policies, procedures, or processes are applicable in this scenario?

Ethics

- What are the relevant ethical issues in this scenario?
- What information would the characters need to make sound ethical decisions?

Identity

- How might characters' social identities affect how this scenario would unfold?
- How do the situation and the information you need change depending on the identities of those involved?

Scenario-Specific Questions

- Who else might Jeremy reach out to before meeting with the students? Whom might the students want present for the meeting?
- What is the catalyst for the RA requesting this meeting? What other factors might Jeremy want to ask about during the meeting with the residents? What is the role of the identity of each roommate in this process? What role do Jeremy's identities play in this scenario?
- Where might Jeremy turn for resources before having the meeting? Where might he look for possible resources to offer depending on how the conversation goes?
- When should Jeremy meet with the students? When should he and they expect a resolution to the situation?
- Why is the RA, rather than the residents, requesting this meeting? Why might each student have the opinion she does about this issue?
- How might the resolution of the roommate situation affect women's center advisory board meetings? How might the resolution affect their living dynamic? How might Jeremy prepare for the meeting in terms of preparing questions, choosing a meeting location, and developing a facilitation plan?

How can the Institutional Intelligence Model help Jeremy prepare for and navigate this conflict?

Conclusion

There are various legal and ethical issues that we must navigate as we serve students. The history that higher education has with students (and staff and faculty) who hold marginalized identities is problematic. As we work to do better today and in the future, we must bear in mind the past and how that past continues to affect law and policy on campus. Ethically, we are obligated to ongoing reflection related to our work and our own identities. We must respect students and their expertise, lived experiences, and identities to support and advocate for them effectively.

As you consider the information in this chapter, we ask that you consider what may be missing. Ask yourself the following questions to build your Institutional Intelligence related to student identity centers in higher education.

- What student identity-based centers and services are we missing?
- What student identity-based centers and services does your campus have?

- What social identities are silent and often marginalized or overlooked on your campus?
- How have student needs related to identity-based centers changed in the past five years? Ten years? Two years?
- How have student centers changed in recent years regarding staffing, funding, and ways of engaging with students and campus?

This chapter shows how identity-based centers emerged—many in the first five years after the passage of the 1965 Civil Rights Act. These centers provide support to students who have historically been excluded from higher education on the basis of the social identities they hold. As the law continues to evolve on issues of student diversity on campus, it is important to pay attention to decisions related to affirmative action. The ripple effect of these decisions remains to be seen in the context of student centers. We must pay attention to current cases such as those related to student organizations and who is afforded membership or allowed to be excluded (e.g., Business Leaders in Christ [BLinC] v. the University of Iowa) and affirmative action on campus (e.g., Students for Fair Admissions, Inc. v. President and Fellows of Harvard College). The ripple effect of these cases on identity-based centers remains to be seen.

We encourage you to consider identity in *all* of the critical scenarios throughout this book. The resources available, the student needs, and the strategies we use to support different individuals depend on who those individuals are and what they need. We have designed these scenarios for you to consider whatever identities are most salient to the conversation you want to have. Changing the identities that people in these scenarios hold can complicate the situations differently. You may find different needs and identify gaps in resources depending on the students, staff, and faculty involved.

11

ADMISSIONS, FINANCIAL AID, AND ORIENTATION

> There are few, if any, better paths out of generational poverty than higher education. Studies estimate the additional lifetime income at over $1 million for a college graduate versus someone with only a high school diploma. We in enrollment management have an obligation to find, and in some cases make up for, the disadvantages that students face based on what high school they attend, what race, ethnicity, nationality, sex, or gender they identify with, and what zip code they were born into. We are the gatekeepers to that path, and the decisions we make every day have the ability to change lives.
>
> —Dr. Chuck Knepfle, Vice President for Enrollment Management, Portland State University

College preparation, access, and navigating higher education begin before admissions. Often, students are influenced by P-12 education and family to think about their goals and career aspirations in college. For many students and families, navigating the admissions application, orientation, and financial aid processes are some elements and markers for students to begin to see themselves as college students. Therefore, we forefront admissions, financial aid, and orientation as the first functional areas highlighted in this text. As students complete college and university admission applications, apply for financial aid, get an admissions acceptance letter, attend an orientation program, and enroll for classes, they put themselves "out there" as people who wish to earn a college degree. This can be personally and financially overwhelming for first-generation and other students.

DOI: 10.4324/9781003442707-14

Chapter Organization

This chapter includes sections on admissions, financial aid, and orientation programs. Each section includes a brief history followed by the role of staff today. Admissions programs have been scrutinized throughout the history of higher education. It is incumbent upon us to engage in ongoing critique and reflection partnered with identifying strategies and solutions to emerging issues. Financial aid has opened the door to college access for students who would not otherwise be able to participate. Again, there are issues (as with every area in higher education), and a goal is for us to wrestle with those issues to find access strategies that are more equitable.

In doing this, we must navigate multiple ethical issues. These include large-scale issues and concerns such as the role of donor contributions. Other ethical issues include the role of standardized testing in college admissions, college student debt, and the role of race-based admissions practices in higher education.

Finally, orientation programs are the welcome wagon of higher education. This work, along with welcome week activities and new student programming, requires partnering with the entire university and potential students and their families to successfully welcome and transition students to campus. Ethical considerations in this area of higher education include student safety, access to and transparency of information, the Family Educational Rights and Privacy Act (FERPA), and ethical considerations of potential corporate partnerships.

Legal and Ethical Considerations

Where do high school students want to go to college? *It depends* on academic experience/future goals, cost, personal and family capital and experiences, and fit. Each of these connects to the functional areas in this chapter. Academic and student affairs practitioners have a range of legal and ethical obligations to (potential) students, families, institutions, and external stakeholders. For example, university policy and federal and state law significantly structure the work of admissions and financial aid staff. Orientation issues intersect with accessibility, accommodations, safety, facilities, and student well-being. The role of parents can be significant in all three of these areas.

From an ethical standpoint, the admissions staff must consider the individual admissions decisions and how these decisions create the university community. Institutional diversity, legacy students, donors, and other factors affect equity on campus and in society. Furthermore, financial aid ethics include additional ethical considerations related to student debt. Orientation programs are some of the first spaces where students assess their sense of belonging on campus. And the degree to which undergraduate orientation leaders cultivate inclusion is essential for individual students and has implications for the institution. The decisions that orientation and new student program staff make about the experience that they create have implications beyond the time that students and families participate in the program. Therefore, legal and ethical considerations must be at the forefront of admissions, financial aid, and orientation programs.

Competencies

Access and transition to higher education deal with complex issues. Whom colleges and universities admit as students has implications related to Advising and Supporting (A/S); Values, Philosophy, and History (VPH); Law, Policy, and Governance (LPG); and Social Justice and Inclusion (SJI). We must consider the history and how it has laid the foundation for admissions and financial aid policies and processes. The SJI competency (see Appendix) inspires us to consider innovative ways to work toward equity and justice in the context of college access. Finally, admissions, financial aid, and orientation staff play some of the university's most critical A/S roles. We recruit, encourage, and welcome students into our new higher education experiences. If we do not excel in that work, the students will not even get started, let alone persist to graduation from college.

Admissions

Harvard established its first admission policies in 1642, six years after it opened. Early on, college students "were examined as to their character, background, and demonstrated proficiency in Latin and Greek. Later, toward the end of the eighteenth century... a working knowledge of arithmetic was added" (Beale, 1970). As Neklason (2019) put it:

> In the school's earliest decades, wealthy white students were not just privileged in admissions; they were essentially the only ones considered... When it was first founded, Harvard based its admissions decisions on subjective judgments of students' character and family background and their proficiency in Latin and Greek.
>
> *(para. 4)*

The Scholastic Assessment Test (SAT)—formerly the Scholastic Aptitude Test—was first administered in 1901 and focused on essay questions on subjects such as Greek, Latin, and physics. The exam took place over five days. Following the influx of students after World War II, the SAT became enmeshed in higher education culture. This was a result of a string of events starting with Alfred Binet's development of a test to quantify intelligence in 1905, U.S. military aptitude testing during World War I, a National Education Association (NEA) endorsement for standardized testing in 1914, and the application of high-speed computing to testing in 1935 (National Education Association, 2020). However, we continue to make "subjective judgments" about admissions on the basis of legacy status, donor relationships with the university, and the prestige of an applicant's high school.

It was not until the late 1940s through the mid-1950s that college entrance requirements were standardized. At that time, colleges and universities began basing admissions on the following:

- High school graduation and class rank
- A minimum number of credits in specific subjects
- A recommendation from the principal
- Personal interview
- Achievement test scores

Critiquing began as early as the 1920s, after the introduction of IQ tests. The main concerns were that the tests measured cultural conditioning rather than intelligence as a biological trait and that no single human ability was more important than all others. Additionally, people feared that "IQ tests could be misused to classify millions of young people as mentally inferior and so to deny them opportunity" (Lemann, 1995, para. 6). In 1948, scholars critiqued standardized tests' social class and racial bias: "Both the tests and the schools are caught in a circular kind of educational philosophy" (Davis & Havinghurst, 1948, p. 302). The authors contended that if we say only certain things matter and design tests to examine knowledge of those things and call that an intelligence test, then we will identify people who conform to the limited definition of intelligence, not intelligent people.

Critique of standardized testing at all educational levels re-emerged in the 1970s with significant concerns about cultural bias, and the test's "perpetuation of status-quo power structures based on race and class" (Manhattan Review, n.d., para. 6) began to gain attention. While there were exam revisions in 1994 and 2005, the Scholastic Aptitude Test (SAT) and the American College Test (ACT) continued to face challenges regarding what they measured in terms of the potential success of college students. As the COVID-19 pandemic swept the world, most institutions have dropped this requirement for college admission. According to Lovell and Mallinson (2022), based on IPEDS (Integrated Postsecondary Education Data System) data, 79% of private non-profit institutions and 83% of public institutions adopted test-optional admissions policies before or during the pandemic. How colleges and universities use standardized tests after the pandemic remains to be seen for the ACT and SAT as well as the Graduate Record Examinations (GRE), which has been dropped or made optional since 2019 by schools such as Harvard, the Massachusetts Institute of Technology (MIT), Princeton, Stanford, and the University of California at Berkeley.

To summarize, in the first 150–200 years of higher education in the U.S., only the sons of the wealthy members of the elite class were admitted based on their completion of specific areas of study. The early to mid-1800s continued the practice, but schools offered remedial courses so long as a student's family could pay tuition, fees, and expenses. With the expansion of higher education through the Morrill Act, admissions exams (written and oral) expanded, and remedial courses continued. From the late 1800s through the early 1900s, colleges and universities required high school diplomas, and academic and testing organizations began to develop intelligence testing. Following the Great Depression, the federal government created financial aid, colleges adopted either open-access or highly selective approaches to admission, and institutions considered students' character for admission.

In the wake of the G.I. Bill following World War II, the need for efficiency in admissions grew as the public saw higher education as something for everyone (at least for all white men) and not just for the elite. From the mid-1960s through 1990, higher education access increased through Pell Grants and the push of social movements. These movements coincided with major court cases such as Brown v. Board of Education and Regents of the University of California v. Bakke (see Chapter 3) and legislation such as the Educational Amendments of 1972 (see Chapter 2). We are too close to the 1990s to identify the subsequent eras of education. However, we can assume that the spring of 2020, when the world – including higher education – dealt with the COVID-19 pandemic, will mark the beginning of the newest era.

Emerging admissions issues from the 1990s until the pandemic included social media, technology, the growth of for-profit education, college student diversity, the increased profile of community colleges, the role of parents, Title IX and sexual misconduct, the continued impact of college sports, litigiousness in higher education (and society in general), and the influence of national politics on higher education. This 30-year period has been one of dynamic change followed by even more condensed (and intense) change and adaptation across higher education in the context of the COVID-19 pandemic. A more precise delineation between different eras will emerge as we gain additional perspective during the pandemic/post-pandemic era(s).

Perhaps one of the most significant admissions issues in recent years is the "Operation Varsity Blues" scandal facilitated by William Rick Singer.

Singer took money from parents to bribe college administrators, admissions officers, testing officials, coaches, and athletics staff members. By manipulating learning disability processes and paperwork, Singer arranged for privileged students to cheat on standardized tests (SAT/ACT). The irony is that standardized tests were designed to advantage those with privilege. However, some families felt they needed to cheat because having a test designed specifically for them was not enough.

Institutional Intelligence Questions

Who: Who makes admissions decisions? Whom have colleges and universities historically admitted? Who has historically been absent or underrepresented? Who writes the admission policy? Who gets exceptions from the "normal" admission criteria? Is having a parent who gave a multi-million-dollar gift to the university and received an admission "favor" any different from that same parent paying off a coach to give their child a scholarship?

What: What is the mission of the institution? What are the accessibility considerations (language beyond English, language unfamiliar to first-generation students/families, visual impairment, and other accessibility considerations) built into the admissions application? What factors do institutions and admissions staff consider when making admissions decisions? What role do trustees, regents, and political leaders have in admissions policies? What relationships exist between community, vocational, technical, and other institutions and four-year institutions that have admissions implications? What additional resources unfairly advantage students with financial privilege (private tutors, test-taking support, college-prep resources, and assistance writing essays)? What obligation does an institution have to make up for past discriminatory practices?

Why: Why has the institution chosen specific criteria—to expand or limit access? To utilize accurate indicators of success and identify students who may need additional resources? To perpetuate advantages to students holding specific identities, legacy status, or financial resources?

Where: Where do students get help with college application processes?

When: When are students offered support and preparation for college-going?

How: How are decisions processed? How have legacy students been historically treated and advantaged? How does an individual's athletic ability factor into college admissions decisions? How is employment valued in terms of a student's ability to manage time and multiple tasks? How have application reviewers been trained to identify non-traditional assets that students will bring to college?

Critical Scenario 11.1 Admissions

Co-Author: Dr. Chuck Knepfle, Vice President for Enrollment Management, Portland State University

Jorge (he/him) is an admissions counselor at Pontiac State University (PSU). He has been in his role for about 18 months, and as summer winds down, he is excited about the students he has helped bring to PSU. One Friday at 2:30 p.m., he gets a call from Joan (she/her), a friend who works for a newspaper in a neighboring community.

"Jorge, I wanted to let you know about something—I'm not calling as a reporter but to share information. Although, of course, if you have any comments you are willing to share, I'd love to hear them." Joan tells Jorge that a recent admit to PSU was convicted of assault, although the student was initially charged with felony assault and battery. Jorge thanks Joan for the information and declines to make any further comments.

Jorge does some research and sees that the student—Alex (he/him)—was convicted after applying to PSU but before being formally admitted. The student did not disclose any criminal history on his application. Technically, the student did not have a criminal conviction to report, and the situation occurred before Alex was officially a PSU student.

The Law

- What are the relevant legal issues in this scenario?
- What institutional policies, procedures, or processes are applicable in this scenario?

Ethics

- What are the relevant ethical issues in this scenario?
- What information would the characters need to make sound ethical decisions?

Identity

- How might characters' social identities affect how this scenario would unfold?
- How do the situation and the information you need change depending on the identities of those involved?

Scenario-Specific Questions

- Who else might need to be informed or contacted (parents if the student is not 18, other offices on campus, community agencies)?
- What are the relevant federal and state laws that might be in place? What (if anything) does the university's student code of conduct say about this situation? Is this a violation, and if so, is the timing of the incident relevant?
- Where is the student living? Is the university obligated to notify the housing staff if Alex lives on campus? His roommates?
- When was the student obligated to share this information? On PSU's admission application? On a housing contract? Did the university require the student to update PSU when he was convicted?
- Under what circumstances can an admission director withdraw an admission offer?
- How does Institutional Intelligence inform what Jorge does next? How can he go about gathering the Institutional Intelligence information he needs to address the situation?

How else might you use the Institutional Intelligence Model to understand campus context factors related to this scenario?

Financial Aid

The history of financial aid dates back to medieval times in Europe when international students would band together to provide support to one another in the same country to pay professors. Financial need led to aid in the form of early work-study programs, access to dining hall leftovers, and giving students licenses to beg to support their education. Early scholarships were not need-based; wealthy families gave students financial gifts. Early European financial gifts to support enterprising but under-resourced poor students came from community members, not institutions. The wealthy gave based on the role modeling of Jesus, who supported the poor (Wilkinson, 2005).

As education took root in the United States, wealthy patrons were responsible for fostering support of elementary and high schools and higher education (with, for example, John Harvard's gift of books and money). The interest from Lady Anne Radcliffe Mowlson's gift to Harvard provided financial aid to these students. Harvard offered the first scholarship in 1643 and student loans in 1838 (Thelin, 2011).

The next major event to impact financial aid came with the Servicemen's Readjustment Act of 1944—the G.I. Bill (see Chapter 2) increased both educational access and costs (Altschuler & Blumin, 2009). As a result of the need for more residence halls, staff, dining centers, classroom space, and faculty, higher education costs increased for all students. In response, the College Examination Board helped develop standardized admission tests and developed the Financial Aid Form through its newly established College Scholarship Service.

The modern era for financial aid in the United States took off following Sputnik and a push for STEM (science, technology, engineering, and mathematics) research. Colleges and universities began offering aid through the 1958 National Defense Education Act (NDEA). Housed in the Office of Education, this aid came from loans for undergraduate and graduate students in scientific and technical education (Thelin, 2011).

Following the establishment of the first federal grant program—the Federal Supplemental Education Opportunity Grant (formerly known as the Education Opportunity Grant and then the Supplemental Education Opportunity Grant)—the Economic Opportunity Act of 1965 (Title IV Programs) was created to provide financial aid support to students with financial need (Thelin, 2011). In 1972, the Basic Educational Opportunity Grant (BEOG) was also established. It would later be renamed after Senator Claiborne Pell as the Pell Grant (Thelin, 2011) to promote access to higher education through need-based grants primarily to undergraduate students. It is important to note that Lois Rice, Director of the College Board at the time the Pell Grant was being created, pushed and actively lobbied for the creation of the program (Rice, 2019). Rice is known as the "mother of the Pell Grant," which has helped an estimated 80 million people go to college (Bates et al., 2022).

Financial Aid Successes

In the 2021 fiscal year, the Federal Pell Grant Program awarded approximately $23.7 billion (Dortch, 2021). The average award has increased yearly since 2011, and more than half of the funds awarded go to families earning less than $20,000 annually (Hanson, 2021). Financial aid is essential to educational access, persistence, and graduation. Goldrick-Rab et al. (2009) found that, based on empirical evidence, more aid leads to an increase in college enrollment and graduation. Additionally, "students have significant unmet financial need suggesting that student financial aid is critical to improving college access and success" (Long, 2008, p. 35).

Financial aid plays a significant role in educational attainment and positively affects college-going and student success in higher education (Goldrick-Rab et al., 2009). Furthermore, Herbaut and Geven (2020) stated, "Outreach and financial aid may help disadvantaged students to access and complete [higher education] if these interventions efficiently address some of the barriers met by disadvantaged students" (p. 2). Recent studies have found that financial aid plays a role in the re-enrollment of Hispanic first-generation students (Latino et al., 2020).

Financial Aid Challenges

Each institution had the autonomy to decide how to award its funds. This individual approach created additional issues. Just as standardized testing was problematic in terms of class and racial bias, so were—on occasion—financial aid awards. Schools sometimes use funds to attract athletes and high-achieving students rather than support poor students (Shermer, 2021). That said, the vast majority of the time, aid has been awarded and utilized as a tool for college access and success. Financial aid increases college retention and graduation (Whalen et al., 2009), and grants increase college graduation rates (Millea et al., 2018).

The Higher Education Act (HEA) of 1965 (see Chapter 2) established the federal government as the primary source of financial aid, specifically under Title IV of the act (the BEOG). This allocated funds directly to colleges and universities. In 1992, the U.S. government implemented the Free Application for Federal Student Aid (FAFSA) as part of the reauthorization of the HEA of 1965 (see Chapter 2).

Through all this, financial aid awards continued to provide less support to women (Moran, 1987) and Students of Color (Long & Riley, 2007), providing the bulk of the aid to white men. With the reauthorization of the HEA in 1972, the government made several changes, including the addition of Title IX to address this inequity.

Despite these additions to the process, problems related to the clarity of the process persisted. The 2008 reauthorization of the HEA addressed these concerns to some degree. Shermer (2021) wrote, "[FAFSA's] convoluted system's consequences became clear when the 2008 HEA reauthorization forced lenders and campuses to turn over more information about who gets what kind of help covering college costs" (para 15).

That said, there are still significant disparities in loans which exacerbate the existing wealth gap between white students and Students of Color—particularly, Black students. Mishory et al. (2019) wrote, "Black families—already disadvantaged by generational wealth disparities—rely more heavily on student debt, and on riskier forms of student debt, than white families do" (para. 2). She adds that these financial disparities continue after students leave school; as a result, a number of factors, including racial income disparity in the workplace and lower family wealth, perpetuate negative financial events such as loan default, higher interest rates, and more debt as graduate students (Mishory et al., 2019). Perry et al. (2021) added, "the disproportionate debt Black students are taking to finance their education is reinforcing the racial wealth gap" (para. 2). Additionally, the student loan forgiveness program proposed by the Joe Biden administration targets the middle class, doing little for borrowers in the lowest income brackets (Tankersley, 2022).

The escalating cost of a college education and high student debt have persisted into the 2000s. Combined with pushback against higher education from legislators growing throughout the first two decades of the 21st century, "Is college worth it?" became part of college conversation in educational, political, and cultural arenas. As the COVID-19 pandemic spread, the government suspended student loan payments to support those with student loan debt and explored new strategies for providing loan forgiveness.

Institutional Intelligence Questions

Who: Who is most at risk for not receiving the aid they need for college? Who is most at risk for incurring significant student debt? Who is responsible for coaching students about student loan responsibilities and implications?

What: What processes does your institution have in place for financial aid guidance? What resources beyond loans are available to students? What are common questions, concerns, or issues related to financial aid?

Where: Where is financial aid located? Where in a student's career will they engage with financial aid staff? Where do most students find resources related to financial aid?

When: When does a student's relationship with financial aid begin? When are critical milestones in a student's relationship with financial aid?

How: How easy is it for students and families to understand FAFSA and other financial aid information in the context of your institution? How are financial aid staff trained and provided ongoing development to excel in their work and support students? How are award decisions made?

Why: Why are some students given more money than others? Why are some students awarded work-study opportunities?

Critical Scenario 11.2 Financial Aid

Co-Author: Amy Burke, Financial Aid Counselor, Clemson University

Carrie (she/her) shares with Barbara (she/her), a financial aid counselor, that her mother has recently passed away. Carrie's father has never been in her life, and she has not had contact with him for the past six years. Carrie is struggling to figure out how to stay in school.

Cody (he/him) is a graduate student doing an internship in financial aid who co-advises a student organization Carrie is in. He mentioned to her that she might be eligible for a "dependency override" based on the "professional judgment" of a financial aid officer. Carrie is not sure she understands what Cody means.

The Law

- What are the relevant legal issues in this scenario?
- What institutional policies, procedures, or processes are applicable in this scenario?

Ethics

- What are the relevant ethical issues in this scenario?
- What information would the characters need to make sound ethical decisions?

Identity

- How might characters' social identities affect how this scenario would unfold?
- How do the situation and the information you need change depending on the identities of those involved?

Scenario-Specific Questions

- Who are other partners on campus with access to financial resources which may be able to help Carrie? Who else has Carrie talked to about her situation?

- What conversation might Barbara want to have with Cody?
- Why would Cody have mentioned "dependency override" and "professional judgment" to Carrie?
- Where might you go to get answers to your *who*, *what*, *where*, *when*, *why*, and *how* questions?
- When are key dates in the financial aid timeline that might affect how Cody can help Carrie? When does Carrie need the money in order to stay in school?
- How has the Financial Aid Office handled similar situations in the past?

What other Institutional Intelligence Model questions does this scenario provoke for you?

Orientation

There is some debate about where the first college orientation took place. While it appears that orientation programs happened in 1888, some authors name Harvard as having the first college orientation program (Strumpf & Shaker, 1993), and others argue that it was Boston University (Drake, 1966). The University of Maine hosted the first week of activities for new students in 1923 (Packwood, 1977). Prior to the 1920s, faculty coordinated these welcome activities. Through the 1950s, as these efforts grew, there were still relatively few student affairs practitioners for any area, including orientation and transition programs for new college students. The evolution of national organizations and events and changes in orientation and related areas is highlighted in Table 11.1.

Schools have also developed more diverse orientation formats to meet the needs of a variety of student populations—transfer students, nontraditional (not direct from high school) students, international students, and student veterans. Additionally, with the COVID-19 pandemic, institutions were forced to adjust from in-person to online. While this was limiting in some ways, navigating this transition also opened up opportunities to engage with students in new and innovative ways. Many staff and faculty learned ways to enhance or supplement in-person orientation experiences.

TABLE 11.1 Milestones in the History of Orientation, Transition, and Retention Field

Year(s)	*Activity*
1888	Harvard and Boston University document the earliest orientations.
1920–1940	Orientation primarily consists of first-year student courses and first-year student weeks.
1948	Orientation directors meet to discuss campus orientation issues (became National Orientation Directors Association [NODA]).
1950s	Orientation programs develop more structure.
1960s	Pre-college programs emerge.
1970s	College student diversity increases on campuses.
1976–1977	NODA chartered as a professional organization and established first Board of Directors.
1980s	Orientation programs begin at colleges and universities as a common practice. Increased focus on orientation accountability and student retention.
1982–1986	In 1982, John Gardener hosted 175 people at the University of South Carolina to discuss first-year students. Would become The National Center for the Study of Freshman Year Experience in 1986 (now the National Resource Center for The First-Year Experience and Student Transition).
1990s–2000s	Increase in hybrid orientation programs focused on orientation, transition, and retention. Students were more consumer-minded. Programs more focused on including parents and family members. Greater variety of programming.

Note: Adapted from J. A. Ward-Roof and K. L. Guthrie (2010). "Reflections on the history of orientation, transition, and retention programs." In J. A. Ward-Roof (eds.), *Designing successful transitions: A guide for orienting students to college* (Monograph No. 13, 3rd ed.). University of South Carolina, National Resource Center for the First-Year Experience and Students in Transition.

Institutional Intelligence Questions

Who: Who are critical partners in planning new student orientation programs? Who facilitates specific orientation sessions? Who helps sponsor orientation activities, and are there legal or ethical considerations related to those partnerships?

What: What are the goals of orientation generally and for specific sessions? What assessment data is collected/available? What are the deadlines related to orientation? What are students' concerns during orientation? What are their concerns during their transition to campus? What are the costs involved in participating, and do those costs potentially prohibit students from participating? What activities are part of orientation, and are there any legal liability concerns related to those activities?

Where: Where are specific sessions held? Where do students/families stay during orientation? Where are they allowed to tour on campus? Where can students with specific questions or concerns get information during orientation events? Given the location of events, are there any accessibility considerations for space or online access that might disproportionately affect students with disabilities?

When: When do orientation events take place?

Why: Why is the orientation schedule set up as it is?

How: How is orientation funded—student fees? How are other activities funded?

Critical Scenario 11.3 Orientation

Co-Author: Dr. Myles Surrett, Associate Vice President for Career, Experiential Learning, and Transitions, James Madison University

Daria (she/her) is an assistant director in orientation and new student programs at Central State University (CSU). She works directly with student orientation leaders (OLs) through the summer and during the welcome week in the fall term. Daria has been at CSU for a year, but her office is down a person this year. As a result, she is responsible for supervising the OLs independently instead of with a partner.

During the third of 12 summer orientation sessions, a story breaks that the university has allowed the dean of the College of Liberal Arts and Sciences to retire after reports that he sexually harassed students. One of your OLs shares that two other student staff members filed complaints against the dean. They are relieved that he is gone but stressed about the news coverage.

On the second day of the session, the OLs are facilitating a meeting for parents of incoming students. The mother of an incoming student asks for specific details about the situation and whether or not her daughter, as someone who will be a student majoring in a liberal arts and sciences program, is safe on campus.

The Law

- What are the relevant legal issues in this scenario?
- What institutional policies, procedures, or processes are applicable in this scenario?

Ethics

- What are the relevant ethical issues in this scenario?
- What information would the characters need to make sound ethical decisions?

Identity

- How might characters' social identities affect how this scenario would unfold?
- How do the situation and the information you need change depending on the identities of those involved?

Scenario-Specific Questions

- Whom does Daria need to notify about this situation? Who else might expect to be informed or involved in responding to this situation?
- What does she need to know to respond at the moment? What does she need to know to follow up with the entire team to support her OLs and continue onboarding new students to campus? What resources will she need to effectively respond to the concerns raised during the parents' session?
- Where else might these questions come up during or after orientation? Where might Daria go to get more information about the situation?
- When should Daria follow up with her supervisor? Are the OLs directly involved? The rest of her team?
- Why is a transparent and honest response needed to the question? Why might Daria not be able to share as much detail as others might like?
- How does Institutional Intelligence inform Daria's outreach to her OLs (including the two women Daria was told to have been directly affected)?

How else can the Institutional Intelligence Model help Daria understand her campus?

Conclusion

Students' formal relationships with institutions begin with admissions. As students accept their admission and transition to campus, they must navigate various personal, administrative, financial, and academic issues. The staff working with these students must familiarize themselves with institutional legal guidelines and ethical practices. This early phase of a student's relationship with the institution will provoke questions from students and families. Understanding the context of your campus and having relationships in place to connect students to relevant resources build your Institutional Intelligence and provide excellent support to students on your campus. By extension, understanding your university is essential to your successful navigation of legal and ethical issues that may emerge in your work.

12

ACADEMICS

> The very foundation of higher education is curiosity and lifelong learning. Everyone across campuses and in partnership with higher education institutions is essentially engaged as students regardless of being labeled 'student,' 'staff,' and/or 'faculty.' Thus, it is important to approach and cultivate opportunities to support each other directly and build knowledge collaboratively through open, data- and experience-driven dialog. For students and academic affairs practitioners, such interactions can be life-changing moments impacting students' careers and lifelong learning skill sets as they become tomorrow's colleagues and leaders.
>
> —Dr. Amy Lawton-Rauh, Associate Provost for Faculty Affairs, Clemson University

Academics are the foundation for higher education. Extracurriculars, housing, dining, recreation services, and parking—yes, EVEN parking—are built around academics. Academic experiences are essential for career preparation, communication, and success after graduation. Higher education prepares professionals, practitioners, researchers, and scholars across various fields and applied areas. Academic support staff—advisors, academic success personnel, and others—go beyond the content of study area and provide support to students on how to learn and successfully work toward their academic goals and promote student success. Therefore, academic support staff are essential in all higher education institutions.

DOI: 10.4324/9781003442707-15

In 2021, about 42% of Americans 25 and older held a college degree at the associate's level or above (Bryant, 2021). Most of those who earned college degrees were white (72%), whereas both Black and Latin* people each accounted for 9% of those degrees, and Asian American people earned 8% of those degrees. In comparison, "other" (2%) and Native American, American Indian, Alaska Native, and Native Hawaiian/Pacific Islander peoples made up 1% of college graduates (Bryant, 2021).

There are gender and racial disparities related to college graduation. In the 2018–2019 academic year, women made up 53% and men 47% of college degree holders 25 and older (Bryant, 2021). Yet those numbers flipped when it came to graduates with business degrees (women 47% and men 53%). Furthermore, in the same year, women earned only 23% of engineering degrees, while men earned 77% of engineering degrees (NCES, n.d.-c). Women earned more degrees in health professions (84%), psychology (79%), and biological and biomedical science (63%), and slightly more women (51%) earned social science and history degrees than men (NCES, n.d.-c).

As we begin to explore the legal and ethical issues related to academics in higher education, it is essential to understand students' identities. There are ethical considerations in terms of who has access to higher education and who has been historically excluded. Consider what Del Pilar and Elston (2022) wrote: "no state has a public higher education system with a student body that reflects its demographic profile" (para. 4). This is an ethical issue for higher education and higher education professionals. The underrepresentation of some student populations in higher education is also perpetuated by some legal and policy issues on campus, in individual states, and across the country.

Additionally, there are ethical issues related to how data is collected regarding gender. The data in most sets is strictly related to the gender binary (men and women) and do not account for other gender identities. Cuellar and Salinas (2022) suggested that in collecting data on diverse student populations, we must acknowledge their various identities and how those identities intersect. Therefore, institutions must revisit their demographic questions for data collection and allow students to self-identify their social identities, including gender, pronouns, race, ethnicity, and nationality (Cuellar & Salinas, 2022).

Student demographic information is relevant to every functional area. We have included it here as the academic support staff are uniquely positioned to support college students. Through their support, students—regardless of their identities—can find their way through higher education, paving the way for those who come next and changing the narrative of colleges and universities.

Chapter Organization

After a brief history of student and academic affairs partnerships, the chapter moves to a focus on academic advising and coaching. Next, we explore additional academic considerations as students are complex and have individual needs as they navigate their courses and degree programs in higher education. We include a section focusing on the important and complex relationships between faculty and students and the ethical and legal implications of those relationships. Each section of the chapter concludes with critical scenarios based on different ways that academic practitioners engage with students.

Legal and Ethical Considerations

Academic legal considerations include the responsibilities that advisors and faculty members have to students regarding academic policies, catalogs, registration, syllabi, and other elements of the academic contract. However, legal issues also emerge as student behavior in the classroom, academic support spaces, and assignments. How these staff members approach law and ethics depends on their students and institutions. We must consider legal issues in the evolving contexts of student populations, technology, and society. For example, what is the academic integrity policy on campus? What happens if a student records a lecture and distributes it via social media? Institutions must communicate academic policies and resources to students, staff, and faculty. Furthermore, employees must communicate appropriately when student behavior, safety, and well-being concerns arise.

Practitioners and faculty must navigate ethical issues related to academics, including student autonomy and parental involvement. Staff can find themselves advising students about what may be best for them when that advice conflicts with what students want for themselves. Examples are course registration, academic major, and academic withdrawal. In these situations, ethics inform what and how we communicate with students.

Additionally, staff and faculty members' behavior can create situations with legal and ethical implications. Issues of sexual misconduct, harassment, racist comments and behaviors, and other problematic and/or criminal behavior can affect students, staff, and faculty, especially those who are and have been targeted, marginalized, and oppressed. For example, when racist comments or behaviors show up in learning environments (i.e., a faculty member engages in racist microaggressions), issues related to academic freedom are sometimes raised as a defense. This example can also create arguments and tensions around freedom of speech on college campuses. Regardless of the sexual misconduct, harassment, or racist comments and behaviors, these will have many ethical and legal implications.

Competencies

In this chapter, we focus on the Student Learning and Development (SLD) competency (see Appendix). Staff in academic affairs work in direct support of the academic mission of an institution. At the foundational level, practitioners must be able to construct and assess learning outcomes and assess teaching and training (ACPA/NASPA, 2015). As practitioners move through this competency, they examine programmatic and institutional initiatives. This chapter provides opportunities to think about how we connect with students and collaborators to support academic success.

History of Student and Academic Affairs Partnerships

Academic support for students has always been part of higher education. Early in U.S. higher education, the faculty (sometimes a single individual who also served as the college president) was responsible for administration, teaching, and monitoring student behavior. Faculties were small, as few families could afford to send their sons to college. Classes began in the summer of 1638 at New College—the first college in the United States in New Towne, MA. New College was renamed after a major donor, John Harvard. New Towne was also renamed Cambridge after the British alma mater of some Puritan residents. The school had a single "master," and the grounds consisted of "a single frame house and a college yard" (Zeidan et al., 2022).

From the beginning, faculty facilitated students' intellectual and moral development (Gallagher & Demos, 1983). Faculty also managed student discipline, academic and otherwise (Brubacher & Rudy, 1997). As the Revolutionary War approached, faculty expected students to be free thinkers responsible for their own choices (Gillispie, 2003). Throughout the 1800s, as college training and academic specialization expanded beyond the preparation of clergy, faculty members guided students on course selection.

Industrial psychology proliferated during World War I, and universities adopted psychometrics as an instrument for vocational guidance and academic advising (Gallagher & Demos, 1983). In *The Student Personnel Point of View* in 1937, the American Council on Education specified Student Personnel Services as responsible for helping students discover their "abilities, aptitudes, and objectives" and assisting each student in determining "his courses of instruction in light of his past achievements, vocational and personal interests, and diagnostic findings" (p. 4). It is worth noting that students are referred to consistently throughout the document by he, him, or his even though coeducation in colleges had existed since the opening of Oberlin Collegiate Institute in December 1833. By 1924, about 74% of college and university students in the United States attended coeducational institutions (Goldin & Katz, 2011).

But we digress. The point here is that higher education was shifting away from moral development drawn from the religious basis at early colleges and universities. Industrial psychology in the U.S. emerged during World War I and proliferated even after World War II. Universities embraced industrial psychology and adopted similar psychometrics and occupational aptitude assessments for academic and vocational guidance (Gallagher & Demos, 1983). The *Student Personnel Point of View* from 1949 stressed that, for students to achieve, the most important thing was success in studies, including the development of proficiency, motivation, time management, study skills, and counseling related to curricular choices (ACE, 1949). These developmental considerations aligned with industrial psychology strategies.

After World War II, student developmental issues, social justice, and access became critical considerations in higher education and set the stage for enhanced academic advising (Gordon, 1992; Komives et al., 1996). As academic advising became more prevalent in higher education, practitioners began sharing information between campuses about student issues, programs, and support strategies.

This information sharing was relatively unrestricted—at least at the federal level—until the establishment of the Family Educational Rights and Privacy ACT (FERPA) in 1974. FERPA afforded students and families more control over students' academic records. These protections include the right of a student (over the age of 18) to keep their academic records from their parents; this can be a situation navigated by academic advising or other student-facing academic staff or faculty.

In 1977, academic practitioners created the National Academic Advising Association (NACADA) to further collaborative work and learning about this functional area (NACADA website, 2021). Today, academic advising builds on previous work and theories. Academic support varies depending on individual campus structure. For example, advising can be centralized or decentralized. Academic support staff and faculty continue to engage students holistically to support their academic and personal success.

Academic Advising and Coaching

Perhaps the most apparent connection between student affairs and academic staff in higher education is embodied in the role of the academic advisor. Advisors are part of academic departments or colleges (when decentralized) or under the office of the provost or student affairs (when centralized). Academic advisors help students develop plans of study, meet degree requirements, understand academic policies and procedures, and get the academic support they need. Academic coaching is distinct from advising, focusing on helping struggling students rather than advising them on registration, although some institutions blend these roles. Academic advising and academic coaching do not compete but complement one another to support student success.

Ultimately, the organization of these services depends on the institutional context. For example, some higher education institutions have academic advising separate from academic coaching. Other institutions combine academic advising, academic coaching, and career advising. An academic success center's services might include academic coaching, tutoring, coordinating a college transition course, and student success workshops on one campus and might include centralized academic advising at another school. Regardless of the organizational structure, these academic services have similar goals: to educate students through advising practices and to help students succeed in individual courses and stay in school, resulting in higher retention and graduation.

Institutional Intelligence Questions

Who: Who advises students about academic requirements for their majors? Who promotes academic success? Who are the academic advisors and academic coaches? Who engages directly with students regarding their academic success?

What: What academic services does your institution offer? What are the roles and job descriptions for academic advisors and academic coaches?

Where: Where are the academic advisors and coaches located (physically and in organizational charts)? Where do students go to find out about academic advising and support resources?

When: When are the most critical times for students to connect with academic advisors? When should students engage with academic coaching and other academic support resources?

Why: Why might some students not engage with academic success centers and staff members? Why are some campus partners connected (or not) with academic advising and support?

How: How is academic support discussed and promoted within your institution? How is academic support discussed and promoted within your area or team?

Critical Scenario 12.1 Academic Advising

Co-Author: Olivia Battinelli, Campus Recruiter, Ernst & Young

Dontral (he/him) is a third-year academic advisor in the School of Management in the College of Business. During one of the fall term's busiest weeks for academic advising, Dontral is booked with appointments for three days straight. In a meeting with Jesse (they/them), Jesse shared that they think they are in the wrong major and want to switch to something else.

After some discussion during which Jesse says they are not sure what they want to major in, they finally say, "Maybe education. Maybe I would like to teach English in a high school." The appointment time is almost up, and Dontral knows he will not have a chance to follow up with Jesse for at least two days.

The Law

- What are the relevant legal issues in this scenario?
- What institutional policies, procedures, or processes are applicable in this scenario?

Ethics

- What are the relevant ethical issues in this scenario?
- What information would the characters need to make sound ethical decisions in this situation?

Identity

- How would characters' social identities affect how this scenario might unfold? Assign the characters specific social identities and go through the scenario. Then change those identities and go through the scenario again.
- How do the situation and the information you would need change?

Scenario-Specific Questions

- Who else might be available to help Jesse in Dontral's office? Whom does Dontral need to tell about Jesse's struggle?
- What are some of the academic implications for Jesse switching from their current major to a different one? What resources are available on campus to help Jesse figure out a new major?
- Where else on campus would it be helpful for Dontral to have relationships to best support students who want to change their majors?
- When are the deadlines for registration?

- Why might Jesse have waited until the advising appointment to bring this up with Dontral? Why might Jesse be struggling with their current major?
- How might Dontral have asked Jesse questions to learn more about why they want to change majors? How might Dontral have created obstacles (intentionally or unintentionally) to Jesse reaching out sooner?

How else can Dontral use the Institutional Intelligence Model to prepare to follow up with Jesse?

Critical Scenario 12.2 Academic Coaching

Co-Authors: Christian Barrientos, Associate Director, Emerging Scholars Office of College Preparation and Outreach, Clemson University, and Janel Acosta, Graduate Assistant, the Center for Leadership and Social Change, Florida State University

Aurora (she/her) is in her first month as the Academic Success Center Assistant Director at Holloway College. She coordinates academic coaching, which helps students develop plans, set goals, identify resources, and address academic concerns. Aurora meets with new students, students on academic probation, and those who want to improve organizational and time management skills. Aurora supervises 10 peer coaches, who must have a 3.00 GPA and be sophomores who have taken at least one full year of courses on campus.

Ezra (he/him) is a new graduate student Aurora supervises. In their weekly one-on-one meeting, Ezra shares a concern about Donald (he/him), a junior. Ezra met Donald because of Donald's academic probation status. Donald has missed the last two appointments they set.

"Donald met with me twice. The first time—the first week of classes—he came prepared with a planner and markers to color code his schedule and the concerns he had. The second time, two weeks later, Donald seemed distracted and unprepared. He said that lately, he has been feeling out of place at Holloway. I haven't seen him for three weeks, and he isn't responding to my messages to reschedule."

The Law

- What are the relevant legal issues in this scenario?
- What institutional policies, procedures, or processes are applicable in this scenario?

Ethics

- What are the relevant ethical issues in this scenario?
- What information would the characters need to make sound ethical decisions in this situation?

Identity

- How would characters' social identities affect how this scenario might unfold? Assign the characters particular social identities and go through the scenario. Then change some of those social identities and go through the scenario again.
- How do the situation and the information you would need change?

Scenario-Specific Questions

- Who else may need to know about Donald's struggles? Who might have additional information about the change in Donald's engagement with Ezra?
- What campus context/Institutional Intelligence would Aurora and Ezra need as they collaborate with Donald on the next steps? What type of institution is Holloway College?
- Where else on campus might a change in Donald's behavior have surfaced?
- When should someone reach out to Donald? When should they be concerned about another lack of response from Donald?
- Why might Donald's lack of response be concerning? What explanations for his lack of response would be less concerning?
- How can Aurora and Ezra find out more on campus and in their unit to effectively support Donald and share departmental and other campus resources?
- What else would it be helpful to know about Holloway College to navigate the situation with Donald?

How else might Aurora or Ezra use the Institutional Intelligence Model to support Donald?

Additional Academic Support

Academic support initiatives include programs, services, and strategies created for students to succeed academically, professionally, and personally. Academic support is used by an institution to "increase the academic achievement for students who may be at risk of diminished academic achievement" (Peterson et al., 2018, p. 2). Academic support provides additional academic and social support to students beyond academic advising. For example, tutoring and mentorship allow students to engage in "motivation, personal individual attention, direct instruction, and error correction to increase students' academic skills" (Peterson et al., 2018, p. 2).

Some institutions and individuals consider academic support to be related only to formal coursework (i.e., tutoring, writing center, math labs, testing center, faculty mentoring, and academic advising). Others see academic support as being closely connected to other personal and social relationships. Academic success can be part of work in counseling and psychological services, international student services, multicultural affairs services, military and veterans' affairs, student accessibility services, mentoring programs, women's centers, LGBTQ+ centers, and fraternity and sorority life, among other resources. Of course, ideally, the network of support for students includes academic advising and success and other student resources on campus.

The U.S. Federal Government, in partnership with the U.S. Department of Education, has also allocated grants for Federal TRIO Programs (TRIO) and Student Support Services (SSS) projects. TRIO is a group of eight outreach and student services programs (Upward Bound, Talent Search, Student Support Services, Veterans Upward Bound, Education Opportunity Centers, Training Program for Federal TRIO Programs, Ronald E. McNair Post-Baccalaureate Achievement Program, and Upward Bound Math-Science). These programs identify and provide services to low-income, first-generation college students and students with disabilities to progress from middle school to postbaccalaureate programs (U.S. Department of Education, 2022). Program grants are awarded to colleges and universities to provide support (e.g., tutoring, advising, coaching, financial aid, and scholarships) and to motivate students to complete college. Staff members working with TRIO programs can be essential student success partners on campus.

As you think about students' academic success, consider the support you received or wish you had received as a college student. Considering our own experiences can help us connect with students and identify opportunities and resources we can offer. This consideration can include thinking about what resources are available but also includes reflecting on our experiences and how those experiences might inform our actions moving forward. Reflection is an essential element of the Institutional Intelligence Model. You carry experience all the time, and drawing from that in intentional and reflective ways enhances your work.

Institutional Intelligence Questions

Who: Who is not receiving academic support? Whom are the academic support programs created for?

What: What academic support does your institution provide? What programming and services provide and promote academic support at your institution?

Where: Where can students, staff, and faculty find academic resources on campus and online?

When: When are academic support programs offered, and when are busy times in these offices?

Why: Why is academic support necessary? Why might it be important to different students in different ways? Why was the academic support at your institution created and for whom?

How: How are students, faculty, and staff engaged in academic support? How does your institution identify students in need of support?

Critical Scenario 12.3 Additional Academic Support

Co-Authors: Halie Swanson, Student Development Coordinator, First Year Experience, Northern Arizona University, and Colby Brown, Career Coach, David Eccles School of Business, University of Utah

Lily (she/her) is a second-year practitioner in the Academic Support Center at Mountain University. In her role, she works to connect students with academic resources such as peer tutors and peer mentors, academic success workshops, and student success tools. Lily directly supervises the peer mentors, who meet with students to discuss academic success strategies such as time management.

Lily also teaches a college transition course for about 30 students each fall semester. In the first week of the course, she asked each student to create a list of challenges they anticipated they might face during the term. Lily specifically said to include academics and not just things like roommates and finding friends. It is now the week after midterms, and she has asked the students to revisit their initial list and make updates about concerns, resources they need, and anything else they want to share.

K.J. (he/they) is a transfer student who came to Mountain University via a bridge program from a local community college. In the first part of this assignment, they wrote that they felt comfortable finding academic resources because they did that at their previous school. They also said they were not worried about time management, as they had already developed those skills. However, after the midterms, K.J. wrote,

I don't know what happened. I feel completely lost. I thought I was working hard enough and managing it all, but I'm a failure. I went to my academic advisor, and he helped me schedule a meeting with a peer mentor. Maybe I'm just a slacker, after all. I'm not sure where to start.

Before reviewing K.J.'s assignment, one of Lily's peer mentors, Maria (she/her), shared her concerns about K.J. with Lily. Maria met with K.J. that morning. K.J. said,

I just don't want to be here anymore. I don't belong here, and no one wants me here. Also, this weekend, I was at a party, and this guy from my building made me feel really uncomfortable. He wouldn't stop touching me, even though I asked him to stop multiple times. I feel like I should just drop out of school so I don't have to deal with this. But please don't tell anyone this. I don't need any help.

Lily thanked Maria for sharing this new information and scheduled a meeting with them after reading K.J.'s assignment.

After K.J. receives a notification about the meeting with Lily, K.J. confronts Maria. He is angry and confused, saying, "What the hell? I told you in confidence, and now my teacher wants to meet with me. I know it was you who told her. I will never be using these resources again."

The Law

- What are the relevant legal issues in this scenario?
- What institutional policies, procedures, or processes are applicable in this scenario?

Ethics

- What are the relevant ethical issues in this scenario?
- What information would the characters need to make sound ethical decisions in this situation?

Identity

- How would characters' social identities affect how this scenario might unfold? Assign the characters specific social identities and go through the scenario. Then change some of those social identities and go through the scenario again.
- How do the situation and the information you would need change?

Scenario-Specific Questions

- Who needs outreach and at what level of priority in this situation?
- What questions does Lily need to ask? What information does Lily need to best support K.J. and Maria?
- Where might Lily want to connect on campus for strategies to navigate the situation? Where might she want to help Maria connect if this situation is distressing for Maria? Where might she refer K.J.?
- Why might Lily share that Maria shared K.J.'s response?
- Why might Lily want to stay directly involved? Why might she prefer to bring in someone else?
- How might Lily's needs be different if she was brand-new to campus? How have similar situations been handled in the past in the office or at the institution?

How else can Lily and Maria use the Institutional Intelligence Model to prepare for further outreach to K.J.?

Faculty

In addition to in-class interactions, faculty and students in higher education engage in various ways. On some campuses, faculty serve as academic advisors. Faculty might also work with students on research projects and in mentoring relationships, serve as references for jobs and graduate school applications, and help students build professional networks. These relationships can vary based not only on the individuals involved but on the area of study or the status of the students involved. For example, graduate students may be more dependent on faculty relationships for assistantships, research opportunities, conference attendance, and other professional development opportunities. It is important to acknowledge that there are power dynamics at play in these relationships.

In its description of professional ethics of faculty, the American Association of University Professors (AAUP) writes, "Professors demonstrate respect for students as individuals and adhere to their proper roles as intellectual guides and counselors... They avoid any exploitation, harassment, or discriminatory treatment of students" (AAUP, 2009, para. 4). Individual institutions also have ethical guidelines and expectations embedded in faculty manuals and policies.

Additionally, what are appropriate boundaries in the important relationships between faculty and students outside of formal academic settings? There is a range of situations where faculty and students need to consider what is appropriate. For example, Chory and Offstein (2017) asked:

> Should a faculty member close [their] door when a student, an emotional student, needs to talk? Should a professor give a student a ride home from school? Should a [faculty member] accept a LinkedIn request? How about a Facebook friend request? Should faculty members frequent bars and coffee shops where their students congregate? Is it appropriate to play sports... with our students? Is it advisable to have a drink with a student at a tailgate before a big game? What is harmless and what is harmful?
>
> *(pp. 29–30)*

These are but a sampling of the complex questions that faculty must navigate in building relationships with students outside the classroom. Consistency in a reading of publications such as *Inside Higher Ed* or *The Chronicle of Higher Education* will reveal ethical and legal issues related to faculty behavior on a weekly or daily basis.

The ethical and legal behavior of faculty includes their actions in research and service, their relationships with colleagues on campus and beyond, and their external relationships as consultants, trainers, and researchers doing grant-funded work. For the purposes of this text, we focus on the faculty–student relationship. In the teaching, research, and service triad, the issues discussed here relate most closely to teaching, but ethical and legal problems can arise both in and out of the classroom and in other formal academic settings.

Another consideration when looking at legal and ethical implications for faculty is the role of academic freedom. Academic freedom is "the indispensable requisite for unfettered teaching and research in institutions of higher education" (AAUP, n.d., para. 1). In practice, this means that faculty should not be limited in their pursuit of knowledge and truth either in their research projects or in how they teach in the classroom. While academic freedom is not without some restrictions, it is an essential element of faculty work in U.S. higher education.

Finally, it is important to remember that identity is an essential factor in ethical behavior. The identities of the faculty and the students have an impact on how these two groups interact with one another. As Reybold (2009) wrote, "the alignment of ethics only with morality and legality is troublesome, as it assumes a common standard for right and wrong" (p. 375). The author continued:

> From this perspective, ethical decisions are straightforward and tangible—to "be ethical" is to follow the rules; to "be unethical" is to break them. But there is nothing simple about ethics in higher education. Ethical decisions are made and evaluated by individuals in relation to other individuals, and all have histories, experiences, and perspectives.
>
> *(Reybold, 2009, p. 375)*

In other words, there are laws and ethics that apply to faculty, and the actions that faculty take in relation to those legal and ethical guidelines are informed both by the identities of the faculty members and by the identities of the students.

Institutional Intelligence Questions

Who: Who are the faculty, and who are the students (identities, positions of power, and influence/vulnerability)?

What: What spaces do faculty and students share, in and beyond the classroom? What expectations do faculty have of students? What expectations do students have of faculty? What steps have been taken to address issues of power in learning partnerships? What are the institutional guidelines and expectations of faculty and faculty behavior? What resources do students have for addressing academic and other concerns about faculty?

Where: Where can students, staff, and faculty find legal and ethical resources on campus and online? Where do student and faculty learning and lives intersect?

When: When are faculty provided information and training related to legal and ethical behavior and obligations? When are students provided information about legal and ethical guidelines related to academics and faculty behavior?

Why: Why do lapses in ethical or legal decision-making occur between faculty and students?

How: How are students, faculty, and staff engaged in academic support? How does your institution articulate legal and ethical guidelines for faculty? For students?

Critical Scenario 12.3 Faculty and Student Engagement

Heather (she/her) is a first-year Latina student affairs graduate student. She was excited to start the program at State U because of the opportunity she would have to work with Dr. O'Connor (he/him). Dr. O'Connor is well known across student affairs as a college access scholar, particularly as access relates to financial aid. As a full professor with tenure, Dr. O'Connor has received a number of research awards and significant grant funding for his scholarship. He was recently recognized as the Bradshaw-Hamlin Endowed Professor of Education for his work. He has built his career at State, where he worked for the past 20 years.

On Monday, the first day of her orientation to the program, all of the faculty attended and introduced themselves. Dr. O'Connor is friendly and encourages students with an interest in research to meet with him. Heather sends an email immediately after orientation that day. She does not get a response by the end of the week but knows it is a busy time of year. She also has Dr. O'Connor for student development theory, so she plans to follow up after class the next week.

In theory class on Tuesday, Dr. O'Connor goes over the syllabus for the course. He highlights the theories they will focus on. When Ruth, an African-American woman, asks why there is so little time dedicated to student identity-based theories, Dr. O'Connor explains that most of this class is about foundational work. "If you look to the third week in October, we spend a full class period on social identity theories. Plus, this is graduate school. You should be doing more reading outside of class based on your interests and questions." Before Ruth could respond, Dr. O'Connor moved on to explaining the main assignments for the course.

After class, Heather waits her turn to talk with Dr. O'Connor. When it is her turn, she says, "Thanks for a great first day. I am so excited to have a class with you." Dr. O'Connor thanked her for the compliment. Heather continues, "I was hoping that I could work with you on a research or writing project while I'm in the program. Do you have any projects going on right now that I can help with?"

"That's great," Dr. O'Connor responds. "I have to run to a meeting right now but send me an email and we can set up a time to meet. Welcome to State!" He smiles at her and hurries out of the room.

Heather talks with her buddy in the program—Beth, a white woman who is a second-year student in the program. Heather shares her excitement and tells Beth about the conversation with Dr. O'Connor. Beth responds,

> Dr. O'Connor isn't great about responding to emails. You might have to write him four or five times. Or you can try to catch him in the office. He has done a lot of media reviews for a regional newsletter with students in my cohort. You might read a few of those before you meet with him. I did one with him last fall. I will send you the link to the newsletter.

Heather immediately reads through the reviews that Beth has sent. As she reads through the reviews, she makes notes about the student co-authors so she can reach out to get their input on how to approach Dr. O'Connor and what the experience was like. Heather meets with five of the students—all of whom are white. She emails Dr. O'Connor again and tries to catch him in his office but misses him the three times she stops by.

As Beth gets ready for theory class the next week, she thinks about how to approach Dr. O'Connor again about her interest.

The Law

- What are the relevant legal issues in this scenario?
- What institutional policies, procedures, or processes are applicable in this scenario?

Ethics

- What are the relevant ethical issues in this scenario?
- What information would the characters need to make sound ethical decisions in this situation?

Identity

- How would characters' social identities affect how this scenario might unfold? Assign the characters specific social identities and go through the scenario. Then change some of those social identities and go through the scenario again.
- How do the situation and the information you would need change?

Scenario-Specific Questions

- Who else might help Heather make contact with Dr. O'Connor?
- What concerns might Heather have about contacting Dr. O'Connor? What concerns might arise as a result of how Dr. O'Connor is teaching theory?

- Where might Heather turn if she continues to have problems connecting with Dr. O'Connor? Where else might Heather find opportunities to engage in scholarship, writing, and research while she is in her program?
- Why might Dr. O'Connor fail to respond to Heather? Why might Dr. O'Connor make the choices he made about the course content?
- Why might Dr. O'Connor's responses (or lack thereof) be received differently depending on the identity of the students with whom he is engaging?
- How might Heather feel as a result of these experiences? How might Dr. O'Connor check in with students to see how the class is going over the course of the semester?

How else can Heather and Ruth use the Institutional Intelligence Model to navigate the classroom and out-of-class relationships in their program?

Conclusion

Students' academic success is at the center of college and university work. As a result, staff and faculty must be aware of legal and ethical issues as they advise, coach, and support. Higher education provides workforce development and preparation while students (ideally) develop critical thinking skills, learn the importance of civic and community engagement, and become more proficient in their communication and teamwork abilities. Students' academic learning is part of those elements and their personal development through higher education.

13

STUDENT LIVING AND WELL-BEING

> As members of the campus community (faculty, staff, graduate interns, and administrators), we are responsible for ensuring the best learning and developmental experiences possible for students at the university. With that in mind, we must act/respond when we become aware of incidents that negatively impact a student's well-being or success. Ethically and legally, we should always act when we become aware of even "minor" incidents—from roommate conflicts to individual behavior concerns. Incidents can escalate. These incidents can place students, us, and the institution in jeopardy for not responding to or addressing concerns once we become aware of them.
>
> —Dr. Reyes J. Luna, Interim Executive Director of Housing Services, California State Polytechnic University, Pomona (Cal Poly Pomona)

Students face incredible challenges today. Some consider academics the focus of the college experience, but students live their whole lives while pursuing their education. Their attendance, participation, grades, and success in class are informed by what goes on in the residence halls, apartments, and communities where they live. Their academic focus is affected by their employment, involvement, and leadership experiences. Their personal and family relationships, health, and various other issues impact their engagement as students.

While Deans of Students and their teams play essential roles on campus, anyone in a student-facing position can be called upon to help students. Student life areas are specific to student experiences and development outside of

DOI: 10.4324/9781003442707-16

the classroom. Those experiences may include students making connections through campus recreation intramural teams coming together to engage in wellness activities or by joining a fraternity or sorority. These areas include those centered on community, such as residence life, student conduct, or a Greek letter organization. While this chapter focuses on fitness, well-being, residential spaces, and functional units often required to respond to emergencies, the discussion here cuts across functional areas. It can be helpful to professionals regardless of the offices in which they work.

Chapter Organization

This chapter focuses on students' well-being outside of class. While students spend about 15 hours per week in classes (Sasso & DeVitis, 2015), that leaves them 153 hours to fill with activities, including eating, sleeping, personal hygiene, working, and studying. Student-facing practitioners engage students in their academic success, lives, and personal development. Students will connect with the programs and services across campus, where they find their niche and discover a sense of connection and belonging. Students will choose a variety of staff to confide in across all their campus experiences when facing challenges.

Legal and Ethical Considerations

Student-living and well-being staff face legal safety, accountability, and policy issues. Their daily work depends on what is happening in their campus communities. These practitioners must balance students' rights with community concerns and be familiar with the Family Educational Rights and Privacy Act (FERPA), the Health Insurance Portability and Accountability Act (HIPAA), the Clery Act, other campus policies, and state and federal laws. Safety issues related to emergencies, facilities, and equipment are particularly salient in recreation, fraternity and sorority life (FSL), and housing. There are also contractual considerations, and practitioners in these and other areas must familiarize themselves with contracts. These documents outline expectations for students and vendors and highlight institutional responsibilities and obligations (for more on contracts, see Chapter 7).

Anytime we have people in community, ethical issues emerge. How do we prioritize different and sometimes competing needs between communities and individuals? How do we allocate resources in equitable ways? If *it depends*, what does it depend on? Practitioners must consider who has privilege and power and how an institution has historically excluded, overlooked, or under-resourced certain student groups and populations.

These and other questions are challenges for student affairs professionals in the functional areas outlined in this chapter.

Competencies

Several American College Personnel Association/National Association of Student Personnel Administrators (ACPA/NASPA) competencies (see Appendix) inform this chapter: Personal and Ethical Foundations (PEF); Law, Policy, and Governance (LPG); Social Justice and Inclusion (SJI); Student Learning and Development (SLD); and Advising and Supporting (A/S). Many new(er) staff begin their work in the areas in this chapter. As a result, these staff members develop their personal and ethical selves while advising students through their learning and development.

The work done in these areas is complex because of the implications for safety and belonging. Significant legal and ethical issues related to facilities, harassment, and hate speech emerge in these spaces. Student learning takes place in classes and training, but students also learn through experiences like roommate conflicts and conduct violation discussions. As a result, these competencies can blend to inform staff work in the functional areas discussed in this chapter.

The Evolution of Student Support on Campus

Student affairs emerged for several reasons from a faculty-run higher education system. The Humboldtian research university model (German in origin and named for its creator, Wilhelm von Humboldt) integrated teaching and research, the freedom to teach and learn, solitude and freedom in the pursuit of truth, and the seminar system to foster a community of teachers and learners (Rainer, 2001). U.S. graduates of German universities returned home, and the research institution model began to take root in the United States, beginning with Johns Hopkins University in 1876. With the establishment of these new types of institutions, many faculty began to see their role solely focusing on teaching and research, not student behavior and other extracurricular activities (see Chapter 14 for more detail).

At around this time, in 1887, Alice Freeman Palmer (former president of Wellesley College) was recruited by University of Chicago President William Rainey Harper to become Dean of Women and Professor of History (Solomon, 1980). She agreed and, in 1892, became—by most accounts—the first Dean of Women in the country (Palmer, 1909). Higher education leaders created Dean of Women positions upon the admission of women and the spread of coeducation across colleges and universities. The role of early Deans of Women was to "advise, assist, and counsel the new 'minority' population on campus, female students" (Schwartz, 1997b, p. 505). Women were a problem to be dealt with and managed. It would be 17 years until Thomas Arkle was named the first dean of men at the University of Illinois (Schwartz, 1997b). Because the U.S. designed higher education for (white) men, dealing with the behavior of men students was not seen as needing specific administrative oversight.

In the early 1900s, health centers, registrars, and career counseling emerged. As a result, the foundational pieces of student affairs divisions were in place. Colleagues formed professional organizations for Deans of Women (National Association for Deans of Women, founded in 1917) and Deans of Men (Conference of Deans and Advisers of Men, founded in 1919 but not named until 1921). Schwartz (1997b) wrote, "The men's meetings were social and clublike in contrast to the professionalism of the national conferences of the deans of women" (p. 510). In contrast, Deans of Women were teaching faculty committed to research and dedicated to training and opportunities for new women deans (Esther Lloyd-Jones, Sarah Strang, and Sarah Sturtevant) at the first graduate preparation program for student affairs, at Teachers College, Columbia University (Schwartz, 1997b).

After World War II, Dean of Women positions began to disappear, and many of the remaining student affairs administrative positions went to men. As Schwartz (1997b) wrote, the G.I. Bill contributed to this shift as it "served as a vehicle by which the college campuses were returned to their 'rightful' owners, men" (p. 516). This shift had long-term implications for student affairs leadership: "On individual campuses, the office of dean of men expanded to become dean for student personnel, dean of students, and vice-presidents for student personnel services during the 1950s" (Schwartz, 1997a, p. 433).

Additionally, the national professional associations evolved. The National Association of Deans of Women was established in 1917. The organization underwent several name changes, finally merging with NASPA in 2000. The National Association of Deans of Men adopted the name NASPA in 1951. ACPA would eventually emerge from the National Association of Appointment Secretaries (NAAS), founded in 1924.

In 1929, the National Association of Deans of Women and Advisors of Girls in Colored Schools was founded, followed by the National Association of Personnel Deans of Men at Negro Educational Institutions in 1935. These organizations formed because segregation prohibited Black and African-American practitioners from joining other organizations but continued because of "a continuing need to help Black students confront problems that related directly to their cultural, economic, and social backgrounds" (Dungy & Gordon, 2011, p.67). These organizations would become the National Association of Student Affairs Professionals (NASAP), founded at

Howard University in 1954 (NASAP, n.d.). While NASAP now has collaborative relationships with NASPA and ACPA, we must acknowledge the history of these organizations and wrestle with how the past informs today and the future.

Campus Recreation

The history of campus recreation began in the mid-1800s. After years of colonial disapproval of play, colleges started engaging in sports like football, boat racing, rowing, and baseball. Sports grew on campuses until the Civil War and returned shortly after that. In the mid-1880s, physical education in school settings began to take root, and intramurals on college campuses followed. Recreational sports originated with the first recognized programs at Ohio State University (Ohio State University Recreational Sports, 2015) and the University of Michigan (University of Michigan, 2015) in 1913; this represented a shift from sports solely as competition to sports as a form of student participation beyond intercollegiate athletics. Through the 1930s, organization, formalization, and control of these activities on campus began to take shape.

In the 1950s, the emergence and value of leisure began to impact the culture—on campus and off. As Margaret Mead (1957) wrote, "After the war, there came, understandably, a desire to recoup these quantitatively perceived losses, to get some joy out of life" (p. 14). During this post-war era, in 1950, the National Intramural and Recreational Sports Association (NIRSA) was founded as the National Intramural Association. Dr. William Wasson "convened a meeting of 20 representatives from 11 Historically Black Colleges and Universities and Dillard University in New Orleans" (NIRSA, n.d., para. 5). Today, the organization is known as NIRSA: Leaders in Collegiate Recreation.

Since the 1950s, campus recreation programs have expanded to include more and more types of activities and more participants. According to Forrester (2014), campus recreation plays an important role in student recruitment and retention. Additionally, students highlight the importance of campus recreation in the collegiate experiences. Studies have examined the role of intramural activities in students' community and belonging (Knifsend et al., 2020; Miller, 2011; Phipps et al., 2015). Sport has historically existed as a means of competition and collaboration, building teams/communities on college campuses and beyond.

As long as there have been college students, they have engaged in activity, fitness, and (mostly) friendly competition. That said, there are many considerations that recreation staff must bear in mind when hosting events, facilitating activities, and fostering student wellness. Student safety and risk management are central to physical activities. Programs must train staff to lead activities like rock wall climbing, outdoor recreation trips, and fitness classes and address emergencies with first aid, CPR, and other training.

Additionally, like all functional areas in student affairs and student-facing work in other areas, creating a welcoming environment is essential. In the case of campus recreation facilities, activities, and trips, who is present and absent? Are Students of Color participating in activities? What about international students? Is there a disparity in the participation of students based on gender identity? How are facilities accessible for students with various physical and cognitive ability levels? More than high participation is required. Additionally, staff must monitor who the participants are to sustain a vital and thriving recreation center.

A unique aspect of campus recreation that is seen less in other areas has to do with the intensity of student competition. In addition to safety and participation, what language is used/tolerated during competition? How is abusive language addressed during an intramural basketball game? How are threats and physical contact beyond the scope of the sport or activity addressed by staff? If anger management is an issue with a specific student, how is their behavior addressed at the moment and managed in future participation? Competition can be exciting and can help develop community and camaraderie. However, it can also provoke negative behavior in some students and undermine the positive experiences of engaging in sports and activities.

Institutional Intelligence Questions

Who: Who are critical partners on campus with this office? Who is present and participating? Who is absent? Who is responsible for coordinating events?

What: What are the special considerations around safety and competition in campus recreation activities? What are the outcomes of recreational activities (learning, well-being, and otherwise)? What is the history of certain events (positive, negative, neutral)? What is the process for reviewing risk management and ensuring appropriate and timely responses to accidents or injuries? What protocols are in place to ensure safety during practice, competition, and travel?

Where: Where are activities held? Where are these spaces accessible to students with diverse identities and abilities?

When: When are activities held? Do those times align with the academic mission of the institution?

Why: Why are these activities important? Why do students participate? Why are resources allocated to these activities?

How: How can staff set graduate student assistants or interns up for success during their time with this unit? How can we facilitate participation in a way that is inclusive and celebrates a broad range of abilities? How are advising, coaching, and training services provided for students in club sports?

Critical Scenario 13.1 Campus Recreation

Co-Authors: Chris Fiocchi, Senior Director of Campus Recreation at Clemson University, and Jordan Bowman, Coordinator of Operations, University of Tennessee at Chattanooga

Diana (she/her) is a student who works as an intramural sports referee/official. She has worked for the Campus Recreation Department at Alpha University for three semesters. She reports to Dave (he/him), a graduate student in recreation services, and Dave reports to Joel (he/him), an assistant director with recreation services.

Alpha has recently tried to engage more intentionally with international students on campus. Alpha is proud of its recruitment and retention of students from China. During a special orientation session for international students, Campus Rec made its space available to familiarize students with activities and recreation opportunities. It provided an overview of many sports and activities, including intramurals offered by the department. As a result, there has been an increase in international student participation on campus, particularly among Chinese students.

Broomball is a unique intramural sport at Alpha. Played on ice, broomball resembles hockey, but participants use broom-like paddles to hit a ball into a goal. The games are held between 10 p.m. and 1 a.m. on weeknights to avoid conflict with the school's hockey team practice.

At a recent game, when Diana was working, there was an altercation between Brock (he/him) and Hu (he/him). Brock claimed Hu fouled him, called his opponent out using a racial epithet, and told Hu to "go back to where you came from!" Diana and Dave were both present and witnessed the exchange.

The Law

- What are the relevant legal issues in this scenario?
- What institutional policies, procedures, or processes are applicable in this scenario?

Ethics

- What are the relevant ethical issues in this scenario?
- What information would the characters need to make the best ethical decisions in this situation?

Identity

- How would characters' social identities affect how this scenario might unfold? Assign the characters particular social identities and go through the scenario. Then change some of those social identities and go through the scenario again.
- How do the situation and the information you would need change?

Scenario-Specific Questions

- Who involved in the game needs outreach or intervention immediately? Whom does Diana need to tell about this issue immediately?
- What are the potential legal, ethical, and safety issues? What do staff need to document? In what order might Joel want to meet with Diana, Dave, Brock, Hu, and the other students present at the incident? What information might divisional leadership or other departments on campus need?
- Where might Diana and Dave talk with players and teams if other games are happening on the ice at the same time?
- When do Diana and Dave need to contact Joel? When might they need to call others to assist with the situation?
- Why might this incident have implications beyond these two players or teams?
- How might staff decide whether the game can continue or not? How should Dave and Joel follow up with recreation staff members (present at this incident or not)? How have similar incidents been handled in the past at Alpha? How would this incident inform upcoming staff meetings or future training?

Using the Institutional Intelligence Model, what other information might Diana and Dave get, and how might they use that information to address this situation and plan for the future to avoid similar incidents?

Fraternity and Sorority Life

FSL is one way that many students seek a sense of belonging. Students are part of a community by affiliating with organizations that ideally foster a shared vision and goals. FSL organizations may involve residential living experiences on some campuses, either on or off campus. Healthy FSL organizations can foster a sense of social connectedness and belonging, develop leadership skills, engage in philanthropic activities, support a chapter's collective academic success, and provide a support network for college students.

The history of fraternities and sororities on college campuses goes back nearly 300 years, beginning as early as 1750, and the first fraternity (Phi Beta Kappa) was established at the College of William and Mary in 1776 (College of William & Mary, n.d.). The first sorority (Gamma Phi Beta) would follow about 100 years later, in 1874, at Syracuse University (Syracuse University, n.d.). The original fraternities and sororities were for white students only. However, other organizations would emerge to serve the needs of other racial/ethnic groups. See Table 13.1 for a list of the first of cultural interest fraternities and sororities.

These organizations are faced with various challenges as they constitute social and academic networks, provide housing and meals, and obligate members to financial and work commitments. Some challenges for FSL students, communities, and staff members working with these organizations include alcohol and other drugs, hazing, inclusivity related to race, gender, sexual orientation, and other identities, mental health, and Title IX/sexual misconduct issues (Boettcher et al., 2018).

FSL chapters that offer housing (on or off campus) face challenges similar to those of residence life and dining programs. With these challenges in mind, various liability, safety, wellness, and student risk issues emerge. Additionally, FSL organizations can take on many of the same risks as student activities, clubs, and organizations. Similarly, the sense of history and tradition in many chapters not only fosters pride and community but also can create challenges for members and organizations alike, as those histories and traditions are often complex and need to be acknowledged and adapted as times change.

Institutional Intelligence Questions

Who: Who are critical partners on campus with this office? Who are the chapter advisors, live-in staff, and alumni who continue to be active with specific chapters?

What: What background do staff in FSL have (student affairs, other)? What is the history of FSL organizations and specific chapters nationally and on a given campus? What does recruitment entail for different

TABLE 13.1 Origins of Cultural Interest Fraternities and Sororities

Cultural interest	*First fraternity*	*First sorority*	*Umbrella organization*	*Notes*
African American/ Black	Alpha Phi Alpha Fraternity, Inc. 1906 Cornell University	Alpha Kappa Alpha, Sorority, Inc. 1908 Howard University	National Pan-Hellenic Council (NPHC)	
Asian American, Pacific Islander, and Desi American	Rho Psi Society 1916 Cornell University	Sigma Omicron P.I. 1930, San Francisco State University	Asian Pacific Islander Desi Association (APIDA)	There are currently 50+ organizations; 11 are APIDA members
Latin*	Phi Iota Alpha Fraternity, Inc. 1898, Rensselaer Polytechnic Institute	Lambda Theta Alpha Latin Sorority, Inc. 1975, Kean University	National Association of Latino Fraternal Organizations (NALFO)	There are currently 45 Latin* organizations; 16 are NALFO members
LGBT	Delta Phi Upsilon Fraternity, Inc. 1985, Florida State University	Beta Phi Omega Sorority, Inc. 2000, Tallahassee Florida		
Multicultural	Pi Sigma Phi Multicultural Fraternity, Inc. 1990, Montclair State & New Jersey City universities	Mu Sigma Upsilon Sorority, Inc. 1981, Rutgers University	National Multicultural Greek Council (NMGC)	
Native American	Epsilon Chi Nu, Inc. 1996, East Carolina University	Alpha Pi Omega 1994, UNC-Chapel Hill		
South Asian	Iota Nu Delta Fraternity, Inc. 1994, Binghamton University	Kappa Phi Gamma Sorority, Inc. 1998, University of Texas, Austin		

Latin* is an all-inclusive term that critically considers the fluidity of social identities of people of Latin American descent or origin. Latin* invites to the conversation those who do and do not identify with Latinx, Latino, and Latina. For example, Latin* considers Latinx, Latiné, Latinu, Latini, Latino, Latina, Latina/o, Latin@, Latin, or Latin American (Salinas, 2020; Salinas & Lozano, 2022).

organizations/chapters? What is the history of FSL on your campus? What is the role of FSL alumni and affiliated donors, legislators, or institutional leaders? What is the role of national organizations for those chapters that are so affiliated? What role or authority do campus practitioners, campuswide Greek councils, and national organizations have in recognizing and self-governing individual FSL organizations?

Where: Where are chapter events held? Where do members live (on campus, off campus, campus-adjacent)? Where are FSL facilities located (on or off campus, part of residence life)?

When: When does formal recruitment for chapters take place? Is it the same time for fraternities and sororities? When does recruitment happen for the Interfraternity Council (IFC), Multicultural Greek Council (MCG), National Panhellenic Conference (NPC), and National Pan-Hellenic Council (NPHC)?

Why: Why do students join these organizations on your campus?

How: How have student leaders and organizational members historically been trained about hazing, sexual assault, alcohol, and other drugs? How effective has that training been? How can staff set graduate assistants or interns up for success during their time with this unit? How are violations of policy handled for these organizations and members? How are the relationships between these organizations and the rest of campus and the surrounding community? How are Greek letter organizations recognized and sustained?

Critical Scenario 13.2 Fraternity and Sorority Life

Co-Author: Cayce Pasko-Stanley, Assistant Director for Fraternity & Sorority Life, Northwestern University

Pearl (she/her) is an experienced professional, having worked in FSL at two different schools. She is in her first year as Assistant Dean of Students and Director of FSL at Mack University. She has built good relationships with her team and many students in her first weeks on campus.

The annual leadership retreat planning committee—comprised almost exclusively of Panhellenic and IFC members—has completed a draft of the upcoming retreat and transition training for new leaders. The previous director created the committee with the intention of getting better access to student feedback and ideas. The retreat will take place early in January after the semester break. Members of NPHC and Multicultural Greek Council (MGC) organizations come to the FSL office to discuss their concerns. Dinah (she/her), a current chapter president, says,

> "The topics are great, and the organization, for the most part, works, but they only have leaders from our organizations presenting on diversity, equity, and inclusion (DEI) topics. White leaders present on leadership, time management, politics, ethics, group dynamics, hazing, 'living your organizational values,' and team building. We have expertise in those areas, so it would be nice for white students to do DEI training and education. We are willing to help, but there is more we can contribute, too."

The other members agree and ask Pearl why they have not been invited to be more involved with planning retreats.

The Law

- What are the relevant legal issues in this scenario?
- What institutional policies, procedures, or processes are applicable in this scenario?

Ethics

- What are the relevant ethical issues in this scenario?
- What information would the characters need to make the best ethical decisions in this situation?

Identity

- How would characters' social identities affect how this scenario might unfold? Assign the characters particular social identities and go through the scenario. Then change some of those social identities and go through the scenario again.
- How do the situation and the information you would need change?

Scenario-Specific Questions

- Who is involved with the governance of FSL organizations on this campus?
- Who funds this retreat?

- Who selects the retreat planning committee members, and what are the selection criteria?
- Who leads the retreat sessions?
- What is the history of peer training and education in the FSL system at this institution?
- What additional support resources may Pearl consider offering to members of NPHC and MGC who may have experienced harm as a result of being excluded?
- What education or follow-up may need to be delivered to IFC/Panhellenic members of the committee as a result of this feedback?
- Where might Pearl go to get more information on the history of relationships between organizations on her new campus?
- When is the deadline for making changes to the upcoming retreat? When should conversations begin about future retreats?
- Why might Pearl's experience at other schools be an asset? Why might it be a challenge?
- How can students go about making changes to committees, events, training, and other activities in FSL involving multiple organizations?
- How have concerns in the past been shared and addressed?
- How can Pearl help foster stronger relationships and better communication and build rapport and trust between different organizations?

What information might Pearl get using the Institutional Intelligence Model to help her navigate the retreat situation and support all the students and organizations involved?

Housing

Housing has been part of higher education from the beginning. Based on the European institutions at Oxford and Cambridge, residence halls were educational spaces for formal and informal learning. Since faculty also lived in the halls, they had the opportunity to supervise students who often traveled a great distance to attend the early colleges (Winston & Anchors, 1993). This living dynamic provided for the emergence of in *loco parentis* as faculty and other school leaders took on responsibility for students who—particularly early on—were not more than 13 or 14 years old (Cohen & Kisker, 2010).

The popularity of residence halls decreased in the late 1800s. While the Morrill Acts of 1862 and 1890 resulted in more colleges and universities, residence halls were not always part of that growth (Winston & Anchors, 1993). By the early 1900s, however, residence hall construction was again on the rise. Even as the impact of the Great Depression unfolded across the country, the Public Works Administration housing division partnered with universities to build residence halls (Winston & Anchors, 1993).

Following World War II, with the implementation of the G.I. Bill, the Housing Act of 1950 inspired a construction wave across higher education (Winston & Anchors, 1993). Student activism on campuses in the 1960s led to changes in residence halls, a decrease in *loco parentis*, and a shift from a housemother system to hall directors and student governance around programming, judicial boards, outreach counselors, and the emergence of resident assistants (RAs) (Schroeder & Mable, 1994). At the same time, the concerns related to housing were less about accommodating students (as there were enough spaces for students on most campuses by then) but instead focused on providing services (Ebbers et al., 1973).

After a period of increasing amenities and using housing as a means of attracting students during competition to increase enrollment, we are now in the midst of new changes. The intense focus on privacy has given way to suite-style spaces and smaller bedrooms to create larger shared spaces that are multi-functional, and the incorporation of technology into living spaces continues to be a priority (Fabris, 2014). Finally, blending academic spaces and experiences into residential communities brings residential living full circle. Instead of separating academic and co-curricular learning spaces, faculty-in-residence and classroom spaces in residence halls are on the rise, just as academic and living spaces and faculty residing with or near students were part of early higher education in the U.S.

Acknowledging the connection between residence life, dining, and facilities is essential. These areas work in tandem, in many cases, as part of a housing program. Each has responsibilities for student safety, well-being, and development. Additionally, staff in these areas can be essential to the student experience.

I (Michelle) once had a faculty member who shared that when his daughter graduated from college, there were two people she wanted her parents to meet. One was the college president. The other was the woman who swiped students' cards in the dining hall. It was this woman the student felt showed the most care and support for her in college.

Additionally, the custodial staff in residence halls can play a significant role in the student experience. Students have shared that custodial staff help to keep them safe by maintaining public spaces, showing care through conversation with them, and playing an essential role by engaging in conversations about life with students (Boettcher et al., 2019a). Additional housing services such as room assignments, summer programming, and front desk operations provide other ways for students to engage via employment and community engagement.

Housing staff deal with the holistic experience of students in higher education. Live-in professional staff frequently engage with students about well-being, academics, sense of belonging, leadership, policy, safety, Title IX, and any other issues that college students face on campus, in class, and in their home communities. Working with students 24/7 when most other campus services are closed, these practitioners are often well networked to resources across campus and provide comprehensive support to the students who live on campus. Nguyễn et al. (2018) wrote that "residence life and housing are two areas in higher education and student affairs that experience the most intersections of law and policy with practice and compliance" (p. 12).

Perhaps these practitioners regularly respond to crises more than any other student affairs staff. These include facilities emergencies (fires and floods), interpersonal crises (dating violence, roommate conflicts, and bias incidents), and medical and mental health issues. This team likely includes undergraduate students employed as live-in paraprofessional RAs or similar roles. This peer leader role is essential to community development and safety and requires additional training, supervision, and support from full-time practitioners.

In addition, the residential communities can look dramatically different across a single campus. Housing programs designate communities by gender, student classification (first-year halls, graduate student, or family communities), and building type (traditional residence halls with community bathrooms as opposed to a suite- or apartment-style living). Learning communities that focus on academic majors or particular interest areas provide additional collaboration and student involvement opportunities. Further, different buildings may have very different facilities—and often different costs. Some halls may be air-conditioned while others are not. Some communities may include office or classroom spaces. The cosmetic and aesthetic design of residence halls and their proximity to campus can vary dramatically. Additionally, some halls may be much closer to the campus than others. These contextual environmental dynamics can impact the roles and responsibilities of staff who oversee these communities.

In navigating issues of community, crises, and college success, residence life staff, graduate, and undergraduate staff must be highly collaborative, knowledgeable about policy and resources, and willing and able to engage in difficult conversations about various topics. Given both the breadth and depth of demands on staff in these areas—particularly staff living in the same communities where they work—training and knowledge are essential. In our constantly changing higher education settings, providing support and guidance to these staff is also central to the success of these units on campus.

Given the live-in status of some faculty and staff, unique issues can arise. With faculty in residence and/or housing staff "on-site" 24/7, those individuals may notice things and identify concerns that do not come up in other functional areas or that live-out or potentially live-on staff may not see. Additionally, there are times when live-in staff or faculty can be involved in issues or even cause issues, again because of their unique circumstances. Living with students in their homes differs from working with students in an office. There are special considerations and potential needs for live-in staff and faculty.

Institutional Intelligence Questions

Who: Who are the key partners on campus with this office?

What: What background or education do staff in this area need (student affairs, other)? What is the relationship between this unit and others on campus and in the larger community? What topical training do staff receive at the beginning of the year? What ongoing training and development do staff have throughout the year? What is the role of student leaders within the community?

Where: Where are specific residential communities located? Where are staff located within that community? Where are community spaces?

When: When are staff on call? When are they provided time away from work?

Why: Why are policies in place (particularly those that may not be common across other institutions in higher education)?

How: How is staff well-being supported? How is collaboration across academic and student affairs functional areas facilitated? How do senior leaders ensure that they do not exploit undergraduate and graduate student staff in unpredictable, time-intensive roles? How are students informed of policies and held accountable for those policies? How are student leaders engaged in managing the community?

Critical Scenario 13.3 Housing

Co-Authors: Dr. Reyes J. Luna, Interim Executive Director of Housing, Cal Poly Pomona, and Dr. Aja C. Holmes, Assistant Dean of Students and Director of Student Living, University of San Francisco

Two roommates have had ongoing issues throughout the fall term. Both students are first-year students in their first semester on campus. Their conflict has become an issue in the larger community. Other students on the floor have taken sides, the roommates have taken turns sleeping on friends' couches, and the roommates have actively engaged with other residents to try to garner support for their perspective on the room issues. Kim (they/them), the RA on the floor, has facilitated two dialogues between the roommates, but both insist that the other should move out of the room.

Kim has documented their work with residents in a thorough but concise manner. Kim sees these as being the main issues:

- Teresa (she/her) does not feel her roommate Shauna (she/her) is doing enough to keep the room clean. Teresa says Shauna does not wash her dishes or take out the trash even though they said in their roommate agreement that they would alternate weeks taking out the trash and would not leave dirty dishes in the room for more than 24 hours.
- Shauna has shared that Teresa has friends visiting at all hours and her boyfriend spends the night at least three times a week. In their roommate agreement, they said that there would be no guests after midnight and that overnight guests were permissible but only when they both agreed to it.
- The roommates have stopped speaking to one another and instead leave notes on each other's desks. Kim has seen the notes, and they have become increasingly hostile as the term has gone on. Teresa's last note to Shauna read, "Your side of the room is a pigsty. Everyone knows it. CLEAN IT UP TODAY!" The last note Shauna wrote in response said, "I'll clean the room when you tell your nasty bf to start sleeping in his own room!"

The Law

- What are the relevant legal issues in this scenario?
- What institutional policies, procedures, or processes are applicable in this scenario?

Ethics

- What are the relevant ethical issues in this scenario?
- What information would the characters need to make the best ethical decisions in this situation?

Identity

- How would characters' social identities affect how this scenario might unfold? Assign the characters particular social identities and go through the scenario. Then change some of those social identities and go through the scenario again.
- How do the situation and the information you would need change?

Scenario-Specific Questions

- Who needs to be involved in conversations with Teresa and Shauna? Who else might need to know about the situation between the roommates?
- What other issues might be at play that Kim has not documented? What are the processes at the institution for resolving roommate conflicts? What is the configuration of Teresa and Shauna's room?
- Where do the students live (newer/popular residence hall community, older community, other)?
- Where did Shauna and Teresa meet? (Are they friends from high school? Have they lived together before?)
- Why is Kim being brought into the situation at this particular point? Why might things have built up or escalated over time?
- How has the roommate tried to resolve the issue themselves?

How might Kim use the Institutional Intelligence Model to identify other resources or strategies to navigate the situation with Teresa and Shauna?

Student Behavior Intervention

In recent years, more campuses have developed offices to provide intrusive support to students outside of traditional student affairs functional areas. These offices deal with a broad range of student concerns and often are at the hub in connecting students to multiple resources as they navigate challenges related to school and life. Student Behavior Intervention offices may have a variety of approaches and responsibilities for student success. They may be known as student assistance programs, case management services, student advocacy and care, or similar titles.

These teams work to mitigate risk and provide support to affected students (Drysdale et al., 2010; Jablonski et al., 2008). Additionally, behavioral assessment is an ongoing process of assessing specific student behaviors, planning interventions, and evaluating processes implemented (Deisinger et al., 2008). When convening or attending student behavioral intervention team meetings, Title IX meetings, and other teams related to responding to distressed students, these staff members often utilize case management strategies that emerge from social work practice.

These staff members focus on issues ranging from homesickness to suicidal ideation. Understanding the complex issues involved is a process that requires building rapport with students beyond a single meeting. These staff must be skilled in listening, documenting, responding, and providing resources to help students self-advocate and problem-solve. They support students to make connections to a variety of resources across campus and in the community to get the support they need. Furthermore, this office must foster relationships with faculty so student assistance staff can address issues in the classroom, academic work, or interactions between students. Other issues that this staff team can help with include the death of a family member, relationship violence, mental and physical health concerns, and general student welfare.

Institutional Intelligence Questions

Who: Who are key partners on campus with this office? Who else might have information about student behavior and issues to serve as collaborators in addressing issues that might arise? Who else must be informed when students or others share issues with a Student Assistance staff member?

What: What background or education do staff in this area need (student affairs, social work, counseling, medical, other)? What questions do staff members in this office need to be prepared to ask students? What questions might these staff members need to ask faculty or staff on campus who are reporting concerns? What information can staff share with faculty or staff who report concerns? What are the differences between a student's relationship with Student Assistance staff and a counselor?

Where: Where is this office located on campus? Where is the director of this office in the organizational chart for the department, division, or institution? Where do these staff members get ongoing training? Where are these staff members obliged to document and report information they receive about different types of incidents (online, forms, to which offices on campus/off campus)? How might where staff have conversations (phone, video conference, email, in person) influence what those conversations entail?

When: When are the busy times of year for this office? When is time built in for staff to care for themselves amid very stressful and time-intensive work? When would you reach out to the student? When would you let others know about this situation?

Why: Why does this functional area exist in addition to student conduct and the counseling center? Why might case management be best positioned to assist the holistic needs of students in some situations?

How: How is information about responding to student concerns documented? How is follow-up done? How quickly should staff respond to people reporting concerns? To students? How do practitioners in this work build and sustain relationships across campus and in the community? How do students find out that this office exists, and how does it provide support? When engaging with students, how do staff triage immediate, underlying, chronic, and crisis issues?

Critical Scenario 13.4 Student Behavior Intervention

Co-Author: Dr. Keith Robinder, Vice President for Student Support, St. Louis Community College, Wildwood Campus

Professor Neal (he/him) is a political science faculty member with an established relationship with the Student Advocacy & Resource Center on campus. He reaches out with a concern for Marcus (he/him), a student in his course. He shares that Marcus's class participation, homework, exam scores, and physical appearance have declined in the past few weeks. Marcus started the semester as a highly engaged and active participant who made significant contributions to class discussion, showed up on time, and scored a 97% and a 98% on the first two exams in the class. Professor Neal shares that Marcus has not turned in the weekly homework assignments for the past three weeks, is often late to class or absent altogether, seems unkempt, and often wears dirty clothes. Marcus no longer volunteers to speak in class, and when called upon, he gives one-word responses or says he does not have anything to add.

Professor Neal has a good rapport with Marcus and recently offered to help him create a plan to salvage the semester. During the meeting, Marcus shared with Professor Neal that he is homeless and no longer has access to the internet, reliable food resources, or safe places to stay. Marcus reported to his instructor that he is not sure he can focus on learning as he struggles to provide for his basic needs.

The Law

- What are the relevant legal issues in this scenario?
- What institutional policies, procedures, or processes are applicable in this scenario?

Ethics

- What are the relevant ethical issues in this scenario?
- What information would the characters need to make the best ethical decisions in this situation?

Identity

- How would characters' social identities affect how this scenario might unfold? Assign the characters particular social identities and go through the scenario. Then change some of those social identities and go through the scenario again.
- How do the situation and the information you would need change?

Scenario-Specific Questions

- Whom might Professor Neal reach out to for strategies on how he can continue to engage with and support Marcus directly? Who may need to know about the challenges that Marcus is facing?
- What university resources and policies are in place to support homeless students? For which community resources might Marcus be eligible? What other issues may be concerns that Marcus has not discussed with Professor Neal?
- Where might Professor Neal connect Marcus with resources? Where are safe places for homeless members of the campus community? Where are safe places for homeless members of the community beyond the institution?
- When does Marcus need to complete work to save his grade in Professor Neal's course? Other courses? When did Marcus begin experiencing homelessness?
- Why might Marcus not have discussed his situation until Professor Neal asked?
- How can Marcus prepare for the next semester, given his circumstances? How can Marcus access resources if transportation is an issue?

How else might Professor Neal use the Institutional Intelligence Model to support Marcus?

Student Conduct

Student conduct is an office unto itself, and work is incorporated into other areas. For example, housing staff may serve as hearing officers, student hearing boards might hear violations in FSL organizations, and academic affairs may oversee academic integrity rather than student conduct offices. For this section, we will focus on student conduct offices, but there are implications for offices and staff across higher education.

Student conduct in the early years of higher education in the United States was focused on morality and encapsulated by *in loco parentis*. An authoritative focus on discipline was established early (Brubacher & Rudy, 1997; Smith, 1994) and continued until after the Civil War. Early students and faculty lived in the same residential spaces, so higher education sought to align intellectual and moral development (Brubacher & Rudy, 1997). A push for students to have a voice in the creation, enaction, and enforcement of policies began in the context of democratization following the Civil War. At the same time, administrators were hired to manage student behavior, replacing the college president and faculty in this function (Dannells, 1997). In 1937's *The Student Personnel Point of View*, student conduct is identified as within the realm of student affairs as the document specifies, "Administering student discipline to the end that the individual will be strengthened and the welfare of the group preserved" (American Council on Education [ACE], 1937, p. 5).

With the implementation of the G.I. Bill, the number of students on campus increased dramatically (Dannells, 1997; Smith, 1994). In 1949, *The Student Personnel Point of View* was revisited. This time the authors went a bit further in their comments about student behavior issues on campus. The ACE report described discipline as "an educational function designed to modify personal behavior patterns and to substitute socially acceptable attitudes for those which have precipitated unacceptable behavior" (ACE, 1949, p. 8).

As a result, a rebellion against *in loco parentis* amid other social, political, and cultural shifts in the larger society began to manifest in higher education. In the 1960s, student access to due process, the appeal of university rulings, and other rights expanded the disciplinary process on college campuses (Lowery, 2011). Additionally, students were afforded some input on campus policy violation adjudication through student involvement on judicial hearing boards (Sims, 1971). These changes to campus conduct processes also expanded the role of courts outside of higher education. They increased tension between students and systems and educational and legalistic approaches to student behavior.

The 1970s, 1980s, and 1990s saw several pieces of legislation (FERPA, the Clery Act, the Violence Against Women Act [VAWA], and HIPAA; see Chapter 2) providing additional guidance to universities about legal expectations and privacy and transparency when it comes to student conduct and safety information. The current century has highlighted conduct issues related to bias incidents, litigation, privacy, social media, threat assessment, Title IX, and other persistent and emerging issues. It may be too early to fully understand what will define the current era of student conduct, but the work continues nonetheless.

Institutional Intelligence Questions

Who: Who are the key partners on campus with this office? Who is the director—an attorney or a student affairs professional? Who hears appeals beyond the conduct office? Who has access to student conduct records?

What: What is the philosophy of the conduct office? What background or education do practitioners in this area have (student affairs, law degree, other)? What issues are most common on campus? What is the student's perception of this office? What training and educational programs does this office provide? What is the relationship of the conduct office with faculty on campus? What types of cases does this office hear? What relationship does this office have with other conduct processes on campus (student hearing boards, residence life, FSL)?

Where: Where do students find information about campus policies and student rights and responsibilities?

When: When are busier times in terms of cases? When are students notified of violations? When are the student code of conduct documents updated? When might parents be notified about student conduct violations?

Why: Why might a student engage with this office? Why might faculty engage with this office? Why might staff engage with this office?

How: How can staff set graduate student assistants or interns up for success during their time with this unit? How does this office function in partnership with university counsel? How are student conduct records maintained? How is FERPA ensured? How is equity prioritized?

Critical Scenario 13. 5 Student Conduct

Co-Author: Adric Hardy, Assistant Dean of Students, Duke University

Rob has come to his conduct meeting regarding a recent incident. Last weekend after the football game, Rob was very intoxicated. He was seen spray-painting "graffiti rock" on the edge of campus with racial epithets. Graffiti rock is the campus expression canvas where students often spray-paint various messages, announcements, and art. When confronted by police, Rob ran away, falling and breaking his ankle. Campus police arrested him and forwarded a report to the student conduct office.

The Law

- What are the relevant legal issues in this scenario?
- What institutional policies, procedures, or processes are applicable in this scenario?

Ethics

- What are the relevant ethical issues in this scenario?
- What information would the characters need to make the best ethical decisions in this situation?

Identity

- How would characters' social identities affect how this scenario might unfold? Assign the characters specific social identities and go through the scenario. Then change some of those social identities and go through the scenario again.
- How do the situation and the information you would need change?

Scenario-Specific Questions

- Who has information about this situation relevant to Rob's conduct meeting? Whom is Rob allowed to bring with him to his hearing?
- Who was harmed as a result of Rob's actions, and how (if at all) can the institution reasonably facilitate the process of repairing that harm?
- What are the potential violations in this situation? What non-conduct concerns might the hearing officer raise with Rob? What role do Rob's attitude, honesty, and forthcomingness play in the hearing/hearing outcome? What type of institution is Rob attending—for instance, is his university a public or private institution? What are the routes of appeal open to Rob depending on this case? What are the judicial history and philosophy related to student conduct on this campus?

- What protections does the First Amendment provide for Rob's speech (if any)?
- Where are students made aware of policies, student code of conduct, and other relevant information? Where can Rob go to get guidance about the conduct process before his hearing?
- When did the incident occur, and when is the hearing?
- How old is Rob? How might Rob respond during the hearing? How might his reaction inform the process and the outcome of the hearing?

How else might the conduct officer, in this case, use the Institutional Intelligence Model to support Rob?

Wellness Programs

Infirmary care was the original approach to student health concerns on college campuses through the first half of the 20th century (Dorman & Christmas, 2002). Between the 1940s and the 1970s, medical care on campuses shifted to primarily outpatient systems. The opportunity to make this shift was driven by immunizations, antibiotics, and other medical advances and concerns about liability issues. College wellness grew out of a shift in the 1970s from college "health education" to "health promotion" (Huey et al., 2020). All of this set the stage for the emergence of college wellness in the 1990s. Health promotion colleagues "helped introduce NASPA... to the inextricable link between the health and well-being of college students and their academic success, retention, and graduation" (Huey et al., 2020, p. 809). As a result, NASPA hosted strategy conferences on topics such as sexual violence, alcohol, mental health, and peer education (NASPA, n.d.-b).

Wellness programs can be housed in several different places, depending on the campus organization. They may fall under campus recreation or be part of the health center. Wellness can encompass stress management, suicide prevention, eating disorders, and education about alcohol and other drugs, among other topics. Wellness is an important and complex area in student affairs. As with campus recreation, knowledge about safety and risk management is essential. For this staff, it is also important to distinguish between confidentiality and privacy (see Chapter 15). Most wellness staff cannot offer confidentiality to students but should be prepared to connect students with confidential resources such as counseling or medical staff.

Wellness programming is often connected to concepts of different wellness wheels with specific life tasks such as spirituality, self-regulation, work, friendship, and love (Sweeney & Witmer, 1991). Staff use variations on this model in well-being programming, residence life programming and curriculum, and other aspects of college student life. Because of the nature of the topics that wellness staff present on, they must be familiar with campus resources. For instance, the staff in this office may do presentations for various student organizations and groups on topics such as anxiety, depression, stress, suicide, and other issues related to mental health. Staff in this area will frequently address potentially sensitive or controversial topics such as alcohol and other substance abuse, reproductive health, safer sex, and preventing sexually transmitted infections, among other topics related to student well-being. Preparing for challenging questions, requests for help, and personal disclosures is essential.

It is essential to consider issues of (in)equity related to wellness practice and access to wellness resources. Identity erasure and racial color-blindness can "create barriers to wellness" for some students (Mosley et al., 2019). Wellness and well-being staff must connect students to resources and follow up with students and partners. Additionally, staff must consider with whom they must share information depending on what students may disclose.

Institutional Intelligence Questions

Who: Who are the key partners on campus with this office?

What: What backgrounds do staff members in this area have? (Student affairs, counseling, medical? Other?) What is the role of students/peer mentors in work done in these areas? What training on ethics do students working in this area receive?

Where: Where are wellness staff most likely to encounter legal and ethical issues? Where do issues arise most frequently through programs, individual meetings, courses, or other times?

When: When are wellness staff obligated to report concerns about students and practitioners? When are the busier times of year for these practitioners?

Why: Why are students often involved in wellness activities? Why might the engagement of specific students make this functional area more vulnerable to litigation?

How: How can staff set graduate student assistants or interns up for success during their time with this unit? How can staff anticipate potential legal and ethical issues?

Critical Scenario 13.6 Wellness Programs

Co-Author: Michael Almond, Assistant Director, Student Volunteerism and Service, Kennesaw State University

The Center for Wellbeing on campus hosts an end-of-the-semester stress-free zone the week before finals each term. The staff host various activities, including meditation, massage, "make your own stress ball," and other events. The events are well attended, and the staff gets to know some students well, as some of the same students attend these events each semester.

Charlie (they/them) is in their second year in the unit as a full-time professional. They have gotten to know Anthem (xe/xem) well through the stress-free zone and other well-being programs over the past two years. Anthem has told Charlie that xe sees them as a mentor and values them as a campus resource.

At the end of the fall term, Anthem comes to the "make your own stress ball" workshop, and Charlie welcomes xem and jokes, "This has got to be your third or fourth time making a stress ball, Anthem. You must wear them out." Anthem laughs and says that xe makes the most of the stressful activities every semester. At the end of the event, Anthem asks if xe can talk to Charlie for a few minutes.

"I cannot go home when the residence halls close this break," Anthem says, tearing up.

"My mom is living with a new boyfriend, and I'm not welcome there. I don't know where to go or what to do. I'm thinking about giving up."

"Giving up on what?" Charlie asks. "On school?"

"Sure," Anthem responds. "On school and everything else."

The Law

- What are the relevant legal issues in this scenario?
- What institutional policies, procedures, or processes are applicable in this scenario?

Ethics

- What are the relevant ethical issues in this scenario?
- What information would the characters need to make the best ethical decisions in this situation?

Identity

- How would characters' social identities affect how this scenario might unfold? Assign the characters specific social identities and go through the scenario. Then change some of those social identities and go through the scenario again.
- How do the situation and the information you would need change?

Scenario-Specific Questions

- Whom should Charlie notify immediately about Anthem's comments?
- What is the protocol on campus for reporting concerns about student well-being?
- Where can Charlie help Anthem connect? What confidential resources are available for Anthem?
- When should Charlie let their supervisor know about this situation? When should Charlie try to contact Anthem again?
- Why is it essential that Charlie not keep this exchange with Anthem to himself?
- How might the incident trigger Charlie?

In what other ways can Charlie utilize Institutional Intelligence, and what additional questions should they be asking related to that framework to give Anthem the best possible guidance and support moving forward?

Conclusion

Many higher education staff attend to students' holistic well-being and learning. These areas contribute to a sense of belonging, engagement in learning, persistence, and success. The functional areas in this chapter intersect as offices where students often engage in various conversations, learning experiences, and activities to help them learn more about who they are and their rights and responsibilities as community members.

Staff in these functional areas provide resources and guidance and challenge students in their learning and growth. Staff must consider legal issues related to contracts, policies, and other guidelines. This work is complex and has significant legal, ethical, personal, professional, and institutional implications. Staff benefit from using the Institutional Intelligence Model as this approach helps practitioners protect students, themselves as employees, and their units and institutions. More importantly, Institutional Intelligence can help ensure complete and high-level care and support through difficult situations.

14

STUDENT INVOLVEMENT

> Involvement in and out of the classroom leads to positive outcomes for students. Positive role models are essential for students' growth and development. Ethical advisors inspire students to emulate their behaviors in their leadership roles. Whether a student is a member or on the executive board, this is true. Student engagement in student organizations, service learning, and study abroad are just a few ways students gain valuable soft and hard skills and foster students' growth to become servant leaders who leave the world better than they found it.
>
> —Tiana Iruoje, Director of Student Engagement and Success, School of Informatics, Computing, and Engineering, Indiana University Bloomington

Students are active in various areas of student affairs as residents in halls on campus, by participating in activities like orientation, through the use of financial aid resources, and by engaging with other resources and opportunities. Many of the most active students are engaged across multiple functional units and are members of or hold leadership positions across various areas. They may be club officers, peer mentors, or student employees in student and academic affairs offices.

One student might be an orientation leader, a member of marching band, a residence hall president, and the creator of a service initiative and be involved in intramural sports activities. Another may be a resident assistant (RA), the president of a club associated with her academic major, a member of a faith practice organization, a tutor at a local elementary school, and a reporter for the campus newspaper. Still, another student may have a part-time job and be

DOI: 10.4324/9781003442707-17

involved significantly with only one organization—the campus lecture series or homecoming planning committee. Student engagement can vary from institution to institution based on the location and engagement opportunities available on a specific campus. Regardless, students can sometimes prioritize these involvements at a cost to their academic work. Putting activities before academics can become ethical issues if students are so overwhelmed that they take academic shortcuts that might constitute academic integrity violations. Or a student who prioritizes a club commitment over their work responsibilities can create other ethical challenges for students.

Managing commitments and priorities are far from the only ethical issues that students navigate regarding campus involvement. This chapter will explore the variety of Institutional Intelligence considerations that academic and student affairs staff and others in higher education must keep in mind as they work to enhance students' campus experiences through activities and involvement.

Chapter Organization

This chapter includes an overview of student involvement which explores its evolution and the changing perspectives of administrative leaders about what involvement outside of going to classes should include. We then move to civic learning and leadership, leadership development, and the university's role in developing citizens to engage with communities during and beyond students' time in higher education. The final section is an additional connection to the community; here, we examine the role of community service and service learning in student activities.

Legal and Ethical Considerations

What are the legal and ethical implications for student involvement? *It depends.* Staff must consider risk management issues, contracts, and off-campus partnerships/vendors as student organizations plan events and activities. Many students learn about fiscal management as organizational treasurers, so staff who work with organizations as advisors must also be attentive to organizational finances. Not every student activity and involvement opportunity goes through a traditional or institutionally recognized student organization. For example, protests, free speech zone events, and other coordinated events on campus obligate staff members to understand free speech and protest issues through the lens of campus policy and local, state, and federal regulations. Finally, the media may cover any event or activity. Academic and student affairs practitioners must be aware of potential implications through social and traditional media coverage. It is imperative to understand whom to notify if events or activities do not go according to plan.

As noted in other chapters, tensions may arise between your beliefs and ethics and those of the larger university. Suppose we are working with students whose approach we agree with and supervisors or other university leadership gives us direction that goes against our ethics and values—what we will do? There will also be times that we do not agree with what students are doing and this can create different ethical challenges. At some point, most of us will be in a position where we have to decide: Do we stand our ground and support the students we are working with, or do we comply with the university so that we remain employed and have the chance to support students in the future?

Competencies

Staff members who work in academic and student affairs develop their professional competence in several competency areas (see Appendix) while helping students developmentally. Practitioners have the opportunity to develop in the area of Personal and Ethical Foundations (PEF) not only in their primary job responsibilities but as advisors and mentors for individual students and student organizations. These roles also help staff identify their strengths and areas for growth in the Leadership (LEAD) competency formally and informally. Social Justice and Inclusion (SJI) are ongoing considerations as practitioners work with students to set and achieve goals and celebrate success while engaging in sustained work to examine who is involved, who is missing, and who is served through student involvement and organizations.

Student Learning and Development (SLD) and Advising and Supporting (A/S) are also areas of development for staff who work closely with student involvement. Out-of-class learning opportunities are a significant part of the college experience. Before even joining, let alone leading an organization, students must choose where they want to spend their time, how they want to be involved, and the contributions they hope to make. Supporting students through that process draws from both SLD and A/S competencies. In advising and mentoring roles, practitioners learn to distinguish between being an organizational leader and being an organizational advisor. This role transition can be particularly challenging for graduate students and newer practitioners who were highly involved leaders as undergraduate students.

An Overview of Student Involvement in Higher Education

Student activities began in the form of literary societies, debate, athletics, and other clubs and organizations. By the end of the Civil War, "the extracurriculum expanded rapidly, offering the undergraduate an unprecedented number of opportunities to fill his leisure hours" (Potter, 1944, p. 125). As these new activities emerged on campus, discussion about whether or not student activities beyond academics should be part of the college experience was, and continues to be, debated in higher education. For example, one point of contention is about the purpose of higher education. In the U.S., it started with the training of clergy. However, it evolved over the next 200 years to include a much more diverse curriculum, different institutional types, and various student activities.

At the same time, student organizations persisted; however, African-American students, white women, and religiously minoritized students, while able in some cases to attend college, were not welcome in campus organizations or the larger campus culture (Allen et al., 1991; Thelin, 2011). Some people in higher education questioned the importance of student organizations and student activities. We see different perspectives on what the college or university experience should include in comments from former Princeton University (and the U.S.) President Woodrow Wilson in 1915 and W. H. Crowley's remarks from his inaugural presidential address to Hamilton College.

Wilson sought to ban Black students from Princeton (a continuation of his racism in action from when he was the U.S. president) and worked against women's suffrage as U.S. president. He also sought to abolish elitism at the university and hired Princeton's first Jewish and Catholic faculty members. He was messy and problematic, as so many people are. Wilson wrote about student activities and extracurriculars as the "side shows" while academics were the "main tent." Wilson (1915) wrote:

> The side shows are so numerous, so diverting—so important, if you will—that they have swallowed up the circus, and those who perform in the main tent [the professors] must often whistle for their audiences, discouraged and humiliated.
>
> Amusement, athletic games, the zest for contest and competition, the challenge there is in most college activities to the instinct of initiative and the gifts of leadership and achievement—all these are wholesome means of stimulation, which keep young men from going stale and turning to things that demoralize. But they should not assume the front of the stage where more serious and lasting interests are to be served.
>
> *(p. 23)*

Wilson was not saying that we do not need student activities, athletics, or other extracurriculars. He says they may have become more important than academics and intellectual pursuits on college campuses.

Then, in 1938, W. H. Cowley, one of the first advocates for the study of higher education, shared the following at his inauguration as the president of Hamilton College (Cowley [1938]):

> The college must be the place par excellence in our society for the highest intellectual motivation and achievement. The college, however, is more than a mind factory... College students do not live and work in isolation but in a social milieu in which their emotions, their morals, and their social outlooks are influenced at least as much by their fellows and their environment as by the courses of instruction which they take. The college, therefore, does not face a choice between intellectual excellence and the education of the whole student. It is not a question of either-or, but of both together.
>
> *(p. 477)*

So the debate was, and so the debate continues.

It is worth noting that Wilson made his comments before the U.S. had joined World War I, and Cowley's were after the war had concluded. After the war, people in the U.S. had significantly more time for leisure. Work hours had decreased from an average of 59 hours a week in 1900 to 48 hours a week by 1929 (Huberman & Minns, 2007). The 1920s were labeled the "Age of Play" (Duffus, 1924) and a "golden age of sport" (Dyreson, 1989).

As always, the college campus reflected the larger society. The Association of College Unions International (ACUI) was founded in 1914 (ACUI, n.d.), just before the first world war, and student organizations and unions grew over the next several decades. At this same time, college enrollment was growing faster than the U.S. population (Jordan & Vakilian, 2013). In addition, college unions were part of the surge in construction made possible by increased financial resources allocated to colleges and universities (Rudolph, 1990).

With the Great Depression and World War II, higher education fell behind economic and war concerns in national priorities. However, between those events, in 1937, the *Student Personnel Point of View* was published by the American Council on Education. This document endorsed the idea of attending to the *whole* student—intellect, spirit, and personality.

By 1949, a revision of the report listed 17 "Elements of a Student Personnel Program" (ACE, 1949, p. 7), three of which focused on student activities. These included activities "designed to induct the student into his new life and environment as a member of the college or university family... group activities arising from the natural interests of students... recreational activities" (ACE, 1949, p. 7). At the same time, extracurricular activities grew in a variety of ways. The U.S. National Student Association (NSA), founded in 1947, would grow to become a powerful organization focused on campus issues, civil rights, and college access (Altbach, 1997).

Student organizations "demonstrated a need for more than the curriculum offered and a need for engagement" (Culver et al., 2013, p. 44). Debate societies and related organizations had already been established. However, the 1930s saw the emergence of student union governing boards and student programming committees as other forms of student activities on campus (Culver et al., 2013) and student leadership programming (ACUI, 1937).

The influx of college students after World War II affected every area of student affairs. Grinnell (1946) wrote that when veterans went into higher education, they would demand "more freedom in student activities... for themselves and for the little man in their midst" (p. 245). As a result, the period following World War II saw college union hours (and staff) increase (Butts, 1971), a resurgence of fraternity and sorority life (Horowitz, 1987), and significant growth in residence hall communities (Pope et al., 2009). Between 1945 and 1950, more than half of all college football players were veterans, and this "helped solidify a public belief that colleges and athletics went hand in hand" (VanOverbeke, 2013, p. 435).

During the 1950s, 1960s, and 1970s, there was increased activism on college campuses related to civil rights, the Vietnam War, and other social issues. Hoge and colleagues (1981) compared college student values between 1952 and 1979 and found that students placed increasing emphasis on "personal freedom in life-style, accompanied by a greater tolerance of others whose life styles are different" (p. 273). This shift was reflected in college activities by increases in diverse student organizations, such as the Congress of Racial Equity, founded in 1942 by students at the Chicago Theological Seminary (Altbach, 1997), which grew in membership and influenced the Student Nonviolent Coordinating Committee (SNCC) founded in 1960, and the Freedom Riders. The Freedom Riders included several Fisk University students encouraged to participate by Fisk student Diane Nash (Urban, 2002).

Some changes on college campuses in the 1960s and 1970s were driven by the Vietnam War and student protests related to the war. Hall (2004) wrote, "Antiwar activists established draft counseling centers to educate men about their options. Thousands resisted the draft through both legal and illegal methods" (p. 14). The National Guard informed the context of violence against protesters on campus. Also, the role of the National Guard on campuses escalated, culminating in the May 4, 1970 shootings of four students on the campus of Kent State University. It is important to acknowledge the South Carolina Highway Patrol killing of three men engaged in a protest at South Carolina State University on February 8, 1968, as well as the killing of two men at Jackson State College (now Jackson State University) on May 15, 1970 (11 days after the shootings at Kent State). In the aftermath of these events, the President's Commission on Campus Unrest reported, "Campus protest has been focused on three major questions: racial injustice, war, and the university itself" (United States, 1970, p. 3). The report concluded with recommendations to law enforcement officials, college administrators, students, and government officials, including that college administrators should develop plans for responding to protests and communicating with police. Students were advised to condemn violent protest (United States, 1970, p. 464).

During the 1980s and 1990s, higher education saw a decline in student involvement and activism. However, this was also when LGBTQI+ organizations began to form and often became "the most visible and active groups on campus" (Stanley, 1983, p. 397). During this time, the role of peer leaders increased in and beyond student organizations, based on the success of undergraduate leadership in orientation leader and resident assistant roles (Ganser & Kennedy, 2012). Additionally, student involvement in organizations, clubs, and student activities was stressed during this time as necessary for students' future careers (Boone et al., 1988; Burggraaf, 1997; Howard, 1986) because organizational and club experiences were a means to develop students' interpersonal skills (Felson, 2001; Rubin et al., 2002).

Since the start of the 20th century, student activities, clubs, and organizations have changed. Our increasingly litigious society often forefronts risk management as institutions seek to distance themselves from student organizations to manage liability (Alexander & Alexander, 2017). Issues of freedom related to campus-based movements and an increasingly polarized society mirrored on campus have created and exacerbated tensions around religion (Coley, 2021) and LGBTQ+ movements (Coley, 2020; Wilson, 2022). Student activism is again an element of student organization participation. This is true for student organizations engaging in work related to the murder of Black and Brown students and citizens (Museus, 2008; Reyes, 2018), safety and facilities issues for Trans* students (Colburn, 2020), and college access for undocumented students (Galindo, 2011, 2012; Nicholls, 2013; Reyna Rivarola & Cisneros, 2021). It is important to remember that there are alternative perspectives on all of these topics. Ultimately, navigating these and other complex issues comes back to "*it depends*," as action depends on institutional culture, region, and other considerations discussed in this text.

Student activities have emerged because of students' needs, demands, and activism. These activities and organizations are embedded in student affairs and valued during the college experience, graduate and professional school admission, and job search after graduation. Involvement in activities is essential to being fully engaged and holistically developed as a student, citizen, employee, and member of the larger community.

Given the various programs, clubs, and activities on college campuses, there are various legal and ethical issues to consider. Who can belong to an organization, and who is excluded? What are the standards for organizational recognition from the university? What are risk management concerns for different organizational activities and events? How are contracts negotiated and enforced with outside entertainers and vendors? As with other issues discussed in this text, *it depends*. The following sections provide opportunities for examining specific aspects of student programming, involvement, and activities through an Institutional Intelligence lens.

Civic Learning and Leadership Programs

Civic learning and leadership programs connect to student development outcomes in higher education. Guthrie and Jenkins (2018) identified "leadership development as both curricular and co-curricular in nature" (p. 57). These areas are complementary and often connected as "[m]ost contemporary college leadership programs reflect a strong philosophical connection to the values of social service, civic responsibility, and the common good" (Dalton & Crosby, 2010, p. 5). These experiences overlap in a variety of ways.

Civic learning and leadership programs foster various skills and student outcomes in support of the mission of higher education broadly. Critical thinking is often central to undergraduate student outcomes in higher education. Leadership and civic engagement experiences foster this development as students explore their roles as leaders and their responsibilities to their communities.

Social responsibility, change, and justice are crucial elements of student learning related to leadership and civic engagement. Just as with leadership, students understand their responsibilities as citizens and that those are paired with obligations to work to create transformative, positive, and sustainable change. In our current context, the challenge comes from differing perspectives on what to change, how to change it, and how to make the change process equitable.

As with other sections in this text, we situate legal and ethical responsibilities related to civic learning and leadership in the Institutional Intelligence Model. We must explore the steps of making good and well-informed legal and ethical decisions in the context of the institution(s) where we work. Additionally, we must consider our relationships, the identities of and connections (or lack of connection) with others in our units and across campuses and communities, and the specifics of emerging issues. Only once we have holistically considered the *who*, *what*, *where*, *when*, *why*, and *how* of a given situation can we move forward and make informed and appropriate decisions.

Institutional Intelligence Questions

Who: Who are critical partners on campus with leadership and civic engagement offices? Are there academic components (i.e., leadership certificate programs) whose faculty and staff can and should be consulted when issues arise?

What: What background does staff in this area have (student affairs, academic/teaching, other)? What does the institutional mission, strategic plan, or other overarching document say about students' civic and leadership development?

Where: Where are these programs situated in the organizational chart for the division?

When: When were leadership programs established? When did leadership emerge as an outcome for different programs—especially if leadership initiatives are decentralized?

Why are students involved in leadership initiatives? Why is leadership highlighted in specific programs or activities?

How: How is leadership defined on a particular campus? How do civic development and citizenship align with student development outcomes at the institutional level?

Critical Scenario 14.1 Civic Learning and Leadership

Co-Author: Victoria Goetzinger, Community Director, the University of North Carolina at Chapel Hill

Kathy (she/her) is a first-year graduate student at Grace Wesleyan University and serves as the graduate assistant for Student Involvement and Leadership Education. A primary aspect of Kathy's role is advising the Student Funding Board (SFB), a student-led board that allocates $100,000 annually to student organizations for travel, speakers, and daily operations. Kathy and the SFB reviewed guiding documents, held mock hearing sessions, and outlined member expectations during the fall retreat.

At the previous SFB meeting, a student organization presented its proposal to bring a guest speaker to campus to discuss his U.S. Senate campaign.

Students rallied on social media to oppose using student fees to give a venue to this speaker and his hateful rhetoric and discriminatory policies impacting marginalized groups—particularly LGBTQI+, undocumented, and international students. Since the proposal was approved, Kathy learned that other student groups organized a protest and counter-protest at the next SFB meeting. Kathy's supervisor, Marc (he/him), informed her he heard the faculty, staff, and community members were also planning to attend, as SFB meetings are open to the public.

Kathy received the following voicemail on her office phone:

> *Hi, Kathy. This is Sam, the editor-in-chief of the student newspaper. We are covering the protest set to take place at this Thursday's Student Funding Board meeting. It has been brought to our attention that the Student Funding Board bylaws were not followed in the passing of Bill 26 about the senate candidate coming to campus. Can you please call me back so I can get your statement?*

The Law

- What are the relevant legal issues in this scenario?
- What institutional policies, procedures, or processes are applicable in this scenario?

Ethics

- What are the relevant ethical issues in this scenario?
- What information would the characters need to make sound ethical decisions in this situation?

Identity

- How would characters' social identities affect how this scenario might unfold? Assign the characters specific social identities and go through the scenario. Then change some of those social identities and go through the scenario again.
- How do the situation and the information you need change?

Scenario-Specific Questions

- Whom can Kathy consult about this issue? Who will need to know about the media's interest in the upcoming SFB meeting?
- To best navigate this situation, what does Kathy need to understand about on-campus policies, SFB procedures, media guidelines, and other issues?

What resources are available to help her understand the situation's complexity?

- Where can Kathy go for guidance and collaborative support so she does not feel alone in managing the emerging situation?
- When does Kathy need to communicate with the students involved in SFB about the different considerations for the upcoming meeting?
- Why might Kathy choose to return Sam's call? Why might she not return Sam's call?
- How can Kathy prioritize everything she needs to do before the SFB meeting?

Using the Institutional Intelligence Model, what other information do Kathy and her supervisor need, and how can they get it to respond effectively to the situation?

Community Service and Service Learning

Civic learning and leadership programs emerged out of student desires to transform culture in pursuit of social justice, particularly during a surge in college student activism in the 1960s. Growing out of the civil rights movement (Kenny & Gallagher, 2002), these initial acts of engagement were student-led and focused on partnering with people and communities outside of higher education. Fast forward, and today's many civic learning, volunteer, and service programs are undergoing appropriate critique as many exploit People of Color (domestic and abroad) who may struggle with poverty as a result of systemic issues of power and race. In some cases, the goal of these programs is to educate privileged white students about issues of poverty and race rather than to transform society and eradicate injustice.

Thus, this work sits at the crux of transformation (in service to historically marginalized and exploited communities) and education (in service to historically centered and privileged communities). With this in mind, we must ground these programs' work and existence in ethical reflection. Whom are we serving? What is the transformation taking place—is it with the students or the communities? If both, is it both in equitable ways?

Irwin and Foste (2021) highlighted elements of Institutional Intelligence in their article on service learning, saying that programs "vary by institutional history and mission" (p. 420). Additionally, programs vary based on history, mission, and the students and communities served. Other

Institutional Intelligence considerations include location (where), scheduling (when), and planning strategies (how). Perhaps the most significant Institutional Intelligence element for practitioners and partners to consider in regard to service and civic learning experiences is *why*. Why is the service being done? Why has a specific community or agency been selected as a partner?

Why are the students choosing to be involved in the first place? Are students actively seeking to create change and transform society to make it more equitable for everyone? Are students choosing a specific civic or service experience because of the location of the service—for example, spring break trips to communities near beaches or opportunities to travel abroad? Are students choosing to be involved to add to their resumes or write about the experience for graduate or professional school admissions essays?

Institutional Intelligence Questions

Who: Who are critical partners on campus and in the community with this office?

What: What service does the community need? What service does the surrounding community need as opposed to communities in distant and perhaps more appealing venues? What are the risk management and legal issues related to travel and service? What training will students receive in advance of the trip? What is the debriefing process?

Where: Where is the service taking place?

When: When do events take place? When do students begin learning and preparing for their trips?

Why: In addition to the why questions outlined above, why are students often involved in these activities? Why do units choose specific service opportunities or partners?

How: How are the voices of the individuals and communities served centered? How are projects identified? How are the priorities of the communities served and the individuals participating balanced?

Critical Scenario 14.2 Community Service and Service Learning

Co-Author: Kate Radford, Director for Leadership Education and Development, Clemson University

Melissa (she/her) and Barb (she/her) are co-student site leaders of a spring break service experience for the Alternative Breaks organization on their campus.

They are working on planning a week-long experience for a rural community in a neighboring state recently devastated by a series of tornadoes. They have researched and decided to focus on the damage done to state and national park areas. The cost to go on the trip is $350 and includes travel, lodging, and most meals.

When they share the plan with their organization, there is resistance. This pushback is not unusual when leaders initially propose trips, but the resistance to this trip is more intense than usual. These were the main issues raised:

- The cost of the experience is too high.
- The service does not directly impact the people in the community as much as other projects in the area might.
- Because this is a rural area that is likely to be cold and wet during spring break, the organization is worried that few students will sign up.
- Melissa and Barb did not consult with local community agencies or representatives when identifying projects for this experience.
- Melissa and Barb need more confidence in connecting the service tasks they imagine to the related social issues or community needs.

Luther (they/them) is the new staff member who advises this organization. How can they use the Institutional Intelligence Model to help Melissa and Barb, as well as the other members, navigate this situation? What changes might Luther make for future iterations of experience planning/proposals for this organization?

Ethics

- What are the relevant ethical issues in this scenario?
- What information would the characters need to make the best ethical decisions in this situation?

Identity

- How would characters' social identities affect how this scenario might unfold? Assign the characters particular social identities and go through the scenario. Then change some of those social identities and go through the scenario again.
- How do the situation and the information you would need change?

Scenario-Specific Questions

- Whom did Melissa and Barb consult in developing this idea? Who at the university needs to be involved from risk management, financial, and student organizational oversight perspectives? Who in the organization, in addition to Melissa and Barb, needs to be consulted about the plan?
- What types of projects have this organization traditionally taken on? What input have members had in deciding the service location? What has the process been for partnering with the local communities affected and the agencies that serve those communities? What commitments have Melissa and Barb already made? To whom?
- Where else do members want to go? Where on campus can Luther go to learn about how this organization and other service groups have planned trips in the past? Where are campus policies about service trips kept?
- When do plans need to be finalized? When are the reservation and transportation deposit deadlines? What other financial or contractual obligations does the group have?
- Why might Melissa and Barb intentionally choose not to consult with the group? Why else might group members be upset about decisions besides the above reasons?
- How can Melissa, Barb, and the organization move forward from this point? How can they take what they have learned from the experience to implement guidelines or policies for future trips?

How else might using the Institutional Intelligence Model have helped Melissa and Barb in advance of planning this trip?

Student Activities

Student activities in higher education in the United States go back primarily to the Civil War era. Student organizations in institutions prior to that focused on religion and character development. The first organizations or "student societies" that emerged were literary and focused on the development of the mind, followed by Greek letter fraternities (see Chapter 13) and debate societies in the 1820s. Since then, student activities have expanded exponentially, informed by current trends and issues, specific student interests, and our world's changing social and technological context.

The National Association of Campus Activities (NACA) and the ACUI are two professional organizations engaged in supporting and developing student activities and student activity practitioners in higher education. Komives (2019) alluded to the concepts behind the Institutional Intelligence Model when she wrote, "The scope of specific activities varies by institutional type, size, and location" (p. 16). According to the CAS (Council for the Advancement of Standards in Higher Education) Standards, campus activities should enhance student cooperation, leadership, and learning—complementing academics at the institution and helping students develop as citizens of the campus and larger society.

Institutional Intelligence Questions

Who: Who are the members and advisors of organizations? Who approves funding and resources for student activities? Who has the authority to sign contracts or collect risk waivers? Who participates in planning events? Who is excluded from planning? Who is excluded from attending?

What: What are the legal considerations for student activities? What are safety concerns for events or travel? What contractual obligations do student activities have or create? What is the history of specific events on campus? What is the overall cost of specific events for individual students?

Where: Where are specific activities held?

When: When do organizations need to get approval for certain activities? When are events held? When are events not allowed?

Why: Why are students involved in specific activities?

How: How can staff anticipate potential legal and ethical issues? How are students able to get involved in events?

Critical Scenario 14.3 Student Activities

Co-Author: Daniel Francis, Director of Community Values, Limestone University

Cooper College is a small, private liberal arts college in a small town in the Northeast. Each spring, the students on campus organize the Cooper Hoopla—an event showcasing school pride, academic programs, and student successes for the year. What originally started as Honors Week to recognize academic, leadership, and personal excellence on campus has grown to be a week of high-profile events for current and potential students, alumni, donors, and the community surrounding the campus. There are no classes on Wednesday, Thursday, or Friday as students dedicate time to college and programmatic events and open houses as well as honors ceremonies and a campus festival.

One of the most significant traditions on campus is the annual Hoopla Whoopla, where organizations from across campus—social, academic, and service—gather on the quad and compete for the best cheer on campus. The event has been a highlight of the spring on campus for more than 90 years. Organizations are allowed to use props but not amplification devices. The Coopyros—the campus pyrotechnics club affiliated with the chemistry department on campus—is often the star of the show, having won the Whoopla the past seven years.

This year, the festival falls on the first warm weekend of the year. After a frigid and snowy winter, Hoopla Week is mild and sunny, and students are very excited. At the Whoopla—a kick-off event on Wednesday night—there is a problem with the fireworks that the Coopyros have set up. Instead of a series of displays, all the fireworks go off at once. While no one is seriously injured, students flee the area, and the rest of the night collapses into a series of disruptions and significant vandalism in the college town area adjacent to campus.

The festival the next day goes well, but again that evening, students are in the community, drinking excessively, tipping over cars, and vandalizing local businesses. University administrators shut down the event on Friday, and campus and community leaders tell students to be off the streets by 8 p.m. Instead of celebratory events through the weekend, there are a series of meetings, town hall conversations, and student organization dialogues about the future of Cooper Hoopla.

Ethics

- What are the relevant ethical issues in this scenario?
- What information would the characters need to make the best ethical decisions in this situation?

Identity

- How would characters' social identities affect how this scenario might unfold? Assign the characters particular social identities and go through the scenario. Then change some of those social identities and go through the scenario again.
- How do the situation and the information you would need change?

Scenario-Specific Questions

- Who is invested in Cooper Hoopla? In what ways? Who is likely to have strong opinions about the future of Cooper Hoopla? Who is affected on campus by Cooper Hoopla and whether it continues? Who is affected off campus by Cooper Hoopla and whether it continues?
- What are the main concerns of university leaders and administrators about the disruptions during Cooper Hoopla? What are the financial implications of continuing or canceling the event in the future? What are the potential student conduct and public safety concerns related to Cooper Hoopla? What are the legal, ethical, and financial implications of canceling or continuing the event? What is the role of security and law enforcement during the event?
- Where might students involved with planning Cooper Hoopla go with their concerns and frustrations about incidents during this year's event? Where might they voice their commitment to sustaining the event in the future?
- When will university leaders need to decide about the future of this event?
- Why would it benefit the university to keep Cooper Hoopla? Why would it benefit the university to suspend or permanently cancel the event in the future?
- How can university leaders ensure that they attend to all constituents affected by continuing or stopping Cooper Hoopla?

How else might using the Institutional Intelligence Model can help college leaders to promote student activities?

Conclusion

Student involvement through organizations, activities, and services can be some of the students' most significant experiences in college. These groups and events are significant to current students, alumni, donors, future students, and community members. Many experiences associated with student involvement become institutional and organizational traditions, rites, and rituals. As with any event or campus activity, there are legal and ethical considerations. Stakeholders and constituents may weigh in when issues arise, expecting others to listen to and act on their recommendations and perspectives and incorporate them into campus life changes. Thus, the complexity of student involvement goes well beyond a specific organization or its members.

15

CONFIDENTIAL RESOURCES

> As professionals in higher education, we center our work on student success. We strive to establish authentic and trusting relationships that guide students to achieve their educational goals. In this context, students may disclose sensitive or private information to those they trust. Often these disclosures are requests for assistance or support, or they could be a cry for help at a point of crisis. Providing coordinated, holistic, and intrusive resources to students in need is better than distinct, disconnected interventions. Collaborating in this context requires us to balance supporting each student's unique needs with our institutional obligation to respect and protect their privacy, particularly when specific professional and ethical standards extend the privilege of confidentiality. Working together to serve the complex needs of today's students demand collegiality, compassion, and excellent judgment.
>
> —Dr. Keith E. Robinder, Vice President of Student Support Programs, St. Louis Community College

As we discussed how to organize this book, we realized that there are many ways that functional areas could be categorized. Additionally, we found that different areas can fall under different umbrellas, varying from one campus to the next. We have not included counseling centers, health centers, spiritual life/campus ministry, or sexual assault victim advocates in the chapter on student wellness; rather, we address them here because of their connection to confidentiality, but we affirm that these areas are definitely about student wellness.

DOI: 10.4324/9781003442707-18

However, something exceptional about these areas sets them apart from other student affairs and higher education functional areas. The staff in these areas are often the ONLY STAFF ON CAMPUS who can offer students CONFIDENTIALITY. You will note some capitalization in the previous sentence. Unless your job is designated as a confidential resource by campus policies and your professional, ethical standards, or licensure requirements, you cannot and should not promise to keep student communication confidential. Professionals should expect to share private information as appropriate with supervisors, colleagues, and other stakeholders who need to know. Too often, people confuse privacy and confidentiality, and this puts employees, institutions, and students at risk.

Chapter Organization

We open this chapter with a discussion on the difference between privacy and confidentiality. People often use these words interchangeably, but the two have significant legal differences. We introduced the Family Educational Rights and Privacy Act (FERPA) and the Health Insurance Portability and Accountability Act (HIPAA) in Chapter 2 and provide more detail about these pieces of legislation in this chapter. Throughout the rest of the chapter, we explore the importance and complexity of student affairs collaborations related to confidentiality, counseling centers, health centers, campus ministry and spiritual life, and sexual assault victim advocate partnerships.

Legal and Ethical Considerations

The Law, Policy, and Governance (LPG) and aspects of the Personal and Ethical Foundations (PEF) competencies (see Appendix) are essential for legal and ethical considerations in this chapter, particularly to understand the importance of working with confidential resources. While there are specific laws to consider, such as FERPA and HIPAA (more about this later in the chapter; also see Chapter 2), student affairs practitioners must be very familiar with campus policies and procedures. There is a significant overlap between campus policy and state and federal law when partnering with medical and counseling professionals, religious advisors, and advocates of sexual assault victims.

It is vital to proactively use the Institutional Intelligence Model to prepare before issues arise. Because of the personal, physical, and emotional stakes of students using confidential resources, learning through trial and error rather than through education ahead of time can significantly harm students. Practitioners must be familiar with their personal and professional ethics and with the ethics of other areas (counseling, health care, religious advisors, and advocates of sexual assault victims) to serve students effectively, legally, and ethically.

Competencies

Working with confidential resources draws upon several professional competencies. In particular, we have to examine our PEF, LPG, and Advising and Supporting (A/S) abilities. Work and communication are essential and complex when student issues involve campus partners in counseling and other confidential areas. Situations with confidential resource partners can inspire us to develop skills at multiple levels and inspire our PEF development as we attend to the well-being of others while cultivating a deeper understanding of how our ethics align with those of our field or institution.

Because of the ethical and professional codes and obligations of confidential resources staff, work involving these areas and partners also carries significant law and policy implications. We may feel that we can provide better responses and more support by knowing the details of a student's situation. Because of confidentiality between a health-care provider and the student, that may not be possible—particularly if the student chooses not to share health-care information. Practitioners must know the policies and laws related to information in all contexts, particularly in working with confidential resources.

Then, we develop essential A/S skills when supporting students through situations with confidential partners. A student who reports sexual misconduct or assault must be heard and provided the power to make their own choices as they navigate forward from their trauma. The A/S competency highlights "partnering with others" and "conflict and crisis" (ACPA/NASPA, 2015, p. 12), which are particularly salient in our work with confidential partners and resources.

Privacy vs. Confidentiality

Simply put, respecting a student's privacy means that an employee will not tell anyone about what the student has shared other than those with a legitimate need to know. Confidentiality means that an employee cannot share information without a student's permission. Examples of confidential information and conversations are physical health records, counseling conversations, and conversations with religious advisors. While there may be some exceptions to each, the point to focus on is that those of us who are not licensed counselors, medical professionals, victim advocates, or religious counselors cannot offer confidentiality.

"Who has a legitimate need to know?" you might ask. Well, let's talk about it. As is the case in so many issues in this book, the short answer is—*it depends*. The longer answer is yours to find out as you understand your institution. Examples of things it could depend on: Do the police or other safety professionals need to be aware of the information based on a regulatory requirement? If a student discloses that they are receiving clinical services at your institutional counseling center and have recently been contemplating suicide, are you permitted to share this disclosure with others? Is what the student shared a potential Clery Act violation that your institution must report (without identifying information) annually?

Navigating Privacy

As a former conduct officer, I (Michelle) talked with students, faculty, and staff about various issues. Some of those were highly personal and often difficult for people to discuss. Sometimes, I thought that a person might be about to disclose something that I would be obligated to report to others. I would stop them if I realized it before the student shared the information. I would say,

> I think you may be about to tell me something that I am obligated to share with my dean and potentially others. Before you go on, I want to make sure you know that you have confidential resources on campus if you would prefer to have this conversation with them before or instead of sharing more about the situation with me.

Now, you would think that would drive students away. That was not my experience. Instead, I tried to help them understand that I was doing everything I could to give them the most control over their situation and what happened next. Sometimes they talked to me. Sometimes they wanted another resource. Sometimes they left and came back later. Sometimes they did not come back to speak with me. Regardless, they had the information they needed to decide how they wanted to move forward.

FERPA and HIPAA

This section builds on the introduction of the FERPA of 1974 and the HIPAA of 1996 offered in Chapter 2. Educational records (often attendance-based) were kept by colleges and universities as early as the 1800s. As the record-keeping evolved, staff retained more detailed and personal information on file. The information was accessible by various people and officials for virtually any reason. Records policies changed in 1974 in the wake of Watergate.

Given a significant decline in the public's trust in the government, Republican Senator James L. Buckley of New York proposed FERPA (also known as the Buckley Amendment). FERPA applies to the privacy of educational records to protect students and families. It is essential to learn what constitutes an educational record in your role. FERPA records *may or may not* include forms, notes from student meetings, and email exchanges, among other things.

It would be another 22 years before an act protecting medical records—HIPAA, or the Kennedy–Kassebaum Act—would be enacted. Generally speaking, HIPAA restricts the release of medical or health records to anyone other than a patient or the patient's "authorized representative"—a minor's parents, for example. HIPAA deals with health care coverage, fraud, taxes, and group health plans, but Title II speaks most directly to the confidentiality of health records when there is insurance billing. Most other records are still protected but under FERPA rather than HIPPA. The focus of HIPPA was not on college students; instead, the driving force was to provide healthcare to more people and make it more efficient—particularly in helping employees retain health care when they change jobs.

While FERPA and HIPAA protect student information, these federal laws exemplify the difference between privacy and confidentiality. FERPA protects student privacy related to their academic records. Records can be shared with others with a legitimate need to know. For example, other higher education institutions may request student transcripts if a student seeks to transfer. Other examples of appropriate legal disclosure are information needed for audit or accreditation, subpoenaed records, or information with financial aid implications.

HIPAA records are confidential as they relate to student health records related to insurance, and FERPA protects most other health-related information as an educational record. Records can be released in situations involving public health concerns, reporting abuse or neglect, or through de-identified data sets for research purposes.

Student Affairs Collaborations Related to Confidential Information

While most student affairs practitioners are not practicing and licensed counselors, health-care professionals, sexual assault victim advocates, or religious advisors, nearly anyone interacting with college students may need to engage with staff in these areas. An academic advisor may have a student share that they are suicidal. A student organization advisor may notice erratic and concerning behavior from a group member. A financial aid staff member may get a concerning email from a student. An instructor for a leadership course may read something in a student paper that raises some red flags that they are in a potentially violent dating relationship. In all of these examples, FERPA allows for the appropriate consultation with or referral to designated confidential resources to connect students to appropriate campus services.

Because of these experiences, we wanted to include this chapter to speak to the art of navigating conversations with confidential resources. We have intentionally chosen the word art because, to serve students best, these conversations and exchanges of information go well beyond a simple checklist. This section focuses on how student-facing student affairs and academic affairs professionals can best partner with confidential resources. Unlike other chapters, the focus is not on counselors, medical professionals, sexual assault victim advocates, and religious leaders on campus but on other functional areas and how staff members can best think through how to engage with the individuals and offices with confidential status.

Counseling Centers

In 1910, Princeton University established the first mental health center to serve college students. These centers expanded across the country, particularly after the influx of students under the Servicemen's Readjustment Act of 1944. The need for cross-cultural and intersectional identity training for counseling staff has also increased as campus diversity (race, gender identity, sexual orientation, immigration status, international students, student veterans, and students with existing mental health concerns) has increased (Clauss-Ehlers & Parham, 2013). In short, the work is becoming increasingly complex.

In some ways, the stigma of seeking help for mental health issues is declining. As we see more examples of individuals engaging in counseling relationships and talking more openly about the need for ongoing mental health support, counseling has become more common. Mental health resources are discussed overtly during orientation and in residence halls, conduct hearings, classrooms, and other campus spaces.

That said, there is no complete transparency regarding students' mental health records—nor should there be. While we often feel that we need as much information as possible to support students, that is not always true. In many ways, when approaching conversations with counseling center staff, a good first question to ask before you meet with them is: Is a student's behavior and how it connects to their counseling relationship something that *you* need to know or that *someone* needs to know?

Nothing prevents us from sharing information a student has disclosed with confidential resources who have positional responsibilities related to the information we have (e.g., counselors and medical professionals). However, we should not expect to get information in return. Instead, consider approaching these exchanges by saying something like,

> Hello, confidential resource colleague. A student shared that they are a client/patient of yours in the counseling center. I know you cannot confirm that, but I have information that may be important for you to know about the student's situation. While this information may inform future steps, I am not expecting that you can share what those steps might include. I just thought it was important for you to have the information that I do.

This approach allows for some centralization of information to best support and assist students.

There may be cases when students want confidential resources to share information. For example, they may ask their counselor on campus to share information with a staff member in Student Advocacy and Care with whom the student has developed a relationship. In these situations, there are forms that the student must sign in order for their counselor to share information. These information releases are specific about what information should be shared and specify a limited time frame for sharing information.

In most cases, when there are strong and healthy partnerships, we should be able to trust our colleagues in counseling to hold more information than we do. Ultimately, our confidential resource partners can know everything that we know relevant to a student's situation without compromising a student's privacy since those partners may have, as FERPA stipulates, "a legitimate need to know." At the same time, we may not be allowed to know everything the counseling staff knows without compromising a student's confidentiality.

For example, say a student comes to you in your capacity as the advisor for a student organization to which they belong. The student discloses that they must resign from their leadership role with the organization because of some struggles. The student says, "I'm meeting with Marty in the counseling center, and he is helping a lot. I need to step away from a few things to make time to deal with some stuff." It might be good for Marty to know that the student is disconnecting from the leadership role with the group, but Marty will not disclose to you what the student is working on through counseling.

In situations where trust and open communication do not exist, it is essential to document what you have shared (or not shared) and why. Sharing that information with a supervisor or other appropriate party is an essential step in documenting what efforts you and others made to help the student.

This process also allows you to track your involvement, action, and communication in the situation. This is important for several reasons, including keeping your supervisor informed, compiling information for future reflection about how a situation was handled and whether current protocols and practices work, and being able to share what you did accurately if legal issues should emerge.

This work is not easy. It is messy, and this messiness defies a checklist response because the best response depends on the situation and the institutional context. It is not always the same response from one situation to the next. The questions you need to ask yourself and how you need to engage in understanding the context of your campus and developing Institutional Intelligence in your role are critical. The more you can do this proactively, the better prepared you will be. By developing Institutional Intelligence, you will have the capacity to ask for help when faced with the unexpected or unknown.

Institutional Intelligence Questions

Who: Who else is impacted by the situation and the student's behavior? Who works through the process (counseling, law enforcement, other student or academic affairs staff, health-care providers, family, roommates, and others)? Who are your go-to people for sharing information (behavioral intervention team, counseling staff, law enforcement, residence life staff, fraternity and sorority life [FSL])?

What: What is the situation you are facing? What is your role (engaging with the student directly, supporting colleagues, working with family)? What resources are available to you? What assets or strengths does the student have that will enhance existing support systems or provide additional support? What information do you have, and what additional information do you need? What direction or guidance have others given you? What is the impact of a student's behavior on a larger community or communities: Is there a threat of harm to self or others?

Where: Where is the student? Where does the student live? Where are concerning behaviors taking place (residence hall, student organization, classroom, on campus, off campus, on social media)? Where do others who might be affected live? Where do they engage with the student?

When: When were you made aware of the situation? When were others made aware? When will you or others act in this situation? When can you communicate with others who may need to be involved?

Why: Why is this an issue (is it a safety concern, a code of conduct violation)? Why have you been consulted? Why is this student's behavior concerning? Why might this behavior be happening? For example, is there an underlying medical or mental health condition?

How: How is the student at the center of the situation doing? How are they involved (or not involved) in seeking solutions and resolutions for the situation? How do you balance other students' and employees' needs to know how the institution responds with their desire to care for the student, curiosity, or fear of the unknown? How have you documented what has happened so far, and what will the following steps be? How have you communicated information to others who may need to be involved? How have you received information from others? How might this information be subject to Freedom of Information Act (FOIA) requests (see Chapter 2)? When confidentiality applies, how do you deal with your fears and concerns about student behaviors? How are you taking care of yourself as you respond?

Critical Scenario 15.1 Counseling Relationships

Co-Authors: Elliott DeVore, Post-Doctoral Psychology Fellow, and Wayne Glass, Mental Health Counseling Graduate Student, Teachers College, Columbia University

Jess (she/her) is an academic advisor in the College of Engineering. She also teaches an orientation course for all new engineering students. A recent assignment in the course was for students to write a paper about who they are, why they are in engineering, and their aspirations for the first semester. Denny (they/them) wrote the following at the end of their paper for the course:

> *My aspirations for this semester are to make it through without killing myself. My counselor on campus didn't seem to like it when I said that to him, but I think it's a good goal. At least, it's one I hope I achieve.*
>
> *I don't see anyone here like me: Puerto Rican, non-binary, and—shall we say—creative in my attire. Most people show up in their jeans and t-shirts and work in groups among themselves—the white guys, I mean. Anyone not white either gets dispersed among the white guy groups or—if there are enough—form a group of their own. The girls in class are the same—dispersed or congregated. And then there is me. It's the whole "picked last for kickball" thing again.*
>
> *I understand a lot of my coursework, but no one wants to work with me, so groups are impossible. I have never felt welcome or part of any group*

assignment. The teachers are not much better. I only had one who introduced herself with pronouns—a TA in a lab. But then she made us introduce ourselves with our pronouns. I got weird looks and giggles when I said my pronouns.

I clearly am not wanted here. I thought—I hoped college would be different, that I might finally find a place to belong. I don't belong on earth. I don't belong in engineering. I don't belong in college.

The Law

- What are the relevant legal issues in this scenario?
- What institutional policies, procedures, or processes are applicable in this scenario?

Ethics

- What are the relevant ethical issues in this scenario?
- What information would the characters need to make sound ethical decisions in this situation?

Identity

- How would characters' social identities affect how this scenario might unfold? Assign the characters particular social identities and go through the scenario. Then change some of those social identities and go through the scenario again.
- How do the situation and the information you need change?

Scenario-Specific Questions

- With whom will Jess want to share Denny's comments? Who has a legitimate need to know about this information? Who can best help Denny? Who else might be impacted by Denny's struggles?
- What other information does Jess need? What resources are available to Denny?
- Where on campus can Jess go for guidance on how to support Denny? Where might Jess help Denny connect to find community and a sense of belonging? Where might Denny go for academic support or major/career counseling?

- When does Jess need to reach out to Denny's counselor (if at all)? When does she need to share the information she has with other staff?
- Why might Denny have chosen this assignment to share their thoughts? Why might Denny have chosen Jess?
- How should Jess document this situation? How should Jess go about sharing it with others?

Using the Institutional Intelligence Model, what additional questions does Jess need to answer regarding Denny's comments and situation?

Health Centers

According to the American College Health Association (ACHA), "In 1861, Dr. Edward Hitchcock was named the medical director of the department of physical education at Amherst College, which is generally given credit as the first college health service" (ACHA, n. d.). Shortly after that, Mount Holyoke College hired a physician-in-residence. Infirmaries and other student health sites and initiatives continued to proliferate. In 1918 (amid a pandemic), additional funding was made available by the U.S. Congress to support health initiatives on campus related to hygiene, health examinations, emergency care, and attention to sexually transmitted infections.

In the wake of the Great Depression and the founding of organizations such as the Blue Cross and the Centers for Disease Control and Prevention (CDC), the nation and higher education struggled to provide health care for students and citizens. In 1954, healthcare professionals came together at the Fourth National Conference on Health in Colleges and recommended a health fee (Christmas, 1995).

More recently, infirmaries have disappeared, and many campuses now house a team of physicians, physician assistants, nurse practitioners, and nurses to provide primary care to students. Wide-spread illnesses, including epidemics and pandemics, have been issues in higher education, from the Black Plague's impact at Oxford University to the COVID-19 pandemic. Additionally, epidemics and other illnesses—such as SARS (severe acute respiratory syndrome) at the beginning of the 20th century, Ebola 15 years later, and measles and meningitis outbreaks on college campuses multiple times over the past 50 years—have forced colleges and universities worldwide to respond. As a result, campus health officials are instrumental in planning responses to events and crises along with other student affairs, academic affairs, and campus administrative leaders.

Today, health centers deal with significant community health issues and also with holistic student well-being, including outreach, education and prevention, general health, immunizations, sexual health, seasonal flu, diet, and nutrition, among other issues commonly provided by public health and private clinics off campus. Additionally, health centers partner with counseling and other campus resources to support student health. Some of the issues they collaborate on are anxiety, depression, stress, sleep issues, alcohol, substance abuse, eating disorders, sexual assault, exercise, nutrition, and many other student health and well-being concerns.

Health Center Partnerships on Campus

As with counseling centers, health center staff cannot and should not disclose to campus partners HIPAA-protected data contained in student health records. Staff may be able to share generalized information, like the number of flu cases they have documented in a week or a month. They may be able to share trends they see on campus regarding student needs or the number of students making appointments. They may share de-identified information about public health concerns, such as exposure to a highly contagious infection in a classroom or residential community. However, when focusing on an individual student, they may be very limited in sharing details.

Again, this should not preclude campus partners from sharing information with healthcare providers. Suppose a student's medical situation potentially impacts a larger community, or their health status is a factor in conduct, housing, or other decisions. In that case, healthcare staff may be able to provide general guidance without sharing specific details. As with so many examples in this book and our work, the answer always is *it depends* when we ask ourselves what can be shared related to a particular case.

Building and sustaining connections with healthcare providers and the health center on campus are vital as with other relationships. A few examples of collaborations between health centers and other areas of student affairs are immunizations required for enrollment, sexual assault nurse examiners (SANEs), urgent care, and physical examinations. Additionally, wellness programming is often part of the health center. Wellness work can include topics such as general well-being, food insecurity, mental health promotion, recovery, sexual health, suicide prevention, and other wellness topics related to the experiences of college students. Understanding our campus health center's services allows us access to essential resources to support students.

Institutional Intelligence Questions

Who: Who is on the staff at your health center? Who can access the center's services (undergraduate students, graduate students, post-docs, faculty, staff, family members, and others)? Who are your primary contacts when you have health-related questions? With whom has your area historically partnered on presentations or training related to health topics? Are students involved with health promotion and wellness on your campus? Who is allowed to transport students to the hospital or other locations in an emergency?

What: What services does the health center on your campus provide, if any? What services are provided by contracted off-campus providers or community-based clinics? What services are covered by student health fees, and what does the university bill students or insurance for? What insurance coverage is required, and do the requirements vary by student type (athletes, distance education students, international students, residential students, graduate students, dependent students living at home)? What healthcare access disparities impact historically underserved communities, such as undocumented or trans students? What are the student health trends or issues your health center is navigating? What points of intersection do you see between the work you do and the work of healthcare providers? What information do you have about student health and well-being that the health center staff on your campus may need? What services are unavailable on campus (pharmacy, sexual assault examinations)?

Where: Where is the health center located? Where does the health center report organizationally—to student affairs, auxiliary services, an institutional medical school, or through a different line—and how does the structure enhance or inhibit collaboration? Where do students go for medical emergencies after hours? Where is the nearest hospital in your community?

When: When is the health center on your campus open? When is health and wellness training for other student affairs staff? When does your campus program around specific health and wellness theme months?

Why: Why do students frequent the health center? Why might students avoid going to the health center (e.g., limited female or racially diverse providers, language barriers, or the lack of trans*-inclusive care)? Why do students engage in wellness organizations and programming? Why do other student affairs partners reach out and consult with health and wellness staff?

How: How is health-related information shared between medical and other student affairs staff? How can student affairs reach out to health center professionals with student concerns? How often do health center staff participate in behavioral intervention team conversations? How is the campus at large made aware of health-related issues at your institution?

Critical Scenario 15.2 Health Centers

Co-Author: Laura Knowles, Registered Nurse, Mary Greeley Medical Center

Aria (she/her) is the assistant director of the Women's Center on campus. She and her graduate assistant for programming, Bret (they/them), are working with a student planning committee for Women's Wellness Week (3W). In a one-on-one meeting, Bret shares a concern they have about one of the students on the committee—Kay (she/her). Bret says that in a recent planning meeting, Kay became very emotional. Bret said students asked whether she was okay and what was wrong, but Kay said it was just something she was working through.

After the meeting, Bret asked Kay whether there was anything they could do for her. Kay said, "I am working through a health issue. Some of the things we talked about tonight just touched a nerve. No one did anything wrong." Bret asked again whether there was anything they could do. When Kay said no, Bret offered to help Kay connect with health center staff if that would be helpful. Kay said, "I am already working with Abbie at the health center. Thanks, though."

Bret shared that they called the health center and asked whether there was an Abbie working with the student, but they could not confirm that.

I told them the situation, and they said they would share the information, but they cannot share a patient's information. That doesn't work for me because I need to know what is going on to help Kay. I don't know what to do if she breaks down in another meeting.

What should Aria's next steps be with the staff at the health center? What, if anything, should Aria tell the director of the Women's Center related to Kay, Bret, and the sequence of events so far?

The Law

- What are the relevant legal issues in this scenario?
- What institutional policies, procedures, or processes are applicable in this scenario?

Ethics

- What are the relevant ethical issues in this scenario?
- What information would the characters need to make sound ethical decisions in this situation?

Identity

- How would characters' social identities affect how this scenario might unfold? Assign the characters specific social identities and go through the scenario. Then change some of those social identities and go through the scenario again.
- How do the situation and the information you need change?

Scenario-Specific Questions

- Who might Aria reach out to for additional information? Who is allowed to share information about students' health situations? Who else might need to be aware of what Kay shared with Bret?
- What does Aria need to know about the health center, the university, and how they have historically supported students when medical information is involved? What things should Aria let the health center staff or the Women's Center director know about Kay, Bret, and the sequence of events so far?
- Where might Aria connect Bret to develop some strategies for supporting Kay? Where else on campus might staff have information about Kay?
- When should Aria share information with other offices? When is the next meeting? When are other scheduled interactions between Bret and Kay or Aria and Kay or Aria and Bret?
- Why might Bret think they need to know Kay's medical information? Why might Kay not have shared specifics about her medical situation with Bret?
- How can Aria help Bret understand the difference between privacy and confidentiality?
- As a supervisor, how should she work with Bret to develop his Institutional Intelligence related to this situation?

As a supervisor, what Institutional Intelligence factors will guide Aria as she works with Bret to support Kay?

Spiritual Life/Campus Ministry

While early education in the United States focused on the training of Protestant clergy, the emergence of religious societies, organizations, and the diversification of campus ministry began with the first recorded student Christian society at Harvard, which had been founded by Puritan colonizers in 1706. Many of the early colleges in the U.S. were religiously affiliated:

Yale (Congregationalist, 1701), Princeton (Presbyterian, 1746), Columbia (Anglican, 1754), Brown (Baptist, 1764), Rutgers (Dutch Reformed, 1766), and Georgetown (Jesuit Catholic, 1789). While specific religions founded many schools, many institutions no longer retain those affiliations. That said, religiously affiliated schools still play an essential role in higher education, and about 9.5% of college students attend religiously affiliated colleges and universities (NCES, 2018).

The emergence of religious organizations began more than 200 years after higher education began in the U.S. According to Pearson and Collins (2001),

> Student Christian Associations arose on campuses in the United States after the American Civil War. They were the predecessors of the modern campus ministry movement... While tolerated by the universities, they were primarily off-campus groups and were not well integrated into the activities of the campuses.
>
> *(p. 4)*

In 1858, the first Young Men's Christian Associations (YMCAs) were established at the universities of Michigan and Virginia (Shedd, 1938). Religious practices were embedded in the routine of early college life before some of these organizations took root on campus. The first Jewish student organization was the Menorah Society at Harvard in 1906 (Sachar, 1945).

Today, the prevalence of religious organizations on campus is essential to students, faculty, staff, and others. These organizations include Intervarsity Christian Fellowship, Navigators, Campus Crusade for Christ (Temkin & Evans, 1998), Buddhism, Islam, and Hinduism (Mailer, 1989). Barton et al. (2020) wrote, "many student religious organizations including Muslim Student Associations, Hillel International, and evangelical parachurch organizations, are experiencing growth in student members" (p. 69). Interfaith initiatives on college campuses are also increasing (Schmalzbauer & Mahoney, 2018).

Unfortunately, as religious diversity has increased, so have acts of religious intolerance. Fosnacht and Broderick (2020) found that 41% of first-year students and 36% of seniors who were members of a non-Christian faith experienced acts of religious intolerance, and 1 in 12 of these first-year students experienced 10 or more incidents, indicating these are not isolated incidents. These incidents can increase for students of particular faith traditions, often in response to world events and national violence.

Students' spiritual growth is embedded in *The Student Personnel Point of View* (ACE, 1949), which states that the education of college students should include *spiritual* as well as physical, social, emotional, and intellectual development. Many wellness models in higher education continue to include spiritual development and self-learning. Li and Murphy (2018) wrote that students have become increasingly engaged with spirituality over the past 20 years. As a result of student engagement in spirituality, the role of religion in the larger society in the U.S. and abroad, and the broader diversity of faith traditions on college campuses, student affairs professionals must be prepared to engage in conversation and action related to religious and spiritual issues on campus.

Student Affairs Partnerships

The institution may not employ many religious advisors and chaplains associated with universities. Religious leaders who are employees are not always housed under student affairs, although their work aligns and intersects with student affairs. These partners frequently have information about students' needs that can enhance the support that student affairs professionals seek to provide (Barton et al., 2020). Indeed, the literature related to these collaborations speaks to Institutional Intelligence. As Barton et al. (2020) wrote, "The nature and outcomes of collaboration between chaplains and student affairs professionals will depend on who the chaplains are and how they are positioned within an institution" (p. 81). When we ask how religious advisors and student affairs professionals work together effectively, the answer is: *it depends.* Barton et al. (2020) assert that knowledge about a specific campus (i.e., Institutional Intelligence) informs chaplains' situational and contextual positions as well as their partnerships with student affairs staff.

Focusing on collaboration and an understanding that religious life is housed on some campuses with student affairs and student life, the remainder of this chapter focuses on the complexities of these relationships. Traditionally, members of a given faith trust their religious leaders and advisors. Members consult with and confide in these advisors without fear that faith advisors will disclose what they have shared.

As religious life on college campuses has become more diverse, and new approaches to fostering religious and spiritual growth among students have taken root, the communication between student affairs and religious life staff members is essential. This communication requires further learning and development around different faith practices and building connections between individual staff members or offices. This interdependence also means understanding the complexities of faith. For example, practitioners should not conflate social or political conservativism with the Muslim faith or evangelical Christianity. Centering students and fostering open access to various resources are essential in work related to student faith as much as in any other area of student learning, growth, development, and wellness.

Institutional Intelligence Questions

Who: Who are the students on your campus? Who are students' religious and spiritual resources on and off campus? Who has been most active around issues of religion and spirituality on your campus?

What: What relationships currently exist between spiritual life and student life/student affairs on your campus? What aspirations do you have for those relationships? What opportunity do you have to effect change and enhance those relationships? What role do staff in spiritual life play in the activities on campus and students' lives in a broad sense? What role do they play in specific situations in the lives of specific students? What history exists related to religious and spiritual practices and organizations on campus? What problematic incidents, microaggressions, or harassment related to religious affiliation have occurred on your campus? How does the university accommodate students when the academic calendar intersects with non-Christian religious holidays, fasting, or other observances?

Where: Where are religious life staff physically located? Where are religious life staff and places of worship/gathering spaces located? Where are spaces across campus for students who need to regularly pray or meditate as part of their religious practices? Where do students learn about resources related to religion and spirituality when they come to campus?

When: When are recurring services and meetings held for different organizations? When are different religious celebrations and events on campus? When do different religious/spiritual organizations collaborate?

Why: Why is religion/spirituality part of the work in your division of student affairs? If it is not, then why not?

How: How are students with religious traditions and spiritual practices served if they do not have a faith community on or near campus?

Critical Scenario 15.3 Campus Ministry and Spiritual Life

Co-Author: Jan Scoville, Regional Learning Dean, Northeast Wisconsin Technical College

Mario (he/him) is the executive director of Campus Ministry, a layperson coordinating different religious and faith events on campus. Dia (she/her)—a student Mario knows well—approaches him, looking for space in her residence hall for a religious practice during an upcoming holiday that requires lighting candles (which is not allowed in the hall). Mario says he will try to identify a space for her.

Mario has noticed that Dia has been quieter and less engaged and missed many events she usually attends at the campus ministry center. He asks if she is doing all right. Dia says she is dealing with issues in her residence hall and has had people write harassing comments about her faith practices on her dry-erase board. When Mario asks for more specifics, Dia shares that she knows who is responsible and has told Esther (she/her)—whom she considers her religious advisor on campus—all of the specifics. Esther (she/her) is a part-time university employee and a trained religious leader who is usually on campus only for weekly services and short-term programming. Dia says that she is not yet ready to file a formal report.

The Law

- What are the relevant legal issues in this scenario?
- What institutional policies, procedures, or processes are applicable in this scenario?

Ethics

- What are the relevant ethical issues in this scenario?
- What information would the characters need to make sound ethical decisions in this situation?

Identity

- How would characters' social identities affect how this scenario might unfold? Assign the character individual social identities and go through the scenario. Then change some of those social identities and go through the scenario again.
- How do the situation and the information you need change?

Scenario-Specific Questions

- Who is considered a religious advisor, according to the university? Who else may need to be informed about the situation in the hall? Who else might be a good person to help Dia?
- What are the issues that need to be addressed? What is the history of partnering between religious advisors and university student affairs/residence life? What are the implications for the community beyond Dia and her roommate related to this situation? What Institutional Intelligence information does Mario need to provide the best legal and ethical response to Dia's situation?

- Where else is Dia connected on campus? Where is Dia's room located in the building? Where might she want (or not want) space for the upcoming holiday?
- When (dates and times of the day) does Dia need the space for her religious practice?
- Why might Dia hesitate to share more information with Mario?
- How can Mario navigate this situation and continue to build a good relationship with Dia? How might he seek support for some of his concerns throughout this situation?

What other Institutional Intelligence questions may Mario want to ask before acting in this situation?

Advocates of Sexual Assault Victims

A final and essential role on campus that can involve confidentiality is the Title IX advocacy staff member or team. Title IX incidents are situations where campus response falls into the *it depends* category. Some campuses have designated their campus advocate as a confidential resource, whereas others have not. You must understand who the confidential resources are on your campus. Additionally, Title IX potentially deals with not only student needs but also campus response, community impact, federal reporting, and various other issues depending on the nature of the incident.

Inconsistency about the location of Title IX staff further complicates their work and collaboration. If there is a specific Title IX office, the advocate may be part of that team. If not, advocates may be in various areas, including student assistance, women's centers, campus police, the dean of students office, human resources, or elsewhere on campus. The confidential resource might also be located off-campus and not affiliated with the institution. Finally, there may not be a Title IX advocate on your campus, although students would still have access to confidential resources through any other areas listed in this chapter. Each incident has challenges, potential partnerships, and resources informed by your institutional context and personal knowledge.

These staff members attend to the specific needs and wants of students in crisis. As a result, they must be well connected with student affairs staff for issues related to housing, student conduct processes, interim actions available to students, counseling, medical care, and other supports. Additionally, safety and security for students sit at the intersection between campus police/safety and housing and other areas of student affairs. There are also academic considerations; the dean of students office staff or student support areas can often assist with those concerns.

The confidential advocate may have information that the student does not wish to share with law enforcement, student affairs, or other resources on campus or in the surrounding community. Additionally, the advocate may know more than roommates, friends, and family. As a result, student affairs professionals need to be aware of processes, procedures, and policies. They must collaborate with victim advocates to ensure that students have all the information they need to make decisions about the next steps after an incident occurs.

Outside of specific incidents, student affairs is often the coordinating area for sexual misconduct, sexual violence prevention, and education around sexual assault awareness (Finley & Levenson, 2018). Additionally, the identities of students experiencing sexual violence inform the choices they may make and the resources available to them. Too often, institutions design sexual misconduct protocols focused on cisgender white women. This approach not only reinforces the stigmatization of other student populations related to sexual violence but limits the breadth and depth of potential support and strategies that can be offered to and developed with students reporting sexual violence.

Institutional Intelligence Questions

Who: Who is/are the confidential victims' advocate(s) on your campus? Who is available in the community to serve as a confidential victim's advocate if there is none on campus? Whom does the advocate collaborate with most frequently? Who is connecting students with the advocate? Who is a "responsible employee" for mandatory reporting regarding the Clery Act?

What: What individuals, teams, offices, units, and areas connect with the confidential victims' advocates? What training is available for students, staff, and faculty about sexual misconduct, victims' options, and advocacy resources on your campus? What options do students have for reporting and acting? What support is available if students do not move forward with formal processes?

Where: Where is the victim advocate located on campus (physically and in terms of functional area)? Where is information provided to students about the victim advocate and sexual misconduct related to campus policies, processes, and resources? What resources are available for students accused of sexual misconduct?

When: When can the advocate be reached (weekdays, 24/7, other)? When should students expect a response if they initiate outreach?

Why: Why was the advocate position created on your campus (in response to a specific incident, legislation, administrative directive, or other)? Why might students want to engage with the victim advocate? Why might student affairs want to connect with this staff member?

How: How can various student affairs partners best support the victim advocate to center on supporting students? How are staff and students trained in "trauma-informed" response practices when students disclose sexual violence or misconduct? How can student affairs and this staff member partner on training, sharing resources, and sharing information as situations arise? How can students connect with this office and this staff member informally outside of reporting incidents on campus? How do confidential victim advocates interface with Title IX, Clery, and other compliance functions? How do staff with differing and sometimes competing institutional priorities work together to support students navigating sexual violence and trauma?

Critical Scenario 15.4 Sexual Assault Victim Advocates

Co-Author: Taylor Tyson-Knapp, Women's Resource Center Coordinator, Texas A&M University

Anne (she/her) is a program coordinator working with the Fraternity and Sorority Life (FSL) Office. One afternoon, a student, Joe (they/them), asks Anne if they can talk with her. Joe starts with, "So, something happened, and I need some help, but I don't want you to tell anyone about it."

Anne immediately says,

> Joe, I am so glad you feel comfortable talking with me. Before you go on, I want to let you know that depending on what you share—particularly if it involves violence you have experienced or thoughts about self-harm, I may be obligated to share the information you share with me. I don't want to put you in a position where you don't have the control you want and need right now. I can help you connect with a confidential resource. While I will protect your privacy and share information only with people who need to be informed, there are people on campus who can offer you confidentiality.

Joe pauses, nods, and then asks who the confidential resources are on campus. Anne shares names, phone numbers, office locations, and services provided for the health center, the counseling center, and the victim advocate on campus, Teresa (she/her). Joe says, "This is really helpful. I think I would be more comfortable talking with a confidential person. What do you know about Teresa?"

Anne shares that Teresa has worked in her current role for several years and has been a great collaborator around training and programming with the FSL office. Anne says, "If you would like, I'd be happy to walk you over and introduce you to Teresa." Joe says that would be great. Anne calls to confirm that Teresa is available and walks Joe to Teresa's office to make the connection.

Over the next two weeks, Anne sees Joe twice—both times at organizational meetings. Joe seems disengaged, and Anne tries to talk to them after the second meeting. Joe says they are busy and cannot talk right now but not to worry that they are doing all right. Anne is worried.

The Law

- What are the relevant legal issues in this scenario?
- What institutional policies, procedures, or processes are applicable in this scenario?

Ethics

- What are the relevant ethical issues in this scenario?
- What information would the characters need to make sound ethical decisions in this situation?

Identity

- How would characters' social identities affect how this scenario might unfold? Assign the characters individual social identities and go through the scenario. Then change some of those social identities and go through the scenario again.
- How do the situation and the information you need change?

Scenario-Specific Questions

- Who may need to know how Joe is engaging (or not) with their FSL organization or other groups on campus?
- What might Anne expect if she shares information with Teresa regarding an update on Joe? What can Anne do to address her concerns about this student?

- Where can Anne get support if she is experiencing stress or anxiety about the situation with Joe?
- When should Anne share information with her supervisor and Teresa about her experiences with Joe at the meetings?
- Why might Joe have preferred a confidential resource in this situation?
- How can Anne continue to support Joe without overstepping?

What other Institutional Intelligence factors should Anne consider as she decides what next steps to take because of her exchange with and concern for Joe?

Conclusion

Significant legal and ethical considerations accompany working as a confidential resource or partnering with those resources on campus. Understanding the difference between privacy and confidentiality is essential to navigating complex situations. Often the reason students reach out to confidential resources is highly personal and emotionally charged and requires ongoing work. Fostering trust and providing safety to students are essential for them to move forward personally and academically.

There are nuances in balancing privacy and confidentiality, and this work takes a significant toll on students and staff. It is essential that staff who navigate these issues be supported to maintain their capacity and well-being. Supervisors are essential in providing time, space, mental health resources, and other support. We provide the best support for students by taking care of ourselves—particularly when we have histories, triggers, stressors, or other factors and experiences that make navigating the complexities of this work more difficult.

16

GRADUATE STUDENTS

> Graduate student assistantships in graduate preparation programs allow students hands-on experience in student affairs, including functional areas, ethics, law, and professional expectations. Graduate supervisors provide experiential learning for students, so they can make informed decisions about whether a particular area is right for them. Supervisors must be intentional with graduate student development. Excellent supervisors ensure they provide guidance and direction, encouraging students to learn about many functional areas and helping graduate students stay current with emerging issues in student affairs, higher education, and beyond.
>
> —Dr. Aja C. Holmes, Assistant Dean of Students and Director of Student Living, University of San Francisco

"Hey, Michelle and Cristóbal," you, the reader, begin, "why are you putting graduate students so late in the book? Is it because they aren't important?"

No, dear reader. Not at all. Instead, graduate students are among the most crucial staff in student and academic affairs, and their positions are some of the most complex on college and university campuses. Graduate students also hold positions across all functional areas discussed in the text.

In fact, as faculty members in higher education and student affairs programs, we enjoy working with graduate students as much as or more than anyone else. Hall-Hertel et al. (2022) wrote that graduate students "are some of the most valuable constituencies of the higher education enterprise" (p. 3). However, there is a lack of literature on holistic support strategies for

DOI: 10.4324/9781003442707-19

graduate students (Sanchez & Beard, 2022), and Shepard and Perry (2022) call for "a common understanding that the culture of the university supports graduate and professional student thriving or creates barriers to it" (p. 226). We saved this chapter until now so that our discussion about graduate student experiences builds on law, ethics, the Institutional Intelligence Model, and the functional areas discussed in earlier chapters.

When I (Michelle) was a relatively new professional, I asked one of my mentors, Dr. Ginny Arthur, the Associate Director of Housing at Iowa State University, how she could stand working with graduate students. I said, "Every couple of years, you have to have the same conversations over and over. And some of the students are very whiny." She smiled and said, "Well, some full-time staff are whiny, too."

Point taken.

Anyway, she explained that working with graduate students was an opportunity for her to be an educator in a unique way as grads figured out who they wanted to be in the work. The graduate students also experienced various student affairs functional area tasks in housing. They might be doing academic advising, leadership development, supervising, co-advising a student organization, or having a conduct meeting at any given time. As a result, she also engaged with graduate students as they figured out what type of work they wanted.

Ginny Arthur said,

> Besides, as a leader, you are always training new staff to move into new roles – if their goal is to move on or up. We are always training new people. The work is cyclical. Grad students are an important part of the cycle in housing and student affairs.

Chapter Organization

After a brief history of graduate students in U.S. higher education, we will discuss five essential elements of the student and academic affairs graduate student experience. First, we talk about the academic experiences of graduate students in student affairs programs. Next, we explore graduate assistantships and the unique elements of graduate student supervision. After that, we examine the role conflict that graduate students face as being both students (who may want to speak out against campus policies) and employees (who may need to exercise caution in criticizing their employers). Last, we discuss graduate students' transition into student affairs as new practitioners upon graduation.

In short, the graduate student experience is complicated, and this chapter focuses on those complexities. Is being a graduate student with an assistantship in student or academic affairs positive or negative? Well, *it depends.* As in the other chapters, we will use the Institutional Intelligence Model to navigate the experience of graduate students working in student and academic affairs.

Legal and Ethical Considerations

Because excellent supervisors, mentors, and faculty embed the competencies into their work and learning with graduate students, significant legal and ethical considerations inform working and learning with graduate students. While not every graduate student will be involved in every legal issue in an office, they can learn from these experiences. We must provide graduate students with opportunities to observe, discuss, and reflect on issues related to contracts, hiring, student accountability processes, records management, crisis response, and other work with significant legal implications.

We all benefit from department or other meetings and class discussions when we pair work with reflection. This is particularly true as graduate students develop their ethical identities in the context of institutional and professional organizational ethical guidelines. A final and important consideration is that as we work with graduate students, we prepare outstanding colleagues for the future. While practitioners and faculty teach, role model, supervise, advise, and mentor graduate students, staff and faculty should seek opportunities to learn from them.

Competencies

Of all the competencies in the chapters, this section is the easiest to write. Supervising, mentoring, and teaching graduate students require us to use *all* competencies (see Appendix). When working in these roles, we must help graduate students develop in each competency area.

Personal and Ethical Foundations (PEFs) get at the core of who we are today and who we aspire to be in the future. Values, Philosophy, and History (VPH) competency is essential to understanding the field of student affairs and the context of higher education. Assessment, Evaluation, and Research (AER) competency is vital to programs and projects. Law, Policy, and Governance (LPG) connects to contracts and job descriptions but is also relevant to the daily work and ways we engage with institutions and individuals. We implement Organizational and Human Resources (OHR) through hiring, evaluation, and termination but also through the structure of organizations. We use Leadership (LEAD) competency to supervise and mentor students and provide them with opportunities to take on leadership roles. We should be embedding Social Justice and Inclusion (SJI) into every aspect of our work, learning, and growth. Student Learning and Development (SLD) applies to the student experiences of graduate students and our work supporting undergraduates and other students through our work responsibilities. Technology (TECH) can often provide experienced practitioners with the opportunity to learn from the expertise of graduate students. Moreover, Advising and Supporting (A/S) informs our work with all students, including the graduate students in our offices and classes.

The History of Student Affairs Graduate Education

Scholars acknowledge that despite much research on U.S. higher education, we have overlooked graduate students in our scholarship (Chism, 1998; Wert, 1998). However, some information provides a better understanding of the role of graduate students in student affairs. For instance, the first graduate assistants began in the late 1600s at Harvard University. Graduate students provided support for students but also received their positions to lighten the faculty load. Faculty members especially wanted to relegate "the much-resented burden of teaching introductory courses" (Geiger, 1997, p. 19).

In the mid-1800s, the German research institution model took root in the U.S. Faculty members wanted more graduate students to help with research. The number of graduate students increased with the establishment of research institutions like Johns Hopkins University (Roper & Hirth, 2005). We discuss this in more detail in Chapter 13, where we explore student living and well-being in higher education.

Columbia University created the first student affairs graduate program and grew out of the work of the Deans of Women. The Columbia University website states, "The Higher and Postsecondary Education Program at Teachers College, Columbia University has prepared students to work or continue study in the field of higher education for over a century, since our program's founding in 1913" (Columbia University, n.d., para. 1). Five years later, at the end of World War I, "the student personnel movement gained national recognition and professional stature" (Brubacher & Rudy, 1958, p. 336).

While the Deans of Women focused on academic preparation, the Deans of Men prioritized apprenticeship over classroom learning (Schwartz, 2000). In the 1924 notes on the proceedings of a meeting of the Deans of Men, a dean reported that the YWCA (Young Women's Christian Association) sponsored discussion groups with fraternity chapters and other groups. The document says, "The [discussion] leaders in most cases are faculty or graduate men" (Schwartz, 2000, p. 24). Neither the 1937 nor the 1949 version of the *Student Personnel Point of View* mentions graduate students (American Council on Education [ACE], 1937, 1949).

Graduate education and graduate assistantships again increased in the 1950s as student enrollment in U.S. higher education grew, particularly in STEM (science, technology, engineering, and mathematics) fields. This growth resulted from the G.I. Bill, the Space Race, and atomic energy research, among other factors (Kaiser, 2002). At the same time, counseling psychology, social and organizational psychology, international education, and post-secondary education programs grew (Columbia University, n.d.). Along with more undergraduate students in higher education, there were more graduate students—including student affairs graduate students—during this time.

In 1961, there was a push to "professionalize" student affairs work through "advanced graduate training and the incorporation of technical know-how" (Williamson, 1961, p. 17). Williamson (1961) further asserted that replacing "technical knowledge for the earlier common-sense approach" (p. 17) to student development would improve effectiveness and could be done without resulting in impersonal relationships between academic and student affairs staff and students.

Throughout the 1960s and 1970s, scholars began studying college student development and, as a result, created theories that would become embedded in student affairs graduate program curriculums (Long, 2012). In the 1980s and 1990s, the college student population became more diverse concerning race, gender, LGBTQ+ students, age, ability, and other identities. In response, higher education and student affairs embraced new modes of learning. At the same time, scholars created new developmental theories based on students other than white men (Long, 2012).

In the 2000s, the diversity of college students continued to increase. Additionally, globalization and internationalization in student affairs played a more significant role than in the past. Furthermore, the role of technology increased, and the American College Personnel Association (ACPA) and the National Association of Student Personnel Administrators (NASPA) added technology as a stand-alone competency in 2015 (ACPA/NASPA, 2015). As we entered the COVID-19 pandemic in 2020, student affairs adjusted to distance, online, and virtual engagement formats. The future will inform what we have learned and how we apply that learning to the future of student affairs.

Throughout the rest of this chapter, we explore the academic program, assistantship, and supervision experiences related to graduate students. We also discuss role conflict, graduate student development, and transitioning into the profession. Because graduate students are essential to student affairs work and the field's future, excelling in our work with and supporting graduate students are central to the ethical and legal situations that student affairs practitioners will navigate moving forward. We cannot overstate the importance of graduate students.

Academic Program Expectations

For most student affairs practitioners, obtaining a master's degree is an initial step to full-time work (Kuk et al., 2007). According to the NASPA Graduate Program Directory, 272 schools offer master's programs related to student affairs and higher education (NASPA, 2020). The CAS (Council for the Advancement of Standards in Higher Education) standards (2020) outline three core areas academic programs in student affairs should include: foundational (history and philosophy), professional (theory, student characteristics, organization/administration, individual and group strategies, and assessment/evaluation/research), and supervised (work, assistantship, and practicum/internship) practice.

Scholars have identified a variety of specific courses included in various student affairs graduate program curricula, including assessment, evaluation, and research (Cooper et al., 2016; Ortiz et al., 2015; Perez, 2016); history (Ortiz et al., 2015); law and ethics (Cooper et al., 2016); diversity, multiculturalism, social justice, inclusion, and equity (Flowers, 2003; Flowers & Howard-Hamilton, 2002; Gayles & Kelly, 2007; McEwen & Roper, 1994; Ortiz et al., 2015; Pope & Reynolds, 1997); organization and administration (Perez, 2016); supervised practice and field experiences (Ortiz et al., 2015); technology (Engstrom, 1999); theory (Ortiz et al., 2015; Perez, 2016); and values (Young & Elfrink, 1991). In addition, as early as 1913, when Columbia started the first student affairs graduate program, students were required to complete a practicum as part of their curriculum (Lloyd-Jones, 1949).

We know that assessment, evaluation, and research, as well as diversity, multiculturalism, social justice, inclusion, and equity, are not synonymous with one another. We have grouped these terms for a summary here. Nevertheless, these terms have different meanings that often inform each other. We can utilize the Institutional Intelligence Model's questions to understand how specific institutions and departments use these terms.

Through student affairs graduate preparation programs, emerging student and academic affairs practitioners learn about historical information and current issues while gaining practical experience. This work is not a simple curriculum, nor is the above a complete listing of all the courses offered through graduate preparation for student affairs. Each graduate program is different, and graduate students must understand their *what* and *where*. What is the purpose of their graduate program? Where are they earning their degree? Some programs might focus on policy, others on research and evaluation, and others aim primarily to develop social justice educators or student affairs practitioners.

That said, how are equity and access actualized in graduate preparation programs? Many student affairs graduate preparation programs have eliminated the Graduate Review Examination (GRE), given the racial bias of standardized tests and the financial burden that taking the exam puts on program applicants. Nevertheless, these systemic inequities go beyond standardized exams. Consider the expenses to students just to be *considered* for positions in programs. These costs include application fees, travel expenses for campus assistantship interviews (if applicable to the program), and expenses related to "professional attire." Furthermore, this is all before a student is offered a position in a graduate program.

Once a student secures admission and an assistantship, those inequities—particularly concerning finances—persist. Many programs require an assistantship—usually with a small stipend—and unpaid labor in the form of practicum and internship(s). A 120-hour internship over a 15-week semester means that students must work eight hours a week *for free*. Students gain valuable academic and professional experience (assuming a good field experience supervisor and a rich set of opportunities). However, this commitment is eight hours per week. These are eight hours a week that students cannot work for pay that they may need for rent, food, and expenses.

Other expectations that student affairs have embedded in its culture exacerbate issues related to economic privilege. "Professional attire" is another expectation with significant implications for working-class and lower–socioeconomic status students. More than once, graduate students have shared that they have been reprimanded or mocked about their attire at their assistantships or field experience sites. Student affairs makes a common and problematic assumption that all students can afford to buy work clothes. Designing strategies to support students across different levels of financial privilege is part of what academic and student affairs staff do for undergraduate students all the time. We need to make sure we are doing the same for graduate students.

Other areas where student affairs programs and assistantships reinforce financial privilege include professional organization membership, conference attendance, and textbook expenses. When we make things affordable for students without financial resources, we make things better for every student. Identifying free or low-cost textbook options is an essential consideration for faculty. Even ensuring that social activities and program celebrations are no- or very low-cost is vital for student affairs practitioners and faculty to walk our talk.

Another consideration is that the larger institutional culture may create barriers and reinforce student inequities. Students of Color at predominantly and historically (and intentionally) white institutions will have labor and stress that white students do not have to navigate. This labor will impact the students' classes, assistantships, field experiences, and individual well-being and safety.

Additionally, programs and functional areas often expect Students of Color, undocumented and DACA (Deferred Action for Childhood Arrivals) students, LGBTQI+ and gender non-conforming students, students with disabilities, and international students to show vulnerability in service to majority populations. These expectations can be particularly true in diversity, equity, inclusion, and justice classes. More likely, we all have been in spaces where white students stay silent or say, "I don't know what to say because I don't want to say the wrong thing." Statements like this imply that it is okay for white students to avoid risk and vulnerability. However, students holding non-majority identities should do most of the talking (and most of the risk-taking).

We have probably also experienced situations where students have spoken and other students (or faculty or practitioners) have disregarded them because they do not have the vocabulary to discuss issues of justice and equity effectively. Students who hold more conservative beliefs or root their perspectives in their religious traditions can be shut down and judged rather than invited into conversations. To advance higher education, it is our responsibility to educate and provide learning opportunities for graduate students to critically examine education and advocate for historically marginalized communities.

Utilizing the Institutional Intelligence Model, we can identify questions to explore the culture of student affairs graduate preparation programs. These questions are helpful for students and informative for faculty and supervisors. Teaching about justice and equity without putting them into practice is hypocritical and harms students—usually those most vulnerable. Additionally, as many programs stress the role of reflection in the experiences they create for students, faculty and staff should be engaging in reflective practice (see Chapter 17).

Institutional Intelligence Questions

Who: Who are the students in your program? Who is missing from the program? Who are your good partners across the university? With which field experience supervisors do students struggle? Who are people you have not historically engaged with that can enhance your program? Who are the people you remain engaged with to the detriment of your program? Who are your faculty and instructors?

What: What strategies do you use to do an equity review centering on students in your program? What experiences do you require that disproportionately negatively impact some students rather than others? What are your program's requirements (i.e., internships and field projects)? What skills or experiences, now missing from your academic program, will students need as they become practitioners? What classes are offered and required in the program?

Where: Where do you recruit students? Where are potential students engaging with your program? Where are current students engaging? Where are there gaps in your curriculum? Where do your resources come from?

When: When do classes meet, and do those times center students, or do they center assistantships or faculty? When are your deadlines for admission and administrative paperwork? When do students have access to faculty? When are the difficult times of the year or challenging terms in the program for students?

Why: Why is your curriculum structured as it is? Why do students choose (or not choose) your program?

How: How does your program address inequity in its processes? How does your faculty role model student-centered work? How are students at the center of your program?

Critical Scenario 16.1 Academic Program Expectations

Co-Author: Dr. Deborah L. Floyd, Professor, Department of Educational Leadership and Research Methodology, Florida Atlantic University

A potential student in the student affairs graduate preparation master's program at Robinson University, Max Barbo (he/him), sent the following email to Dr. Francis (she/her), the program coordinator.

Dear Dr. Francis,

I am very excited about applying for the master's program at Robinson University. I have heard amazing things about the faculty, the Division of Student Affairs, and the students in the program. As I prepare for a career in student affairs, I am looking for the best next step for me, and I believe that Robinson is part of that journey.

As a first-generation, working-class student, I have paid my way through my undergraduate education. As a result, I need to be as financially responsible as possible as I move on to graduate education. I wanted to reach out and see if you can help or direct me to someone else about the following questions:

- *Is there any* chance to apply for a waiver of the application fee?
- If admitted academically, is it possible to do a Zoom or other remote interview *instead of coming to campus for assistantship interview days?*
- *I anticipate that I will need employment beyond my assistantship in order to cover my living expenses. Are there any limitations for graduate students regarding outside employment?*

I understand that most field experiences are unpaid, but is it possible to negotiate a paid internship? Since I need to work to cover expenses, I am concerned about meeting this experiential requirement since I need to have paid work, including internships.

Thank you for your assistance. I was relieved to see that your program does not require the GRE, as that would have been an expense I would likely not have been able to afford. The Robinson program was recommended to me by an alum of the program—Faye Stevens. She was the advisor to the Student Government Association [SGA] at my undergraduate institution and has been a mentor to me as SGA Vice President. Faye has also been an incredible support in terms of my academics, next steps after graduation, and future career. Thank you for your help.

Sincerely, Max Barbo

The Law

- What are the relevant legal issues in this scenario?
- What institutional policies, procedures, or processes are applicable in this scenario?

Ethics

- What are the relevant ethical issues in this scenario?
- What information would the characters need to make sound ethical decisions in this situation?

Identity

- How would characters' social identities affect how this scenario might unfold? Assign the characters specific social identities and go through the scenario. Then change some of those social identities and go through the scenario again.
- How do the situation and the information you need change?

Scenario-Specific Questions

- Who decides about application fees (program, department, college, graduate school)? Who needs to be consulted before waiving fees?
- What is the policy about paid internships? What assistantships pay more (stipends but perhaps also room and board) than others? What are the

most important facts surrounding the case? What are the critical issues in this case? What are your possible courses of action? (Respond, ignore, delegate?) What information do you need to respond to this inquiry?

- Where are the offices that offer assistantships in the program? Where can students get more information about the compensation and responsibilities for each assistantship?
- When do students find out about assistantship offers? When do they need to decide once they receive an offer?
- Why does the program require an assistantship and multiple field experiences?
- How has the program managed these issues in the past? How have students navigated these challenges?

What other questions should Dr. Francis consider asking the Institutional Intelligence Model before responding to Max's email?

Graduate Assistantships

Given the importance of supervised practice for graduate students discussed earlier in this chapter and the role of theory-to-practice embedded in most student affairs programs (Creamer & Winston, 2002), graduate assistantships are a crucial aspect of graduate student preparation. In these situations, the assistantship is not a job as much as it is an extension of the academic experience. While graduate students work in assistantships, they might receive a full or partial tuition waiver and often a stipend (Dewberry, 2005; Flora, 2007).

Supervisors and other academic and student affairs practitioners must remember that students are in their assistantship roles to learn first and foremost. Graduate assistants' primary responsibility is as students, not employees. If someone comes to campus to study and has an assistantship as part of their academic program, they are primarily students. They are first and foremost employees if they work at a university and also take courses.

When student or academic affairs units approach graduate students as cheap labor, the students' educational experiences are erased or minimized. Keppler (2010) wrote that graduate students help during budget crises as they take on the work of vacated full-time positions. Similarly, Creamer and Winston (2002) warned that when units use graduate student labor to manage costs, intentional supervision, coaching, and mentoring become secondary to holding students accountable for completing work tasks.

Assistantships should center on the graduate student as a learner. Requiring assistantships and field experiences embeds the notion of theory-to-practice in the student's learning and development experience. By having a workspace where students work with college students, student and academic affairs graduate students can connect what they are learning in class to real situations.

Financial Considerations

Using graduate student labor because it is cheaper than a full-time employee is problematic; also, cheap labor from graduate students can be exploiting graduate students. We encourage you to consider the wage and insurance benefits that graduate assistants receive at your institution, aside from other benefits (professional development, partial meal plan, free t-shirts, etc.). For many graduate students, that stipend—after taxes—is the only income they will have to live on during their graduate programs.

Consider the implications that your work culture has on students' finances. Boettcher et al. (2020) wrote about the financial impact of staff lunches or potlucks, expected contributions to gifts for colleague retirements or baby showers, and other dollars supervisors tell grad students to allocate from their stipends to participate in work events and be a good team player. Class is present in student affairs in several ways, from meeting for coffee to socializing after work and attending campus and other events together—all of which can have financial implications (Ardoin & Martinez, 2019). Again, take the time and examine the culture of your institution, unit, and team. How is it designed to support graduate assistants, and what can you do to resolve issues of inequity?

Institutional Intelligence Questions

Who: Whom are you consulting when determining work hours and schedules for graduate students? Whom are students expected to serve? Whom are you hiring (or not hiring) as part of your team?

What: What are your needs and expectations of graduate students? What are the responsibilities and expectations in your position description? What compensation and professional development support do you provide to graduate assistants in your areas? What role do students play in outlining their experiences in graduate assistantships?

Where: Where will students work? (Do they have their own offices?) Where is the graduate space located in relation to high-traffic areas, their supervisors, other graduate students, and other resources?

When: When are students expected to be at work? When do students get vacation? When will students have a chance to engage with practitioners across their unit, department, and division?

Why: Why is this position/work best filled/completed by a graduate student instead of a full-time employee? Why would students be drawn to this opportunity?

How: How can students get more information about the position experience? How will students get information from others who have held this assistantship? How are students supported in their work (supervision and mentoring)?

Critical Scenario 16.2 Graduate Assistantships

Co-Authors: Madison Beine, Coordinator for Orientation Programs, University of Oregon, and Alexis Swider, Assistant Director of Involvement for Fraternities and Sororities, Elon University

Cory (he/him) is finishing his first semester of grad school and is a graduate assistant for his university's multicultural center. While he loves his work and gets along well with the rest of the staff, he has become increasingly overwhelmed as the semester progresses. Cory's contract stated he would work 20 hours per week, but lately he has been working closer to 25 or 30 hours. He is excited about the projects he is working on, but the heavy workload has started infringing on his schoolwork and personal life. Cory also feels uncomfortable that he is working so many unpaid hours.

Cory is scared to bring up his hours because he does not want to jeopardize the good relationship with his supervisor Malia (they/them). When Cory finally broaches the topic in a one-on-one, Malia expresses their disappointment. According to them, working overtime and not being compensated are just parts of working in student affairs.

Cory leaves the meeting feeling very down and confused. He does not want to let down Malia or the rest of the team but also is unwilling to work many hours without getting paid. Cory begins to question whether student affairs is the right career for him.

The Law

- What are the relevant legal issues in this scenario?
- What institutional policies, procedures, or processes are applicable in this scenario?

Ethics

- What are the relevant ethical issues in this scenario?
- What information would the characters need to make sound ethical decisions in this situation?

Identity

- How would characters' social identities affect how this scenario might unfold? Assign the characters specific social identities and go through the scenario. Then change some of those social identities and go through the scenario again.
- How do the situation and the information you need change?

Scenario-Specific Questions

- Who are other resources, and what other offices does Cory need to find and connect with to chart a plan forward?
- What else does Cory need to know to succeed in his role without his labor being exploited? What information or training does Malia need to better support Cory while ensuring that all of the center's work is done? What do Malia and Cory need to understand, and how might they begin working to transform the culture of overwork in student affairs?
- Where might additional training and development come from for Malia as a supervisor or Cory as a graduate assistant?
- When are ideal times for graduate students to raise issues about hours and other work considerations with their supervisors?
- Why might Malia believe that overwork is just part of student affairs?
- How do the institutional and student affairs cultures set the stage for this exchange? How can students learn about the culture of an office before they begin their assistantships? How can supervisors help students understand office culture? How might this culture of overwork negatively impact Malia and other full-time staff in addition to graduate assistants?

How might Cory and the team use the Institutional Intelligence Model questions to examine the experience of graduate students as well as the impact that this culture has on full-time practitioners?

Graduate Assistant Supervision

If you review the list of curricular elements earlier in this chapter, you will notice that we do not include supervision. Research has shown that academic programs assume that students get supervision training and education through assistantships and work experiences. Often, work settings assume that students have been trained in supervision through the academic program (Calhoun & Nasser, 2013; Holmes, 2014; Winston & Creamer, 1997). As a result, many first-time supervisors are developing skills on the job as they work with their first supervisees.

Stock-Ward and Javorek (2003) categorized graduate students as "Level One" supervisees. The authors suggest that, among the considerations for supervisors of graduate students, establishing a supportive supervision relationship is crucial. This relationship should initially stress positive feedback, offer ongoing feedback, set clear expectations, specify paperwork to be completed, and provide opportunities for students to observe more experienced staff and for supervisors to observe staff at work.

In the case of graduate students, supervision can be particularly complex. Graduate students are learning who they are, learning what functional areas interest them, and being socialized as practitioners. At the same time, they are developing their philosophies of integrity and ethics. While most graduate students are transitioning from undergraduate to graduate education, others are returning to graduate school after full-time workforce experience. Many graduate students are also learning to be organizational advisors rather than leaders. This contributes to students' socialization on specific campuses and anticipatory socialization into student affairs more broadly (Weidman et al., 2001).

Assistantship Experiences and Responsibilities

Graduate assistantships serve as a "mechanism for students' professional socialization" (Perna & Hudgins, 1996, p. 2). Ideally, graduate assistant experiences help emerging practitioners develop skills across professional competencies (Flora, 2007; Perna & Hudgins, 1996). Understanding the graduate program culture at your institution is essential in supervising graduate students and offering them support.

Using the Institutional Intelligence Model can help you as you work to understand the culture. What are the graduate student responsibilities and experiences in your department and your institution? How are the graduate program and your area partnered to create developmental opportunities for graduate students?

Most graduate assistantships have a set number of hours. The number of hours in a student's contract is what supervisors have stated they expect and what graduate students agreed to. To violate this regularly is both unethical and potentially a contractual violation that exposes a department and university to the risk of a lawsuit. What are the hours for graduate assistants in your area? What are the expectations for work during breaks, vacations, and sick leave? Supervisors who might tell graduate students, "You are a student, so you don't get benefits," and then later say, "You're not a student, so you work during breaks," need to exercise caution as these messages are contradictory, hypocritical, and exploitive.

Graduate assistantship experiences should attend to not only the position responsibilities and daily work routine but also issues of professional development (Flora, 2007; Perna & Hudgins, 1996). What is the culture of support related to graduate student development? How do the practices in your area align with or diverge from those in other graduate assistantship areas? Is there additional funding for students to attend conferences, build their professional libraries, or get specific training or credentials? Do you allow students work time to attend professional development events? Are there other ways you support the professional developmental experiences of graduate students?

Graduate assistants and supervisors can partner to develop a supervisory plan by considering Institutional Intelligence factors. What will meetings look like? When will graduate assistants get feedback? How will a student know whether they are being successful in their assistantship? Discussing expectations is an excellent time to explore campus culture and build Institutional Intelligence. Other opportunities for graduate assistantship supervisors to implement Institutional Intelligence discussions include weekly supervision meetings, discussing expectations, and discussing learning about other campus cultures during the job search.

Institutional Intelligence Questions

Elements in developing a supervision plan can be built using the Institutional Intelligence Model prompts.

Who: Who is the supervisor, and who is the graduate student? Who else can serve as a resource (mentor, collaborator, or peer) for graduate students in the workplace? Who is served through this assistantship? Who is the leader or director of the unit? With whom will the supervisor help the new graduate assistant connect in the unit, department, division, and the larger university in the first 90 days?

What: What are the job responsibilities? What are the responsibilities of the supervisor and workplace to the student? What professional development opportunities are there? What are the expectations of the supervisor and the supervisee? What experience does the supervisor have? What is this position's compensation, professional development funding, and vacation/break schedule? What experience and supervision style does the supervisor bring to the work with the graduate student? Besides regularly scheduled annual evaluations, what ongoing feedback will the supervisee receive (and when)?

Where: Where will supervision meetings take place? Where can the graduate student go with questions if the supervisor is unavailable?

When: Where will mutual expectations be set and revisited? When will supervision meetings take place? When can the graduate student expect feedback outside of the formal evaluation? When will expectations be revisited over each semester?

Why: Why was this person chosen to be the supervisor of this graduate student? Why was this graduate student offered this assistantship?

How: How will mutual expectations be set? How often will supervision meetings happen, and how long will they last? How will they be rescheduled if a conflict emerges? How will students raise concerns about supervision or the assistantship experience? How will supervisors raise concerns about performance and communication? How do the job responsibilities provide students with opportunities to work on specific ACPA/NASPA competencies? How will feedback be shared and discussed?

In addition, supervisors and graduate students should create a professional development plan, and supervisors should do an overview of the formal evaluation (and provide the graduate student with that evaluation early in their first month on the job). In order to attend to the student holistically, the supervisor and student should identify strategies for providing care and support for the graduate student and how the student will share their needs related to support. Students should also be provided opportunities to give feedback to their supervisor about the supervision, work responsibilities, and other factors related to the work site and the student's experience. Also, you can use the NASPA and ACPA competencies to develop professional development opportunities and evaluate graduate students.

Critical Scenario 16.3 Graduate Assistant Supervision

Co-Authors: Dr. Aja C. Holmes, Assistant Dean of Students and Director of Student Living, University of San Francisco, and Dr. Reyes J. Luna, Interim Executive Director of Housing, Cal Poly Pomona

Patty (she/her) is an experienced hall director who supervises two graduate assistants (GAs). In addition to attending individual supervision meetings, she meets with both GAs weekly. They discuss how the resident assistant (RA) staff is doing, building and departmental initiatives, and regularly check in as a leadership team.

In a meeting at the end of October, Sara (she/her) and Joe (he/him) discussed some challenges with the RA staff team and strategized how to address issues. Sara says, "Patty, we are so lucky to have you as a supervisor. We appreciate all the time you give us."

Joe nods and adds,

> Elliott is having a really tough time with his supervisor, Gretchen. Last week when they met was the first time Gretchen hasn't canceled or rescheduled their supervision. Elliott said they have met only twice so far this year. Anyway, Gretchen said, 'I notice that you aren't volunteering for additional work beyond your set hours. I worry that it makes you look like you're not a team player.' She said it could impact his references and what they say about him when he graduates.

Sara adds,

> And she isn't letting him leave until the university closes at the end of the semester. I thought we were able to leave as soon as the halls closed. I hope that is still true since I have a flight home the day after closing.

The Law

- What are the relevant legal issues in this scenario?
- What institutional policies, procedures, or processes are applicable in this scenario?

Ethics

- What are the relevant ethical issues in this scenario?
- What information would the characters need to make sound ethical decisions in this situation?

Identity

- How would characters' social identities affect how this scenario might unfold? Assign the characters specific social identities and go through the scenario. Then change some of those social identities and go through the scenario again.
- How do the situation and the information you need change?

Scenario-Specific Questions

- Who is Patty's supervisor? Who is Gretchen's supervisor? Who else may be impacted by the difference in staff supervision between Patty's team and Gretchen's?
- What questions should Patty ask to inform what action she should take based on the Institutional Intelligence Model and what Sara and Joe have shared? What additional information might Patty have access to? What is the history of staffing during academic breaks in the department?
- Where are the guidelines about staff expectations and supervision?
- When should Patty talk to Elliott? When should she talk to Gretchen? When should she talk to her supervisor?
- Why might Patty choose not to get involved in the situation Sara and Joe shared? Why might she choose to get involved?
- How can Patty address this situation without potentially compromising what Elliott may have shared with Sara and Joe?

How else might individuals in this situation use the Institutional Intelligence Model to understand the culture and work toward equity?

Role Conflict

Journey with us back to one of the age-old questions facing our profession: Are graduate assistants employees or students? The answer, of course, is "Yes,"—but it can also be, "*It depends.*" We need to wrestle with the complexity of the graduate student situation for ethical and legal reasons. Generally speaking, a person's primary role in higher education is determined by the reason they are on campus. This was mentioned earlier, but if a person has a full-time job and takes classes, they are at the university first and foremost as an employee. If a person has a job but would not have that job without being enrolled as a student (i.e., a graduate assistant), that person is a student.

That said, graduate students are transitioning from their roles as undergraduates (in most cases) to being graduate students. They are learning about different academic expectations, new ways of having relationships with faculty, and the difference between being an undergraduate student leader and an advisor, mentor, or supervisor as a graduate student. Similarly, graduate school is a time to learn about the difference between being students engaging in protest and critique of the institution where they go to school and being employees whose freedom to criticize is more limited in many cases.

As Grube et al. (2005) wrote, "By accepting a position as a graduate assistant, a graduate student enters into a mixed role of responsibility by serving as both a professional and a student" (p. 153). Similarly, Nguyen and Yao (2022) wrote, "Graduate students' lives are messy and complicated, and their academic, personal, and professional lives are difficult to disentangle" (p. 241).

Graduate assistants are simultaneously students and employees but often are put in whichever category is most convenient to the institution or their assistantship unit. Communicating with students about their primary role as students on campus needs to be consistent across assistantships and between assistantships and the academic program. Class and academic obligations need to take priority over assistantship or field experience activities. Full-time staff sometimes dismiss graduate students' ideas when they raise concerns about a policy or process. Supervisors may tell them they are "just students" or will be at the institution for only two years. Supervisors, faculty, and other full-time staff may also tell them they do not understand the historical and political culture of the campus.

Another time the dichotomy of the graduate assistant's position surfaces is during campus protests. Functional area leaders may tell graduate students that they are employees and should not participate or may be welcome to participate since they are students. It is crucial to set graduate students up for success by discussing issues of Institutional Intelligence related to assistantship expectations, campus culture, and history, and examining the legal and ethical implications of acting—or not—in the face of injustice or inequity on campus.

Institutional Intelligence Questions

Who: Who are your graduate students (holistically—identities held, experience, goals in life)? Who is going to be supervising your graduate student(s)? Who else influences the learning and growth of students?

What: What graduate program(s) are students in? What are the tasks you need students to accomplish? What experiences do students want to have? What is the history of graduate student involvement/protest on your campus? What is the current culture on your campus? What expectations have you outlined in collaboration with graduate students about their intersecting identities as employees and students?

Where: Where does your student hope to be developmentally at the end of their graduate program? Where do they want to work upon graduation (functional unit, institutional type, geographic region)? Where is your student free to be themselves and openly share their opinions? Where might they be more limited or face the consequences for sharing or critiquing too much?

When: When can you provide space for graduate assistants to air their concerns about their experiences, unit/division, and campus? When can you provide resources to help students transition from student to employee?

Why: Why is this opportunity a good one for a graduate student? Why is the designated person the best person to supervise this graduate student?

How: How can a supervisor set the graduate student(s) they supervise up for success? How has the supervisor been trained and prepared to supervise graduate students?

Critical Scenario 16.4 Role Conflict

Co-Author: Dr. Fred Tugas, Associate Dean of Students, Old Dominion University

Diane (she/her) is a second-year graduate student in the student affairs master's program at Hammond University and works in the multicultural student center. She is the only second-year graduate assistant in the office, but two first-year students also have assistantships in the center. Diane has built strong relationships with her co-grads and the students she serves. She co-advises several student organizations and has helped teach courses on difficult dialogues and diversity in higher education. Diane has received both campus and regional organization recognition for her dedication, support of students, and innovative approaches to programming and education related to social justice, equity, and college access.

Diane co-advises the Hammond Equity Liaison Program (HELP) with her direct supervisor. HELP is a student organization focused on partnering with staff, administrators, and faculty to address campus social justice and equity concerns. In a recent meeting, the students brought up a series of issues on campus. These incidents include racial epithets written on dry-erase boards of Students of Color in residence halls, a truck of unidentified men throwing beer cans at three Black women walking on campus, fliers placed on cars on campus questioning the legal status of Latin* students and calling for them to be removed from the institution.

Recently, an Asian American student was assaulted near campus.

These incidents have been the subject of much discussion and debate (much of it vitriolic) on social media. At a recent meeting, HELP had been planning a peaceful protest of Delano Hall—the main administrative building on campus which houses the offices of the president, the provost, and the vice president of student affairs. After the assault, the students begin the protest immediately.

Jared (they/them) is the vice president of HELP and has served as an equity liaison with the Dean of Students around campus issues and on several task forces at the university. Jared texts Diane as the students begin to gather in front of Delano. "We are starting the protest. Can you come over and help us get things coordinated? There is not a lot of organization yet, but we're tired of waiting for the university to do something. We're doing something ourselves."

The Law

- What are the relevant legal issues in this scenario?
- What institutional policies, procedures, or processes are applicable in this scenario?

Ethics

- What are the relevant ethical issues in this scenario?
- What information would the characters need to make sound ethical decisions in this situation?

Identity

- How would characters' social identities affect how this scenario might unfold? Assign the characters specific social identities and go through the scenario. Then change some of those social identities and go through the scenario again.
- How do the situation and the information you need change?

Scenario-Specific Questions

- Whom might Diane turn to for advice about engaging (or not) with the protest? Whom would Diane want to let know that the protest will be happening? Who might be other graduate students, staff, or faculty on campus with whom Diane might share the protest information? Who is Diane's direct supervisor, and who is her supervisor's supervisor?
- What is the campus history of student protests and graduate assistants' involvement in those protests? What have Diane and her supervisor discussed about campus protests? What campus policies might relate to the protest?
- Where is Delano Hall located on campus? Where have students been meeting to plan the protest? Where might information about the protest show up (online, social media, mainstream media)?
- When should Diane respond to Jared? When should Diane let others know about the emerging situation?
- Why might the response to one protest be different from another?
- How can Diane attend to her stress, anxiety, and personal needs as the protest unfolds? How can Diane provide resources and support to the undergraduate students involved in the protest? How can Diane navigate the student/employee line in this situation?

What other information does Diane need, and how can she get that using the Institutional Intelligence Model as she decides what her next steps should be?

Transitioning into Full-Time Roles

Another important element that the graduate student experience provides for emerging student affairs staff is to begin the transition into full-time roles. This transition includes building a professional network among cohort members, faculty, academic and student affairs staff on campus, and professional organizational involvement. Renn and Jessup-Anger (2008) identified the following goals for the graduate experience to prepare new staff: creating a professional identity, navigating cultural adjustment, maintaining a learning orientation, and seeking advice. Haley et al. (2011) found similar themes in their study of student affairs graduate students; through their programs, students develop in their professional roles while building a sense of belonging, relationships, and self-agency.

Specifically, regarding graduate students, Strayhorn (2019) wrote, "Understanding how students come to choose a particular graduate school may provide clues to meeting their needs, which, in turn, is likely to increase their chances of success" (p. 126). Asking about a student's motivations is an easy starting point for supervisors, peers, and faculty to begin understanding and supporting the graduate students with whom they work and learn. By simply asking, "Why did you choose student affairs? Why did you choose to come here?", we learn about people as individuals and the experiences they bring with them to campus.

For example, some of us were student leaders at our undergraduate institution, and an academic or student affairs practitioner said, "You know you can do this for a living." Others work in student affairs because of gaps in our undergraduate experiences. We may have needed something, and someone helped us, and we want to do that for others. Still, others come to student or academic affairs because *no one* helped us, and we want to ensure that does not happen to anyone else. Regardless of what brings us to the work, there are several considerations we must keep in mind as we support graduate students' transitions into full-time positions.

As student and academic affairs graduate students advance through their academic programs, engage in the job search, and begin new roles, they engage in "anticipatory socialization" (Duran & Allen, 2020; Lombardi & Mather, 2016; Perez, 2016). Anticipatory socialization prepares graduate students and new practitioners to adjust to their new full-time student affairs practitioner roles. The Institutional Intelligence Model fits in anticipatory socialization as that transition time is when we begin to explore the culture of institutions where we might like to work (Boettcher, 2019). By learning about our campuses, we become more confident in our roles and our abilities to support students and one another, or as Strayhorn (2019) wrote, "socialization begets belonging" (p. 132) and "belonging begets success" (p. 133).

Professional organizations also play a significant role in graduate student socialization. However, if graduate students ask which organization(s) to join, the answer must be "*It depends*." For student affairs practitioners, the two umbrella organizations are NASPA and ACPA. Others may be drawn to functional area organizations such as ACUHO-I (Association of College and University Housing Officers—International) for housing, NODA (originally National Orientation Directors Association) for orientation and new student programs, NACADA (National Academic Advising Association) for academic advising, CSCC (Council for the Study of Community Colleges) for community colleges, NCORE (National Conference on Race and Ethnicity in Higher Education) for race and ethnicity, or ASHE (Association for the Study of Higher Education) for researchers. Belonging is vital in academic programs and academic and student affairs fields. Additionally, a sense of belonging in professional organizations helps graduate students develop social connectedness. Furthermore, supervisors, faculty, and mentors can help students build connections and a professional network. Finally, the cost of memberships and annual conferences and events impacts students' ability to join.

There are legal and ethical issues regarding the job search for job-seekers, employers, mentors, and supervisors who support graduate students. For example, for job-seekers who are offered multiple jobs at once, it is a challenge to decide when to accept an offer. If you accept an offer from one school and then get an offer from a school you ranked more highly, what will you do? If you pass on the preferred school, there are implications. If you back out of an offer you have already accepted, there are implications. Both personal and professional ethics will guide you in deciding what to do (see Appendix).

Institutions posting jobs must consider their approach to campus travel reimbursement. Does the institution pay, or do the candidates pay? If the candidate pays, will they get reimbursed, and how long will it take for them to get their reimbursement? If the candidate pays, your institution is further privileging candidates with financial means to travel. Then there are the institutions that pay if a candidate accepts an offer or is not offered a job, but if the candidate is offered and declines, then the candidate pays. Who came up with that? That reimbursement process seems sketchy in an ethical sense, doesn't it? There could be a legitimate reason a school has to take that approach. The important thing is that institutions have explicit policies to share with candidates.

Institutional Intelligence Questions

Who: Who are your go-to people as you enter a job search? Who will give you good feedback on resumes and cover letters and tell you what to expect in an interview? Who can support you through the ups and downs of the search process? Who are people outside your program and institution who can provide you with other perspectives?

What: What are your non-negotiables in a position (e.g., location, salary, time with students, and job responsibilities)? What if you get an offer to start a position before the semester ends (implication for your office/ team and expenses to pay for coursework as a non-student)? What do you want your life to look like outside of the job? What can you learn from others who have worked in a specific office or campus? What are the questions you want to ask during your interviews?

Where: Where do you want to work? Where can you go to get more information on a specific campus? Where do you want to be six months (or a year or five years) from now as a professional?

When: When do you feel you need to have a job? When do you want to begin your search?
Why: Why do you want to join a specific organization?
How: How can you help students with a sense of belonging in their program and the profession?

Critical Scenario 16.5 Transitioning into Full-Time Roles

Co-Author: Drew Johnson Office of Student Life Coordinator for Academic Initiatives and Assessment, Syracuse University

DeJuan (he/his) is an associate director of student activities. He has individual meetings with all of the graduate assistants in his area at least twice a semester. At the end of the fall term, DeJuan is meeting with Tiana (she/her), a second-year graduate student. Tiana's supervisor left early in the year, and that position remains vacant, but she has been meeting periodically with DeJuan (about once a month).

DeJuan asks Tiana to come for their next meeting, prepared to discuss her future beyond graduation. In their meeting, Tiana shared that she is very nervous about the job search process—particularly from a financial perspective. She says that a co-grad in the department, Rob (he/him), has pressured her to attend a national convention to make potential job connections. The convention is in Chicago, a flight away from their institution, and the registration, hotel, and other costs will be significant. This is particularly stressful given that she knows she will have other search expenses as she looks for her first full-time position.

When Tiana expressed her concerns about the financial cost of the experience, her grad colleague Rob told her to get a hotel room with five or six other people. However, when Tiana says she is uncomfortable with that, Rob responds, "Well, as my mentor told me, you have to go through it. It's what we all do at some point. It's just part of being a graduate student in student affairs."

To ease her tensions, Rob suggests that Tiana help him put together a workshop for all the graduate students in the unit to talk about their searches and build connections for upcoming conference rooming. When Tiana shares that adding this to her current workload at the busy end of the semester will put her over her assistantship hours, Rob replies,

> See, Tiana? This is another example of you not being a team player. I don't get resistance to these opportunities from anyone else I work with. You are always so focused on hours that it seems like you don't want to do the work. An attitude like this could potentially impact your references, you know. We all work more hours than we are scheduled. It's part of being in student affairs.

She asks DeJuan for help dealing with Rob and for information about any financial assistance available to support her conference attendance.

The Law

- What are the relevant legal issues in this scenario?
- What institutional policies, procedures, or processes are applicable in this scenario?

Ethics

- What are the relevant ethical issues in this scenario?
- What information would the characters need to make sound ethical decisions in this situation?

Identity

- How would characters' social identities affect how this scenario might unfold? Assign the characters specific social identities and go through the scenario. Then change some of those social identities and go through the scenario again.
- How do the situation and the information you need change?

Scenario-Specific Questions

- Whom should DeJuan talk to about this situation? What other resources can DeJuan connect Tiana with?
- What are the legal and ethical issues in this scenario? What are equity issues at the office, unit, division, and institutional levels to be addressed?
- Where might DeJuan go to find out more about the culture among the graduate student cohort?
- When (if at all) should DeJuan talk to Rob, follow up with Tiana, and have a conversation with other graduate students in his area?

- Why might this incident be indicative of more significant issues on campus? Why might Rob feel compelled to guide Tiana and assess her performance as he did?
- How can DeJuan support both Tiana and Rob in their experiences and development? How can DeJuan minimize disruption to his team while maintaining professional integrity?

What other Institutional Intelligence questions should DeJuan be asking before responding to Tiana?

Conclusion

Graduate students are the future of academics and student affairs. They learn in class but learn just as much or more out of class through assistantships, field experiences, and observing other practitioners. Often it is in assistantships and field experiences where students have a chance to learn about legal and ethical issues in practice. Supervisors, faculty, and mentors are responsible for fostering environments where students can explore, take (reasonable) risks, fail safely, learn, succeed, and develop. To excel as graduate student resources, practitioners and faculty must attend to students holistically as role models and reflect on what has happened, is happening, and may happen in the future. As we said earlier in this chapter, working with graduate students is some of our most critical work. We must invest in them by being as prepared as possible for that work.

SECTION 4

Reflection and Recommendations

17

REFLECTIVE PRACTICE THROUGH HUMAN RESOURCES AND CHANGE

Here it is, the almost end of the book. Unless you are reading this chapter first, in that case, here it is—the first chapter you are reading in the book. Regardless of how you read this book, this chapter will help you reflect on the legal and ethical implications of higher education issues and challenges. We hope this chapter also provides opportunities for growth and change through reflective practice.

The information throughout the functional area chapters in this text explores *thinking before acting* using the Institutional Intelligence Model. This chapter uses the model to focus on thinking *before*, *during*, and *after* we act using two aspects of work: human resources and crisis. We decided to focus on human resources and crisis because every campus faces these issues and the legal and ethical implications connected to those situations.

Chapter Organization

This chapter begins with an overview of why we chose to examine change specifically through human resources and crisis lenses. We move on to human resources and look at the job search, hiring processes, and onboarding. Our crisis discussion focuses on the before, during, and after stages of crises. Specifically, in working through issues after a crisis, we discuss incident review and reflection and the role of reflection in the recovery stage following a crisis.

DOI: 10.4324/9781003442707-21

Legal and Ethical Considerations

Legal and policy issues are involved in both human resources and crisis work. For human resources, there are legal considerations related to compensation and benefits, fair labor, family leave, protected class issues, safety, and other issues regarding hiring, firing, and the work environment. We discuss legislation related to many of these topics in Chapter 2; however, given the complicated relationships of graduate students to their institutions, the relevance of many of these issues varies from one campus to another. What factors must higher education consider when it comes to a crisis on campus? *It depends* on what kind of crisis the institution is facing. Crises can include campus threats, financial crises, interpersonal violence, mental health concerns, natural disasters, public health issues, or other alarming issues or behaviors. Each situation has its implications in terms of individual and community legal action. Additionally, campus policies affect human resources and change, which practitioners must be familiar with and follow.

The ethics of change are complicated. The more we know who we are, our institutions' values, and how our ethics inform our interaction with others (individuals and groups), the more prepared we are to navigate change while abiding by our ethics. The reality in academic and student affairs is that we may know how we will react only once we face specific situations. We must be as prepared as possible to navigate those moments.

Competencies

The principal competencies (see Appendix) related to human resources and change are nearly the same. Organizational and Human Resources (OHR) competency is a primary consideration when doing job searches and navigating change related to staffing. Furthermore, both human resource issues and change involve Leadership (LEAD); Law, Policy, and Governance (LPG); and Social Justice and Inclusion (SJI) competencies. Leaders manage change which affects all aspects of higher education organizations. Through any change—staffing, crisis, or otherwise—leaders must consider issues of law and equity.

Change: Why Human Resources and Crisis?

Human resources decisions and crises highlight the role of change in higher education. Higher education, like the world, is constantly changing, adapting, learning (or not), and moving ahead (or not), informed by both obstacles and opportunities. Heraclitus said a person could never step in the same river twice. Over time, it is not the same river, and the person is not the same from one moment to the next, either. Anyone who has left their alma mater and returned to work there knows that institutions and our relationships with them change.

Too often, we see change as negative. Change can always result in something positive, even if the catalyst is negative. Change should be an opportunity to evolve and grow. We should not maintain the status quo or "go back to the way things were" after every crisis. There is no progress and evolution without change. Additionally, change is no longer limited to institutional leaders. Lester (2020) wrote, "Our collective understanding of who should be defined as leaders and who should be engaged in change management has broadened to be more inclusive of individuals and groups across organizations" (p. iii).

Change does not happen in isolation. Change can be something to dread and resist or something to embrace. The answer to "How do we deal with this change?" is "*It depends.*" How we deal with change depends on what is changing. Navigating change while maintaining our ethics and integrity is difficult, as we often make mistakes in new situations since we have not encountered them before. How we plan for, respond to, and reflect on the change ultimately matters. For example, no one wants to lose a great colleague or would wish for a global pandemic. Regardless, we must reflect on and learn to adapt to these situations. Institutions change, and we must keep up with those changes, which is part of the Institutional Intelligence Model. Lane (2007) wrote, "The ability to cope with constant change is now a key requirement for success in life and work" (p. 85). Acknowledging that change happens, we will explore how to ethically and legally negotiate staffing issues and campus crises as catalysts for positive transformation.

Crisis

So what exactly do we mean by "crisis" in the context of this book? Harper et al. (2006) wrote, "A campus crisis is an event, often sudden or unexpected, that disrupts the normal operations of the institution or its educational mission and threatens the well-being of personnel, property, financial resources, and reputation of the institution" (p. 5). The authors go on to identify three types of crises: disasters (a large-scale event that may disrupt campus and community, such as a tornado or pandemic), crises (events that affect only the campus, such as a residence hall fire), and critical incidents (affects only the campus but could become a disaster if not addressed and limited to campus, such as a bomb threat). In this text, we use the word "crisis" to encompass large-scale campus/community events, significant campus-only events, and smaller-scale events that can escalate.

We also acknowledge that interpersonal situations (i.e., harassment, interpersonal violence, sexual misconduct, stalking, and threats) can have a community impact both on and off campus. Interpersonal incidents often require coordinated responses between partners such as campus police, residence life/housing, and counseling staff. In our thinking, these incidents have the potential to escalate and often impact other students in the surrounding community (i.e., roommates, friends, neighbors, and peers in student organizations). As a result, we are including those situations in our concept of crisis.

Every institution is currently navigating multiple crises. While this is true at any time, we know it is true at this moment as institutions figure out the implications of the COVID-19 pandemic. This chapter can help organizations, leaders, and responders to ask essential questions about their current situation. Furthermore, this chapter can help organizations and units not simply return to normal but implement things we have learned while anticipating, engaging, and reflecting.

The crisis section of this chapter is divided into four parts—before, during, and the two phases after. We split a crisis into reviewing the process and recovery and staff support. The crisis review phase helps individuals, teams, and organizations address ongoing needs and concerns, providing time for broader reflection after an incident. The second and most often overlooked aspect of crisis response is post-incident recovery. Recovery shows up in several ways—personal recovery of those impacted directly, personal recovery of those impacted as responders, and recovery of the teams and the organization. Too often, while we work to ensure support for students and others directly impacted by crises, we overlook the importance of supporting staff who may be directly or indirectly affected. Sometimes, supervisors ask staff to move from crisis back to regular work mode without being given time to process, rest, and work toward healing. This last section of this chapter outlines questions we need to ask to take care of ourselves and our teams through and beyond crises.

Setting the Stage: Law, Ethics, and Institutional Intelligence

We have discussed legal and ethical considerations and described the Institutional Intelligence Model throughout this text. This section reminds us of these vital elements as we discuss change within higher education. Here, we highlight the critical role that student and academic affairs staff play. This work has significant implications for individuals, units, and organizations.

Legal Considerations

Legal issues are a growing concern for student affairs professionals, but few employees have formal or extensive training on legal issues related to recruitment, hiring, or employment (Tolman & Calhoun, 2019). This knowledge should start with graduate preparation programs. However, studies have shown that many programs lack sufficient coursework in law (Cooper et al., 2016; Cuyjet et al., 2009), although it is among the coursework most recommended for inclusion in student affairs graduate programs (Herdlein, 2004). The information in this text helps fill this gap by using critical thinking and application rather than memorization and repetition.

Recent scholarship has highlighted the role of context, further making a case for Institutional Intelligence concerning legal and ethical issues. For example, Ryder et al. (2022) wrote that student affairs professionals "noted that where they worked mattered to their experience with legal structures... They also noted how much institutional approaches to legal structures varied from one institution to another" (p. 120). As mentioned throughout this text, thinking about what you need to know rather than expecting a checklist of "what to do if" items for legal and ethical issues is the most effective way to approach job search, hiring, crisis, and any other student affairs issue with legal implications. Spoiler alert: almost all student affairs issues have legal implications.

Ethical Considerations

While we often focus on legal issues, worry about litigation, and stress the role of policy and law, our ethics have a much more significant impact on the work most of us do. Not every action we take has legal implications. However, *whom* we serve, *what* we do, *where* we work or turn for help, *when* we act, *why* we do certain things and not others, and *how* we engage with students and other partners and constituents are all ethical decisions that we make multiple times a day. Sundberg and Fried (1997) wrote, "making ethical choices and thinking through ethical issues are at the very core of our work" (p. 67). The ongoing development of ethics by higher education practitioners requires complex thinking (Reybold et al., 2008), tools, and training to make ethical decisions (Gueras & Garofalo, 2002). It is a reflective and daily process (Wilcox & Ebbs, 1992). By implementing the Institutional Intelligence Model, practitioners have another tool they can use to act ethically in the context of the specific institution where they work.

The Institutional Intelligence Model

We designed the Institutional Intelligence Model to help higher education professionals navigate issues of context on individual campuses. Practitioners can understand their specific campuses by asking *who*, *what*, *where*, *when*, *why*, and *how* questions. In this chapter, we build on not only establishing understanding but using this model to sustain and continue to foster an understanding of campus through change.

For example, an experienced academic advisor may have an established contact in the Dean of Students Office (DSO) if she needs to reach out with a concern about a student. She may have worked with a particular person on multiple student issues and knows she can go to that person with questions or concerns. If her DSO contact leaves the institution or there are other staffing changes in the DSO, she will want to check in and see who her new contact should be. This change means re-establishing rapport, trust, and communication to continue her work supporting students.

As a result, the Institutional Intelligence Model is a tool that practitioners can use at any point in their careers and at any institution—including one where they work for an extended time. Change, as we have indicated, happens. It often is neither positive nor negative but it simply is. We must adapt and keep up with changes to do our work effectively, legally, and ethically.

Human Resources

While the Institutional Intelligence Model focuses on navigating places, individuals navigate institutions, environments, culture, jobs, and relationships among people. The people involved in student and academic affairs, as much as leaders, politics, geography, or any other institutional factor, determine the university's culture. It is often said that the most important decisions we make are choosing the people we hire. Winston et al. (2001) remind us that "[t]he successful administration of a student affairs division is primarily determined by the competence of the staff members who fill positions" (p. 7).

Generally, we engage in staffing processes either to look for a job or to hire someone, so that is how we divided this section. Some things are the same for job seekers and hiring teams, but there are also differences. The Institutional Intelligence Model helps us navigate both. The model will help applicants develop questions to understand the institutional culture before deciding whether to accept a job. The model can help draft interview questions for search committees and hiring decision-makers to understand potential hires' skills, experiences, and adaptability. In the following sections, we consider job searches and their legal and ethical implications from the perspectives of those seeking and hiring.

We encourage you to remember the idea of change as you read through these sections. During a job interview, people are not asked, "How do you deal with total stability and steadiness because everything is in balance and nothing ever changes on this campus?" Instead, people asked, "How do you deal with change?"

Job Search

We encourage you, as a jobseeker, to do two things we are often discouraged from doing as student and academic affairs staff. First, brag. What we mean by this is that you should speak boldly and confidently about your related work experiences and accomplishments. You want to be able to highlight your skills and show how they are transferable as you apply for new roles. All skills are transferable. Celebrate your successes and let potential new colleagues get excited about working with you. Second, make the job search all about *you*. Too often, we are encouraged to put other people or work tasks ahead of ourselves. The job search is not the time to do that. Instead, think about the life you want and how a new job might fit into that life (as opposed to thinking about how you might carve out life around a new job). In order to engage in your search holistically and be successful in the process, you need to engage in reflective practice.

We must consider our questions and the Institutional Intelligence Model questions as we move into new roles. Reflecting on some of the questions below can be useful when starting a new position. However, they can also be helpful as both graduate students and experienced professionals begin to prepare for the job search.

Who are you ethically? What experiences do you have with legal issues? Developing an ethical philosophy can help prepare you to write your cover letter and answer interview questions. Who are you, and what are your core values as a student affairs professional? How do those values show up in your work? How do your values align with the position(s) you applied for? Below are some starter questions to get you as an individual thinking about who you are, what you bring, and what you are looking for when it comes to student affairs or student-facing positions in higher education.

Proactive *who* questions focus on the people involved in your work—including you. Think about yourself. Thinking about who you are, your position, and what you have to offer is essential. Preparing can help you avoid difficulties down the road in a specific position and your career.

Putting Preflection into Action: The Search

As we move through these processes, we encourage you to be preflective. Whereas reflection happens after an event or process, reflective practice has tremendous value before you begin a process. We refer to this as "preflection."

So, where do you start? Updating the resume? Scanning websites and postings for jobs you might consider? Ask others what they think about the jobs you are considering and whether you are qualified. While many of these can be part of your practice, Boettcher et al. (2019b) suggested the following as starting points of reflection in the job search:

> (1) What have you done and want to do regarding your work (practice)? (2) With whom do you want to work—both students and colleagues (people)? Furthermore, (3) Where do you want to work regarding the institutional type, culture, and the surrounding community (Place)? After reflecting on your individual needs and preparing for the transition, you will be better prepared to engage in the act of professional dreaming in the context of exploring job change.
>
> *(p. 95)*

If you have done the preflection about yourself as discussed earlier in the chapter, you should be ready for these common interview questions:

- Tell us about yourself and why this position interests you.
- How would you describe your leadership style?
- What strengths do you bring to a team?
- How do you handle change?

We are not offering the questions with a purely philosophical purpose. There are practical reasons for doing this. Engaging in preflective work sets you up to give a strong interview. It also sets you up to find the right next opportunity for yourself as you navigate your career.

Imagine you are about to finish your student affairs graduate preparation program. You sit down to write your cover letters and are thinking ahead to phone interviews and campus visits. By reflecting on the questions above about yourself and others, you can begin to define who you are and the groups with whom you have worked. Too often, students (and professionals) go into interviews hoping to "wow" the search committees with their personalities and experience. Of course, everyone wants to do well in an interview, but it is also our responsibility as candidates to ask questions of search committees and others during the interview process. Asking questions is also essential, as we each want to find a place where we can thrive and be successful and respected by a community of mutually supportive colleagues. We also want to work at a place where our values align with those of the organization. The Institutional Intelligence Model can help candidates create questions to ask the search committee, potential colleagues, and campus partners. The model is also helpful after the interview as applicants reflect on it while making final decisions. Consider the following preflection questions about your own experiences and needs as you consider applying for jobs and before your interview:

Who: Who have you successfully worked with in the past?
What: What role do you play on a team? What do you expect of your colleagues or supervisor? What teams give you energy (or drain you of energy)? What students do you want to work with? What foundational values are you looking for in a unit or institution? What are your core values and ethics?
Where: Where do you turn when you have questions about your work? Where have you been successful in the past (type of institution, type of team)?
When: When have you been most successful? When have you struggled?
Why: Why does this position interest you? Why make a job change now?
How: How do you hope to grow in this role? How do you hope to use your existing skills and talents? How will you determine whether this is the right opportunity for you? How do you look for your ethics and values to align with the mission of the institution where you work?

These and other questions can help you start a preflection for the job search.

Putting Preflection into Action: The Interview

Using the job search as a context to try out preflection, we focus on questions about what we need to know and what training or preparation we need. The questions below address things you may want to ask during a campus interview. Before taking a job, you have to consider whether you want that job. When you interview for a position, you are both interviewee and interviewer. You want them to get to know you and see what you will contribute, but you also want to know whether this is the right opportunity. Consider the following:

Who: Who is the supervisor? Who is your supervisor's supervisor? Who are your potential new colleagues? Who are the students you will get to interact with?
What: What foundational values are you looking for in a unit or institution? What are some current student issues on campus? What is your supervisor's supervisory style? What does support during stressful times look like in this office?
Where: Where has this team been successful in the past? Where will your organization focus time and resources in the future? Where are areas for improvement for your team?
When: When has this organization been successful? When has it struggled? When (and how) has this institution negotiated legal or ethical issues in response to incidents on campus?

Why: Why is this job open? Why did the last person leave?
How: How do you see your organization's foundational values enacted in your work? How do you support staff during challenging times? How have campus leaders responded to violence, protest, or other controversial events on or beyond campus?

Prepare to respond during an interview when asked, "So, do you have any questions for us?" By the way, you should *always* have questions for interview committees when applying for a job. Ask what you want to know, and it will serve you well in the long run.

Hiring Processes

The hiring process begins well before a new team member's first day of work. As in the previous section, hiring managers and search teams need to consider several context issues to do the best job possible for the team, the institution, the students, and the new employee. As a former staff member leaves, consider whether that position needs to be filled if there are potential reorganization decisions that can better serve the unit, students, other constituents, and other issues related to the unit. Additionally, it is important to think about and develop a hiring timeline and a diversity plan and consider how this hire fits in the context of other vacancies or positions to be filled. For example, if a position is vacant and that supervisor's position is also vacant, do you fill the supervisor position first so they can help hire their team, or do you work to have the positions filled simultaneously? This and other questions will emerge as the hiring process is developed.

Once you have engaged in that reflective process, it is time to review the position description and post the job. A clear and thorough job description serves both the organization and the candidates. What will the person be doing, what opportunities are there for autonomy, and with whom will the person be partnering are essential considerations? As Dalton (2003) wrote, "Trying to hire the right candidate for a position with an ill-defined job description is like trying to find an unfamiliar destination without a road map" (p. 406).

Posting the position is the next important consideration. Where are you posting the ad, and how do your choices affect the diversity of the candidate pool? What are you highlighting in the position listing since it likely will not include a complete job description? How are you addressing issues of equity and transparency related to salary and other considerations? There are legal and ethical considerations throughout this process.

Identifying the search committee is another step in the process. Who is on the committee? What positions, social identities, experience, and knowledge of this role does each member have? How will each person engage with the new staff member once they are on campus? Is the search committee composed of people who will be able to answer questions that candidates might have throughout the process? Do the members of the search committee work well together?

Additionally, will the hiring decision rest with the committee or someone else? If a single person makes the decision, will that person be on the search committee or give guidance in an initial meeting about the needs? Dalton (2003) suggested that the hiring decision-maker/future supervisor of the person to be hired "should be as specific as possible about the necessary qualifications and the most important responsibilities of the position" (p. 407). This information will help the committee agree on candidates and bring forward those individuals most likely to succeed in the role.

Other considerations through the job search include interviewing top candidates (often via phone or virtually first and then in-person through an on-campus visit), checking references, making the offer, and orienting the new staff member to campus and the role. There are many legal and ethical considerations throughout each of these steps. Making sure committee members and hiring decision-makers are familiar with the university and other employment policies and procedures is essential. The Institutional Intelligence Model can help leaders, teams, and individuals involved in the search process make informed, legal, and ethical decisions. Examples follow in the next section.

Institutional Intelligence Questions

Who: Who is on the search committee? Who will have access to applications, search committee information, and other materials related to the search? Who is the decision-maker for this hire? Who are campus partners that should be included in the on-campus interview?

What: What are the responsibilities of the search committee, and what authority will they have in the final hiring decision? What are the university guidelines or training required of search committee members (privacy, implicit bias training, and other preparation required)? What are the expectations for on-campus interviews (time with students, a presentation)?

Where: Where should applicants be directed if they have questions about the position or the search? Where will candidates submit materials?

When: When (and from whom) will the committee get its orientation for this search? When will references be contacted?

Why: Why is this position posted at this particular time of year? Why has each committee member been selected, and what are they expected to bring to the process?

How: How will this search recruit diverse candidates and address equity issues? How much time will involvement in this search take? How will the search committee give feedback? How will the interviews be structured (phone, virtual, in-person)? How many candidates can the committee bring to campus?

Onboarding

When onboarding new staff, there are questions that supervisors of new staff need to ask and be prepared to answer. Instead of focusing on ourselves as individuals at this stage, we should think systematically and systemically as we welcome and incorporate new team members. Helping new staff understand who plays what role in an office or across campus positions incoming team members to work more effectively and efficiently from the beginning.

Institutional Intelligence Questions

Who: Who are key campus partners with whom they need to foster relationships? Who in the unit or on campus is exceptionally knowledgeable about institution and community resources? Who is the best resource for new staff about protocol when law enforcement or other emergency response is required? Who in the communication chain immediately needs to know about situations, and whom is it okay to brief later?

What: What do new hires need to know about how legal and ethical issues intersect with their new role? What are standard office and departmental processes? What do you expect of the new staff member? What do they expect of their supervisor and colleagues? What are the office culture and norms? What are expectations around attire, work hours, working remotely, and letting staff know when you leave for lunch or a meeting elsewhere on campus?

Where: Where are meetings held? Where are supplies kept?

When: When will a new staff member's supervisor provide feedback? (Is there a standard 30-, 60-, or 90-day review?)

Why: Why did you hire this candidate (to validate new employees)?

How: How is feedback given to the staff member? How do history and culture inform the work that they will do? How does vacation time accrue? How does a new staff member go about requesting vacation or sick leave?

In conclusion, the hiring process is extensive and time-consuming for job-seekers and staff looking to hire new employees. Being intentional from the very start sets individuals, teams, units, and organizations up for success. Additionally, a good search process fosters a positive reputation for organizations across student affairs, which has the potential to continue a pipeline of talented employees in the future.

Crisis

Campus crises can include natural disasters, medical emergencies, active shooter situations, bomb threats, financial emergencies, student deaths, hate events, campus protests in response to incidents or campus culture, and other situations. Rollo and Zdziarski (2007) wrote, "History has shown that campus crises have had a significant impact on higher education—our students, their families, and society as a whole" (p. 22). Regardless of the crisis level, each of us must adapt to change in the face of crises. We may need to reprioritize work tasks to attend to the emergent needs of students and families, or we may need to reorganize our work because of a pandemic or facilities emergencies that requires us to relocate.

Authors have written about the ability of colleges and universities to adapt in the face of crisis (Rollo & Zdziarski, 2007). We have seen this recently in the context of the COVID-19 pandemic when institutions closed residence halls, shifted classes to virtual spaces, and made other adjustments very quickly. Often student affairs professionals are the first to respond to crises on campus (Treadwell, 2017).

Shaw (2018) wrote that student affairs departments look for crisis management and emergency response skills when hiring employees at all levels. Student and academic affairs practitioners who work most closely with students play critical roles during crises and are valued by institutions and across the field of student affairs. Among the skills that student affairs staff are expected to bring to work are crisis planning and communication skills (Merriman, 2008). The legal and ethical issues in a crisis vary tremendously. There are issues of safety, communication, action/reaction, policy, and process at every point in a campus incident.

Given that crisis response is a role that student affairs and other student-facing professionals on campus are increasingly called upon to play, what work does each of us do in a crisis? *It depends.* Some staff may respond directly; their crisis work could involve coordinating emergency housing or ensuring that staff members follow safety protocols. For others, crisis work may involve supporting students and coordinating with faculty about missed classes. For yet others, our crisis work may involve facilitating communication and information sharing related to updates about situations on campus. The legal responsibilities of this communication will vary depending on the incident in terms of timeliness, format, and content of the information shared. Regardless of what the incident is or what our roles are, there are three phases of crisis work where utilizing Institutional Intelligence reflection strategies is important:

- Before an incident occurs.
- As an incident is unfolding.
- After an incident has taken place.

Catullo et al. (2009) wrote, "best practices suggest institutions develop plans that address all three phases of a crisis: precrisis, crisis, and postcrisis" (p. 317). Before an incident, we are in planning mode. During an incident, we manage situations and respond to individuals, and after an incident, we review what we did and incorporate time for recovery. There are legal and ethical considerations in each phase, as we explore below.

Before an Incident

Too often, crisis management in higher education is reactive rather than proactive (Catullo et al., 2009; Zdziarski, 2006). It is essential to anticipate crises and plan accordingly to be prepared (Stein et al., 2007). Given the oversight of planning before an incident, this section will focus on some key questions to ask in order to understand your role, institutional context, and other issues related to crisis response.

Consider thinking about your role, strengths, and job responsibilities as you seek to understand crisis response and your role in it at your institution. "Who are you?" is the central question. Your role includes your job position, title, and where you are in the organizational chart. Position matters, and most of us learn that by either overstepping ourselves or undervaluing an administrator or leader at some point.

Who you are is more than that. Who you are in terms of the social identities you hold, your reputation, and the way you respond in challenging and stressful situations are additional aspects of your identity related to your role in a crisis. Who you are matters in terms of how you see yourself and how others see you. Individuals and groups may perceive you differently: colleagues vs. students, parents vs. supervisors, or the women's center staff vs. public safety. Knowing those perceptions in advance will help you respond most effectively when situations arise.

In addition to knowing yourself, you must anticipate incidents where you may be asked to assist. Examples are mental health, alcohol and drug issues, and other health concerns for students or family members. Domestic and relationship violence issues and stalking and harassment may also be situations you address. Additionally, natural disasters and public health concerns may call for campus response. Finally, active shooter incidents, bomb threats, and other acts of mass violence can impact communities in higher education settings. Each of these situations has specific legal and ethical considerations related to safety; state, local, and federal law; contracts between institutions and individuals; and the level of care we provide to students, staff, and faculty on our campuses.

While each of these and other types of incidents may draw from similar areas of expertise on campus, different functional areas may play different roles depending on health and safety issues. What are the settings or communities most directly affected (i.e., student organizations, residence and fraternity and sorority life, academics and classroom spaces, off-campus student living communities)? It is essential that the appropriate functional areas be included and that those individuals and units with the most expertise have input and provide guidance related to emerging issues. Leadership should incorporate strategic thinking into planning before, responding during, and reflecting after campus incidents.

Institutional Intelligence Questions

Who: Who are your campus crisis partners? Who are the people or groups you serve through your work? Who is your core team? Who is best served by our processes and policies? Who is neglected by our processes and policies? Who is at risk? Who is missing as part of the conversation? Who is missing as part of the work?

What: What legal and ethical guidelines inform the campus response to a particular situation? What is the written plan for crisis response on your campus? What sorts of crises are common in your area, on your campus, and for your student population? What training have you had, and what training do you need to be prepared to deal with crises? What resources do you need readily available in case of a crisis (i.e., phone numbers, online information, and other information/resources)? What crisis protocols are in place for your area or on your campus? What policies or procedures must you be familiar with in preparation for crisis response?

Where: Where do you need to report information about crises or emergencies? Where are points of intersection between the work of institutional employees and community agencies (e.g., law enforcement, health-care providers, and other resources on and off campus)?

Why: Why might your campus and community be more prone to certain crises than others? Why have emergency response teams been convened on your campus recently?

When: When does crisis training happen in your department/on your campus? When have campus crises historically taken place at your institution? When will you be in positions to be more likely to respond to crises (in an on-duty role, during major campus events, or in your work with student organizations)?

How: How has your office/team partnered to educate staff and students about potential crises? How has your unit been involved in crises in the past?

During an Incident

Most of this book focuses on using Institutional Intelligence in the context of emerging issues, challenges, crises, events, and opportunities. In particular, the issues faced by staff in housing and conduct (see Chapter 13) and those who work with partners who are confidential resources (see Chapter 15) on campus may be responding regularly to crises/potential crises. Rather than revisiting those topics, we will highlight the foundational Institutional Intelligence questions you must ask when responding.

Institutional Intelligence Questions

Who: Who is directly involved or impacted by the incident? Who is involved in the immediate response on and off campus? Who needs to be informed as the situation unfolds? Who is the media contact? Who is coordinating the ongoing response to an incident (the dean of students, chief of police, director of the health center, a representative from the president's or provost's office)? Who will be the primary contact for students (and potentially families) directly involved following the initial event or incident? Who will provide follow-up to campus partners after the incident? Who will provide information to families?

What: What are the legal and ethical considerations in this particular crisis? What training do you have relevant to this crisis? What is the protocol for situations like the one you are facing? What other information do you need for your response? What ongoing services and resources (i.e., counseling, health services, housing/dining, other) do individuals and communities impacted need? What information do you need to share with students, families, and campus partners? What documentation and reporting are needed?

Where: Where is the incident occurring? Where can you direct students for assistance related to safety, housing, food, counseling, and emergency funding? Where are calls from parents, and the public, being managed?

When: When were you made aware of the situation? When were you able to respond?
When and how often will emergency response, behavioral intervention, and other crisis teams meet? When can students expect the necessary resources to be made available? When can people and teams expect updates?

Why: Why are you involved? Why did you and others respond the ways that you did? Why were certain people involved and others not? Why did you make specific decisions during the crisis?

How: How did others respond? How do you plan to move forward? How do you need to document and report on the issues and processes involved? How will you know when the situation is resolved?

As with other lists of questions throughout this text, these are not all-encompassing questions. These are things you can use reflectively and need to be ready to ask and often answer quickly at the moment as situations arise. Additionally, each situation is unique and will generate additional in-the-moment questions that you need to ask yourself and others.

After an Incident: Review

There comes the point in every crisis when you have completed the bulk of the response work. At that time, it is essential to reflect on how to improve protocols, practices, and actions for better responses in the future. Each college and university should have a customized post-incident reflection process. Reviewing a crisis is an essential part of the crisis management process. Reflecting on crises offers individuals and organizations a chance to learn and improve (Meyers & Holusha, 1986; Ulmer et al., 2007). Much of the post-crisis reflection focuses on these aspects of learning and improvement. Additionally, the review has policy and law implications.

A thorough and effective review of a crisis can help ensure that we do not repeat mistakes or encounter similar problems as we manage future events (Lebow, 1987; Pauchant & Mitroff, 1992; Ulmer et al., 2007). How we respond to individual situations has a tremendous impact on future situations. Zdziarski et al. (2021) provided an extensive crisis debriefing checklist, including the following items:

1. Map a timeline.
2. Log major events (through interviews and document review) and develop an appendix (including images, diagrams, resources, a list of those impacted, and other relevant items).
3. Document findings, including lessons learned.

4. Specify recommendations for the future (including timeline and who is responsible for following through on each recommendation).
5. Communicate findings and changes to internal and external stakeholders.

Reflection after a crisis should include reflecting on cultural considerations—another opportunity for us to apply Institutional Intelligence. This process needs to inform what worked and to identify needed changes. Zdziarski et al. (2021) recommended organizing a post-incident review using the five Ws embedded in the Institutional Intelligence Model.
Institutional Intelligence Questions

Who: Who was involved? Whom did we overlook or underserve? Who led each aspect of the response? Who should take leadership or responsibility in the future? Who excelled in this situation, and how can they utilize those strengths in the future? Who outside the crisis response team can help plan for the future?

What: What decisions and actions had legal implications? What laws and policies guided the response to the situation? What broader campus, institutional, community, and cultural challenges surfaced during the event? What transformations and innovations are possible because of lessons learned from this event? What campus culture traits initiated or exacerbated the event, situation, or crisis? What policies, processes, expectations, directives, and procedures do we need to review? What did we do well? What have we learned? What do we need to change for the future? What is the debriefing plan? What concerns do constituents have about the response?

Where: Where did the incident occur? Where did we send students and other constituents for shelter, safety, food, and additional information? Where were crucial responders and resources located, relocated, and made available?

When: When did leaders, units, and other responders make decisions? When will debriefing happen, and how will it be facilitated?

Why: Why were decisions made? Why were certain people involved and others not? Why did the crisis occur in the first place?

How: How did this situation happen? How did we respond? How effective was that response? How will we adjust and adapt based on what you learned during this incident? How can you, your team, and your partners make positive changes at your institution? How did we live up to our ethical obligations as individuals, units, and institutionally?

Institutions want to follow the law. Part of the post-incident reflection focuses on law and ethics around the incident or crisis. However, there is more to post-incident processing than assessing compliance or reviewing processes, protocols, practices, and responses. We explore the recovery phase of reflection in the next section.

After an Incident: Recovery

We acknowledge that, in many ways, no major incident on campus is ever over. After a situation occurs, students, staff, and others may need more time—even months or years—during which they may need ongoing support and resources. While we are often good at providing ongoing support and follow-up to students, we do not always excel in doing the same for staff. Attending to issues of self-care or other support related to post-incident recovery is often absent from crisis processes (Holzweiss & Walker, 2018).

Many things need to happen outside of the specific incident to provide recovery and closure for students and others affected. How does your team or institution attend to individual and community healing? What is the process for returning to pre-crisis policies and procedures or communicating new policies and procedures informed by the incident? What has the university planned in order to bring closure to the event (ceremonial activities, commemorations, memorials, recognitions, vigils, or other activities)? What communal and individual opportunities will the university and your team provide, facilitate, and attend to assist with the recovery and healing after an incident?

Leaders and organizations must consider many groups in this recovery process. We must support those directly impacted (students, family, staff, faculty) and provide space for grief, healing, reconnection, and other vital processes. Additionally, communities, organizations, and units will need help recovering from incidents. Just as with individuals, we must provide resources for them.

Finally, attending to individual staff and other responders to crisis events is essential and often overlooked. This care is an ethical issue. Caring for people—particularly those involved in crisis and stressful situations—is the responsibility of supervisors and leaders. The work you do is demanding. Too often, leaders ask you to go directly from one crisis to the next or manage multiple crises simultaneously. Being aware of what individuals are facing and providing time for healing and recovery, and rejuvenation to continue the work are essential.

Attending to your teams is crucial for individuals and teams engaged in work with significant legal and ethical implications and crisis response. In student-facing academic and student affairs jobs, the culture socializes and conditions us to put others first. For many of us, helping others is a primary drive for the work we do.

In order to be equipped, ready, and able to provide our support and advocacy, *we* must also be supported. If leaders need a more pragmatic reason beyond "It is your responsibility to care for your people," we would offer that the more taxed people are, the more likely they are to make mistakes with legal and ethical implications. If you want a team that can do good work, you must care for them.

With staff doing the work in mind, we provide a final set of Institutional Intelligence questions for engaging in reflective practice. In this case, the questions center on student employees, staff, and faculty involved in this work.

Institutional Intelligence Questions

Who: Who is involved in the crisis? Who is managing multiple crises or a crisis alongside other major projects? Who is available to assist so that those most directly involved have time and space for recovery? Who needs additional training for the future?

What: What crisis follow-up work or meetings can we delegate to staff members not as directly involved in the crisis? What routine work tasks do we offload to another staff member? What are the status and needs of the responders involved—undergraduate, graduate students, full-time employees, campus/community responders, student affairs professionals, academic affairs professionals, and faculty members? What are the unique needs of each? What meetings can we cancel to provide space for recovery? What work tasks can we cancel or postpone providing space for recovery? What language are leaders using to require recovery and structure it formally? What campus policies do we need to revisit in the context of the recent incident?

Where: Where can those involved in providing support and response to situations go for support through the physical, mental, and emotional issues they may be navigating as they engage in response to student crises, emergencies, events, and issues on campus?

When: When do you begin the recovery process around incidents? When do you cross-train to ensure that regular job tasks can be attended to if a team member is involved in a crisis?

Why: Why might different people have different recovery needs?

How: How are resources people need different or similar for staff dealing with a specific incident instead of an accumulation of stress, anxiety, or other issues from a series of incidents over time? How do leaders and organizations inform staff about resources? How are supervisors trained to ensure staff take time away from work after significant incidents? How is the team developed so others can pick up more routine work and tasks for individuals called upon to respond to crises? How do you focus on recovery and healing if an entire unit is involved in a crisis? How did our actions align with our institution's values and ethics as individuals?

If teams move beyond debriefing after incidents, they can build better processes and protocols for the future. Additionally, by attending intentionally to the staff most impacted by crisis work, the culture can be rebuilt in human-centered ways with an ethic of care informing the practice. The questions in this chapter can help colleges and universities build healthier work experiences, departments, and individual staff members.

There are real financial implications for doing this work well. Attending in ethical ways to individuals, communities, and events minimizes the risk of lawsuits. Investing in cultural reflection on campus after an event can help amplify voices that have historically been silenced or minimized. Cultural reflection through the implementation of the Institutional Intelligence Model has the potential to address underlying issues so that similar crises or responses to those crises do not repeat themselves.

Conclusion

At the beginning of the chapter, we mentioned Heraclitus and his idea about change related to rivers and people. Heraclitus also said, "The only constant in life is change." Whether it is a new job for you or you are on a search committee to hire a new colleague, your team and your institution will constantly be changing. People create change. Crises create change. Law and ethics create change. We can resist change—either lose the battle or be left behind as other institutions progress—or we can embrace change. We can thrive based on the lessons learned. By examining our campus contexts and continually developing our Institutional Intelligence, we can carry forward all the best things about higher education and work to change the things that hold our colleges and universities back. Instead of trying to return to the way things used to be, we can move boldly forward with care for those around us to create something better.

18

AFTERWORD

The Future and Continuing the Work

You have reached the Afterword of this book. What did you think? How many chapters did you skip? What did you learn? Hopefully, the answers to those questions are, "It's the most amazing book on this topic I have ever read," "I didn't skip ANY chapters. It was so compelling, I couldn't put it down!", "I learned so much. This book has transformed my thinking. Thank you. Thank you. Thank you."

If those are your responses, well then, you are very welcome.

However, if your answer is "*it depends*," we know you have read and understood the message of this text, including the Institutional Intelligence Model. Since you might have different answers, permit us a few closing remarks.

Utility of the Institutional Intelligence Model

As we were writing this book, we both shared the concept of Institutional Intelligence with the classes we were teaching. We wanted to see whether the idea worked and resonated with students doing academic and student affairs work. In one class I (Michelle) taught, I gave students a couple of very vague scenarios: "A parent called" and "A student reports a conflict." I then asked students to identify the most important *who*, *what*, *where*, *when*, *why*, and *how* questions related to the situation. This approach lets them practice figuring out how to anticipate and plan (think before acting) for situations they might encounter in new positions or on new campuses.

After that class, I received an email from a student named Sydney. She shared that after class, she and her roommate, Michael (also a student in our class),

DOI: 10.4324/9781003442707-22

continued to practice this exercise in the context of their roommate relationship. In responding to the prompt: "Michael said something," they came up with the following questions using the Institutional Intelligence Model:

Who do you think you are?
What is THAT supposed to mean?
Where did you get the audacity to say such a thing?
When are you moving out?
Why did you start this?
How dare you?

While these questions are a bit more hostile and pointed than what we envisioned for the model, they exemplify that the model works in various situations. It also shows that students will actively engage with the Institutional Intelligence Model even if they are smart-alecky about it. Most importantly, this is an example of the ease of utility of this model. It shows that, while used in a joking way by Sydney and Michael, the model is transferable. We have since used the model to provide some structure for other assignments. It is something we have found students and practitioners understand, can relate to, and can fairly easily put into practice.

The Future

This section acknowledges the ever-changing nature of student and academic affairs and the changing nature of higher education informed by society, culture, politics, and all the other stuff in the world. With those ideas in mind, we close with some thoughts for the future and one strategy to continue the thinking, work, and conversation. How do we learn first and act second? As you have read throughout the text, the Institutional Intelligence Model is one suggestion we have.

In Chapter 11, we noted that whatever the future of higher education holds, the COVID-19 pandemic proved just how quickly higher education could change and adapt if it has to. It taught us all about technology, relationships, and the complexity of student engagement in the world today. Of course, legal issues emerged—students who sued universities for tuition and fees because of the pivot online; a drop in student enrollment; programming switch to mostly online; and faculty and staff experience burnout—among other issues.

The more significant issues we deal with and continue to face are ethical issues, and our ethics will help us navigate the future. As with the rest of the book, we will share questions rather than answers as we consider the future.

If you have not learned anything else in this book, the answer to big questions is "*It depends.*" Only when we take those big questions from the global to the local and look at our practices at our own institutions can we generate answers and create authentic, transformative, and sustainable change.

Ask Yourselves

- Whom do we admit to institutions?
- Who in our area, state, and country has access to the internet, computers, or quiet space to do work or attend virtual classes?
- Who is teaching and developing syllabi for classes?
- Who is making decisions for our institutions?
- What are we doing to provide more access to more students?
- What do we each believe about the value of human beings in higher education?
- What can we do to make higher education safer for students, staff, and faculty?
- What did we learn from the COVID-19 pandemic, and are we continuing to learn?
- Where are we putting our resources?
- Where do we look for input during strategic planning, crises, or change?
- When should we seek legal advice?
- When do we participate in institutional traditions and culture?
- Why do we continue to hold exclusive rather than inclusive institutions in such high regard?
- Why do we reward universities that keep lots of people out instead of letting lots of people in?
- How do we address issues of educational access?
- How do student and academic affairs enact their values in the expectations of students, staff, and faculty?
- How do we show genuine and holistic care for employees?
- How do we know whether it is time to make a career change (new position, new institution, outside of higher education)?

Continuing the Conversation

We opened the book by introducing a space for you to share your thoughts. We know that a book is a one-way communication. However, we do not want to stop with this book. We welcome your ideas and encourage you to share your wisdom with us as we continue to wrestle with the ideas in this book. What are your critical scenarios? What experiences have you had that we all need to think about? If you are willing to partner with us in continuing the work and have scenarios to share, please submit them to **institutionalintelligencebook@gmail.com**. We want to get more ideas, challenges, and questions out to people doing the work. We intentionally partnered with practitioners because they know what is happening on their college campuses. We hope you will be a collaborator and share your ideas. We will publish these scenarios on our professional websites (https://www.mlboettcher.com and https://www.drcrissalinas.com).

Students, whom did we miss in these scenarios, and what else should we be discussing? New and emerging practitioners, what are you seeing and experiencing, and where should we go next? Experienced practitioners, where do you see challenges, and when do you see things changing in the future? Administrators and leaders, when do we set aside the idea of "going back to normal," and why do we insist on thinking that the way things were was good? Faculty, how do we teach with technology and care to build on what we have learned in different class spaces?

Our shared space is open to everyone. We value and want to hear from you all.

The Authors

Michelle

I was a practitioner at Iowa State University for 12 years (five years in housing and seven in student conduct). I earned my undergraduate and doctoral degrees there. I developed Institutional Intelligence to understand relationships between the Dean of Students Office and our partners. I continually learned about my relationships with colleagues. I cannot take what I knew there and give it to others. I could not even bring all of what I had learned as a student affairs practitioner at Iowa State to my role as a faculty member at Clemson University.

All of this to say, we cannot give answers, best practices, or any form of detailed checklist about how to navigate legal and ethical issues as a final takeaway. Instead, we offer you the Institutional Intelligence Model for you to consider as you think about your work at your institution with the students and other constituents who inform the work you do. This model will help you anticipate, navigate, and contemplate your institution and how you can effectively abide by legal and ethical guidelines in your work wherever you choose to go.

Cristóbal

As stated earlier, writing a book has been challenging. I would not have been able to accomplish this by myself. I thank Michelle for her dedication and patience and for challenging me to engage more in this work. Our weekly meetings have fostered our learning from each other, afforded us space to develop new ideas, and given us a chance to share our experiences. During each meeting, we used the Institutional Intelligence Model to guide our conversations.

I reflected a lot on my experiences at Iowa State University as a graduate student and student affairs professional and my experiences as a faculty member at Florida Atlantic University. For example, at Iowa State University, I learned about relationship-building with people (*who*); mainly, I learned about racial relationships. By understanding and knowing the *who*, I often got to the *what*, *when*, *where*, *why*, and *how*. Now, as a faculty member, I have learned to embrace the *who*, *what*, *when*, *where*, *why*, and *how*. When I try to figure things out and wonder what I should do, the answer begins with *it depends*. In figuring out what *it depends* on, I consider *who*, *what*, *when*, *where*, *why*, and *how*. This approach also helps me adapt to change. I continue to engage in conversation with Michelle and other colleagues, am conscious of my awareness and emotions, engage in critical reading, thinking, and writing, and have given myself time to think before I act and to reflect along the way.

As you read this book, I hope you become more aware of and develop your own Institutional Intelligence. Our awareness is a powerful part of understanding Institutional Intelligence.

Gratitude

This is the most important part of the book. We are forever indebted to the critical scenario co-authors. Some of you got a message from us, responded within an hour (or less), accepted the invitation to participate as co-authors, and shared your feedback within 24 hours. How amazing is that? We are grateful to every one of you for your time and insight. This book would have very little utility without your insights and expertise. We owe you. We know that. Let us know what we can do to repay you. Not monetarily, though, okay? We are not making any money from this book.

Thank you for agreeing to be part of this project. By agreeing to be part of this book, you have elevated the quality of the scenarios and the text as a whole. We hope we do the same to you through this book and beyond.

Janel Acosta
Michael Almond
Christian Barrientos
Olivia Battinelli
Abigail Beadle

Madison Beine
Dax Boatwright
Jordan Bowman
Colby Brown
Amy Burke
Elliott DeVore
J'Lissabeth Faughn
Chris Fiocchi
Deborah L. Floyd
Daniel Francis
Wayne Glass
Victoria Goetzinger
Adric Hardy
Aja Holmes
Tiana Iruoje
Larissa Jenkins
Drew Johnson
Chuck Knepfle
Laura Knowles
Andrew Kutcher
Amy Lawton-Rauh
Jared Logan
Reyes Luna
Meredith McDevitt
Brad Menard
Cayce Pasko-Stanley
Anna Pietrzak
Kate Radford
Alonso Reyna Rivarola
Keith Robinder
Jan Scoville
Myles Surrett
Halie Swanson
Alexis Swider
Fred Tugas
Taylor Tyson-Knapp
Catrina Wagner
Wen Xi

Our gratitude as well to John Lowery for your thoughts on the text and feedback as you read our work. Finally, thank you so much to Mimi Benjamin and Jody Jessup-Anger for your reading and feedback on the text.

Thanks especially for the final read. We thought we were finished and you caught a few things we are glad did not make it into this text. You made this a much better book.

Thank you,
Michelle and Cristóbal

APPENDIX

ACPA/NASPA Professional Competencies

Reprinted with permission

Competency area	*Description*	*Professional development*
Personal and Ethical Foundations (PEF)	Involves the knowledge, skills, and dispositions to develop and maintain integrity in one's life and work; this includes thoughtful development, critique, and adherence to a holistic and comprehensive standard of ethics and commitment to one's own wellness and growth. Personal and ethical foundations are aligned because integrity has an internal locus informed by a combination of external ethical guidelines, an internal voice of care, and our own lived experiences. Our personal and ethical foundations grow through a process of curiosity, reflection, and self-authorship.	Foundational outcomes emphasize awareness and understanding of one's values and beliefs, especially as related to professional codes of ethics and principles for personal wellness. Professional development to advanced-level proficiency involves higher-order critique and self-awareness, applications to healthy living and professional practice, and modeling, mentoring, and facilitating the same among others.
Values, Philosophy, and History (VPH)	Involves knowledge, skills, and dispositions that connect the history, philosophy, and values of the student affairs profession to one's current professional practice. This competency area embodies the foundations of the profession from which current and future research, scholarship, and practice will change and grow. The commitment to demonstrating this competency area ensures that our present and future practices are informed by an understanding of the profession's history, philosophy, and values.	Progression from foundational to advanced-level proficiency for this competency area largely involves movement from basic understanding of VPH to a more critical understanding of VPH as applied in practice and then to the use and critical application of VPH in practice.

Assessment, Evaluation, and Research (AER)	Focuses on the ability to design, conduct, critique, and use various AER methodologies and the results obtained from them, to utilize AER processes and their results to inform practice, and to shape the political and ethical climate surrounding AER processes and uses in higher education.	Professional growth in this competency area is broadly marked by shifts from understanding to application and then from smaller-scale applications focused on singular programs or studies to larger-scale applications that cut across departments or divisions. Many advanced-level outcomes involve the leadership of AER efforts.
Law, Policy, and Governance (LPG)	Includes the knowledge, skills, and dispositions relating to policy development processes used in various contexts, the application of legal constructs, compliance/policy issues, and the understanding of governance structures and their impact on one's professional practice.	Progression from foundational to advanced-level proficiency reflects shifts from understanding to critical applications enacted primarily at the departmental level to institutional-level applications that are mindful of regional, national, and international contexts.
Organizational and Human Resources (OHR)	Includes knowledge, skills, and dispositions used in the management of institutional human capital, financial, and physical resources. This competency area recognizes that student affairs professionals bring personal strengths and grow as managers through challenging themselves to build new skills in the selection, supervision, motivation, and formal evaluation of staff; resolution of conflict; management of the politics of organizational discourse; and the effective application of strategies and techniques associated with financial resources, facilities management, fundraising, technology, crisis management, risk management, and sustainable resources.	In addition to the shift from understanding to application, professional development within this competency reflects shifts in the scale, scope, and interactivity of the human and organizational resources with which one works.

Competency area	*Description*	*Professional development*
Leadership (LEAD)	Addresses the knowledge, skills, and dispositions required of a leader, with or without positional authority. Leadership involves both the individual role of a leader and the leadership process of individuals working together to envision, plan, and affect change in organizations and respond to broad-based constituencies and issues. This can include working with students, student affairs colleagues, faculty, and community members.	Professional growth within this competency area reflects shifts from knowledge to critical application and then to fostering the development of leadership within and among others.
Social Justice and Inclusion(SJI)	While there are many conceptions of social justice and inclusion in various contexts, for the purposes of this competency area, it is defined here as both a process and a goal which include the knowledge, skills, and dispositions needed to create learning environments that foster equitable participation of all groups while seeking to address and acknowledge issues of oppression, privilege, and power. This competency involves student affairs educators who have a sense of their own agency and social responsibility that includes others, their community, and the larger global context. Student affairs educators may incorporate social justice and inclusion competencies into their practice through seeking to meet the needs of all groups, equitably distributing resources, raising social consciousness, and repairing past and current harms on campus communities.	Professional development within this competency areas assumed that student affairs educators need to understand oppression, privilege, and power before they can understand social justice. Intermediate- and advanced-level outcomes reflect social justice–oriented applications in practice and then interconnections between leadership and advocacy.

Student Learning and Development (SLD)	Addresses the concepts and principles of student development and learning theory. This includes the ability to apply theory to improve and inform student affairs and teaching practice.	At the foundational level, SLD involves a critical understanding of learning and development theories and their use in constructing learning outcomes. Intermediate and advanced proficiency involves greater application in utilizing various forms of programs and applications within increasingly large and complex venues.
Technology (TECH)	Focuses on the use of digital tools, resources, and technologies for the advancement of student learning, development, and success as well as the improved performance of student affairs professionals. Included within this area are knowledge, skills, and dispositions that lead to the generation of digital literacy and digital citizenship within communities of students, student affairs professionals, faculty members, and colleges and universities as a whole.	Professional growth in this competency area is marked by shifts from understanding to application as well as from application to facilitation and leadership. Intermediate- and advanced-level outcomes also involve a higher degree of innovation in the use of technology to engage students and others in learning processes.
Advising and Supporting (A/S)	Addresses the knowledge, skills, and dispositions related to providing advising and support to individuals and groups through direction, feedback, critique, referral, and guidance. Through developing advising and supporting strategies that take into account self-knowledge and the needs of others, we play critical roles in advancing the holistic wellness of ourselves, our students, and our colleagues.	Progression from foundational to advanced-level proficiency involves the development of higher-order capacities for listening, addressing group dynamics, managing conflict and crisis situations, and partnering with other professionals, departments, and agencies.

ACPA/NASPA (2015).

REFERENCES

AAUP. (2009). Statement of professional ethics. https://www.aaup.org/report/statement-professional-ethics

AAUP. (n.d.). Advancing academic freedom. https://www.aaup.org/our-work/protecting-academic-freedom

American Council on Education (ACE). (1949). *The student personnel point of view* (Rev. ed.) American Council on Education Studies Series 6, 13(13).

ACHA. (n.d.). This history of ACHA. https://www.acha.org/ACHA/About/History/ACHA/About/History.aspx?hkey=29e97485-0afd-49fa-a061-b4dd3ac5fa29

ACPA. (n.d.). Statement of ethical principles and standards. https://myacpa.org/wp-content/uploads/2020/12/Ethical_Principles_Standards.pdf

ACPA – College Student Educators International [ACPA], & NASPA – Student Affairs Administrators in Higher Education [NASPA]. (2015). *Professional competency areas for student affairs educators.* Washington, DC: ACPA – College Student Educators International and NASPA-Student Affairs Administrators in Higher Education. https://www.naspa.org/images/uploads/main/ACPA_NASPA_Professional_Competencies_FINAL.pdf

ACPA/NASPA. (2015). *ACPA/NASPA professional competencies rubrics.* ACPA – College Student Educators Internationals and NASPA – Student Affairs Administrators in Higher Education. https://www.naspa.org/images/uploads/main/ACPA_NASPA_Professional_Competency_Rubrics_Full.pdf

Aggie Traditions. (2021). Bonfire memorial. https://www.tamu.edu/traditions/remembrance/bonfire-memorial/index.html

Alexander, K. W., & Alexander, K. (2017). *Higher education law: Policy and perspectives* (2nd ed.). Routledge.

Allen, W. R., Epps, E. G., & Haniff, N. Z. (1991). *College in Black and White: African American students in predominantly White and in historically Black public universities.* SUNY Press.

Altbach, P. G. (1997). *Student politics in America: A historical analysis.* Transaction Publishers.

Altschuler, G., & Blumin, S. (2009). *The GI Bill: The new deal for veterans.* Oxford University Press.

American Association of Colleges and Universities. (2022). Essential learning outcomes. https://www.aacu.org/initiatives/value-initiative/essential-learning-outcomes

American Council on Education. (1937). *The student personnel point of view* (American Council on Education Studies, series 1, no. 3). Author.

American Council on Education. (1949). The student personnel point of view. *Student Personnel Work, 13*(8), Series IV. https://www.naspa.org/files/dmfile/Student_Personnel_Point_of_View_1949.pdf

American Council on Education. Committee of Student Personnel Work. (1949). *The student personnel point of view* (Rev. ed.: American Council on Education Studies, series 6, no. 13). Author.

Ardoin, S., & Martinez, B. (2019). No, I can't meet you for an $8 coffee: How class shows up in workspaces. In B. J. Reece, V. T. Tran, E. N. DeVore, & G. Porcaro (Eds.), *Debunking the myth of job fit in higher education and student affairs* (pp. 97–118). ACPA.

Associated Press. (2018, June 30). *MSU paid $18,000 for security for Richard Spencer event.* Detroit Free Press.

Association of College Unions International. (1937). Unions start training for group leadership. *The Bulletin, 5*(4), 2.

Association of College Unions International. (n.d.). History. https://www.acui.org/about/who-we-are

Ayres, I., & Foster, S. (2007). Don't tell, don't ask: Narrow tailoring after Grutter and Gratz. *Texas Law Review, 85*(3), 517–582.

Barr, M. J. (Ed.). (1988). *Student services and the law: A handbook for practitioners.* Jossey-Bass.

Barton, R., Cadge, W., & van Stee, E. G. (2020). Caring for the whole student: How do chaplains contribute to campus life? *Journal of College and Character, 21*(2), 67–85.

Bates, K. G., Jennings-Brown, T., Demby, G., Cala, C., & Perry, A. J. (2022, September 7). In 50 years, the Pell Grant has helped over 80 million people go to college. Code Switch. NPR.

BBC. (2017, February 23). Not best of times for US - Supreme Court Justice Ginsburg. https://www.bbc.com/news/world-us-canada-39065535

Beale, A. V. (1970). The evolution of college admission requirements. *The National ACAC Journal, 15*(3), 20–22.

Benitez Jr., M. (2010). Resituating culture centers within a social justice framework. In L. Patton (Ed.), *Culture centers in higher education: Perspectives on identity, theory, and practice* (pp. 119–134). Stylus Publishing.

Bennett, W. (1971). The Afro-American cultural center. *Harvard Journal of Afro-American Affairs, 2*(2), 18–29.

Benson, R. W. (1984). The end of legalese: The game is over. *New York University Review of Law and Social Change, 13*, 519–572.

Boettcher, M. L. (2019). Navigating organizational culture in the job search. *College Student Affairs Journal, 37*(2), 99–113.

Boettcher, M. L., Perez, C., & Salinas, C. (2018). Preventing hazing: Promising practices for college and university administrators and professionals. In C. Salinas, & M. Boettcher (Eds.), *Critical perspectives on hazing in colleges and universities: A guide to disrupting hazing culture* (pp. 137–151). Routledge.

Boettcher, M. L., Earnest, K., Eason, A., & Lewis, L. (2019a). The cultivation of support networks by Students of Color in a residence hall setting at a predominantly White institution. *Journal of College & University Student Housing*, *45*(2), 30–46.

Boettcher, M. L., Walker-Donnelly, K., & Nunamaker, T. (2019b). Reflections and resources to support navigating transitions. *New Directions for Student Services*, *166*, 95–104.

Boettcher, M. L., Adelson, L., Jamison, A., & Kniess, D. (2020). It was never normal: Building new and better post-pandemic support for student affairs graduate students. *About Campus*, *25*(4), 15–19.

Boland, W. C. (2018a). The Higher Education Act and minority serving institutions: Towards a typology of Title III and V funded programs. *Education Sciences*, *8*(1), 1–19.

Boone, L. E., Kurtz, D. L., & Fleenor, C. P. (1988). CEOs: Early signs of a business career. *Business Horizons*, *31*(5), 20–24.

Boland, W. C. (2018b). The Higher Education Act and minority serving institutions: Towards a typology of Title III and V funded programs. *Education Sciences*, *8*(1), 1–19.

Briggs, P., & Ammigan, R. (2017). A collaborative programming and outreach model for international student support offices. *Journal of International Students*, *7*(4), 1080–1095.

Brighouse, H. (2019). How can we understand "liberal arts education"? Mellon Foundation. https://mellon.org/news-blog/articles/how-can-we-understand-liberal-arts-education/

Brown, L. W. (1974). Something for me, my family, the race, and mankind. *The Radcliffe Quarterly*, *60*(1), 17–19.

Brown v. Board of Education, 347 U.S. 483 (1954).

Brown v. Board of Education, 349 U.S. 294 (1955).

Brubacher, J. S., & Rudy, W. (1958). *Higher education in transition: An American history, 1636-1956*. Harper.

Brubacher, J. S., & Rudy, W. (1997). *Higher education in transition: A history of American colleges and universities* (4th ed.). Transaction Publishers.

Bryant, J. (2021, November 11). How many Americans have a college degree? *Best Colleges*. https://www.bestcolleges.com/news/analysis/2021/07/01/how-many-americans-have-college-degrees/

Burgess, E. (2019). *The Niceties*. Samuel French.

Burggraaf, W. (1997). Management skills from different educational settings. *International Journal of Educational Management*, *11*(2), 65–71.

Burris, N. (2022). Our history: Spectrum Center. University of Michigan. https://spectrumcenter.umich.edu/article/our-history

Butts, P. (1948, December). Why a union for a war memorial? *Bulletin*, *41*(4), 6–7.

Butts, P. (1971). *The college union idea* (1st ed.). Association of College Unions International.

Byrne, K. Z. (2000). The role of campus-based Women's Centers. *Feminist Teacher, 13*(1), 48–60.
Calhoun, D. W., & Nasser, R. M. (2013). Skills and perceptions of entry-level supervision. *Georgia Journal of College Student Affairs, 29*(1), 20–34.
Carasik, L., & Bachman, J. S. (2019). Destroying Indigenous cultures in the United States. In J. S. Bachman (Ed.), *Cultural genocide: Law, politics, and global manifestations* (pp. 97–117). Routledge.
Cardoza, B. N. (1921). *The nature of the judicial process.* Yale University Press.
Carnegie Classification of Institutions of Higher Education. (n.d.). Basic classification description. https://carnegieclassifications.iu.edu/classification_descriptions/basic.php
CAS. (2020). Master's level higher education student affairs professional preparation programs. *Council for the Advancement of Standards in Higher Education.* https://www.cas.edu/store_product.asp?prodid=66
Catullo, L. A., Walker, D. A., & Floyd, D. L. (2009). The status of crisis management at NASPA member institutions. *NASPA Journal, 46*(2), 301–324.
Chang, A., Fuller, J., & Handel, S. (2021). 'Theft at a scale that is unprecedented': Behind the underfunding of HBCUs. *NPR.* https://www.npr.org/2021/05/13/996617532/behind-the-underfunding-of-hbcus
Cheesman, N. E., Kinsey, I. B., Laguer, I., & Shaw, M. D. (2008). Assessing Latina/o cultural nourishment: The role of university cultural centers. *Journal of the Indiana University Student Personnel Association, 36*, 9–22.
Chickering, A. W. (1969). *Education and identity.* Jossey-Bass.
Chism, N. V. (1998). Preparing graduate students to teach: Past, present, and future. In M. Marincovich, J. Prostko, & F. Stout (Eds.), *The professional development of graduate teaching assistants* (pp. 1–18). Anker Publishing Company.
Chory, R. M., & Offstein, E. H. (2017). "Your professor will know you as a person": Evaluating and rethinking the relational boundaries between faculty and students. *Journal of Management Education, 41*(1), 9–38.
Christmas, W. A. (1995). The evolution of medical services for students at colleges and universities in the United States. *Journal of American College Health, 43*(6), 241–247.
Clauss-Ehlers, C. S., & Parham, W. D. (2013). Landscape of diversity in higher education: Linking demographic shifts to contemporary university and college counseling center practices. *Journal of Multicultural Counseling and Development, 42*(2), 69–76.
Cohen, A. M., & Kisker, C. B. (2010). *The shaping of American higher education: Emergence and growth of the contemporary system* (2nd ed.). Jossey-Bass.
Colby, A., Kohlberg, L., Gibbs, J., Lieberman, M., Fischer, K., & Saltzstein, H. D. (1983). A longitudinal study of moral judgment. *Monographs of the Society for Research in Child Development*, 1–124.
Colburn, S. (2020). Beyond the bathroom wars: Increasing gender-free restroom access in libraries. *College & Research Libraries News, 81*(8), 387–390.
Coley, J. S. (2020). Reframing, reconciling, and individualizing: How LGBTQ activist groups shape approaches to religion and sexuality. *Sociology of Religion*, 81(1), 45–67.

Coley, J. S. (2021). Mobilizing for religious freedom: Educational opportunity structures and outcomes of conservative Christian campus activism. *Research in Social Movements, Conflicts, and Change, 44*, 175–200.

College of William & Mary. (n.d.). History of William and Mary. https://www.wm.edu/offices/deanofstudents/services/communityvalues/studenthandbook/history_of_william_and_mary/index.php

Columbia University. (2021, September 28). *Columbia University LGBTQ+ resource guide.* https://provost.columbia.edu/sites/default/files/content/Faculty%20Advancement/LGBTQ%20Resources/Guide%20-%20Section%203.pdf

Columbia University. (n.d.). About. https://www.tc.columbia.edu/organization-and-leadership/higher-and-postsecondary-education/about/

Cooper, T. L. (1998). *The responsible administrator: An approach to ethics for the administrative role.* Jossey-Bass.

Cooper, J., Mitchell Jr., D., Eckerle, K., & Martin, K. (2016). Addressing perceived skill deficiencies in student affairs graduate preparation programs. *Journal of Student Affairs Research and Practice, 53*(2), 107–117.

Cowley, W. H. (1938). Intelligence is not enough. *Journal of Higher Education, 9*(1938), 469–477.

Creamer, D. G., & Winston, R. B. (2002). Foundations of the supervised practice experience: Definitions, context, and philosophy. In D. L. Cooper, S. A. Saunders, R. B. Winston, J. B. Hirt, D. G. Creamer, & S. M. Janosik (Eds.), *Learning through supervised practice in student affairs* (pp. 1–34). Routledge.

Cuellar, M. G., & Salinas, C. (2022). Latin* college students' diversity and intersectionality: Future direction for research and practice. In M. Bonous-Hammarth (Ed.), *Tales of two cities in a system: Bridging marginality in higher education* (pp. 55–83). Palgrave Millan.

Culver, V., Ziadie, N., & Cowherd, D. (2013). From debating societies to union boards. *Journal of the Student Personnel Association at Indiana University, 41*, 43–61.

Cuyjet, M. J., Longwell-Grice, R., & Molina, E. (2009). Perceptions of new student affairs professionals and their supervisors regarding the application of competencies learned in preparation programs. *Journal of College Student Development, 50*(1), 104–119.

Dalton, J. (2003). Managing human resources. In S. R. Komives, & D. B. Woodard (Eds.), *Student services: A handbook for the profession* (4th ed., pp. 397–420). Jossey-Bass.

Dalton, J. C., & Crosby, P. C. (2010). How we teach character in college: A retrospective on some recent higher education initiatives that promote moral and civic learning. *Journal of College & Character*, 11(2), 1–10.

Dalton, J. C., Crosby, P. C., Valente, A., & Eberhardt, D. (2009). Maintaining and modeling everyday ethics in student affairs. In G. S. McClellan (Ed.), *The handbook of student affairs administration* (pp. 166–186), Jossey Bass.

Dannells, M. (1997). From discipline to development. Clearinghouse on Higher Education. https://eric.ed.gov/?id=ED408920

Davie, S. L. (2002). *University and college women's centers: A journey toward equity.* Greenwood Press.

Davis, W. A., & Havinghurst, R. J. (1948, April). The measurement of mental systems. *The Scientific Monthly, 66*(4), 301–316.

Deisinger, G., Randazzo, M., O'Neill, D., & Savage, J. (2008). *The handbook for campus threat assessment and management teams.* Applied Risk Management, LLC.

de la Peña, E., Patel, P., & Harris, B. (2018). Paying homage to college and university women's centers: Gender justice work in the center for diversity and inclusion. In B. Bethman (Ed.), *University and college women's and gender equity centers: The changing landscape* (pp. 114–122). Routledge.

Del Pilar, W., & Elston, D. E. (2022, November 9). Higher ed is failing Black and Latinostudents.https://www.insidehighered.com/views/2022/11/09/higher-ed's-promise-dims-students-color-opinion

Dewberry, D. R. (2005). Unions, vitamins, exercise: Unionized graduate students. *College Student Journal, 39*(1), 627–636.

Dorman, J. M., & Christmas, W. A. (2002). Primary care issues in college health. In H. S. Turner, & J. L. Hurley (Eds.), *The history and practice of college health* (pp. 104–117). The University Press of Kentucky.

Dortch, C. (2021). Federal Pell Grant Program of the Higher Education Act: Primer. Congressional Research Service. https://crsreports.congress.gov/product/pdf/R/R45418

Drake, R. W., Jr. (1966). *Review of the literature for freshman orientation practices in the U.S.* (Report No. CG 004 110). American College Personnel Association.

Drysdale, D., Modzeleski, W., & Simons, A. (2010). *Campus attacks: Targeted violence affecting institutions of higher education.* Washington, DC: United States Secret Service, United States Department of Education, and Federal Bureau of Investigation. http://www.secretservice.gov/ntac.shtml

Duffus, R. L. (1924, December 20). The age of play. *The Independent, 113*, 535.

Dungy, G., & Gordon, S. A. (2011). The development of student affairs. In J. H. Schuh, S. R. Jones, & S. R. Harper (Eds.), *Student services: A handbook for the profession* (5th ed., pp. 61–79). Jossey-Bass.

Duran, A., & Allen, E. (2020). Exploring how professional associations socialize student affairs graduate students and new professionals. *Journal of Student Affairs Research and Practice, 57*(2), 132–147.

Dyreson, M. (1989). The emergence of consumer culture and the transformation of physical culture: American sport in the 1920s. *Journal of Sport History, 16*(3), 261–281.

Ebbers, L. H., Marks, K. E., & Stoner, K. L. (1973). Residence halls in U.S. higher education: A selective bibliography. Series Bibliography No. 4.

Eden, S. (2014, November 26). The burning desire of Texas A&M. *ESPN.* https://www.espn.com/espn/feature/story/_/id/11937545/texas-bonfire-burns-fifteen-years-collapse-kills-12-students

Elmore, K., Saia, T., & Thomson, E. A. (2018). Special feature: An introduction to disability cultural centers in US higher education, part 1. *Association on Higher Education and Disability.* https://www.ahead.org/professional-resources/publications/hub/hub-nov-2018/hub-nov-2018-special-feature-disability-cultural-centers

Engstrom, C. M. (1999). Promoting the scholarly writing of female doctoral students in higher education and student affairs graduate programs. *NASPA Journal, 36*, 264–277.

Equity in Athletics Data Analysis. (n.d.). The tools you need for equity in athletics analysis. https://ope.ed.gov/athletics/#/

Espinosa, L. L., Turk, J. M., Taylor, M., & Chessman, H. M. (2019). Race and ethnicity in higher education: A status report. American Council on Education. https://vtechworks.lib.vt.edu/bitstream/handle/10919/89187/RaceEthnicityHighEducation.pdf?sequence=1&isAllowed=y

Eubank, B. (2021, September). Texas NAACP, students file federal civil rights complaint over "The Eyes of Texas". *KVUE ABC News*. https://www.kvue.com/article/news/education/university-of-texas/eyes-of-texas-song-ut-austin-civil-rights-complaint-naacp/269-47d475da-c140-448c-a247-9aa5652207d6

Evans, N. J., Forney, D. S., & Guido-DiBrito, F. (1998). *Student development in college: Theory, research, and practice*. Jossey-Bass.

Evans, N. J., Broido, E. M., Brown, K. R., & Wilke, A. K. (2017). *Disability in higher education: A social justice approach*. Jossey-Bass.

Exec. Order No. 10925, Fed. Reg. (March 6, 1961).

Fabris, P. (2014, December 28). 6 trends steering today's college residence halls. *Building Design + Construction*. https://www.bdcnetwork.com/6-trends-steering-todays-college-residence-halls

Farrell-Cole, P. L., & Cabrales, J. A. (2020). Designing a collective, ethical, and equitable student success culture in Hispanic-serving institutions. In A. M. Hornak (Ed.), *Ethical and legal issues in student affairs and higher education* (pp. 134–167). Charles Thomas Publisher.

Fearn-Banks, K. (2017). *Crisis communication: A casebook approach* (5th ed.). Routledge.

Felson, L. (2001). Undergrad marketers must get jump on networking skills. *Marketing News*, *35*(8), 14–15.

Finley, L., & Levenson, J. (2018). The untapped resources of faculty in campus sexual violence prevention: Issues and recommendations. *Journal of Aggression, Conflict and Peace Research*, *10*(2), 123–133.

Flora, B. H. (2007). Graduate assistants: Students or staff, policy or practice? The current legal employment status of graduate students. *Journal of Higher Education Policy and Management*, *29*(3), 315–322.

Flowers, L. A. (2003). National study of diversity requirements in student affairs graduate programs. *Journal of Student Affairs Research and Practice*, *40*(4), 604–614.

Flowers, L. A., & Howard-Hamilton, M. F. (2002). A qualitative study of graduate students' perceptions of diversity issues in student affairs preparation programs. *Journal of College Student Development*, *43*, 119–123.

Fluke, S., O'Connor, A., Hoff, N., & Peterson, R. L. (2014). Academic support, strategy brief. Student Engagement Project, University of Nebraska-Lincoln and the Nebraska Department of Education. http://k12engagement.unl.edu/academic-supports

Foote. K. (2005). Excerpts from home away from home. In F. L. Hord (Ed.), *Black culture centers: Politics of survival and identity* (pp. 183–210). Third World Press and Association of Black Culture Centers.

Forrester, S. A. (2014). *The Benefits of Campus Recreation*. NIRSA.

Fosnacht, K., & Broderick, C. (2020). Religious intolerance on campus: A multi-institution study. *Journal of College and Character*, *21*(4), 244–262.

Fossey, R., & Crow, G. M. (2011). The elements of a good case. *Journal of Cases in Educational Leadership, 14*(3), 4–10.

Frankl, V. E. (1984). *Man's search for meaning* (Rev. ed.). Washington Square Press.

Future Focused Learning. (2021). The critical thinking cheatsheet multipack. http://get.futurefocusedlearning.net/critical-thinking-cheatsheet

Galindo, R. (2011). Embodying the gap between national inclusion and exclusion: The testimonios of three undocumented students at a 2007 congressional hearing. *Harvard Latino Law Review, 14*, 377.

Galindo, R. (2012). Undocumented & unafraid: The DREAM Act 5 and the public disclosure of undocumented status as a political act. *The Urban Review, 44*(5), 589–611.

Gallagher, P. J., & Demos, G. D. (Eds.). (1983). *Handbook of counseling in higher education*. Praeger.

Ganser, S. R., & Kennedy, T. L. (2012). Where it all began: Peer education and leadership in student services. *New Directions for Higher Education, 157*, 17–29.

García, A. G. (2017). Defined by outcomes or culture? Constructing an organizational identity for Hispanic-serving institutions. *American Educational Research Journal, 54*(1S), 111S–134S.

García, R., & Hinojosa, Y. I. (2020). Encounters with frictions: Engaging resistance through a strategic neutrality. In D. P. Richards (Ed.), *On teaching neutrality: Politics, praxis, and performativity* (pp. 295–302). Utah State University Press.

Gayles, J. G., & Kelly, B. T. (2007). Experiences with diversity in the curriculum: Implications for graduate programs and student affairs practice. *Journal of Student Affairs Research and Practice, 44*(1), 193–208.

Geiger, R. (1997). Research, graduate education, and the ecology of American universities: An interpretive history. In M. Nerad, R. June, & D. S. Miller (Eds.), *Graduate education in the United States* (pp. 8–33). Garland Publishing, Inc.

Gilligan, C. (1977). In a different voice: Women's conceptions of self and morality. *Harvard Educational Review*, 47(4), 481–517.

Gillispie, B. (2003). History of academic advising. *NACADA Clearinghouse*. https://nacada.ksu.edu/Resources/Clearinghouse/View-Articles/History-of-academic-advising.aspx

Goettsch, J., Linden, A., Vanzant, C., & Waugh, P. (2018). Positioning campus women's and gender equity centers for success: Structural issues and trends. In B. Bethman, A. Cottledge, and D. M. Bickford (Eds.) *University and College Women's and Gender Equity Centers* (pp. 8–16). Routledge.

Goldin, C., & Katz, L. F. (2011). Putting the "Co" in education: Timing, reasons, and consequences of college coeducation from 1835 to the present. *Journal of Human Capital, 5*(4), 377–417.

Goldrick-Rab, S., Harris, D. N., & Trostel, P. A. (2009). Why financial aid matters (or does not) for college success: Toward a new interdisciplinary perspective. In J. C. Smart (Ed.), *Higher education: Handbook of theory and research* (pp. 1–45). Springer.

Gonzalez, K. P. (2000). Toward a theory of minority student participation in predominantly white colleges and universities. *Journal of College Student Retention, 2*(1), 69–91.

Gonzalez, A. (2022). Creating coalitions: Culture centers, anti-Asian violence, and Black Lives Matter. *Journal of College and Character, 23*(2), 180–187.
Gordon, V. N. (1992). *Handbook of academic advising*. Greenwood Press.
Grinnell, J. E. (1946, May). When the G.I. goes to college. *The Journal of Higher Education, 17*(5), 246.
Grubbs, S. (2006). The administrative oversight of campus religious groups in the Southeast. *Journal of College and Character, 7*(8), 1–17.
Grube, S. A., Cedarholm, K., Jones, C., & Dunn, M. (2005). Master's student life: The balance between student and professional. *College Student Affairs Journal, 24*(2), 152–161.
Gueras, D., & Garofalo, C. (2002). *Practical ethics in public administration*. Management Concepts.
Guiffrida, D. A., Marquez Kiyama, J., Waterman, S. J., & Museus, S. D. (2012). Moving from cultures of individualism to cultures of collective in support of students of color. In S. D. Museus, & U. M. Jayakuma (Eds.), *Creating campus cultures: Fostering success among racially diverse student populations* (pp. 68–87). Routledge.
Guillory, R. M. (2009). American Indian/Alaska Native college student retention strategies. *Journal of Developmental Education, 33*(2), 14–16.
Guthrie, K. L., & Jenkins, D. M. (2018). *The role of leadership educators: Transforming learning*. Information Age Publishing, Inc.
Haley, K. J., Hephner, B., & Koutas, P. (2011). New school, new job, new life: Supporting the transition of student affairs graduate assistants. *Journal of College Orientation and Transition, 18*(2), 5–19.
Hall, M. K. (2004). The Vietnam era antiwar movement. *OAH Magazine of History, 18*(5), 13–17.
Hall-Hertel, K., Brandes, L. C. O., & Shepard, V. A. (2022). Introductions: Context, research, and applications. In V. A. Shepard, & A. L. Perry (Eds.), *A practitioner's guide to Plsupporting graduate and professional students* (pp. 3–16). Routledge.
Hanson, M. (2021, November 18). Pell grant statistics. *Education Data Initiative*. https://educationdata.org/pell-grant-statistics
Harper, S. R., & Hurtado, S. (2007). Nine themes in campus racial climates and implications for institutional transformation. *New Directions for Student Services, 120*, 7–24.
Harper, K. S., Paterson, B. G., & Zdziarski II, E. L. (2006). *Crisis management: Responding from the heart*. National Association of Student Personnel Administrators.
Herbaut, E., & Geven, K. (2020). What works to reduce inequalities in higher education? A systematic review of the (quasi-) experimental literature on outreach and financial aid. *Research in Social Stratification and Mobility, 65*, 100442.
Herder, L. (2022, May 13). The struggle for dual identity: MSI grant restrictions. *Diverse Issues in Higher Education*. https://www.diverseeducation.com/institutions/msis/article/15291994/the-struggle-for-dual-identity-msi-grant-restrictions-and-the-aapi-community
Herdlein, R. J. (2004). Survey of chief student affairs officers regarding relevance of graduate preparation of new professionals. *NASPA Journal, 42*(1), 51–71.

Higher Education Amendments of 1998. (n.d.) https://www.congress.gov/bill/105th-congress/house-bill/6

Hinojosa, Y. I., & De León-Zepeda, C. (2019). Rhetorical tools in Chicanx though: Political and ethnic inquiry for composition classroom. In I. Baca., Y. I. Hinojosa, & S. Wolff Murphy (Eds.), *Bordered writers: Latinx identities and Literacy practices at Hispanic serving institutions* (pp. 77–103). SUNY Press.

Hirt, J. B. (2006). *Where you work matters: Student affairs administrators at different types of institutions.* University Press of America.

Holmes, A. C. (2014). *Experiences of supervision skill development among new professionals in student affairs* (Doctoral dissertation, Iowa State University).

Holzweiss, P., & Walker, D. (2018). Higher education crises: Training new professionals for crisis management. *College Student Affairs Journal, 36*(1), 124–135.

hooks, b. (2010). *Teaching critical thinking: Practical wisdom.* Routledge.

Horowitz, H. L. (1987). *Campus life: Undergraduate cultures from the end of the eighteenth century to present.* University of Chicago Press.

Howard, A. (1986). College experiences and managerial performance. *Journal of Applied Psychology Monograph, 71*(3), 530–552.

Huberman, M., & Minns, C. (2007). The times they are not changin': Days and hours of work in Old and New Worlds, 1870–2000. *Explorations in Economic History, 44*(4), 538–567.

Huey, M. J., Crihfield, C., & Jopp, D. (2020). The second fifty years: A history of the American College Health Association. *Journal of American College Health, 68*(8), 798–814.

Humphrey, E., Janosik, S. M., & Creamer, D. G. (2004). The role of principles, character, and professional values in ethical decision-making. *National Association of Student Personnel Administrators [NASPA] Journal, 41*(4), 675–692.

Hurtado, S. (2007). Linking diversity with the educational and civic missions of higher education. *The Review of Higher Education, 30*(2), 185–196.

Hutcheson, P. A. (2020). *A people's history of American higher education.* Routledge.

Irwin, L. N., & Foste, Z. (2021). Service-learning and racial capitalism: On the commodification of People of Color for white advancement. *The Review of Higher Education, 44*(4), 419–446.

Jablonski, M., McClellan, G., & Zdziarski, E. (2008). *In search of safer communities: Emerging practices for student affairs in addressing campus violence.* New Directions for Student Services. Jossey-Bass.

Jenkins, T. S., & Walton, C. L. (2008). Student affairs and cultural practice: A framework for implementing culture outside the classroom. In S. R. Harper (Ed.), *Creating inclusive campus environments: For cross-cultural learning and student engagement* (pp. 87–101). NASPA.

Jordan, M., & Vakilian, C. (2013). History of the Association of College Unions International. *Journal of the Student Personnel Association at Indiana University, 41*, 3–24.

Jou, D. (2022). Exchange rates: A history of international students in the US. *The Washington Post.* https://www.wsj.com/video/exchange-rates-a-history-of-international-students-in-the-us/BB681A06-E345-4232-848E-68445B9F8CE6.html

Kaiser, D. (2002). Cold War requisitions, scientific manpower, and the production of American physicists after World War II. *Historical Studies in the Physical & Biological Sciences, 33*(1), 131–159.

Kaplin, W. A. & Lee, B. A. (1995). *The law of higher education: A comprehensive guide to legal implications of administrative decision-making*. Jossey-Bass.

Kaplin, W. A., & Lee, B. A. (2014). *The law of higher education* (5th ed.). Jossey Bass.

Kenny, M. E., & Gallagher, L. A. (2002). Service-learning: A history of systems. In M. E. Kenny, L. A. K. Simon, K. Kiley-Brabeck, & R. M. Lerner (Eds.), *Learning to serve: Promoting civil society through service learning* (pp. 15–29). Kluwer Academic Publishers.

Keppler, K. (2010). Alternate budgetary sources during budget recessions. *New Directions for Student Services*, *2010*(129), 29–41.

King, P. M., & Kitchener, K. S. (1994). *Developing reflective judgment: understanding and promoting intellectual growth and critical thinking in adolescents and adults. Jossey-Bass Higher and Adult Education Series and Jossey-Bass Social and Behavioral Science Series*. Jossey-Bass.

Kitchener, K. S. (1986). Teaching applied ethics in counselor education: An integration of psychological processes and philosophical analysis. *Journal of Counseling & Development*, *64*(5), 306–310.

Knifsend, C. A., Green, L. A., & Clifford, K. L. (2020). Extracurricular participation, collective self-esteem, and academic outcomes among college students. *Psi Chi Journal of Psychological Research*, *25*(4), 318–326.

Kohlberg, L. (1973). Continuities in childhood and adult moral development revisited. In *Life-span developmental psychology* (pp. 179–204). Academic Press.

Kohlberg, L. (1984). *The psychology of moral development: The nature and validity of moral stages (Essays on moral development, Volume 2)*. Harper & Row.

Komives, S. R. (2019). Engagement with campus activities matters: Toward a new era of educationally purposeful activities. *The Journal of Campus Activities Practice and Scholarship*, *1*(1), 14–25.

Komives, S. R., Woodard, Jr., D. B., & Associates. (1996). *Student services: A handbook for the profession* (3rd ed.). Jossey-Bass.

Kaplin, W. A., Lee, B. A., Hutchens, N. H., & Rooksby, J. H. (2020). *The law of higher education* (6th ed., Student version). Jossey-Bass.

Kozel, M. (2008). American Indian student services. *UND Departmental Histories*. 61. https://commons.und.edu/departmental-histories/61

Kuh, G. D., & Whitt, E. J. (1988). *The invisible tapestry. culture in American colleges and universities*. (Report No. 1, 1988). ASHE-ERIC Higher Education, Association for the Study of Higher Education. https://files.eric.ed.gov/fulltext/ED299934.pdf

Kuk, L., Cobb, B., & Forrest, C. (2007). Perceptions of competencies of entry-level practitioners in student affairs. *NASPA Journal*, *44*(4), 664–691.

Lake, P. (2011). *Foundations of higher education law & policy*. NASPA.

Lane, I. F. (2007). Change in higher education: Understanding and responding to individual and organizational resistance. *Journal of Veterinary Medical Education*, *34*(2), 85–92.

Latino, C. A., Stegmann, G., Radunzel, J., Way, J. D., Sanchez, E., & Casillas, A. (2020). Reducing gaps in first-year outcomes between Hispanic first-generation college students and their peers: The role of accelerated learning and financial aid. *Journal of College Student Retention: Research, Theory & Practice*, *22*(3), 441–463.

Lebow, R. J. (1987). Is crisis management always possible? *Political Science Quarterly*, *102*(2), 181–192.
Lee, E. (2015). *The making of Asian America: A history*. Simon & Schuster.
Lee, R., & Ahtone, T. (2020, March 30). Land-grab universities: Expropriated Indigenous land is the foundation of the land-grant university system. *High Country News*. https://www.hcn.org/issues/52.4/indigenous-affairs-education-land-grab-universities
Lemann, N. (1995, September). The great sorting. *The Atlantic*. https://www.theatlantic.com/magazine/archive/1995/09/the-great-sorting/376451/
Lester, J. (2020). *Tools in a toolbox: Leading change in community colleges*. American Council on Education. https://www.acenet.edu/Documents/Tools-in-a-Toolbox.pdf
Levin, J. (2020, June). The damning history behind UT's 'The Eyes of Texas' song. *Texas Monthly*. https://www.texasmonthly.com/arts-entertainment/ut-austin-eyes-of-texas-song-racist/
Li, N., & Murphy, W. H. (2018). Religious affiliation, religiosity, and academic performance of university students: Campus life implications for US universities. *Religion & Education*, *45*(1), 1–22.
Liddell, D. L., Cooper, D. L., Healy, M. A., & Stewart, D. L. (2010). Ethical elders: Campus role models for moral development. *About Campus*, *15*(1), 11–17.
Liu, W. M., Cuyjet, M. J., & Lee, S. (2010). Asian American student involvement in Asian American Culture Centers. In L. D. Patton (Ed.), *Culture centers in higher education: Perspectives on identity; theory; and practice* (pp. 26–48). Stylus Publishing.
Lloyd-Jones, E. (1949). The beginnings of our profession. In E. G. Williamson (Ed.), *Trends in student personnel work* (pp. 260–264). University of Minnesota Press.
Lombardi, K. M., & Mather, P. C. (2016). Understanding anticipatory socialization for new student affairs professionals. *College Student Affairs Journal*, *34*(1), 85–97.
Long, B. T. (2008). What is known about the impact of financial aid? Implications for policy. *An NCPR Working Paper*. National Center for Postsecondary Research.
Long, D. (2012). The foundations of student affairs: A guide to the profession. In L. J. Hinchliffe, & M. A. Wong (Eds.), *Environments for student growth and development: Librarians and student affairs collaboration* (pp. 1–39). Association of College & Research Libraries.
Long, B. T., & Riley, E. K. (2007). Financial aid: A broken bridge to college access? *Harvard Educational Review*, *77*(1), 39–63.
Lovell, D., & Mallinson, D. (2022, February). How test-optional admissions expanded during the COVID-19 pandemic. Urban Institute. https://www.urban.org/sites/default/files/2022-02/how-test-optional-college-admissions-expanded-during-the-covid-19-pandemic_0.pdf
Lowery, J. W. (2011). Student conduct. In N. Zhang (Ed.), *Rentz's student affairs in practice in higher education* (4th ed., pp. 196–230). Charles C. Thomas.
Mailer, A. S. (1989). Recent data on religious identity of college freshmen: A note. *Jewish Social Studies*, *51*, 317–321.

Manhattan Review. (n.d.). The history of SAT. https://www.manhattanreview.com/sat-history/

Martin, J. E., & Janosik, S. M. (2004). The use of legal terminology in student conduct codes: A content analysis. *Journal of Student Affairs Research and Practice*, *42*(1), 36–50.

Maslow, A. H. (1968). *Toward a psychology of being*. D. Van Nostrand Company.

Mathieson, K. (2003). Elements of moral maturity. *Journal of College and Character*, *4*(5), 1–9.

Mayers, A. (1992). The history of Americans with disabilities act: A movement perspective. *Disability Rights Education & Defend Fund*. https://dredf.org/about-us/publications/the-history-of-the-ada/

McEwan, P. J., & Belfielf, C. R. (2010). Native American mascots and alumni giving. In C. R. King (Ed.), *The Native American mascot controversy: A handbook* (pp. 127–142). Rowman & Littlefield.

McEwen, M. K., & Roper, L. D. (1994). Interracial experiences, knowledge, and skills of master's degree students in graduate programs in student affairs. *Journal of College Student Development*, *35*, 81–87.

McGee, K. (2021, May). Tensions boil at UT-Austin over "The Eyes of Texas," where students are refusing to work and a man with a gun crashed a virtual event. *The Texas Tribune*. https://www.texastribune.org/2021/05/04/eyes-of-texas-ut-austin/

McLendon, M. K., Hearn, J. C., & Mokher, C. G. (2009). Partisans, professionals, and power: The role of political factors in state higher education funding. *Journal of Higher Education*, 80, 686–713.

Mead, M. (1957). The pattern of leisure in contemporary American culture. *The Annals of the American Academy of Political and Social Science*, *313*(1), 11–15.

Merriam, S. B. (2009). *Qualitative research: A guide to design and implementation*. Jossey-Bass.

Merriman, L. S. (2008). Managing parent involvement during a crisis. In K. C. Carney-Hall (Ed.), *Managing parent partnerships: Maximizing influence, minimizing interference, and focusing on student success*, New Directions for Student Services, *122*, 57–66.

Meyers, G. C., & Holusha, J. (1986). *When it hits the fan: Managing the nine crises of business*. Houghton Mifflin Co.

Millea, M., Wills, R., Elder, A., & Molina, D. (2018). What matters in college student success? Determinants of college retention and graduation rates. *Education*, *138*(4), 309–322.

Miller, J. J. (2011). Impact of a university recreation center on social belonging and student retention. *Recreational Sports Journal*, *35*(2), 117–129.

Mishory, J., Huelsman, M., & Kahn, S. (2019, September 9). *How student debt and the racial wealth gap reinforce each other*. The Century Foundation. https://tcf.org/content/report/bridging-progressive-policy-debates-student-debt-racial-wealth-gap-reinforce/?session=1

Moran, M. (1987). Student financial aid and women: Equity dilemma? *ERIC Digest*, 1–4.

Morrill Act. (1862). Act of July 2, 1862 (Morrill Act), Public Law 37-108, which established land grant colleges, 07/02/1862; Enrolled Acts and Resolutions of

Congress, 1789-1996; Record Group 11; General Records of the United States Government; National Archives.

Mosley, D. V., Gonzalez, K. A., Abreu, R. L., & Kaivan, N. C. (2019). Unseen and underserved: A content analysis of wellness support services for bi+ people of color and Indigenous people on U.S. campuses. *Journal of Bisexuality*, *19*(2), 276–304.

Museus, S. (2008). The role of ethnic student organizations in fostering African American and Asian American students' cultural adjustment and membership at predominantly white institutions. *Journal of College Student Development*, *49*(6), 568–586.

Museus, S. D., & Jayakuma, U. M. (2012). *Creating campus cultures: Fostering success among racially diverse student populations.* Routledge.

Museus, S. D., Griffin, K. A., & Quaye, S. J. (2019). Forward. In S. J. Quaye, S. R. Harper, & S. L. Pendakur (Eds.), *Student engagement in higher education: Theoretical perspectives and practical approaches for diverse populations* (3rd ed.). Routledge.

NACADA website. (2021). https://nacada.ksu.edu/About-Us.aspx

NASAP. (n.d.). History. https://www.nasap.net/about/history/

NASPA. (2020). Graduate Program Directory. https://apps.naspa.org/gradprograms/search.cfm

NASPA. (n.d.-a). Standards of professional practice. https://www.naspa.org/images/uploads/main/Standards_of_Professional_Practice.pdf

NASPA. (n.d.-b). NASPA strategies conferences. https://www.naspa.org/events/strategies

National Center for Education Statistics. (2018). https://nces.ed.gov/programs/digest/d19/tables/dt19_303.90.asp

National Center for Education Statistics. (2022). College navigator. https://nces.ed.gov/collegenavigator/?s=all

National Center for Education Statistics. (n.d.-a). Fast facts: Expenditures. https://nces.ed.gov/fastfacts/display.asp?id=75

National Center for Education Statistics. (n.d.-b). Fast facts: Historically Black colleges and universities. https://nces.ed.gov/fastfacts/display.asp?id=667

National Center for Education Statistics. (n.d.-c). Fast facts. https://nces.ed.gov/fastfacts/display.asp?id=37

National Center for Educational Statistics. (2021). College enrollment rates. https://nces.ed.gov/programs/coe/indicator/cpb

National Education Association. (2020, June 25). *History of standardized testing in the United States.* https://www.nea.org/professional-excellence/student-engagement/tools-tips/history-standardized-testing-united-states https://nces.ed.gov/programs/digest/d21/tables/dt21_331.30.asp

National Survey of Student Engagement. (n.d.). What does NSSE do? https://nsse.indiana.edu/nsse/

NCAA. (2021a). College athletes continue to graduate at record highs. https://www.ncaa.org/news/2021/12/2/general-college-athletes-continue-to-graduate-at-record-highs.aspx

NCAA. (2021b, June 30). NCAA adopts interim name, image and likeness policy. https://www.ncaa.org/news/2021/6/30/ncaa-adopts-interim-name-image-and-likeness-policy.aspx

NCAA. (n.d.). The college athlete model. https://www.ncaa.org/sports/2021/2/8/about-taking-action.aspx

Neklason, A. (2019, March 18). Elite-college admissions were built to protect privilege. *The Atlantic*. https://www.theatlantic.com/education/archive/2019/03/history-privilege-elite-college-admissions/585088/

Nguyen, D. J., & Yao, C. W. (2022). *A handbook for supporting today's graduate students*. Stylus Publishing.

Nguyễn, D. H. K., Ward, L., & Lowery, J. W. (2018). Contemporary legal issues in college and university student housing: Introduction to the 2018 special issue. *Journal of College Teaching and Student Housing*, *44*(3), 8–13.

Nguyen, M. H., Espinoza, K. J., Gogue, D. T. L., & Dinh, D. (2020). Looking to the next decade: Strengthening Asian American and Native American Pacific Islander serving institutions through policy and practice. https://files.eric.ed.gov/fulltext/ED608022.pdf

Nicholls, W. J. (2013). *The DREAMers: How the undocumented youth movement transformed the immigrant rights debate*. Stanford University Press.

NIRSA. (n.d.). https://nirsa.net/nirsa/about/

Northeastern Illinois University. (2022). El Centro. https://www.neiu.edu/about/neiu150/el-centro

Ohio State University Recreational Sports. (2015). Recreational sports historical timeline. http://www.recsports.osu.edu/who-we-are/rec-sports-historical-timeline

Ortiz, A. M., Filimon, I., & Cole-Jackson, M. (2015). Preparing student affairs educators. *New Directions for Student Services*, *151*(2015), 79–88.

Packwood, W. T. (Ed.). (1977). *College student personnel services*. Charles C. Thomas Publisher.

Palmer, G. H. (1909). *The life of Alice Freeman Palmer*. Houghton Mifflin.

Patton, L. D. (2005). Power to the people! Black student protest and the emergence of Black culture centers. In F. L. Hord (Ed.), *Black culture centers: Politics of survival and identity* (pp. 151–163). Third World Press and Association of Black Culture Centers.

Patton, L. D. (2006). The voice of reason: A qualitative examination of Black student perceptions of Black culture centers. *Journal of College Student Development*, *47*(6), 628–646.

Patton, L. D. (2010). *Cultural centers in higher education: Perspectives on identity, theory, and practice*. Stylus Publishing.

Patton, L. D. (2019). Engaging students of color. In S. J. Quaye, S. R. Harper, & S. L. Pendakur (Eds.), *Student engagement in higher education: Theoretical perspectives and practical approaches for diverse populations* (3rd ed., pp. 17–38). Routledge.

Patton, L. D., Ranero, J., & Everrett, K. (2011). Engaging in multicultural student services. In D. L. Stewart (Ed.), *Multicultural student services on campus: Building bridges, re-visioning community* (pp. 63–80). Stylus Publishing.

Pauchant, T.C. and Mitroff, I. (1992). *Transforming the crisis-prone organization: Preventing individual, organizational and environmental tragedies*. Jossey-Bass.

Pearson, F. C., & Collins, W. R. (2001). Senior student affairs officers' perceptions of campus-based student religious organizations. *Paper presented at*

Annual Meeting of the National Association of Student Personnel Administrators. Seattle, WA.

Pennamon, T. (2019, July 9). Emerging HSIs step up to serve Hispanic, Latinx students. *Diverse Issues in Higher Education*. https://www.diverseeducation.com/demographics/latinx/article/15105018/emerging-hsis-step-up-to-serve-hispanic-latinx-students

Perez, R. J. (2016). A conceptual model of professional socialization within student affairs graduate preparation programs. *Journal for the Study of Postsecondary and Tertiary Education*, *1*, 35–52.

Pérez-Encinas, A., & Ammigan, R. (2016). Support services at Spanish and US institutions: A driver for international student satisfaction. *Journal of International Students*, *6*(4), 984–998.

Perna, L. W. & Hudgins, C. (1996 October 31–November 3). The graduate assistantship: Facilitator of graduate students' professional socialization. [Paper presentation]. *ASHE 1996 Conference*, Memphis, TN.

Perry, A. M., Steinbaurm, M., & Romer, C. (2021, June 23). *Student loans, the racial wealth divide, and why we need full student debt cancellation*. The Brookings Institute. https://www.brookings.edu/research/student-loans-the-racial-wealth-divide-and-why-we-need-full-student-debt-cancellation/

Phipps, C., Cooper, N., Shores, K., Williams, R., & Mize, N. (2015). Examining the relationship between intramural sports participation and sense of community among college students. *Recreational Sports Journal*, *39*(2), 105–120.

Piaget, J. (1932). *The moral judgment of the child*. Kegan Paul, Trench, Trubner & Co.

Pittman, E. (1994). Last word. Cultural centers on predominantly White campuses: Campus, cultural, and social comfort equals retention. *Black Issues in Higher Education*, *11*(10), 104.

Pope, R. L., & Reynolds, A. L. (1997). The student affairs core competencies: Integrating multicultural awareness, knowledge, and skills. *Journal of College Student Development*, *38*, 266–277.

Pope, R. L., Mueller, J. A., & Reynolds, A. L. (2009). Looking back and moving forward: Future directions for diversity research in student affairs. *Journal of College Student Development*, *50*(6), 640–658.

Postsecondary National Policy Institute. (2021, June 1). Factsheets: LGBTQ students in higher education. https://pnpi.org/lgbtq-students-in-higher-education/

Potter, D. (1944). Debating in the colonial chartered colleges. *Teachers College Record: The Voice of Scholarship in Education*, *46*(1), 125–145.

Predominantly Black Institution Act, 2007. https://www.congress.gov/bill/110th-congress/house-bill/4216/text

Quaye, S. J., Harper, S. R., & Pendakur, S. L. (Eds.). (2019). *Student engagement in higher education: Theoretical perspectives and practical approaches for diverse populations* (3rd ed.). Routledge.

Rainer, C. W. (2001). *Humboldt International. Der Export des Deutschen Universitätsmodells im 19 und 20*. Schwabe & Co.

Rankin, S., Garvey, J. C., & Duran, A. (2019). A retrospective of LGBT issues on US college campuses: 1990-2020. *International Sociology*, *34*(4), 435–454.

Renn, K. A., & Jessup-Anger, E. R. (2008). Preparing new professionals: Lessons for graduate preparation programs from the national study of new professionals in student affairs. *Journal of College Student Development*, *49*(4), 319–335.

Rest, J. (1994). Background: Theory and research. In J. Rest, & D. Narvaez (Eds.), *Moral development in the professions: Psychology and applied ethics* (pp. 1–26). Lawrence Erlbaum Associates, Inc.

Reybold, L. E. (2007). The social and political structuring of faculty ethicality in education. *Innovative Higher Education, 2008*(32), 279–295.

Reybold, L. E. (2009). Faculty ethics: Ideal principles with practical applications. *Journal of Veterinary and Medical Education, 36*(4), 375–381.

Reybold, L. E., Halx, M. D., & Jimenez, A. L. (2008). Professional integrity in higher education: A study of administrative staff ethics in student affairs. *Journal of College Student Development, 49*(2), 110–124.

Reyes, D. V. (2018). *Learning to be Latino.* Rutgers University Press.

Reyna Rivarola, A. R., & Cisneros, J. (2021). Undocuqueer. In K. Strunk, & S. A. Shelton (Eds.), *Encyclopedia of queer studies in education* (Vol. 4, pp. 750–755). Brill.

Rhatigan, J. J., & Schuh, J. H. (2003). Small wins. *About Campus, 8*(1), 17–22.

Rice, S. (2019). *Tough love: My story of things worth fighting for.* Simon & Schuster.

Rollo, J. M., & Zdziarski, E. L. (2007). The impact of crisis. In E. L. Zdziarski, N. W. Dunkel, & J. M. Rollo (Eds.), *Campus crisis management: A comprehensive guide to planning, prevention, response, and recovery.* Jossey Bass.

Roper, C. D., & Hirth, M. A. (2005). A history of change in the third mission of higher education: The evolution of one-way service to interactive engagement. *Journal of Higher Education Outreach and Engagement, 10*(3), 3–21.

Rousseau, D. (1990). Quantitative assessment of organizational culture: The case for multiple measures. In B. Schneider (Ed.), *Frontiers in industrial and organizational psychology* (Vol. 3, pp. 153–192). Jossey-Bass.

Rubin, R. S., Bommer, W. H., & Baldwin, T. T. (2002). Using extracurricular activity as an indicator of interpersonal skill: Prudent evaluation or recruiting malpractice? *Human Resource Management, 41*(4), 441–454.

Rudolph, F. (1990). *The American college and university: A history.* University of Georgia Press.

Ruggerio, V. (2015). *Thinking critically about ethical issues.* McGraw-Hill Education.

Rutgers University. (2022a). Paul Robeson Cultural Center. http://prcc.rutgers.edu

Rutgers University. (2022b). Paul Robeson Cultural Center History. http://prcc.rutgers.edu/history/

Ryder, A., Kimball, E., Hasting, J. D., & Slauzis, D. (2022). Creeping legalism: How external demands reshape student affairs practice. *College Student Affairs Journal, 40*(1), 115–129.

Sachar, A. L. (1945). The B'nai B'rith Hillel Foundations University. *American Jewish Year Book, 47*(1945), 144–152.

Salinas, C. (2018). Transforming academia and theorizing spaces for Latinx in higher education: Voices perdidas and Voces de poder. *International Journal of Qualitative Studies in Education, 30*(8), 746–758.

Salinas, C. (2020). The complexity of the "x" in Latinx: How Latinx/a/o students relate to, identify with, and understand the term Latinx. *Journal of Hispanic Higher Education, 19*(2), 149–168. https://doi.org/10.1177/1538192719900382

Salinas, C., & Boettcher, M. (Eds.). (2018). *Critical perspectives on hazing in colleges and universities: A guide to disrupting the hazing culture.* Routledge.

Salinas, C., & Guerrero, V. (2018). Tokenizing social justice. In P. Sasso, & J. DeVitis (Eds.), *Colleges at the crossroads: Taking sides on contested issues* (pp. 161–179). Peter Lang.

Salinas, C., & Lozano, A. (2022). History and evolution of the term Latinx. In E. G. Murillo, D. Delgado Bernal, S. Morales, L. Urrieta, E. Ruiz Bybee, J. Sánchez Muñoz, V. B. Saenz, D. Villanueva, M. Machado-Casas, & K. Espinoza (Eds.), *Handbook of Latinos and education* (2nd ed., pp. 249–263). Routledge.

Salinas, C., Boettcher, M., & Plagman-Galvin, J. (2018). A document analysis of anti-hazing policy. *Oracle: The Research Journal of the Association of Fraternity/Sorority Advisors, 13*(1), 32–50.

Sanchez, M., & Beard, T. (2022). Graduate student engagement and campus programming. In V. A. Shepard, & A. L. Perry (Eds.). *A practitioner's guide to supporting graduate and professional students* (pp. 122–128). Routledge.

Sandeen, A., & Barr, M. J. (2014). *Critical issues for student affairs: Challenges and opportunities*. Jossey-Bass.

Sanders, K. N. (2016). Black culture centers: A review of pertinent literature. *Urban Education Research and Policy Annuals, 4*(1), 30–38.

Sanlo, R. L., Rankin, S., & Schoenberg, R. (2002). *Our place on campus: Lesbian, gay, bisexual, transgender services and programs in higher education*. Greenwood Press.

Sasso, P., & DeVitis, J. L. (2015). *Today's college students: A reader*. Peter Lang.

Schmalzbauer, J., & Mahoney, K. A. (2018). *The resilience of religion in American higher education*. Baylor University Press.

Schroeder, C. C., & Mable, P. (1994). *Realizing the educational potential of residence halls*. Jossey-Bass.

Schwartz, R. A. (1997a). How deans of women became men. *The Review of Higher Education, 20*(4), 419–436.

Schwartz, R. A. (1997b). Reconceptualizing the leadership roles of women in higher education: A brief history on the importance of deans of women. *The Journal of Higher Education, 68*(5), 502–522.

Schwartz, R. A. (2000). Francis F. Bradshaw: A southern student personnel pioneer. *College Student Affairs Journal, 20*, 75–82.

Shankman, M. L., & Allen, S. J. (2009). *Emotionally intelligent leadership: A guide for college students*. John Wiley & Sons.

Sharaievska, I., & Harmon, J. (2021). Contemporary college students. *SCHOLE: A Journal of Leisure Studies and Recreation Education, 36*(1–2), 1–3. https://doi.org/10.1080/1937156X.2020.1773974

Shaw, M. (2018). Teaching campus crisis management through case studies: Moving between theory and practice. *Journal of Student Affairs Research and Practice, 55*(3), 308–320.

Shedd, C. P. (1938). *The church follows its students*. Yale University Press.

Shepard, V. A., & Perry, A. L. (2022). Conclusion: Toward thriving. In V. A. Shepard, & A. L. Perry (Eds.), *A practitioner's guide to supporting graduate and professional students* (pp. 220–228). Routledge.

Shermer, E. T. (2021, May 3). 75 years of reforms have failed to fix our college financial aid system. *The Washington Post*. https://www.washingtonpost.com/outlook/2021/05/03/seventy-five-years-reforms-have-failed-fix-our-college-financial-aid-system/

Shotton, H., Yellowfish, S., & Cintron, R. (2010). Island of sanctuary: The role of the American Indian culture center. In L. Patton (Ed.), *Culture centers in higher education: Perspectives on identity, theory, and practice* (pp. 49–62). Stylus Publishing.

Shuford, B. C. (2011). Historical and philosophical development of multicultural student services. In D. L. Stewart (Ed.), *Multicultural student services on campus: Building bridges, re-visioning community* (pp. 29–37). Stylus Publishing.

Sims, O. L. (1971). Student conduct and campus law enforcement: A proposal. In O. L. Sims (Ed.), *New directions in campus law enforcement: A handbook for administrators*, (pp. 26–30). The University of Georgia Center for Continuing Education.

Smith, D. B. (1994, Winter). Student discipline in American colleges and universities: A historical overview. *Educational Horizons*, *72*(2), 78–85.

Snarey, J. R. (1985). Cross-cultural universality of social-moral development: A critical review of Kohlbergian research. *Psychological Bulletin*, *97*(2), 202–232.

Solomon, B. M. (1980). *In the company of educated women: A history of women in higher education in America*. Yale University Press.

Southeastern Community College v. Davis, 442 U.S. 397 (1979).

Spectrum Center. (n.d.). University of Michigan. https://spectrumcenter.umich.edu/article/our-history

Stanford History. (n.d.). About. https://facts.stanford.edu/about/

Stanley, W. R. (1983). The rights of gay student organizations. *Journal of College and University Law*, *10*(3), 397–418.

van Stee, E. G., Cadge, W., & Barton, R. (2021). How do colleges and universities support chaplaincy? The causes and effects of different institutional approaches. *Journal of College and Character*, *22*(2), 134–155.

Stein, C. H., Vickio, C. J., Fogo, W. R., & Abraham, K. M. (2007). Making connections: A network approach to university disaster preparedness. *Journal of College Student Development*, *48*(3), 331–343.

Sternberg, R. J. (1985). *Beyond IQ: A triarchic theory of human intelligence*. Cambridge University Press.

Stewart, D. L. (2011). *Multicultural student services on campus: Building bridges, re-visioning community*. Stylus Publishing.

Stock-Ward, S. R., & Javorek, M. E. (2003). Applying theory to practice: Supervision in student affairs. *NASPA Journal*, *40*(3), 77–92.

Stoner, E. N. II, & Lowery, J. W. (2004). Navigating past the "spirit of insubordination": A 21st century model student conduct code with a model hearing script. *Journal of College and University Law*, *14*, 359–382.

Strayhorn, T. L. (2019). *College students' sense of belonging: A key to educational success for all students* (2nd ed.). Routledge.

Strumpf, G. & Shaker, G. (1993) Trends and issues in orientation programs. In M. Upcraft, E. Lee, and associates (Eds.) Designing successful transitions: A guide for orienting students to college. *The Freshman Year Experience*, *13*(1), 37–44.

Sundberg, D. C., & Fried, J. (1997). Ethical dialogues on campus. In J. Fried (Ed.), *New Directions for Student Services, No. 77. Ethics for today's campus: New perspectives on education, student development, and institutional management* (pp. 67–79). Jossey-Bass.

Sweeney, T. J., & Witmer, J. M. (1991). Beyond social interest: Striving toward optimal health and wellness. *Individual Psychology, 47*, 527–540.

Syracuse University. (n.d.). History: Syracuse University Greek life history. https://experience.syracuse.edu/greek-life/about-us/history/

Tandberg, D. A., & Griffith, C. (2013). State support of higher education: Data, measures, findings, and directions for future research. In M. B. Paulsen (Ed.), *Higher education: Handbook of theory and research* (pp. 613–685). Springer.

Tankersley, J. (2022, August 25). Biden's student loan plan squarely targets the middle class. *The New York Times.*

Temkin, L., & Evans, N. J. (1998). Religion on campus: Suggestions for cooperation between student affairs and campus-based religious organizations. *Journal of Student Affairs Research and Practice, 30*(1), 58–66.

Terenzini, P. T. (1993). On the nature of institutional research and the knowledge skills it requires. *Research in higher Education, 34*(1), 1–10.

Texas A & M. (n.d.). Aggie code of honor. https://student-rules.tamu.edu/aggiecode/

The University of Texas System. (2022). About the University of Texas System. https://www.utsystem.edu/about

The Women's Center. (2022). About: The Women's Center. University of Minnesota. https://womenscenter.umn.edu/about

Thelin, J. R. (2011). *A history of American higher education* (2nd ed.). Johns Hopkins University Press.

Thelin, J. R. (2019). *A History of American Higher Education* (3rd ed.). Johns Hopkins University Press.

Tolman, S., & Calhoun, D. (2019). Pedagogical approach to developing the hiring practices of higher education administrators. *Georgia Journal of College Student Affairs, 35*(1), 63–83.

Torres, V., Howard-Hamilton, M. F., & Cooper, D. L. (2003). Identity development of diverse populations: Implications for teaching and administration in higher education. *ASHE-ERIC Higher Education Report, 29*(6), 1–125.

Treadwell, K. L. (2017). Learning from tragedy: Student affairs leadership following college campus disasters. *Journal of Student Affairs Research and Practice, 54*(1), 42–54.

Tribally Controlled Community College Assistance Act, H.R. 11104 (1978). https://www.congress.gov/bill/95th-congress/house-bill/11104?s=1&r=58

U.S. Department of Defense. (2019). 75 years of the GI Bill: How transformative it's been. https://www.defense.gov/News/Feature-Stories/story/Article/1727086/75-years-of-the-gi-bill-how-transformative-its-been/

U.S. Department of Education. (2022). Federal TRIO Programs – Home Page. U.S. Department of Education. https://www2.ed.gov/about/offices/list/ope/trio/index.html

U.S. Department of Education. (n.d.). List of postsecondary institutions enrolling populations with significant percentage of undergraduate minority students. https://www2.ed.gov/about/offices/list/ocr/edlite-minorityinst.html

U.S. Department of Justice. (2017). Report to the President: On issues raised by the Virginia Tech tragedy. https://www.justice.gov/archive/opa/pr/2007/June/vt_report_061307.pdf

U.S. News Rankings. (2021). https://www.usnews.com/best-colleges

UCLA. (2019a). Sharing our story. UCLA Asian American Studies Center. https://www.aasc.ucla.edu/sharingourstories/default.aspx

UCLA. (2019b). Mission. UCLA Asian American Studies Center. https://www.aasc.ucla.edu/about/default.aspx#ourhistoricalmission

Ulmer, R. R., Sellnow, T. L., & Seeger, M. W. (2007). *Effective crisis communication: Moving from crisis to opportunity.* SAGE Publication.

United States. President's Commission on Campus Unrest. (1970). *Campus Unrest: The report of the President's Commission on Campus Unrest.* US Government Printing Office.

University of Michigan. (2015). 100 years of recreational sports. Introduction to the A.A. http://recsports.umich.edu/timeline/874/100-years-recreational-sports

University of Minnesota (2023, June 27). The women's center. University of Minnesota web site. https://womenscenter.umn.edu/about

University of Wisconsin-Madison. (2022). The history of ISS. https://iss.wisc.edu/about/the-history-of-iss/

Urban, D. J. (2002). The women of SNCC: Struggle, sexism, and the emergence of feminist consciousness, 1960-66. *International Social Science Review, 77*(3/4), 185–190.

VanOverbeke, M. A. (2013). "Out of the quietness, a clamor: 'We want football!'": The California state colleges, educational opportunity, and athletics. *History of Education Quarterly*, 53(4), 430–454.

Virginia Tech Review Panel. (2007, April 16). *Mass shootings at Virginia Tech.* https://scholar.lib.vt.edu/prevail/docs/VTReviewPanelReport.pdf

Vrontis, D., & Thrassou, A. (2007). A new conceptual framework for business-consumer relationships. *Marketing Intelligence & Planning, 25*(7), 789–806.

Ward-Roof, J. A., & Guthrie, K. L. (2010). Reflections on the history of orientation, transition, and retention programs. In J. A. Ward-Roof (Ed.), *Designing successful transitions: A guide for orienting students to college* (Monograph No. 13, 3rd ed.). University of South Carolina, National Resource Center for the First-Year Experience and Students in Transition.

Weidman, J. C., Twale, D. J., & Stein, E. L. (2001). Socialization of graduate and professional students in higher education. *ASHE-ERIC Higher Education Report, 28*(3). Jossey-Bass.

Wert, E. (1998). Foreward. In M. Marincovich, J. Prostko, & F. Stout (Eds.), *The professional development of graduate teaching assistants* (pp. xvii–xxii). Anker Publishing Company.

Whalen, D., Saunders, K., & Shelley, M. (2009). Leveraging what we know to enhance short-term and long-term retention of university students. *Journal of College Student Retention: Research, Theory & Practice, 11*(3), 407–430.

White, B. (2007). Student Rights: From in loco parentis to sine parentibus and back again – Understanding the Family Educational Rights and Privacy Act in higher education. *BYU Education & Law Journal, 2007*(2), 321–350.

Wilcox, J. R., & Ebbs, S. L. (1992). *The leadership compass values and ethics in higher education.* The George Washington University.

Wilkinson, R. (2005). *Aiding students, buying students: Financial aid in America.* Vanderbilt University Press.
Williamson, E. G. (1961). *Student personnel services in colleges and universities.* McGraw-Hill.
Wilson, W. (1915). What is a college for? In K. Young, N. Foerster, & F. A. Manchester (Eds.), *Essays for college men 2nd series* (pp. 3–28). Henry Holt & Company.
Wilson, R. (1995). The G.I. bill and the transformation of America. *National Forum, 75*(4), 20.
Wilson, E. K. (2018). The legal foundations of white supremacy. *DePaul Journal for Social Justice*, 11(2), 1–14.
Wilson, A. (2022, April 14). Hundreds of students protest in support of LGBTQ+ community, after controversial social media post. *WSPA*. https://www.wspa.com/news/local-news/hundreds-of-students-protest-in-support-of-lgbtq-community-after-controversial-social-media-post/
Winston, R. B., & Anchors, S. (1993). *Student housing and residential life.* Jossey-Bass.
Winston, R. B., & Creamer, D. G. (1997). *Improving staffing practices in student affairs.* Jossey-Bass.
Winston, R. B., & Saunders, S. A. (1998). Professional ethics in a risky world. In D. L. Cooper, & J. M. Lancaster (Eds.), *New Directions for Student Services, No. 82. Beyond law and policy: Reaffirming the role of student affairs* (pp. 77–94). Jossey-Bass.
Winston, R. B., Torres, V., Carpenter, D. S., McIntire, D. D., & Petersen, B. (2001). Staffing in student affairs: A survey of practices. *College Student Affairs Journal, 21*(1), 7–25.
Wintermute, D. (2021, November 4). College guide for Indigenous and Native American students. *Best Colleges.* https://www.bestcolleges.com/resources/indigenous-native-student-guide/
Wolcott, R. J. (2018, March 1). Richard Spencer at Michigan State: Community braces for white nationalist leader. *Lansing State Journal.* https://www.lansingstatejournal.com/story/news/local/2018/03/01/michigan-state-community-white-nationalist-leader-richard-spencer-msu-livestock/380682002/
Yosso, T. J., & Lopez, C. B. (2010). Counterspaces in a hostile place: A critical race theory analysis of campus culture centers. In L. D. Patton (Ed.), *Culture centers in higher education: Perspectives on identity, theory, and practice* (pp. 83–104). Stylus Publishing.
Young, R., & Elfrink, V. (1991). Values education in student affairs graduate programs. *Journal of College Student Development, 32*, 109–115.
Young, L. W., & Hannon, M. D. (2002). The staying power of Black cultural centers. *Ethnic News Watch, 18*, 104.
Zdziarski, E. (2006). Crisis in the context of higher education. In K. Harper, B. Paterson, & E. Zdziarski, II (Eds.), *Crisis management: Responding from the heart* (pp. 3–24). National Association of Student Personnel Administrators.
Zdziarski, E. L., Rollo, J. M., & Dunkel, N. W. (2021). Where do we go from here? In E. L. Zdziarski, N. W. Dunkel, & J. M. Rollo (Eds.), *Campus crisis management: A comprehensive guide for practitioners* (2nd ed., pp. 335–340). Routledge.

Zeidan, A., & Editors of Encyclopaedia Britannica. (2022, April 6). Harvard University. *Britannica*. https://www.britannica.com/topic/Harvard-University
Zeveloff, J. (2016, September 6). There's a brilliant reason why Van Halen asked for a bowl of M&Ms with all the brown candies removed before every show. *Insider*. https://www.insider.com/van-halen-brown-m-ms-contract-2016-9

INDEX

Pages in **bold** refer to tables, and pages followed by "n" refer to notes.

For Product Safety Concerns and Information please contact our EU
representative GPSR@taylorandfrancis.com
Taylor & Francis Verlag GmbH, Kaufingerstraße 24, 80331 München, Germany

www.ingramcontent.com/pod-product-compliance
Ingram Content Group UK Ltd.
Pitfield, Milton Keynes, MK11 3LW, UK
UKHW022311250926
475702UK00046B/703
* 9 7 8 1 6 4 2 6 7 4 3 2 3 *